Homiletical Commentary on the Book of Nehemiah

William Henry Booth, J. H. Goodman, S. Gregory

BIBLIOLIFE

THE

PREACHER'S COMPLETE HOMILETICAL

COMMENTARY

ON THE

OLD TESTAMENT

(ON AN ORIGINAL PLAN),

With Critical and Explanatory Notes, Indices, Etc., Etc

BY VARIOUS AUTHORS.

———◦———

London:

RICHARD D. DICKINSON, 89 FARRINGDON STREET.

1880.

HOMILETICAL COMMENTARY

ON THE

BOOK OF NEHEMIAH.

BY

REV. W. H. BOOTH, REV. J. H. GOODMAN,

AND

REV. S. GREGORY.

————•————

𝔏𝔬𝔫𝔡𝔬𝔫:

RICHARD D. DICKINSON, 89 FARRINGDON STREET.

1880.

PREFACE.

THIS book is one of a series on the Old Testament, projected by Mr. R. D. DICKINSON of Farringdon Street. The object of the series is to lend occasional aid to busy men. If the following pages should help such in the *homiletic* treatment of an unread Book of the Bible, they will have accomplished their purpose.

HOMILETIC COMMENTARY

ON

NEHEMIAH.

INTRODUCTION.

I. Biographical Sketch. Nehemiah was the son of Hachaliah (ch. i 1), and brother of Hanani (ch. vii. 7). His father had not availed himself of the permission to return to his fatherland, withheld probably by possessions and honours acquired in the land of captivity. He was apparently of the tribe of Judah, since his fathers were buried at Jerusalem, and Hanani his kinsman seems to have been of that tribe (ch. ii. 3 ; vii. 2) Some think he was of priestly descent, because his name appears at the head of a list of priests in Neh. x 1—8 ; but it is obvious from ch. ix. 38, that he stands there as a prince, and not as a priest. The expression in v. 18, that Nehemiah " offered sacrifice," implies no more than that he provided the sacrifices. Whilst acting as cupbearer in the royal palace at Shushan, in the 20th year of Artaxerxes Longimanus, or B. C. 446, he received tidings of the mournful and desolate condition of the returned colony in Judea, and obtained permission of the king to make a journey to Jerusalem, and there to act as lieutenant or governor. Being furnished with this high commission, which included letters to the satraps and subordinates, and enjoying the protection of a military escort (ii. 9), Nehemiah reached Jerusalem in the year B. c 446, and remained there till B. c. 434, being actively engaged for 12 years in promoting the public good (v 14). During this time Nehemiah refused to receive his lawful allowance as governor, in consideration of the poverty of the people, and moreover maintained at his own expense a table for 150 Jews, at which any who returned from captivity were welcome. He returned to Persia B c. 434, but hearing of new abuses having crept in during his absence revisited Judea, where he effected various reforms. It is not unlikely that he remained at his post until about B. c. 405, towards the close of the reign of Darius Nothus That he lived to be an old man is thus quite probable from the sacred history, and this is expressly declared by Josephus, who states that he died at an advanced age Of the place and year of his death nothing is known

II. Authorship of Book. Generally attributed to Nehemiah. The central part (vii. 6—xii. 31) is somewhat different in style. The writer does not speak in the

B

first person as elsewhere, and there seems to be a different use of the Divine names, *Jehovah, Adonai, Elohim.* These differences are no proof against Nehemiah's authorship. The same feature occurs in Daniel. All Old Testament writers use documents of which they were not the authors. Chap. vii. 6—73 is professedly a register which Nehemiah found and inserted. Chap. viii—xi. 30, may have been composed by Ezra and incorporated by Nehemiah into his work. Chap. ix. 5—38 is a prayer probably composed by Ezra, and chaps. x. 1—27 , xi. 3—26 contain lists of names doubtless extracted from public annals. Chaps. viii, ix. 3, and x. 28, xi. 2, may have been written either by Nehemiah or some contemporary Levite. They relate to priestly matters in which the civil governor could not appear as the most prominent person.

III. Date of Book. Probably compiled by Nehemiah after the 32nd year of Artaxerxes. Supposing him to have written it about 10 years before his death, and about thirty years after his first visit to Jerusalem, we arrive at the year B. C. 415, at which time it would be possible for him to relate and describe all that is contained in the canonical Book of Nehemiah.

IV. Object of Book. Briefly to describe what Nehemiah effected at one time by direct personal effort, at another in conjunction with Ezra. As Nehemiah's efforts for the civil welfare of the people were but a continuation of those by which Zerubbabel the prince, Joshua the high-priest, and Ezra the scribe had laid the foundation of the community of returned exiles, so does his Book form the continuation and completion of that of Ezra, and may be regarded as its second part and sequel. It is not only similar in style, but has the same historical object, viz —to show how the people of Israel after their return from the Babylonish captivity, were, by the instrumentality of Nehemiah, fully re-established in the Land of Promise.

V. Canonicity of Book. Never seriously disputed. Nowhere quoted in the New Testament. Generally included in the Book of Ezra.

VI. Language and Style. Similar to that of the Chronicles of Ezra. Some few words and forms are not found elsewhere in Scripture, but the general Hebrew is exactly that of books purporting to be of the same age. Several words occur only in this Book as, *Sahvar* (to inspect), *Mogal* (a lifting up), *Tahalukah* (a procession), *Mikrah* (reading), and a few more. The text of Nehemiah is generally pure and free from corruption, except in the proper names, in which there is considerable fluctuation in the orthography, both as compared with other parts of the same Book, and with the same names in other parts of Scripture.

VII. Contemporaneous History. *Samaritan.* The Samaritans were not descendants of the ten tribes, but a purely heathen people who at first included Jehovah in the number of their gods, and by degrees, under the influence of their relations with the Jews, came to worship him as the only true God. They were not however recognized by the Jews as having any part in God's inheritance. Their attitude was bitterly hostile to the Hebrews, and their power to hinder increased by the fact that as native heathen they would be trusted by the Persian monarch. Sanballat was their chief at this time. *Hebrew.* Judea was thinly populated by the returning exiles. Jerusalem, an open village, exposed to all the attacks of its neighbours. The temple rebuilt by Ezra was still unfinished. A few isolated dwellings existed amidst the rubbish which lay in such great heaps about the city that the way round it was impassable. The prophet Malachi closed the Old Testament canon towards the end of Nehemiah's life *Persian.* Artaxerxes I (surnamed Longimanus, on account of his long hands) was king. Persia was in its zenith of splendour and power, although the elements of decay were already beginning to work in the empire. Artaxerxes had come to the throne through the assassination of his father Xerxes by Artabanus the chief of the guard. At the instigation of Artabanus he put his brother Darius to death as the murderer of his father, but on discovering the designs of Artabanus against himself he slew the double traitor. He then subdued a revolt headed by his brother Hystaspes, reduced rebellious Egypt, and made peace with Greece. The empire then enjoyed a period of quiet which may be regarded as the culminating point of its glory, during which the events of Nehemiah's history occurred.— *Lange. Roman.* Herodotus flourished B. C. 450. Rome governed by Censors, and Peloponnesian war B. C. 431. Roman empire was rising into power. *Grecian.* Pericles flourished at Athens, B. C 461—429. Socrates, Xenophon, and Thucydides were contemporaneous with Nehemiah. Plato was born B C. 429, the year in which Pericles died, and about fourteen years before Nehemiah's probable death.

VIII. Contents of Book.

1. *ANALYSIS.*

(i.) *Preparation for the wall building.*

    1. Nehemiah's grief and prayer (ch. i.).

    2. Nehemiah's petition to the king (ch. ii. 1—8).

    3. Nehemiah's journey (ch. ii. 9—11).

    4. Nehemiah's inspection and appeal (ii. 12—20).

(ii.) *The wall building.*

    1. The stations (ch. iii.).

    2. The opposition from without (ch iv).

    3. The opposition from within (ch. v.).

    4. The craft of the enemies (ch. vi).

    5. The guarding of the gates (ch. vii. 1—4).

    6. The genealogy (ch. vii. 5—73).

(iii.) *Discipline of the new community.*

    1. The public reading of the law (ch. viii. 1—12).

    2. The preparations for the feast of tabernacles (ch. viii. 13—16).

    3. The feast of tabernacles (ch. viii. 17, 18).

4. The special fast (ch. ix , x).

5. The distribution of the inhabitants (ch. xi.).

6. The Levitical genealogy (ch. xii 1—26).

7. The dedication of the walls (ch. xii. 27—43).

(iv.) *Later reforms.*

1. Levitical apportionments (ch. xii. 44—47).

2. Separation from strangers (ch. xiii. 1—3).

3. Nehemiah's reforms 12 years later (ch. xiii. 4—31).

2. INCIDENTAL REFERENCES.

We learn incidentally the prevalence of usury, and of slavery as its consequence ; the judicial use of corporal punishment (xiii. 25); the continuance of false prophets (vi. 7, 12, 14); the restitution of the Mosaic provision for the maintenance of the priests and Levites, and the due performance of the Temple service (xiii. 10); the freer promulgation of the Holy Scriptures by the public reading of them (viii. 1); and the more general acquaintance with them arising from their collection into one volume, and the general stimulus given to the art of reading among the Hebrews during their residence in Babylon ; the reviving trade with Tyre (xiii 16) ; the agricultural pursuits, and wealth of the Jews (v 11 ; xiii. 5) ; the tendency to take heathen wives, indicating possibly a disproportion in the number of Jewish males and females (x. 30 ; xiii. 3); the danger the Hebrew language was in of being corrupted (xiii. 24); the hereditary crafts practised by certain priestly families, e. g. the apothecaries, or makers of sacred ointments and incense (iii. 8), and the goldsmiths, whose business it probably was to repair the sacred vessels (iii. 8), and who may be regarded as the ancestors of the money-changers in the Temple (John ii. 14) ; and statistics, reminding us of Domesday-Book, concerning not only the cities and families of the returned exiles, but the number of their horses, mules, camels, and asses (vii.)—*Smith.* The list of returned captives who came under different leaders from the time of Zerubbabel to that of Nehemiah (amounting in all to only 42,360 adult males, and 7,337 servants), which is given in ch. vii., conveys a faithful picture of the political weakness of the Jewish nation as compared with the times when Judah alone numbered 470,000 fighting men (1 Chron. xxi. 5). This explains the great difficulty felt by Nehemiah in peopling Jerusalem with a sufficient number of inhabitants to preserve it from assault (vii. 3 ; xi. 1). It is an important *aid* too, in understanding the subse-quent history, and in appreciating the valour and patriotism by which they attained their independence under the Maccabees. The account of the wall-building contains the most valuable materials for settling the topography of Jerusalem to be found in Scripture.

CHAPTER I.

EXPLANATORY NOTES.] **1. The words**] (Heb. Divray). See 1 Kings xi. 41, where the same word is rendered "acts." **Hachaliah**] His ancestral home was Jerusalem (ii 3) Hence he was probably of the tribe of Judah. Having amassed a fortune, and gained a position at Susa, he was unwilling to avail himself of the permission to return to his fatherland. By his influence he had probably opened a way for the advancement of his still more distinguished son. **Chisleu**] The third month of the civil, and ninth of the ecclesiastical year, coinciding with parts of our November and December. **In the twentieth year**] That is, of the reign of Artaxerxes I., surnamed Longimanus (Long-handed), B. C 446. **Shushan**] Sometimes called Susa or Suses, the capital of Persia, situated in the plains of the Tigris, was from the time of Cyrus the winter palace of the king, and residence of the Court. Xenophon, Plutarch, and others, mention both Babylon and Ecbatana as its seat during some part of the year. The province of Susiana is now called Kusistan. Shuster, its capital, contains 15,000 inhabitants. The Susian palace was a magnificent building, remarkable for its "pillars of marble, its pavement of blue, red, white, and black, and its hangings of white, green, and blue, which were fastened with cords of fine linen and purple to the pillars" (Est i. 6). The palace was furnished with couches of gold and silver, on which the guests reclined when they banqueted. The drinking vessels were also of solid gold (v. 7). The present ruins of Susa cover a space a mile square, the portion of which near the river Shapur is probably "Shushan the palace." **2. Hanani**] Brother by blood relationship (vii. 1), afterwards appointed one of the assistant governors of Jerusalem (vii. 2). **That had escaped**] They had been allowed to return by the edict of Cyrus (Ezra 1) **Came**] The distance from Jerusalem to Susa is more than 1000 miles, and at the usual rate of travelling would occupy 45 days. In winter it would occupy at least 2 months. Ezra with his caravan was four months on his journey from Babylon to Jerusalem (Ezra vii 9). **3. The wall of Jerusalem is broken down**] In ruins, not utterly razed, or it could not have been built in 52 days. Nebuchadnezzar had broken it down 142 years before (2 Kings xxv. 10), and the attempt to rebuild had been stopped by Smerdis 76 years before this date. **4 God of heaven**] (Elohe-hash-shamayim), a phrase not confined to writers of Babylonish period (Gen. xxiv. 3, 7; Jonah i. 9) It distinguished Jehovah from the gods of earth formed of material substances. The style is repeated in Rev xi. 13 (ὁ Θεὸς τοῦ οὐρανοῦ). **5. Terrible**] Awe-inspiring (Heb. Norah). **That keepeth covenant and mercy**] Lit. "that keepeth the covenant of mercy." "The great and terrible God," is borrowed from Deut. vii. 21, and "that keepeth," &c. from Deut. vii 9. **6. Let thine ear be attentive, &c**] A phrase derived from Solomon's prayer (1 Kings viii. 29). Refers to the greater attention paid by the ear when the eyes are open towards the source of the sound. **8. The word which thou commandedst thy servant Moses**] Not the words, but the spirit of the promise, is given (Lev. xxvi. 39—42). **11. The king's cupbearer**] (Heb. Mashkeh, one who gives to drink. Greek οἰνοχόος, wine-pourer). The office one of great honour and confidence, since it gave an opportunity of being near the king's person. It gave Nehemiah an opportunity of increasing his fortune, a circumstance which afterwards very much facilitated his mission — *Hengstenberg.* The chief butler or cupbearer to the king of Egypt was the means of raising Joseph to his high position. Rabshakeh, who was sent by Sennacherib to Hezekiah, appears from his name to have fulfilled a like office in the Assyrian court.—*Gesenius.* Cupbearers are also mentioned as amongst the attendants of Solomon (1 Kings x. 5 ; 2 Chron. ix. 4).

HOMILETICAL CONTENTS OF CHAPTER I.

Ver. 1—11. Characteristics of a True Reformer.
  „ 1. Goodness superior to Circumstances.
  „ 2 Aggressive Benevolence.
  „ 3. The baneful consequences of Sin.
  „ 4. Unselfish Sorrow.
  „ 4. Fasting.
  „ 5—11. Intercessory Prayer
  „ 5—11. Prayer for Church Revival.
  „ 5. The Majesty and Mercy of God.

Ver. 6. Importunity in Prayer
  „ 7. Forgotten Sins remembered.
  „ 8. God's Memory.
  „ 8, 9. Punishment and Penitence.
  „ 10. Electing Grace.
  „ 10. Modest Goodness.
  „ 11. Unanswered Prayers.
  „ 11. Man's Equality before God

CHARACTERISTICS OF A TRUE REFORMER.

i. 1—11. *The words of Nehemiah, the son of Hachaliah.*

NEHEMIAH the civilian, as contrasted with Ezra the ecclesiastic, is brought forward in this Book as the patriot deliverer of his people. His training had fully qualified him for the onerous position he was called to occupy. He may be regarded as a typical reformer. No blot can be found on his character, no guile in his spirit. Note concerning this typical reformer :

I. His motives are pure. Personal ambition is sunk in desire for the public good. Selfish motives are abandoned for generous impulses. Reward is unthought of. Truth and freedom are sought for, oblivious of personal gain 1. *He accepts royal distinction that he may advance his people's interests.* He had risen from an exile captive to be a royal cupbearer by the force and moral worth of his character, in spite of jealousy and an alien creed. The title "Tirshatha," or commander, had been given him, and he became one of the most powerful subjects of the Persian monarch This honour, though won by personal merit, is not employed in the service of personal ambition, but in the interests of his oppressed kinsmen and fellow-citizens. Royal distinction may only be accepted by a true reformer conditionally, (1) *That no vital principle is sacrificed.* The Jew must not become a heathen either in morals or worship. The mandates of a monarch must not override the monitions of conscience. Truth must not bow to expediency. The knee must not bend to either Baal or Dagon. The "Golden Image" cannot be recognized, even though the fiery furnace be the alternative. Nehemiah sacrificed no vital principle in accepting royal favour. He remained true to his nation and loyal to his God. He was known as a sympathizer with the cause of the oppressed exiles. The deputation from Judea came to him openly at the royal palace, fearing no molestation Openly he received and welcomed them. Conditionally, (2) *That it is made subservient to his people's good.* Apart from this, Nehemiah's exalted separation from his oppressed fellow-countrymen would have been unpatriotic and selfishly mercenary. At Shushan he was really serving them better than he could have done at Jerusalem. For (1) he was learning the principles of government at the very seat and centre of the most powerful government of the world. In the royal palace, and under a right royal sovereign, he was gaining a royal spirit. Thus had God prepared other great leaders for their life work. Joseph and Moses in the court of Pharaoh learned lessons which were invaluable to the chosen seed. (2) He had access to the monarch himself. Such a boon was no small privilege, and eventually led to events of the utmost importance. 2. *He employs what influence he may possess for the benefit of his people's cause.* His position gave him considerable influence at Court, which he wielded, not, as most would have done, for his own personal aggrandizement, but for the benefit of his people's cause. Thus, like Joseph and Esther, he was able to influence royal decrees in favour of the Hebrew exiles. Most of the Jews were unable to approach Artaxerxes' person, but the office of Nehemiah gave him an introduction which he was not slow to use for his country and people. Some have opportunities of usefulness denied to others. They have the eye, the ear, the favour of the great. They should use these not for selfish purposes ; but to mention truths which elevated persons seldom hear, to recommend religion which they generally misunderstand, to plead for those who are seldom represented in royal circles. Personal influence is one of the talents for which we are responsible to God. How are we using it? Jerome tells us that Nebridius, though a courtier and nephew to the empress, never made suit but for the relief of the poor afflicted. Terence, one of the generals of the emperor Valens, being bidden to ask what he would, asked nothing but that the Church might be delivered from her Arian foes Thereupon, says Theodoret, the emperor tore into shreds his petition and bid him ask again, when he replied he would never ask anything for himself if he might not prevail for the Church. 3. *He is always ready to relinquish personal luxury for the public good.* If he enjoys honour and emolument on his brethren's behalf, the moment their interests demand their surrender the sacrifice must be made. Herein consists difference between genuine and spurious patriotism. The one delights in self-sacrifice , the other feeds on ambition. Such self-denial is required

(1) if the suffering can be the better served. Hitherto it had not been so. The time had now come when Nehemiah can only serve them by coming amongst them. Duty summoned him from the ease and luxury, to the privation and ceaseless toil of Jerusalem, and he "conferred not with flesh and blood," but gave up all at once. Such self-denial is required (2) if personal honour be associated with the people's oppression. The true patriot cannot serve two masters, or be loyal to two antagonistic principles. If the sovereign be a tyrant, *his* place is with the people. The side of the oppressed is alike the side of justice and of mercy. The bread of luxury is then mildewed with the tears of the slave, and the wine of the banquet mingled with the blood of the rack. Thus are all faithful servants of God called upon to lay down their goods, and their lives, *if need be*, in defence of the Church. For this cause Isaiah gave his body to be sawn asunder. For this cause Jeremiah was cast into a filthy dungeon, and Daniel into a den of lions. For this cause Paul pleaded his cause in chains at Jerusalem and Rome before Festus, Felix, and Agrippa ; and Jesus before Annas, Caiaphas, Herod, and Pilate, and for this cause John the Baptist lost his head. He that will lose his life thus shall certainly find it. In this respect Nehemiah was a type of Christ, who "though he was rich, for our sakes became poor," &c. (2 Cor viii 9).

Illustration :—Turner, the greatest of English landscape painters, had a generous nature. He was one of the hanging committee of the Royal Academy. The walls were full, when Turner's attention was attracted by a picture sent in by an unknown provincial artist. "A good picture," he exclaimed, "it must be hung up and exhibited" "Impossible," responded the committee. "The arrangement cannot be disturbed, quite impossible." "A good picture," reiterated Turner, "it must be hung up ;" and finding his colleagues as obstinate as himself, he took down one of his own pictures and hung up this in its place.

II. His sympathies are generous. 1. *His ear is open to the cry of distress.* Though rich he listens attentively to the story of woe : though occupying a high position he gives heed to the wants of his poorer brethren. Communion and sympathy are the instincts of a true and genuine patriotism. Nehemiah was not a mere passive listener, for he "asked them concerning the Jews." He entered into particulars, and was minute in his inquiries. The inquiry of an uninterested or half-interested person, would have been alike curt and cursory. Court life and duties had not deadened his human sympathy. "The good man heareth the cause of the poor," says Solomon (Prov. xxix.). The duty of every good man to consider his complaint, and pity and help him. 2. *His heart is deeply affected by the tidings which he receives.* "The remnant are in great affliction and reproach," &c The tidings were not entirely new, but probably sadder than he had anticipated Hence his great distress. His patriotism not a mental deduction only, but a mighty passion of the soul. He is not only a human, but a *humane* being. A prince, a commander he may be ; put pre-eminently a *man* and a *brother.* "The enthusiasm of humanity" was not unknown even in this remote age. Here is (1) a sudden outburst of generous sympathy and sorrow. "I sat down and wept." Passionate grief usually the least enduring. Not so this. (2) Sorrow increasing rather than diminishing as time wears on. "I mourned certain days," *i. e.* four months, from November to April. Here is another Rachel weeping, &c. ; another Jeremiah exclaiming "Oh that my head were waters," &c. (Jer. ix. 1). (3) Sorrow accompanied by abstinence from food. "And fasted." This another mark of the reality and pungency of his grief. Ahab may go to the mountain-top to eat and be merry. Elijah must go into solitude, and pour out his complaint to God. David finds "his heart is smitten and withered like grass, so that he forgets to eat his bread" (Ps. cii. 4). A sorrow that rolls in luxury and revels in delightsome pleasure and appetizing food is but a poor counterfeit. 3. *He resolves to identify himself with the cause of the oppressed.* His sympathy does not effervesce in tears. His will is won, and he at once sets about planning their relief. A true reformer must not stand aloof. Isolation is the law of selfishness Association is the secret of influence. The plans he forms may involve the sacrifice of all, a long and perilous journey, and even the monarch's frown, but he shrinks from nothing that can advance his people's cause.

Illustrations :—At the siege of Mons, during the career of the great Marlborough, the Duke of Argyle joined an attacking corps when it was on the point of shrinking from the contest ; and pushing them open-breasted he exclaimed, " You see, brothers, I have no concealed armour · I am equally exposed with you. I require none to go where I refuse to venture. Remember you fight for the liberties of Europe, which shall never suffer by my behaviour." This spirit animated the soldiers. The assault was made, and the work was carried —*Percy* " Sympathy is a debt we owe to sufferers. It renders a doleful state more joyful. Alexander the Great refused water in a time of great scarcity, because there was not enough for his whole army. It should be amongst Christians, as amongst lute-strings, when one is touched the others tremble. Believers should be neither proud flesh, nor dead flesh."—*Seeker.*

III. His spirit is devout. Nehemiah no godless reformer seeking for his countrymen emancipation from an alien yoke and nothing more. He sought the moral, as well as the material welfare of the chosen seed. 1. *He recognizes the existence and authority of the world's Guardian and Governor.* He who seeks to eliminate God from human affairs is no true patriot. This not a mere dogma, but a regulative principle with Nehemiah. Divine sovereignty not fiction, but solemn fact. He believed in a God of Providence. "To own God as fashioning every link in the complicated chain of our history ; to discern his hand in the least as well as in the greatest ; to realize a Providence which overrules what is evil, as well as orders what is good, a Providence which restrains the unwilling whilst it leads the obedient, a Providence so transcendent, that none and nothing can thwart it, so minute, that none and nothing can escape it, a Providence which directs the insect's wing and the atom's flutter, as well as the planet's course and the archangel's flight, to do this clearly, constantly, experimentally, is an attainment in the Divine life as rare as it is precious. We must interweave these assurances with the tissue and texture of our lives , they must enter as an essential element into the formation of our purposes, and into the conduct of our pursuits It is thus that we must ' walk with God.' "—*Stowell.* 2. *He acknowledges Divine aid to be superior to all other.* (1) As the most powerful of all. If Omnipotence be on his side nothing can withstand. So reasoned Nehemiah. Hence he flies to the source and fountain-head of *all* power. He appeals to the throne of the universe before appealing to any lower tribunal. He who enlists the aid of the Lord of Sabaoth commands not only myriads of ministering spirits, but all the forces, destructive and benignant, of the universe. (2) As controlling all other aid. Nehemiah will presently approach the earthly monarch, whose spirit is in the hands of the King of kings. This he knows, hence seeks Divine assistance in making successful suit. He desires God's aid that he may ask (*a*) for the right *thing,* (*b*) at the right *time,* (*c*) in the right *manner.* He who thus seeks human interposition through Divine agency will find the Divine will working in his favour through human instrumentality. No aid can be so effectual as that of Omnipotence. 3. *He regards prayer as the appointed means by which Divine aid is to be secured.* Does not make his belief in the omniscience of Divine Providence a ground for personal indolence, or restraining prayer. The true patriot no fatalist. By prayer and supplication he makes known his request unto God (Phil. iv. 6). This prayer, recorded for our instruction, is one of the model prayers of the Bible (1) Reverent in its attitude towards God (v. 5). (2) Persistent in pressing its suit (v. 6). (3) Penitent in tone and temper (v. 6, 7). (4) Scriptural in argument (v. 8, 9). (5) Child-like in spirit (v. 10, 11). (6) Definite in aim (v. 11).

Illustrations —Augustus Cæsar possessed such an attachment to his country that he called it *his own daughter,* and refused to be called its master, because he would rule it not by fear, but by love. After his decease, his disconsolate people lamented over him, saying, " O would to God that he had never lived, or that he had never died." A Lacædemonian mother had five sons in a battle that was fought near Sparta, and seeing a soldier that had left the scene of action, eagerly inquired of him how affairs went on " All your five sons are slain," said he " Unhappy wretch!" replied the woman : " I ask thee not of what concerns my children, but of what concerns my country " " As to that all is well," said the soldier " Then," said she, " let them mourn that are miserable. My country is prosperous, and I am happy." (*a*) A great chasm opened in the Roman Forum, which the soothsayers said could not be filled but by that which was most valuable to the State Marcus Curtius, an eminent soldier, mounted his war-horse, and full-armed rode into the gulf, a noble sacrifice for his country

GOODNESS SUPERIOR TO CIRCUMSTANCES.

i. 1. *I was in Shushan the palace.*

I. High social positions are not generally favourable to eminent piety. 1. *Because luxury and liberty tend to lust and licence.* Court morals are proverbially corrupt. When wealth to purchase is united with authority to command, selfish ambition and sensual indulgence too often ensue In high life the temptations to self-pleasing are generally too strong for unaided human nature. Long prosperity breeds a plague of dust, as does prolonged fair weather in the Italian valleys. Dust that blinds the eyes of the soul, and chokes the spirit with earthly cares. 2 *Because the pride of human pomp is inimical to the spirit of true religion.* Palaces are above most places theatres of human exaltation and proud display. Religion does not flourish amidst human pomp and pride. By the lowly birth of the Son of God, heaven has poured its contempt upon the mere accidentals of greatness True religion is by the very humility of its nature antagonistic to the spirit of the world Nebuchadnezzar could not withstand this spirit. In his prosperity and pride he exclaimed, " Is not this great Babylon that I have built," &c (Dan iv 30). In his humiliation he regained that religion which he had lost in his exaltation. 3 *Because affluence is apt to beget independence of God.* When Jeshurun waxed fat he kicked (Deut xxxii 15). When God's chosen people prospered they forgot God (Isa. li. 13 ; Judg. iii. 7) A sense of need brings men near to God. When the lap is full, God is forgotten. Hence the words of Christ, " How hardly shall they that have riches," &c (Mark x. 23). Rich men have often to be made poor before they will acknowledge God. Merchant has most reason to watch and pray in the day of his prosperity. Easier to bear

the ebb of disappointment than the floodtide of success. Most reason to watch when we think ourselves most secure A poor Christian remarked when receiving unexpected relief, " Oh ! what a blessed thing it is to be poor, that one may see the hand of God so plain." The hand of God often concealed from the rich in the very affluence of its gifts ; whilst to the pious poor quite naked Hezekiah was humbly grateful when he exclaimed after the slaughter of the hosts of Sennacherib, " The living, the living, he shall praise thee, as I do this day" (Isa. xxxviii 19), yet the sad record of his after days is, " But Hezekiah rendered not unto the Lord, according to the benefit done unto him : for his heart was lifted up" (2 Chron xxxii. 25) " It was as much as we could do to keep our feet upon the splendid mosaic floor of the palace Giovanelli, at Venice ; but we found no such difficulty in the cottage of the poor glass-blower in the rear Observation shows that there is a fascination in wealth which renders it extremely difficult for the possessors of it to maintain their equilibrium ; and this more especially where wealth has been suddenly acquired ; then, unless grace prevent, pride, affectation, and other mean vices, stupefy the brain with their sickening fumes, and he who was respected in poverty becomes despised in prosperity. What man can help slipping when everybody is intent on greasing his ways, so that the smallest chance of standing is denied him. The world's proverb is, " God help the poor, for the rich can help themselves," but it is just the rich who have most need of Heaven's help Dives in scarlet is worse off than Lazarus in rags, unless Divine love shall uphold him —*Spurgeon*. 4. *Because the multiplication of cares tends to deaden spirituality* Increase of wealth means increase of anxiety. Milton has taught us by his picture of the man with the muck-rake that secular cares readily become all-engrossing, and turn the eyes away from the crown of life. The Hebrew word for riches signifies "*heavy*," for riches are a burden, and they that will be rich do but load themselves with thick clay. "There is a burden of care in getting them, of fear in keeping them, of temptation in using them, of guilt in abusing them, of sorrow in losing them, and a burden of accounts at last to be given up concerning them."—*Henry.* "As poison works more furiously in wine than in water, so corruptions betray themselves more in a state of plenty than in a state of poverty."—*Secker.* Mr. Cecil called to see a rich hearer, and said, "I understand you are very dangerously situated." The man replied, "I am not aware of it." "I thought it probable you were not, and therefore called upon you. I hear you are getting rich; take care, for it is the road by which the devil leads thousands to destruction" 5. *Because the commands of an earthly monarch are liable to clash with the mandates of Jehovah.* The earthly king who has no fear of God before his eyes, will not be likely to respect the claims of a Higher Court. He will consequently have no conscience for sacred things, and will be likely to ignore such conscience in his subjects. But the servant of Jehovah has no choice. He must say with the noble three, "We will not serve thy god" (Dan. iii. 18); and with Peter and John, "Whether it be right in the sight of God to hearken unto you more than unto God, judge ye" (Acts iv. 19). With Daniel and John the Baptist he must obey God rather than man, though death be the consequence. Thus is the path of the just beset with perils in the high places of power and pomp

Illustration :—"Philip, Bishop of Heraclea, in the beginning of the fourth century was dragged by the feet through the streets, severely scourged, and then brought before the governor, who charged him with obstinate rashness in disobeying the imperial decrees: but he firmly answered, ' My present behaviour is not the result of rashness, but proceeds from my love and fear of God, who made the world, and whose commands I dare not transgress. I have hitherto done my duty to the emperors, and am always ready to comply with their just orders, according to the doctrine of our Lord Jesus Christ · but I am obliged to prefer heaven to earth, and to obey God rather than man.' The governor on hearing this speech immediately passed sentence on him to be burnt, and the martyr expired, singing praises to God in the midst of the flames."

II. Piety is not impossible in any position of life. 1. *Inward grace is stronger than outward circumstances.* The temptations to slothful ease and self-indulgence may be fearfully strong, but not stronger than Divine grace. The seductions of luxury and the witchery of pleasure may charm with enticing subtlety, but cannot ensnare the man who is faithful to his God, and like Nehemiah recognizes "the good hand of his God" "Greater is he that is in you than he that is in the world" (1 Jno. iv. 4). "In the world ye shall have tribulation, but in me ye shall have peace" (Jno. xvi. 13). Illustrate by Bunyan's picture, in the Interpreter's house, of fire on which Satan poured water and Christ oil. "If a letter were to be addressed to that most influential word, *circumstances,* concluding thus — 'I am, Sir, your very obedient, humble servant,' the greater part of the world might subscribe it."—*Horace Smith.* 2. *The God of providence is also the God of grace.* Where he places, there he can and will sustain If God puts Nehemiah into the Persian palace, he will support him there. Nowhere are faithful witnesses more needed than in the high places of the earth. The nearer the fount of social influence, the greater the power for good or evil. Grace is adapted to providential circumstances.

Illustration :—The trees are adapted to the demands of their position The fir of the northern hills defies the wintry blast by reason of its strong roots which penetrate the crevices of the soil. The tall palms send their roots down three feet into the earth, and then spread out, securing a firm anchorage, and are able to stand the sweep of the desert winds. The roots of the pine are spread over the surface, but it grows in less exposed situations. The mangrove which fringes the estuaries and lagoons of the tropics, exposed to the tides, on a shifting soil, supports itself by sending roots from its trunk and lower branches down into the muddy ground, so that the whole has the appearance of a tree propped up by artificial stakes. We may infer that a like adjustment of strength to situation pervades the moral world.

3. *Many of the holiest characters in history have been found in the most unfavourable situations.* Joseph in Pharaoh's court with an adulterous queen; Moses in the same court; Obadiah under Jezebel and Ahab, David exposed to the evil influence of Saul; Daniel and Mardocheus in the court of Ahasuerus; all served God faithfully though exposed to the most trying ordeals. In the New Testament we find Christians in every station of life: Zenas the lawyer, Erastus the chamberlain, Paul the tent-maker, Luke the physician, Zaccheus the tax-gatherer, Peter the fisherman, and Joseph the carpenter. Learn from this fact, (1) not to condemn bodies and professions of men indiscriminately. (2) Not to make our business an excuse for ungodliness. Some lines of life are indeed much less favourable to morality and religion than others; they afford fewer helps and more hindrances than others; and this consideration should powerfully influence those who have the disposal of youth. But where the providence of God places us, the grace of God can keep us. "These," says God, "had the same nature, were partakers of the same infirmities, and placed in the same circumstances with yourselves. But they escaped 'the corruption that is in the world, through faith.' They found time to serve me. 'Go thou and do likewise.'"—*Stowell.* "Amidst the sternest trials, the most upright Christians are reared. The Divine life within them so triumphs over every difficulty as to render the men, above all others, true and exact. What a noble spectacle is a man whom nothing can warp, a firm, decided servant of God, defying hurricanes of temptation!"—*Spurgeon.* Grace makes itself equally at home in the palace and in the cottage. No condition necessitates its absence, no position precludes its flourishing. One may compare it in its power to live and blossom in all places, to the beautiful blue-bell of Scotland, of which the poetess sings :—

" No rock is too high, no vale too low,
For its fragile and tremulous form to grow :
It crowns the mountain with azure bells,
And decks the fountain in forest dells :
It wreathes the ruins with clusters grey,
Bowing and smiling the livelong day."

III. Positions perilous to piety should be avoided except at the special call of Providence. 1 *Material prosperity should always be regarded as subordinate to spiritual vitality.* (1) It really is so. It matters little what be our position in this world. It matters everything what is our position in the next. "What shall it profit," &c. (Mark viii. 36). Things which are seen are temporal, things which are not seen are eternal" (2 Cor. iv. 18). What man thinks, of no consequence; what God thinks, everything. The life of earth, whatever be its character, soon terminates, the life of eternity never. (2) He who acts upon this principle gains in the end. Lot chose the fertile plain of Sodom, and preferring temporal gain lost all. Moses "chose rather to suffer affliction with the people of God," &c., and became their chosen leader (Heb. xi. 25). Solomon asked neither long life nor riches, but he lost neither in choosing religion (1 Kings iii. 11). (3) Through neglecting to act upon this principle piety has often been lost. Many a worldly marriage has ruined a promising Christian. Many a hopeful life has been wrecked upon the rocks of uncurbed ambition. He who places the world first and heaven second will soon make ambition everything and religion nothing. "Caligula with the world at his feet longed for the moon, and could he have gained it, would have coveted the sun. It is in vain to feed a fire which is the more voracious the more it is supplied with fuel. He who seeks to satisfy his ambition has before him the labours of Sisyphus, who rolled up a hill an ever-rebounding stone, and the task of the daughters of Danaus, who are condemned for ever to fill a bottomless vessel with buckets full of holes. Could we know the secret heart-breaks of those who have forsaken religion for the sake of gratifying ambition, we should need no Wolsey's voice crying, 'Fling away ambition,' but should flee from it as from the most accursed blood-sucking vampire which ever uprose from the caverns of hell."—*Spurgeon.* Pope Adrian VI. had this inscription on his monument, "Here lies Adrian VI., who never was so unhappy in any period of his life as at that in which he was a prince." 2 *No one has a right to tempt God by unnecessarily exposing himself to temptation* This sin of presumption, against which Paul warned Corinthians (1 Cor. x. 9). Christ met it in the wilderness in the form, "Cast thyself down." God will not protect those who rashly presume upon his guardianship. Mockery to pray, "Lead us not into temptation," if we run into it unbidden. When we needlessly expose ourselves we entice sin and court failure. "Temptations are enemies outside the castle, seeking entrance" If there be no false retainer within who holds treacherous parley, there can scarcely be even an offer. No one would make overtures to a bolted door, or a dead wall. It is some face at the window that invites proffer. The violence of temptation addressed to us is only another way of expressing the violence of the desire within us. It costs nothing to reject that which we do not wish. and the struggle required to overcome temptation measures the strength in us of the temptable element. Men ought not to say, "How powerfully the devil tempts!" but, "How strongly I am tempted."—*Beecher.* 3 *Providence will protect those whom it calls to perilous duty* (1) The path of duty is sometimes a path of danger. Christian visitors at home endanger their lives amongst the poor, and Christian missionaries abroad amongst the heathen. Not only bodies, but souls are endangered through the prevalence of surrounding

vice, which Christian workers must come into contact with (2) Special guardianship is exercised over those whose providential path is one of danger. God will not leave them. Disciples in storm were not deserted because they had gone at Christ's bidding. Nehemiah, Daniel, Joseph were untainted by court life because they were surrounded by Jehovah's Shield. (3) We should be careful not to mistake presumption for providential guidance. Many have done so and fallen. Peter walking on the water an instance.

Illustration —A gentleman who wished to test the character of some men who had offered themselves for the situation of coachman, took them to a narrow road which bordered on a deep precipice, and inquired of them how near to the dangerous verge they could drive without fear. One named a few inches, another still fewer. The gentleman shook his head, and dismissed them. He could not risk his life with them A third was asked, "How near this edge can you drive in safety?" He drew back replying, "I should drive as far from it as possible. The place is dangerous. I should avoid it altogether." He was employed, because he could be trusted not to run into needless peril.

Illustration :—A soldier named Miller felt a strong desire to be a minister though still unconverted After his conversion he felt a renewal of this desire. In the battle of Wilderness he was badly wounded, and remained 24 hours on the field The surgeon refused to operate upon him, because death was inevitable. He was removed to Fredericksburg, again examined, and his wounds pronounced fatal. To a friend he said, "The surgeon says I must die; but I do not feel that my work is done yet. When I gave myself up to God last winter I promised him that I would labour for his cause in the Gospel ministry I feel that he has a work for me to do, and that man is immortal until his work is done" A few days after a third consultation of doctors was held, whose decision was, "You will recover; but it is the most miraculous escape we have ever seen." After many months' confinement he was able to begin his preparation for the ministry.

AGGRESSIVE BENEVOLENCE.

i. 2. *I asked them concerning the Jews, &c.*

I. True Benevolence is an active principle. 1. *It seeks that it may save the lost* Not content with remaining at home, it goes after the suffering Nehemiah not altogether ignorant of state of Jews, nor accurately acquainted

with it. He solicits particulars. Goes out of his way to discover need that he may assist it The close cross-examination to which deputation were subjected proved the thorough earnestness of questioner Christ great example of active benevolence, alike in the whole work of redemption, and the details of his mortal life. The Church works in same spirit. It comes "not to be ministered unto, but to minister." The true Christian cries out, "The love of Christ doth me constrain, to seek the wretched sons of men." 2. *Its motive therefore is love rather than duty.* Benevolence without love is cold as ashes. Uncharitable charity a ghastly mockery. Stern duty seldom prompts true charity. This must spring from love alone. Benevolence follows the example of him who "was rich, but for our sakes became poor," &c. A child looking into the face of a lady who had relieved and nursed her in sickness artlessly asked, "Are you God's wife?" God is love, and true benevolence is lovingly God-like.

II. True Benevolence is not deterred from painful investigation through fear of possible sacrifices. 1. *It seeks to know the worst.* Nehemiah not satisfied with superficial knowledge. He probed the national sore. True benevolence acts in the same spirit. It fathoms the abyss that it seeks to close; it probes the wound it seeks to heal (1) Philanthropy deals with the worst human ailments. It shrinks from no contagion, and shuns no patient however loathsome. Its home is the hospital and fever ward. (2) It grapples with the blackest facts of human history, and sheds light upon darkest, foulest blots in human nature. Nothing daunts, nothing drives it to despair. For the most hopeless there is hope; for the worst there is mercy. (3) It seeks to alleviate the direst sufferings of the Church. No breach too wide to be healed. No Church too dead to be revived. No persecutions too cruel to be endured. It seeks not to heal lightly or suddenly, but thoroughly. 2. *It shrinks from no sacrifice.* Nehemiah was aware that he could not relieve his brethren without great personal sacrifice. Not only wealth, but probably position, and perhaps even life, would have to be surrendered. This did not deter him. Self-sacrifice the mark of true benevolence. Hireling charity shuns this test.

(1) Money, (2) Time, (3) Personal ambition all freely given up for the sake of the suffering Church.

Illustration :—When a teacher was wanted by Dr. Mason of Burmah for the war-like Bghais, he asked his boatman, Shapon, if he would go; and reminded him that instead of the fifteen rupees a month which he now received, he could only have four rupees a month as teacher After praying over the matter he came back; and Dr. Mason said, "Well, Shapon, what is your decision? Can you go to the Bghais for four rupees a month?" Shapon answered, "No, teacher: I could not go for four rupees a month; but *I can do it for Christ.*" And for Christ's sake he went.

III. True Benevolence is not easily discouraged. 1. *It regards no case as absolutely hopeless.* Jerusalem and its inhabitants were in a pitiable plight, yet Nehemiah did not sit down in despair. He wept, it is true, but he prayed, and for four months he continued to pray with an importunity that nothing could discourage. Humanity may be very corrupt, but not hopelessly so. The Church may be at a low ebb, but the lowest ebbing point is nearest the flowing point. The night was very dark, but 'tis ever darkest before the dawn. Benevolence knows that what is impossible with man, is possible with God. (1) It helps not only the needy, but the most needy. (2) It believes in the possible regeneration of human nature, however degraded. (3) It believes in the possible revival of the Church, however encrusted with superstition or formalism. 2. *It recognizes the infinite resources of Jehovah.* If looked earthward only, been discouraged. Would have exclaimed mournfully, "Who is sufficient," &c. But looking heavenward its eye rests upon the unspeakable riches of God in Christ. Remembering the Divine omnipotence it has no fear. It remembers the infinite resources, (1) of Divine pity, (2) of Divine power, (3) of Divine pardon. None need despair, even when engaged in the most arduous work for such a master as God (a) His wealth is boundless. The universe belongs to him (b) This infinite wealth is treasured up for the benefit of his needy servants. (c) This boundless wealth is accessible to all who need it, and apply in faith.

Illustrations:—(a) "It is said of the Lacedæmonians, who were a poor and homely people, that they offered lean sacrifices to their gods, and that the Athenians, who were a wise and wealthy people, offered fat and costly sacrifices; and yet in their ways the former always had the mastery over the latter. Whereupon they went to the oracle to know the reason why those should speed worst who gave most. The oracle returned this answer to them—That the Lacedæmonians were a people who gave their *hearts* to their gods, but that the Athenians only gave their *gifts* to their gods." Thus a heart without a gift is better than a gift without a heart.—*Secker.*

St. Theresa, when commencing her homes of mercy with only three half-pence in her pocket, said, "Theresa and three half-pence can do nothing, but God and three half-pence can do everything." Dr. Judson laboured diligently for six years in Burmah without baptizing a convert. At the end of three years, he was asked what evidence he had of ultimate success. He replied, "As much as there is a God who will fulfil all his promises." A hundred churches and thousands of converts already answer his faith. We will suppose that some opulent person makes the tour of Europe. If his money fall short he comforts himself with the reflection that he has a sufficient stock in the bank, which he can draw out at any time by writing to his cashiers. This is just the case spiritually with God's elect. They are travellers in a foreign land remote from home. Their treasure is in heaven, and God himself is

their banker. When their graces seem to be almost exhausted, when the barrel of meal and cruse of oil appear to be failing, they need but draw upon God by prayer and faith and humble waiting. The Holy Spirit will honour their bill at first sight, and issue to them from time to time sufficient remittances to carry them to their journey's end. "I have heard of a Spanish ambassador, who, coming to see the treasury of Saint Mark in Venice, fell a-groping at the bottom of the chests and trunks, to see whether they had any bottom, and being asked the reason why he did so, answered, "My Master's treasure differs from yours, and excels yours in that his have no bottom, and yours have." All men's mints, bags, purses, and coffers may be quickly exhausted and drawn dry; but God is such an inexhaustible portion that he can never be drawn dry: all God's treasures, and his mints and his bags, are bottomless. Thousands of millions in heaven and earth feed upon him every day, and yet he feels it not: he is still giving, and yet his purse is never empty. he is still filling all the court of heaven, and all the creatures on earth, and yet he is a fountain that still overflows. There are some who say, that it is most certainly true of the oil at Rheims, that though it be continually spent in the inauguration of the kings of France, yet it never wastes: but whatever truth is in this story, of this I am most sure, that though all the creatures in both worlds live and spend continually on Christ's stock, yet it never wasteth.—*Brooks.*

THE BANEFUL CONSEQUENCES OF SIN.

i 3. *The remnant that are left . . . are in great affliction and reproach, &c.*

This state of things would never have come to pass, but for the disobedience and idolatry of the children of Israel. It was the natural and inevitable fruit of their own sin. Not mere unfortunate calamity, but punitive and penal discipline. From the text we learn,—

I. That sin brings misery upon human souls. "In great affliction," *i. e.* misery, want, privation. Suffering always follows sin in the nature of things. 1. *Because sin is a violation of law.* Sin transgresses the eternal law of righteousness, which cannot be broken with impunity. Its penalty is pain, and eventually death. Law-breakers everywhere must suffer. (1) See this in relation to laws of health. Violate those laws by unwholesome food, self-indulgent excesses, absorption of poison, and derangement or death will ensue. (2) See this in relation to the laws of society. Ill-manners provoke exclusion. None defy these rules without paying penalty.

(3) See this in relation to national laws. What mean our courts of justice, our prisons and penal settlements, but that law cannot be transgressed without suffering (β) 2. *Because sin separates from God.* Its very nature, essence, is antagonism to God. Wherever it reigns it produces tastes and dispositions contrary to the will of God. Now God is the author of all happiness. The opposite of happiness is misery. Man severed from God like branch cut from tree, or limb torn from body. The man who has not made peace with God cannot be happy, because the "wrath of God abideth on him." No real peace when hostile to God. 3. *Because sin creates discord.* Where there is discord there is misery. Sin works discord— (1) In the individual. It stirs up evil passions against the reign of conscience. No internal peace until the Stronger has cast out the strong man armed who usurps his place in the heart. Christ

alone can " say to our warring passions,
peace." (2) In the Church. It provokes
enmity between man and man, and
different sections of the one great body of
Christ. (3) In the world. It lifts up
the war sign, and mingles nations in the
bloody embrace of strife. When sin
comes to an end men shall learn war no
more. Want of harmony always painful.
Inharmonious colours pain the eye, and
inharmonious sounds jar upon the ear.
All discord is the enemy of peace and
pleasure.

**II. Sin brings reproach upon the
Church.** " In great affliction *and reproach.*" The Jews were not only in a
desolate condition, but were taunted by
the Samaritans with being in that condition. " Sin a reproach to any people "
(Prov. xiv. 34), especially to the Church
—for, 1. *It destroys her power, and
paralyzes her efforts.* Spirituality secret
of Church's power. Stripped of this,
she is like Samson shorn of his locks.
An unholy Church is a mournful spectacle, a miserable ruin. The Church at
Jerusalem was now demoralized through
her unspirituality and want of faith.
2. *It provokes the taunts of blasphemy.*
Church's enemies always vigilant. Did
not hesitate to throw insinuation in her
teeth. " Where is now their God ? "
" As it is a pitiful sight to see a prince
or nobleman cast from his dignity, spoiled
of his honour, lands, and goods, and
forced to become a carter, and drive the
plough, or lie in prison ; so surely it
must needs move any heathen man, to
see the city where he and his elders were
born and buried to be overthrown, lie
open to all enemies, unfenced with walls
or gates, and inhabited only by a few
cottagers, and no better than the poorest
ragged hamlet in the country."—*Pilkington.* 3. *It encourages the growth of
infidelity.* Sceptics, both intellectual and
sensual, not slow to point to Church's
failure in support of their boastful pretensions. Perhaps the Church's failures
and discords have done more to
strengthen atheism than any books or
arguments levelled against religion.

III. Sin removes national defences.
" The walls are broken down." This
material dismantling only a type of the

national demoralization which had taken
place. 1. *Unity is a national defence.*
(1) A nation divided against itself can
no more stand than a city, whereas a
thoroughly united people can resist almost any attack from without. (2) Sin
undermines national unity by sowing
discord and jealousy, and creating party
feeling. It sets all the classes of society
against each other (masters and servants,
landowner and labourer), and seeks to
stifle charity and forbearance. 2. *Bodily
vigour is a national defence.* (1) It
saves from poverty in time of peace.
Strong manhood a security against penury
if united with temperance and industry.
(2) It enables resistance to become effectual in time of war. Sensuality undermines manhood, and unfits for arduous
toil in peace or war. Refer to Franco-
German war as instance. French people
were socially demoralized by vice.
Their manhood was undermined. Religion teaches the sanctity of the human
body, and thus preserves it from prema-
ture corruption. 3. *Domestic purity is
a national defence.* What the family
life is, the national life will soon become.
Domestic fidelity begets a sense of responsibility. It promotes healthy moral
tone. This, backbone of a nation's
vigour. Sin encourages lust and breaks
down all social barriers, and thus robs a
nation of one of its most powerful bul-
warks. 4. *Force of character is a
national defence.* This made England
what she is, and America. It is this
which gives weight to our words and
actions in foreign courts and countries.
Force impossible where sin reigns.
Why ? Because no true cohesion where
no godliness. An unholy life is under
no regulating principle, but at the
mercy of passions and desires. Where
there is internal anarchy, and no central
principle of rectitude ruling the conduct,
there can be no true decision or moral
force in the life (*a*)

**IV. Sin dishonours national govern-
ment.** " The gates thereof are burned
with fire." City gates not only for resistance, but also the seat of government.
There the assembly of chiefs gathered ;
there criminals were tried ; there justice
was administered, and important subjects

discussed. Compare " Ottoman Porte," where word for gate is synonym for government; also, " on this rock will I build my church, and the gates of hell shall not prevail against it." Here "gates" equivalent to kingdom. The demolition of the city gates suggests—
1. *That the administration of justice was neglected.* Crime ran riot. There was no security, no confidence, no defence, therefore none dare seek redress where none could be obtained. Bribery and terrorism the offspring of lax morality. The moral sense deadened, justice impossible. 2. *That the inroads of enemies were unchecked.* No barriers to midnight marauders. Whole nation manifestly paralyzed and dispirited. National honour and independence trodden in the dust. " The walls are destroyed, and the gates burned," when the rulers and ministers do not their duty, but care for other things. And as this wretched people had justly, for their disobedience, neither walls left to keep out the enemy, nor gates to let in their friends, but were all destroyed; so shall all godless people be left without godly magistrates to govern them, and live in slavery under tyrants that oppress them, and be led by blind guides that deceive them.—*Pilkington.* The Jews to this day when they build a house (say the Rabbins) leave one part of it unfinished in remembrance that Jerusalem and the temple are at present desolate; or they leave about a yard square unplastered on which they write the words of the Psalmist, " If I forget Jerusalem," &c. (Ps. cxxxvii.); or else the words, " Zechor Lechorbon," " The memory of the desolation."

V. Sin brings a blight upon the whole land. When Adam sinned, the earth, which was before decked with fruits, brought forth weeds The wickedness of Sodom punished not only by the destruction of its inhabitants, but by the desolation of the land, so that even the air is so pestilent that birds fall dead as they fly over it. The whole country of Palestine, " a land flowing with milk and honey," for the sins of the Jews has become barren, as David said, "The Lord turneth a fruitful ground into a barren, for the wickedness of the dwellers in it" (Ps. cvii.). Jerusalem was not only destroyed now, but afterwards by Vespasian, whose general, Titus, left not " one stone standing on another" (Matt. xxiv. 2). " Herein behold the vileness of sin, that not only man, but the earth, stones, cities, trees, corn, cattle, fish, fowl, and all fruits are perished, punished and turned into another nature, for the sin of man : yea, and not only worldly things, but his holy temple, law, the ark, the cherubims, mercy-seat, Aaron's rod, and holy jewels, are given into the hands of a heathen king, because of the disobedience of his people."—*Pilkington.*

Illustrations.—(a) When Nicephorus Phocas had built a wall about his palace for his own security in the night-time, he heard a voice crying to him, " Oh ! emperor, though thou build thy walls as high as the clouds, yet if sin be *within* it will *overthrow all.*"

(β) " Suppose I were going along the street, and were to dash my hand through a large pane of glass, what harm should I receive ? You would be punished for breaking the glass Would that be all the harm that I should receive ? No, you would cut your hand with the glass So it is with sin. If you break God's laws, you will be punished for breaking them ; and your soul is hurt by the very act of breaking them."

Unselfish Sorrow.

i. 4.   I sat down and wept, and mourned certain days.

I. The occasion of his grief. "When I heard these words I sat," &c. 1. *Not personal loss.* Men mourn when death enters the home and robs them of their loved ones ; when privation comes and strips them of their luxuries ; when disappointment blights their ambition ; when disease or accident deprive them

of vigorous health. Nehemiah's grief not caused by any of these things. He was in no danger at present of losing either friend, or substance, or good name. Nor would he thus have mourned if he had. 2 *Not spiritual despair.* He certainly discovered imperfections in his life not before observed, but nothing to drive him to religious despair. Condemnation and shame follow the awakening of conscience. His not asleep. Religious declension had not estranged him from God. He had walked with God even in the palace 3 *But public calamity.* " When I heard *these words* I sat down and wept." What words? Those by which his brother had just described the "affliction and reproach" into which the Church at Jerusalem had fallen. (1) His brethren were in distress. His human sensibilities not blunted by the formalities of court life. Poor relations not to be forgotten when fortune favours us (2) The Church was desolate. This as important to a good man as if his own home was burnt or wrecked (3) The holy city was in ruins. Other cities had been razed to the ground, and he felt no grief like this. Babylon, a much greater city, had been taken by Cyrus not long before ; Samaria, their neighbour, by Sennacherib and Shalmaneser But this was "the holy city " (Matt. iv.). Over its final destruction Christ wept (Luke xix) It had been beautified with temple, priests, and holy ordinances; and strengthened by many worthy princes and laws, and was a wonder to the world. Its fall was synonymous with the disgrace of true religion. (4) Sin was triumphant. The sin of unbelief and moral impotence within, and of blasphemy and boastful arrogance without. Persecution and poverty are the Church's glory ; but impotence and discord her eternal shame " Where is the Lord God of Elijah ? " her enemies asked ; and in bitter irony are ever ready to exclaim, " See how these Christians love one another ! " When God's cause languishes and his Church is dishonoured it is time for good men to weep. In time of common calamities " Should we then make mirth ? " (Ezek. xxi. 10).

Illustrations —" The Romans severely punished one that showed himself out of a window with a garland on his head in the time of the Punic war, when it went ill with the commonwealth. Justinus, the good emperor of Constantinople, took the downfall of the city of Antioch by an earthquake so much to heart that it caused him a grievous sickness, A. D. 527. When Pope Clement and his cardinals were imprisoned by the duke of Bourbon in St Angelo, Cæsar in Spain forbade all interludes to be played. In England the king was exceedingly sorry, and Cardinal Wolsey drained the land of twelvescore thousand pounds to relieve and ransom the distressed pope, for whom he wept grievously."—*Trapp.*

II The characteristics of his grief.

1. *It was intense.* " I sat down and wept." Probably he had stood to hear their story. Now his heart melts like wax. His grief is overwhelming. Falling into his seat he gives vent to a flood of weeping. Not the transitory ruffling of the emotions, nor mere sentimental sympathy elicited by a tale of woe His brethren's sorrows became his own. Jeremiah's prayer answered, " Oh that my head were waters," &c. (Jer. ix. 1). With David, he "watered his couch with his tears " The sins of his people became in some measure his own. In this see faint type of Christ, who " bore our griefs," &c Faint anticipation of that " man of sorrows," who "offered up prayers and supplications with strong crying and tears" (Heb. v. 7) in the garden of Gethsemane. 2. *It was enduring.* "And mourned certain days." Not the evanescent passion of superficial sorrow, but the deep soul-stirring grief of a noble and generous nature. Blind and violent sorrow generally dies away like the noisy crackling of thorns in the fire. Its very intenseness makes its brevity. Grief that has a deep and abiding provocation dies not thus. It contemplates the future as well as the present. The past it mourns, but seeks help for the future. Nor can it be appeased until the disgrace is wiped away, and deliverance found. Like Mary, it waits at the sepulchre until the angel appears to assure it of the resurrection of buried hopes 3. *It was self-denying.* " And fasted." Not the comfortable and self-indulgent grief that makes the very sorrow an excuse for sottish excess. All such grief bears a lie upon its face The mind affects the body. Severe mental strain, whether of agony or rapture, weakens appetite and kills desire. *Real heart-pain is always ascetic in its bodily aspect.* The grief of the hypocrite or half-hearted is self-indulgent and short-lived because superficial. The grief of an earnest man of

truth is terrible and irresistible because of its self-forgetfulness Fasting is (1) Often associated with profound grief in Scripture (2 Sam. i. 12; xii. 16—21; Ps. xxxv 13; lxix 10; Dan vi 8, Jonah iii 5). (2) May be the natural attendant of grief, or the outward symbol of its presence (3) Is recognized and commended in Scripture as a religious exercise (1 Sam vii 6, Jer. xxxvi 9, Matt. vi. 17, Acts x 30; 1 Cor. vii 5)

III The issue of his grief. "And prayed before the God of heaven." Herein consists difference between godly and selfish sorrow. The one ends in blank despair, the other finds relief in prayer The passionate writhing of a rebellious heart dares not look up. It leads to suicide and madness. Note, 1. *Grief is sanctified by prayer.* Pain no inherently sanctifying or softening virtue. Only when borne in faith and godly resignation does it leave a blessing It then becomes sacred, and softens the heart, like dew upon mown grass, or showers on the thirsty soil Submissive and prayerful sorrow one of the most gracious experiences that can happen to man. 2. *Grief is relieved by prayer* "Be careful for nothing, but in everything by prayer and supplication," &c (Phil. iv 6) In prayer the burden is cast upon One who is able and willing

to bear it. If men find their burdens and anxieties lighter when they speak of them to their fellows, surely the relief must be greater when they unburden their mind to God, who is not only willing, but able to succour. Pent up mountain torrents are turbulent and furious, open streams are calmer, and more placid in their flow 3 *Grief is made fruitful by prayer* Sorrow without an outlet produces not good, but harm. It renders the spirit morose, and comforts no mourner. Only when grief is poured into the ear of God can it bear any good fruit A saint's tears are better than a sinner's triumphs Bernard saith "Lachrymæ pœnitentium sunt vinum angelorum." "The tears of penitents are the wine of angels" St. Lawrence Justinian, Patriarch of Venice, says: "He cannot help sorrowing for other people's sins, who sorrows truly for his own" St. Augustine. "We mourn over the sins of others, we suffer violence, we are tormented in our minds." St. Chrysostom "Moses was raised above the people because he habitually deplored the sins of others. He who sorrows for other men's sins, has the tenderness of an apostle, and is an imitator of that one who said· "Who is weak, and I am not weak? Who is offended, and I burn not?" (2 Cor. xi. 29).

FASTING.

i. 4. *And fasted.*

I Occasions of fasting. 1. Afflictions of the Church (Nehemiah). 2 National judgments (Joel). 3 Domestic bereavement (David). 4. Imminent danger (Esther). 5 Solemn ordinances (Paul and Barnabas set apart).

II The design of fasting 1 *To assist penitence.* "To afflict the soul," a phrase often employed in connection with abstinence (Lev. xvi 29; Isa. lviii. 5) Without spiritual repentance bodily mortification worthless, and meaningless. 2. *To mortify bodily lusts and promote heart purity* Fasting not end, but means Not essential to holiness; only an accidental of our fallen state. No fasting in heaven, because

no fleshly corruptions Without falling into Manichean heresy, which makes sin necessarily inherent in the human body, we must regard the body as an enemy to spirituality Paul did, hence, "I keep under my body," &c (1 Cor. ix. 27) 3 *To humble and give sympathy with the poor.* Opulent classes sympathize too little with struggling poor, because do not understand meaning of want. If practise occasional abstinence, and really *suffer* hunger, can better understand what others suffer constantly.

III The duty of fasting 1 *Forms part of general principle of self-denial essential to true discipleship* "If any man will be my disciple let him take up his cross daily," &c (Luke ix 23) This duty not to be despised because some abuse it. Because some make it meritorious, no reason why we should neglect it altogether. Most sacred ordinances (Lord's Supper) have been most grossly perverted, and most gracious privileges most grossly abused. Counterfeits only prove the value of true coin. 2. *Implied, and therefore enjoined, by words of Christ*. "This kind goeth not out but by prayer and fasting" (Matt. xvii. 21). 3. *Enforced by the example of Christ*. In all things he our pattern. What Christ sanctioned by his own act cannot be considered as either superfluous, or superstitious. Point all objectors to him. 4. *Associated in Scripture with the bestowal of great blessings*. Nineveh spared when the inhabitants prayed, and mourned, fasting (Jonah iv. 11). Ahab pardoned when he humbled himself with fasting (1 Kings xxi. 29). Christ promises heavenly reward to those whose fasting is sincere (Matt. vi. 16).

IV. The manner and degree of fasting. 1. *Sometimes total abstinence from food for a time* (Esther iv. 16). 2. *More often abstinence from superfluous food* (Dan x. 3).

V. The spirit in which to fast. 1. *With sincere humility*. Ostentation condemned by Christ (Matt. vi. 16). Uncharitableness or peevishness often accompany the exercise and deprive it of all sweetness and profit. It may become a source of pride and a cover for sin. 2. *With true repentance*. This the essential principle of all abstinence. *The sacrifice of the will* is the truth forthshadowed. This only one outward sign of the complete surrender of the will in all things. Nothing meritorious. Only means to an end. That end the

complete subjection of flesh to spirit, of the carnal nature to the spiritual. If it be objected, "You should pay attention to the weightier matters of morality and benevolence," we reply: "These ought ye to do, and not to leave the others undone." These outward things, as kneeling, weeping, and fasting, are good helps and preparations unto prayer. As Sarah continued three days in fasting and prayer, that the Lord would deliver her from her shame (Tobit iii); so Tobias maketh it a general rule, saying: "Prayer is good joined with fasting." Ecclesiasticus says (xxx. 5): "The prayer of him that humbleth himself pierceth the clouds, and she will not be comforted until she come nigh, nor go her way until the highest God have mercy upon her."

Illustrations.—Neander says, "Although the early Christians did not retire from the business of life, yet they were accustomed to devote many separate days entirely to examining their own hearts, and pouring them out before God, while they dedicated their lives anew to him with uninterrupted prayers, in order that they might again return to their ordinary occupations with renewed zeal and earnestness. These days of holy devotion, days of prayer and penitence, which individuals appointed for themselves, were often a kind of fast days. They were accustomed to limit their corporal wants on those days, or to fast entirely. That which was spared by their abstinence was applied to the support of their poorer brethren."

"There are Christians whose 'flesh,' whether by its quantity, or natural temperament, renders them sluggish, slothful, wavering, and physically by far too fond of the 'good things' of the table and the wine-cellar. That sort of Christian pressingly needs fasting, ay, thorough fasting. Brave, large-hearted Martin Luther nobly confessed *his* need, and nobly acted it out, not without strife and 'lusting.' Of fasting as a whole, and as applying to all, it may be said that while it has been perverted into a pestilent superstition, yet, in the words of Bishop Andrews, 'There is more fear of a pottingerful of gluttony, than of a spoonful of superstition.'" —*Grosart.*

INTERCESSORY PRAYER.

i. 5—11.   *And prayed before the God of heaven.*

Prayer variously designated *invocation, petition, supplication,* or *intercession,* according to the aspect in which it is regarded. The subject of this paragraph is *intercessory prayer, i. e.* prayer offered by one human being on behalf of another. That such intervention is admissible, and effectual in the Divine economy, is evident from the teaching of Scripture. 1. *It is frequently enjoined* (Numb. vi. 23—26; Job xlii. 8; Ps. cxxii. 6; Jer. xxix. 7; Joel ii. 17; Matt. v. 44; Ephes vi. 18;

1 Tim. ii. 1; Jas. v 14; 1 Jno. v 16). *2. Illustrations of its efficacy abound.* Abraham (Gen. xvii. 18—20; xviii 23; xx. 7—18). Moses (Exod viii 12—31; ix. 33, xvii 11—13, xxxii 11—34). Jacob (Gen. xlvii. 7, xlix.). David (2 Sam xii. 16). Ezra (ix. 3—15) Job (i 5, xlii. 10). Elijah (1 Kings xvii. 20—23) Peter (Acts ix 40) Paul (Acts xxviii. 8).

I. Here is intercessory prayer, based upon a true conception of the Divine character. 1 *It regards him as the majestic ruler of the world* "O Lord God of heaven, the great and terrible God." *Great* in power and government. *Terrible* in judgment and punishment. Such views of the Divine majesty calculated to inspire reverence and wholesome fear. Would check any tendency to presumption, and place the supplicant in a true position at the Divine *footstool* (Ps. xcix. 5, cxxxii 7) 2 *It regards him as the faithful and compassionate Father of his children.* (1) *Faithful,* "that keepeth covenant" Some parts of covenant unconditional; a promise concerning seasons (Gen. viii 22); destruction of the world (Gen. ix 14—17). Some conditional upon moral conduct (Josh. vii 11; xxiii. 16) (2) *Compassionate,* "and mercy" (Exod. xx 6). (3) *To his children.* "Them that love him, and keep his commandments." This, beautiful description of filial spirit. The motive principle and the manifest conduct both indicated. First, inward affection, "that love him;" then, outward obedience, "that keep his commandments" The first revealing itself by the second. The second the offspring of the first. "That he may at once both tremble before him, and trust upon him; he describeth God by his goodness as well as by his greatness, and so helpeth his own faith by contemplating God's faithfulness and loving-kindness."—*Trapp.*

II. Here is intercessory prayer, untiring in its importunity and unselfish in its benevolence. 1. *Unwearied in its importunity* "Which I pray before thee now day and night" (v. 6). Four months elapsed between the commencement of his intercession in Chisleu (i. 1), and the beginning of its fulfilment in Nisan (ii 1). Night and day, *i. e.* unceasingly, did Nehemiah press his suit. Such importunity sure to prevail. Inspired by the Holy Ghost, commended by the Saviour, and encouraged by the word of God, it cannot fail eventually (Acts xii 5; 2 Cor. xii. 8, 1 Thess. iii. 10). "The kingdom of heaven suffereth violence," &c (Matt xi. 12). Parable of the unjust judge (Luke xviii. 5). Perseverance necessary not because God reluctant to hear, but because men are slow to value his gifts. When we rightly appreciate God's mercies he bestows them freely, not before. The "Jews divide their day into *prayer, work,* and *repast;* neither will they omit prayer for their meat or labour The Mahommedans, what occasion soever they have, either by profit or pleasure, to divert them, will pray five times every day, and upon the Friday (which is their Sabbath) six times. How few and feeble are our prayers in comparison, either for ourselves or our brethren in distress" 2. *Unselfish in its benevolence.* Much anguish of mind, and self-sacrifice, accompanied the urging of this prayer. Rest forsook his frame and slumber his eyelids (Ps. cxxxii. 4; Prov. vi 4) His whole soul so thoroughly stirred that he cared neither for sleep nor food. Such intercession has all the marks of sincerity, and every probability of success.

III Here is intercessory prayer, accompanied by self-abasement and contrition "And confess the sins of the children of Israel, which we have sinned against thee, both I and my father's house have sinned" (v 6). From the spirit and language of this prayer we learn—1. *That close approaches to God reveal unsuspected moral defects in the character even of good men.* "I and my father's house have sinned" Though a sincere believer and servant of Jehovah, Nehemiah now discovered and remembered personal and family sins which bowed him to the earth in sorrow. The more closely he approaches the "Holy One who cannot look upon sin" (Heb i 13), the more distinctly and painfully does he perceive his unworthiness and demerit. Thus was it with Manoah (Judg xiii), and Isaiah (Isa vi.), and St. John (Rev. i) When want real power in times of urgent need they discover their weakness. When daring suppliants press up to the steps of the mercy-seat they discover stains previously unsuspected. Comparatively innocent they may be (as Nehemiah was), but not without sin, and such as needs to be confessed and pardoned. 2. *That the discovery of moral defects teaches good men their common depravity and mutual need of Divine mercy.* "Confess the sins of the children of Israel which *we* have sinned" (v. 6). He discovers that in God's sight there is "no difference." He needs mercy and deserves wrath as much as they. Their sins are identified with his own. The supplicant who pleads for others' sins, as though he had real contact with them, and felt their burdensomeness, will prevail. He who pharisaically thanks God that he is not as other men, in his prayers will not succeed much. When we can say, "of whom I am chief," God will pardon both us and those for whom we intercede 3. *That the discovery of moral defects deprives good men of all right to intercede for others on the ground of their own merit.* The holiest may not approach the throne of Mercy in his own name, or make his relationship to God a ground of appeal. Only *one* name, *one* plea, will avail The *name* and *blood* of Christ are our grounds of appeal. The promise and character of God were theirs of old. "For thy name's sake" was the Old Testament form of "For Christ's sake" in the New. When *we* have done our utmost we are only unprofitable servants dependent upon Divine forbearance, and can perform no works of meritorious supererogation. 4. *That the discovery of moral defects brings good men into that state of humility which is essential to success in prayer.* "To that man will I look; even to him that is poor and of a contrite spirit, and trembleth at my word" (Isa. lxvi. 2) Self-sufficiency renders God's arm powerless to hear or help. Self-despair, which casts itself at the feet of God, saying, "If thou canst do anything, have compassion," is sure to meet with a ready response. Human weakness commends itself to Divine omnipotence and compassion. Our impotence is our strongest recommendation to God.

IV. **Here is intercessory prayer fortifying itself with strong arguments, and appealing to the most powerful motives** 1. *It makes the promise of God its ground of appeal.* "Remember, I beseech thee, the word which thou commandedst thy servant Moses" (v. 8; Deut. iv 25—31; xxx. 1—10). No argument so powerful with God as "*Remember.*" When men honour *God's Word,* he will not be slow to hear *their words.* When the prayer of faith builds upon the word of promise it rests upon a sure foundation "God not a man that he should lie, or the son of a man that he should repent" (Numb. xxiii. 19). 2. *It regards the verification of one word as a reason for expecting the fulfilment of another* "If ye transgress, I will scatter you . . . If ye turn, I will gather you" (v. 8, 9). Half the prophecy had been carried out; Nehemiah claims the fulfilment of the other half. "*All* the promises of God are yea" (2 Cor. 1 20). "No variableness or shadow of turning with God" (Jas. 1. 17) He who kept his covenant with Noah will keep it with his posterity to the end of time. 3 *It regards the verification of maledictions as a ground for expecting the still more certain fulfilment of bene-dictions.* If the *curses* were literally carried out, how much more willin ly will the great Father bestow the promised *blessings.* If in chastising he was faithful, surely he will not be less so in healing and restoring. The *fact* of their dispersion becomes the basis of his claim for their restoration. He who is faithful in that which he does unwillingly, will not be less faithful in that which he delights to do. If, because of his word, he punished, because of his word he will show mercy. 4. *It appeals to the relationship existing between God and his chosen people* "These are *thy* servants, and *thy* people" (v. 10). Can he who has borne with them so long and so tenderly desert them now? The paternal heart is appealed to. If an earthly parent acknowledges this as the most powerful sentiment in his nature, how much more the heavenly. Had he not said, "Can a woman forget her sucking child, that she should not have compassion on the son of her womb? Yea, they may forget, yet will I not forget thee" (Isa xlix. 15). 5. *It repudiates a disloyal* *or presumptuous motive.* "Thy servants, who desire to fear thy name" (v. 11). Not that they might boast and defy the God who had delivered them, as their fathers had done, not that they might free themselves from a heathen yoke only ; but that they might fear and worship the God of Israel. Blessings that are to be laid on God's altar when received will not be long withheld   6 *It makes past deliverance the ground of present expectation.* "Whom thou hast redeemed by thy great power, and by thy strong hand." The memory of the exodus from Egypt, and the victories of the wilderness and Canaan, excites the hope that God will again interfere on behalf of his people   The remembrance of those years of the right hand of the Most High, stimulates Nehemiah's prayer. Thus should the past ever instruct the present. He who studies the Church's history will find ample material for the nourishment and strengthening of his faith in God.

V. Here is intercessory prayer accompanied by diligence in the performance of daily duties   "And grant him mercy in the sight of this man. For I was the king's cupbearer" (v 11)   The most earnest supplication not exonerate from personal effort, and the discharge of necessary duties   Prayer not to be made a substitute for work   The suppliant must relax no painstaking effort, and watch for the openings of Providence   Every step must be taken as though all depended on our own effort, and yet in entire dependence on Divine guidance. Thus may we in a sense answer our own prayers. Not necessary to leave ordinary spheres of work   Nehemiah asks Divine guidance in regular duty, that the monarch may be induced to grant him the petition which he was anxious to present at the first favourable opportunity.

Illustrations :—One of the holiest and most devoted of modern missionaries, who after surmounting almost insuperable obstacles, at length completed his translation of the Scriptures into a language of surpassing difficulty, inscribed upon the last page of his manuscript these words :—" I give it, as the result of long experience, that prayer and pains, with faith in Christ Jesus, will enable a man to do anything."

Æschylus was condemned to death by the Athenians, and about to be executed   His brother Amyntas had signalized himself at the battle of Salamis, where he lost his right hand.   He came into court, just as his brother was condemned, and without saying a word, held up the stump of his right arm in the sight of all   The historian says that, "when the judges saw this mark of his sufferings, they remembered what he had done, and for his sake pardoned the brother whose life had been forfeited."

"At the time the Diet of Nuremberg was held," says Tholuck, "Luther was earnestly praying in his own dwelling ; and at the very hour when the edict was issued, granting free toleration to all Protestants, he ran out of his house, crying out, ' We have gained the victory.' "

Rev. Charles Simeon wrote to a friend : "With the hope of ultimate acceptance with God, I have always enjoyed much cheerfulness before men ; but I have at the same time laboured incessantly to cultivate *the deepest humility* before God   I have never thought that the circumstances of God having forgiven me, was any reason why I should forgive myself ; on the contrary, I have always judged it better to loathe myself the more, in proportion as I was assured that God was pacified toward me (Ezek xvi 63).   Nor have I been satisfied with viewing my sins, as men view the stars on a cloudy night, one here, and another there, with great intervals between ; but have endeavoured to get, and to preserve continually before my eyes, such a view of them as we have of the stars in the brightest night the greater and the smaller all intermingled, and forming as it were one continuous mass   There are but two objects that I have desired for these forty years to behold ; the one is my own vileness, the other is the glory of God in the face of Jesus Christ ; and I have always thought that they should be viewed together, just as Aaron confessed all the sins of the children of Israel, whilst he put them on the head of the scape-goat. The disease did not keep him from applying the remedy, nor the remedy from feeling the disease."

PRAYER FOR CHURCH REVIVAL.

i. 5—11. *And prayed before the God of heaven, &c.*

I. Prompted by love for the Church   1. *Therefore persistent.* "Day and night " This love not fickle, or easily discouraged. "Many waters cannot quench love" (Cant. viii. 7).   Not fruitless emotion, but practical in its aim   2 *Therefore fervent.* "Wept and mourned." The love deep, not superficial ; therefore the prayer was fervent. This love, previously slumbering, now fully awakened, therefore prayer intense. This love, now sorely tried; therefore fervent prayer required.

II Recognizes the personal unworthiness of the petitioner. "Both I and my father's house have sinned" This confession consistent with the priestly intercession of those who stand before God in the people's name. Jewish high priests "offered sacrifice first for their *own sins*, and then for the sins of the people" (Heb. vii. 27). Must come not as having any right to intercede, but as magnifying God's mercy.

III Is full of faith "Remember the word" (v 8) 1 *Notwithstanding the Church's declension.* Sin not overlooked, or ignored, but viewed in the light of Divine mercy. Confessed, pardoned, and forsaken, it no longer becomes a hindrance. God will not remember against them his people's sin when they repent thereof. 2 *Because of the veracity of the Divine promise* "I will gather" This, basis of all hope then and now When pleading the promises, should do so in faith, nothing doubting, for "God hath magnified *his word* above all his name" (Ps cxxxviii 2). This promise embraces—(1) The assurance of mercy after chastisement. "I will scatter . . . I will gather" (viii. 9). (2) The renewal of former kindness. "Whom thou hast redeemed by thy great power, and by thy strong hand" (v. 10) (3) The vindication of the Divine name and honour "These are thy servants, and thy people" (v. 10).

Illustrations —It is related of an ancient king that he never granted a petition that was offered with a trembling hand, because it marked a want of confidence in his clemency. "Have faith in God" (Mark xi 22).

A pious sick man in the western part of New York, used to pray for the preachers and the churches of his acquaintance daily at set hours In his diary were found entries like this, " I have been enabled to offer the prayer of faith for a revival in such a place " So through the list. It is said that each church was soon enjoying a revival, and nearly in the order of time named in the diary.

THE MAJESTY AND MERCY OF GOD.

i 5. The great and terrible God, that keepeth covenant and mercy.

From this sublime invocation we gather—

I That there is perfect harmony in the attributes of the Divine nature God is one. His nature indivisible. Men speak as though justice were necessarily opposed to mercy. No necessary antagonism A God all mercy would be a God not only unkind, but unjust. Mistake to speak of mercy triumphing over justice. Mercy harmonizes with justice, never annihilates it. God is just, and "yet the justifier of him that believeth" (Rom. iii. 26). In the pardon of a sinner we see the vindication of Divine justice no less than the magnifying of Divine mercy; and Divine mercy unites with Divine justice in the destruction of the finally impenitent No wrath so fearful to contemplate as "the wrath of the *Lamb*" (Rev vi. 16)

II. That the Divine attributes are equally enlisted in the work of human salvation. Salvation as much an act of justice as of mercy. The holiness of God an important factor in the production of both repentance and regeneration. By the view of holiness, sin is discovered in its true colours By the indwelling of the spirit of holiness, sin is destroyed and eradicated. "Mercy and truth are met together" (Ps. lxxxv. 10) Hence Watts has truthfully sung—

" Here the whole Deity is known; nor dares a creature guess,
Which of the glories brightest shone; the justice or the grace "

III That the harmony of the Divine nature is the only true basis of moral goodness 1 *The contemplation of Divine compassion alone tends to antinomianism.* Mercy may be magnified at the expense of the moral law. God willing to forgive, but equally willing to defend against and deliver from sin itself. Guard against danger of so magnifying Divine mercy as to make sin a light offence. God's law is, " Sin shall not have dominion over you." " Reckon ye yourselves to be dead unto sin" (Rom. vi.). Then, as a merciful provision, " If any man sin we have an advocate," &c. (1 Jno. i.). 2. *The contemplation of the Divine holiness alone tends to legalism.* By viewing the spotless purity of the Divine character, and the rigid requirements of Divine law, apart from the gracious promises of Divine mercy, a spirit of legal bondage, or self-righteous asceticism, is engendered. Hence spring meritorious works, penances, and self-inflicted flagellations and other useless tortures. " Not by works of righteousness which we have done, but according to his mercy he hath saved us" (Tit. iii. 5). 3. *The contemplation of the unity of the Divine nature is essential to the formation of a true moral character.* The spotless purity and immaculate holiness of the Divine nature deter from iniquity, and the violation of God's law; whilst the tender mercy and loving-kindness of his nature encourage the penitent to crave pardon and grace.

IV. That the harmony of the Divine nature furnishes the only true ideal of moral goodness. 1. *Human goodness is at best one-sided.* Some virtues developed at expense of others. Few Christians are fully and evenly matured. One aspect of moral goodness cultivated to the exclusion of others. Men follow too much their natural disposition in this. The gentle are apt to cultivate the passive graces alone, whilst the bold forget to clothe themselves with the meekness and gentleness of Christ. 2. *Divine goodness alone is perfectly impartial.* God both majestic and merciful; infinitely high, yet infinitely condescending. No exaggeration, nor inequality, nor partiality characterizes his nature or his government. His purity unsullied, his peace unruffled, his dignity uncompromised, his fidelity unchallenged, &c.

V. That notwithstanding the har- mony of the Divine nature, men come into contact with different aspects of that nature according to their moral condition. As the magnet draws to itself certain metals similar in nature, and rejects certain others alien from it; so do men in their various characters attract different phases of God's nature. 1. *A penitent spirit is necessary to the experience of Divine mercy.* Only such will seek it; only such require it: only such are capable of receiving and living in the enjoyment of it. 2. *An obedient spirit is necessary to the continued experience of God's favour.* Paternal benedictions only promised to those who possess a filial spirit. " If ye love me, keep my commandments, and I will pray the Father," &c. (Jno xiv. 15). Disobedience always incurs Divine displeasure, and obscures the light of the Father's countenance. 3. *A rebellious spirit will infallibly provoke the exercise of Divine wrath.* "The soul that sinneth, it shall die" (Ezek xviii. 4). " God cannot look upon iniquity" (Deut. xxxii. 4). His character is pledged to active antagonism to evil. Sin not punished now as it deserves, because this is "the day of salvation;" and the mediatorial intercession of Christ holds back the thunderbolts of righteous anger.

Illustrations :—A Jew entered a Persian temple, and saw there the sacred fire. He said, " How do you worship fire?" He was told. Then the Israelite replied, " You dazzle the eye of the body, but darken that of the mind; in presenting to them the terrestrial light, you take away the celestial." The Persian then asked, " How do you name the Supreme Being?" " We call him Jehovah Adonai; that is, the Lord who was, who is, and who shall be." " Your word is great and glorious, but it is terrible," said the Persian. A Christian approaching, said, " We call Him Abba, Father." Then the Gentile and the Jew regarded each other with surprise, and said, " Your word is the nearest and the highest; but who gives you courage to call the Eternal thus?" " The Father Himself," said the Christian, who then expounded to them the plan of redemption. Then they believed, and lifted up their eyes to heaven, saying, " Father, dear Father;" and joining hands, called each other brethren.— *Krummacher.*

IMPORTUNITY IN PRAYER.

i. 6.   I pray before thee now day and night.

I. Natural 1. *If it be the expression of real need.* When children want, they ask; when they feel deeply, they ask earnestly. This prayer protracted through four months, yet not mere repetition of words. Difference between real and artificial want : one listless in prayer, the other importunate. Conscious want asks and asks again. Prayer not to be regarded as end, but means. Many reverse this order. Nehemiah did not pray for sake of prayer, but for sake of object sought. 2. *If it be the expression of urgent need.* When we suffer pain we cry out. Starving man always importunate. The more needy the more earnest. Sinners under conviction of sin, groan and wrestle in agonizing importunity until they find relief. Christians wrestle with "strong crying and supplications" until they prevail. Sailors in a sinking vessel and miners in the prospect of certain death pray with real importunity because they are in urgent extremity. In the same spirit should we approach the throne of grace ; for our need is the same, though we may not feel it. 3. *If it be the expression of hopeful need.* None can persevere earnestly in a cause known to be hopeless Hope cheers on the most despairing. Without hope nothing arduous could be undertaken. This inspires prayer. It looks to the goal, and anticipates eventual success. This hope must have a true foundation, and not rest on desire or possibility only. The word of God is the only secure foundation on which it can build (v. 8).

II. Necessary. 1. *In order that the suppliant may be rightly affected.* Nothing truer than that success in prayer depends on spirit of suppliant. Importunity promotes—(1) Tenderness, (2) Spirituality, (3) Humility, (4) Zeal. Often the petitioner is not morally fit to receive the grace or gift desired. Prayer purifies the heart, sanctifies the will, and removes hindrances out of the way. 2. *In order that the gifts may be rightly appreciated.* God will not cast his pearls before swine. He will only give when his gifts are valued What we seek for long and earnestly, we value highly when we gain. What easily won, lightly esteemed and easily lost. This true of money, lands, home, child, &c The more hardly money is earned, the more carefully it is used. Those who have never earned, but inherited wealth, generally become spendthrift, because ignorant of value of money. Home only possesses its full significance to those who have crossed oceans and continents, and endured perils on land and sea to reach it That life the most precious to the parent which has been oftenest snatched from the jaws of death. Gifts nearly lost, or dearly bought, are counted to be most precious and priceless. 3. *In order that God's conditions may be fulfilled.* (1) Faith required. "He that cometh unto God," &c. (Heb. xi. 6) (2) Whole-hearted earnestness required. "When they seek me with their whole heart" (Ps. cxix. 2). (3) Submission to the Divine will required. "Thy will be done." All these conditions are promoted by continued importunity.

III. Scriptural. 1. *The Bible enjoins it by precepts the most explicit.* (Deut. iv. 7. 1 Ch. xvi. 11. 2 Ch. vii. 14. Job viii. 5 Ps i. 15; lxxxi 10; cxlv. 18. Prov. ii. 3. Isa. xxx. 19; lviii. 9. Jer. xxxi. 9. Lam ii. 19. Matt. vii 7. Luke xviii. 1. Rom. xii 12. Phil. iv. 6. 1 Thess v. 17.) 2 *The Bible encourages it by examples the most striking.* (Gen. xviii. 32; xxxii 26. Exod xxxii. 32. Deut. ix. 15. Judges vi. 39. 1 Sam. i. 10 ; xii. 23. Ezra ix. 5. Ps xvii. 1; xxii. 2 Dan vi 10, ix 3. Matt. xv. 23 ; xx. 31. Acts vi. 4 ; xii. 5. 2 Cor. xii. 8. 1 Thess. iii. 10

IV. Successful Though long delayed the answer came, and Nehemiah's importunity was amply rewarded 1. *Not in the sense that God's will can be affected by man's importunity.* That will is perfect and immutable "I am God, I change not" (Mal. iii. 6). If that will were variable there could be no confidence amongst men. The government of the world would rest upon no firm and solid foundation. Whilst the Divine *will* can never be changed, the *exercise* of that will may be affected by human conditions. The Father's will is to save the whole race; for "he willeth not the death of the sinner;" but according to the laws which he has appointed for man, his will is limited by certain conditions which must be fulfilled before he can exercise that will. The same occurs in earthly relations. A wise father has a spendthrift son, whom he loves and would gladly treat with lavish generosity, but that he knows it would be his ruin. That son becomes reformed, and (not the father's will, for that has remained the same, but) the father's treatment of his son is altered accordingly. He can now do what he had the heart and will to do before, but not the judgment. 2. *Not in the sense that God is reluctant, and can be overcome by human persuasion.* This, a common error. Seen not so much in distinct affirmation as in public prayers, religious literature, and devout conversation. For our sakes, not for God's sake, importunity required. Parable of unjust judge only designed to teach *one salient truth,* viz. the necessity for unwearying devotion in prayer, not the unwillingness of God to hear. The Old Testament passages (Gen. xviii. 32, Exod. xxxii. 32), which represent God as apparently reluctant, and eventually persuaded, are anthropomorphic. God's actual, practical government of the universe is amenable to the intercessions of the righteous. Certain blessings are promised only in answer to "effectual fervent prayer" (Jas. v. 16). 3. *In the sense that importunity and prevalence are mysteriously, but certainly, connected.* The "how" we may not be able to define, but the fact we cannot deny. The process here as elsewhere is mysterious, but the result is patent to all thoughtful and devout minds. Who can explain the connection between the seed and the plant, or between mind and matter? The presence of a mystery does not destroy our faith in the fact. "Elias was a man subject to like passions as we are; yet he prayed," &c. (Jas. v. 17). Let them deny the facts who can; and they are worth many arguments.

Illustrations :—Prayer pulls the rope below, and the great bell rings above in the ear of God. Some scarcely stir the bell, for they pray so languidly; others give an occasional pluck at the rope· but he who wins with heaven is the man who grasps the rope boldly, and pulls continuously with all his might.—*Spurgeon.*

"If from the tree of promised mercy thou
Wouldst win the good which loadeth every bough,
Then urge the promise well with pleading cries,
Move heaven itself with vehemence of sighs;
Soon shall celestial fruit thy toil repay—
'Tis ripe, and waits for him who loves to pray.
What if thou fail at first, yet give not o'er,
Bestir thyself to labour more and more;
Enlist a brother's sympathetic knee,
The tree will drop its fruit when *two* agree;
Entreat the Holy Ghost to give thee power,
Then shall the fruit descend in joyful shower."

FORGOTTEN SINS REMEMBERED.

i. 6. Both I and my father's house have sinned.

I. Sins forgotten are not necessarily sins forgiven. 1. *Wicked men soon forget their sins.* This arises from indifference to the nature and consequences of sin. Sin becomes a trifling matter easily committed, readily forgotten. Not therefore either forgotten or forgiven by God. "I have spilled the ink over a bill, and so have blotted it till it can hardly be read, but this is quite another thing from having it blotted out, for that cannot be till payment is made. So a man may blot his sins from his memory, and quiet his mind with false hopes, but the peace which this will bring him is widely different from that which arises from God's forgiveness of sin through the satisfaction which Jesus made in his atonement. *Our* blotting is one thing, God's *blotting out* is something far higher."—*Spurgeon.* 2. *Good men may forget their sins.* They often do. Nehemiah had done. Not heinous and wilful sins, for such they do not commit. "He that committeth sin is of the devil" (1 John). Sins of ignorance and of inadvertence, as well as of unbelief, &c., may be committed even by believers, and then forgotten—(1) Through neglecting faithful self-examination, (2) Through an uneducated or half-enlightened conscience, (3) Through a low moral sense.

II Forgotten sins often hinder prayer. They did so in Nehemiah's case. Not until his own and his father's sins had been acknowledged and pardoned could he prevail in prayer. What earnest Christian not had similar experience? The spirit of prayer mysteriously absent; oft repeated requests strangely unanswered. On carefully searching have found the hidden sin and put away the hindrance. (1) They deprive the soul of the spirit of supplication. (2) They act as barriers preventing access to God.

III. Forgotten sins often interfere with Church prosperity. No blessing for the Church at Jerusalem until these sins and theirs had been confessed and put away. Achan and his wedge of gold brought shame and defeat upon the armies of Israel. Secret evils cherished often cause great disaster and moral feebleness to the Church. 1. *By depriving her of that joy which is her strength.* "The joy of the Lord is your strength." Without the clear assurance of the Divine favour joy impossible. When Church depressed and doubting, her work languishes 2. *By hindering God's blessing from attending her efforts.* Without his benedictions all the Church's enterprises must fail. Paul may plant, Apollos may water, but God gives the increase.

IV Forgotten sins are often remembered in seasons of gracious visitation. When God comes near and manifests himself as refiner's fire, his servants are quick to discern, and sensitive to feel their most hidden faults, for —1 *Revivals of religion promote self-examination and abasement.* 2. *Revivals of religion create a higher moral sense.*

V. Forgotten sins must be confessed when brought to remembrance. 1. *Vicariously.* Not only own sins but sins of brethren and family, and Church. If we pray for them God will give them repentance and they will be saved. "They shall be made willing in the day of his power." 2 *Separately.* As, in the text, Nehemiah confesses their sins by name, so should all earnest suppliants acknowledge their failures, not in general terms only, but in detail and separately. This will produce clear views of sin in all its reality, and will deepen the sorrow of a sincere repentance. 3. *Accompanied by prayer for mercy.* This, great end of confession, viz that guilt be cancelled, and sins remitted. Confession in itself no virtue, unless it spring from a desire for pardon, and a determination to shun the cause of sin in the future.

GOD'S MEMORY.

i. 8. *Remember, I beseech thee, the word that, &c.*

I God's memory is infallible 1 *Its records are accurate.* No human records are so. Errors in everything human. Memory of man fails, and deceives him. God's memory absolutely infallible, because he alone can see things as they really are. 2. *Its records are impartial.* Prejudice and personal bias enter into all human histories. This bias often quite unconscious and unavoidable. Perfect disinterestedness impossible under existing limitations of human life. God only can look down from the serene heights of immaculate purity, and impartially record the transactions of men. 3 *Its records will form the basis of man's acquittal or condemnation at the Day of Judgment.* The verdict pronounced by Christ in the case of the seven Asian churches, a prelude of the General Judgment of all churches and peoples. Each letter commences with, "I know thy works" (Rev ii.), implying that the judgment pronounced is infallibly true. Such momentous issues, as *eternal life* and *eternal death*, could not depend upon anything less than an infallible record of the whole period of earthly probation ; and none but God can furnish such a record. Not one shall be unrighteously condemned. No miscarriage of justice can possibly occur at that tribunal.

II. God's memory is omniscient. Hence the appeal, "Remember." 1. *It takes cognisance of the most obscure events as well as the most public.* No deed of darkness or act of cruelty unobserved. No cup of water or widow's mite given without the notice of at least One Eye. "What was done in secret shall one day be proclaimed on the housetop." "All things are naked and open to the eyes of him." "Hell is naked before him, and destruction" (Job xxvi. 6). 2. *It is acquainted with the most microscopic details of human life.* Not only does he observe and regulate suns and starry systems in their orbits, but the most infinitesimal animalculæ live and move and have their being under his eye. If he be anywhere, he is everywhere ; if he be in anything, he is in everything. If he order the seraph's flight, he ordains the sparrow's fall : if he tells the number of the stars, he numbers the very hairs of the heads of his saints. The minuteness of Providence its perfection. Since he is above all, and through all, and in all, let us look to him *for* all, let us look to him *in* all. 3 *It fathoms the most secret thoughts and motives.* "Thou compassest my path," &c., "for there is not a word in my tongue, but lo, O Lord, thou knowest

it altogether" (Ps. cxxxix.). Thoughts unbreathed in word are recorded in his memory : and motives unsuspected by the most intimate friend are there written down.

III. God loves to be reminded of his word. "Remember, I beseech thee, the word which thou commandedst thy servant Moses" (v. 8). 1. *Not that he needs to be reminded of it.* Strictly speaking God can neither remember nor forget, for all things are present with him. Figuratively he is said to do both (Isa. lxii. 6, 7). 2. *Not that he desires to forget.* He delights to honour the word of his promise, and is "not slow concerning his promise, as some men count slackness" (2 Pet. iii. 9) 3. *But because he loves to see his children believing his word.* All men love to be trusted. Parents especially delight to see their children exercise the most implicit trust in their veracity. God also seeks to be trusted, and is pleased when his word is believed. Christ's upbraiding couched in these words · "O slow of heart to believe" (Luke xxiv. 25).

Illustration :—"There is a recent application of electricity by which, under the influence of its powerful light, the body can be so illuminated as that the workings beneath the surface of the skin may be seen. Lift up the hand, and it will appear almost translucent, the bones and veins clearly appearing. It is so in some sense with God's introspection of the human heart. His eye, which shines brighter than the sun, searches us, and discovers all our weakness and infirmity." —*Pilkington.*

PUNISHMENT AND PENITENCE.

i 8, 9. *If ye transgress, I will scatter you, &c.*

Here we trace that sequence which is everywhere taught in Bible, viz. :

I. That sin is invariably followed by punishment 1. *Sometimes with loss of temporal good.* "I will scatter you abroad." The loss of national status and social integrity followed loss of God's favour. They are to-day a standing witness to all the world of the faithfulness of Jehovah's word. Josephus says that in his time they had grown so wicked, that if the Romans had not destroyed and dispersed them, without doubt either the earth would have swallowed them up, or fire from heaven would have consumed them. This kind of punishment not always inflicted. Wicked men flourish and grow rich, yet their end is miserable enough. 2. *Always with loss of spiritual blessing.* "Friendship of world enmity against God." God's favour only secured and continued by separation from sin. Withdrawal of Divine approval must follow deviation from path of Divine precepts. 3. *Hereafter with the loss of all good.* Hell is most frequently referred to as a loss, the negation of all that is dear and sweet and to be desired ; loss of heaven, of peace, of God's presence, of opportunity, of gracious influences of the Holy Spirit, in word, the *loss of the soul.* The loss of *hope* bitterest ingredient in cup of despair. Sin not always *manifestly* punished in this world ; but always *really* so   In the next life the punishment will be manifest to all the universe. Sin *shall not* go unpunished.   " The thought of the future punishment for the wicked which the Bible reveals is enough to make an earthquake of terror in a man's mind. I do not accept the doctrine of eternal punishment because I delight in it. I would cast in doubts if I could, till I had filled hell up to the brim : I would destroy all faith in it : but that would do me no good ; I could not destroy the thing   Nor does it help me to take the word ' everlasting,' and put it into a rack like an inquisitor, until I make it shriek out some other meaning , I cannot alter the stern fact."   " The pea contains the vine, and the flower, and the pod in embryo : and I am sure when I plant it, that it will produce them and nothing else.   Now every action of our lives is embryonic, and according as it is right or wrong, it will surely bring forth the sweet flowers of joy, or the poison fruits of sorrow. Such is the constitution of this world ; and the Bible assures us that the next world only carries it forward. Here and hereafter ' whatsoever a man sows, that shall he also reap.' "—*Beecher.*

II. That true penitence is invariably followed by pardon.   " But if ye turn unto me, and keep my commandments," &c.   The sequence carried out in this history.   National repentance was followed by national restoration to God's favour and forfeited privileges. 1. *True repentance implies the forsaking of evil.* This, first step. Greek words (metameleia, and metanoya) signify change of purpose, and change of thought. Not mere desire or emotional sorrow : but deep contrition resulting from clear view of heinous character of sin. Only when Jews abandoned idolatry and heathen associations could they be received again as God's heritage. 2. *True repentance implies turning to God.* By sin do men turn from God . by repentance they return and cleave to him. Judas an instance of insincere repentance , he turned from his sin, but turned not to God, but went straight into arms of despair   Peter's true repentance urged to the feet of his offended Saviour, where he found mercy. 3. *True repentance includes a determination of future obedience.* This mentioned as a condition in God's promise, and quoted in Nehemiah's prayer, " if ye turn unto me, *and keep my commandments," &c.* Evangelically keep them, for with a legal obedience none can do so. The penitent must have at least an earnest desire and firm resolve to do them as far as he can by God's grace. 4. *Pardon is as certain to follow true penitence as punishment sin.* Both rest upon God's " I will." His threatenings and his promises both stand true. If he fulfil the curses, he will certainly fulfil the benedictions   If punishment has followed sin, we may confidently look for mercy to follow the forsaking of sin. God not less ready to restore than to scatter. 5. *Pardon is accompanied by the restoration of forfeited privileges.* " Yet will I gather them from thence, and will bring them into the place which I have chosen, to set my name there " (v. 9). Not only would they be redeemed from exile and captivity, but re-established in Jerusalem, and enjoying all the privileges of God's special providence and protection. When sinners turn to God they receive all the evangelical blessings of the New Testament Covenant through Christ. Adoption, assurance, sanctification, heirship, heaven, are all theirs, through faith in Jesus Christ.

Illustrations —" ' Let him take hold of my strength, that he may make peace with me   and he shall make peace with me '   I think I can convey the meaning of this passage by what took place in my own family within these few days   One of my children had committed a fault, for which I thought it my duty to chastise him.   I called him to me, explained to him the evil of what he had done, and told him how grieved I was that I must punish him for it.   He heard me in silence, and then rushed into my arms, and burst into tears.   I could sooner have cut off my arm than have struck him for his fault ; he had taken hold of my strength, and had made peace with me "—*R. Tolls*

The first physic to recover our souls is not cordials, but corrosives ; not an immediate stepping into heaven by a present assurance, but mourning and lamentations, and a bitter bewailing of our former transgressions. With Mary Magdalene, we must wash Christ's feet with our tears of sorrow, before we may anoint his head with " the oil of gladness "—*Browning*.

Like *Janus Bifrons*, the Roman god looking two ways, a true repentance not only bemoans the past, but takes heed to the future. Repentance, like the lights of a ship at her bow and her stern, not only looks to the track she has made, but to the path before her. A godly sorrow moves the Christian to weep over the failure of the past, but his eyes are not so blurred with tears, but that he can look watchfully into the future, and, profiting by the experience of former failures, make straight paths for his feet.—*Pilkington*. Repentance without amendment is like continual pumping at a ship, without stopping the leak.

ELECTING GRACE.

i. 9—10. *Now these are thy servants, and thy people.*

I. A chosen place. "The place that I have chosen to set my name there." 1. *Historically, Jerusalem.* By God's appointment this city is called the "holy city;" because he chose it for the dwelling-place of his people, and the site for his temple. Hence the Psalmist: "The Lord hath chosen Zion, he hath chosen it for a dwelling-place for himself: this is my resting-place for ever: here will I dwell, because I have chosen it" (Ps. cxxxii.). For this reason it was holy, though the people by their wickedness had defiled it. Other towns and countries have been chosen by God to play an important part in working out his gracious purposes in the redemption of man, as Bethlehem, Nazareth, Babylon, Rome, &c. Jerusalem exalted above all other cities. The place, however, can make no one holy or acceptable before God: for "he chose not the man for the place's sake, but the place for the man's sake"—*Pilkington*. 2. *Typically, the Church militant.* The Christian Church is now to the world what the holy city was of old. There God dwells, and appoints his ordinances and manifests his glory. As in the holy city so in the Christian Church, there may be worldlings and aliens who nominally belong to the Church, but really have no right or portion therein. Membership in the Church does not necessarily involve spiritual life in the New Testament any more than it did in the Old Testament dispensation. "The Church is God's workshop, where his jewels are polishing for his palace and house, and those he especially esteems, and means to make most resplendent, he hath oftenest his tools upon"—*Leighton*. "Hypocrites are not real members, but excrescences of the Church, like falling hair or the parings of the nails are of the body "—*Salter*. 3. *The Church triumphant.* The Church militant and the Church triumphant really one; like a city built on both sides of a river. There is but a stream of death between grace and glory. Heaven is the final home of God's chosen people. There he has recorded his name, and there doth he dwell in unclouded light. Often called the *New Jerusalem.*

II. A chosen people. "These are thy servants and thy people." His by separation from the surrounding heathen, by redemption from Egypt, by special and unnumbered favours. From these words we may gather who are God's elect. 1. *God's elect are they who recognize him as Lord.* "Thy servants." Entering his service they obey his behests, and in all things submit to his will. As servants who are diligent and dutiful have a right to the care and protection of their masters, so Jehovah's servants may reckon upon his providence and grace. Let the obedience and joyfulness of our lives proclaim the character of the God we serve, else the world may say of us, as Argoland, king of Saragossa, said of certain lazars and poor people, whom he saw at the table of Charlemagne when he came to be baptized, " that he would not serve a God who did no more for his servants than had been done for those poor wretches." 2. *God's elect are they who recognize him as their king.* "And thy people." As such they render him legal homage, and honour all his laws, because they love his person. And as earthly subjects look up to their monarch and his government for protection and relief, so do the subjects of the King of kings look up to him for assistance and deliverance in their extremity. 3. *God's elect recognize him as their great*

Redeemer. "Whom thou hast redeemed," &c. Israel *only* thus redeemed, none others could claim this mark of electing grace If not redeemed, then non-elect Same mark of Divine election still holds good. Whatever men may imagine, only those are elect who show by their life that they have come' out of spiritual bondage Note concerning this redemption, (1) That it was *a Divine work.* "*Thou* hast redeemed." An act worthy of God : impossible to any one but God · reflecting highest glory on the character of God. Nothing less than Divine power, joined with infinite love and unerring wisdom, could have accomplished the world's redemption through the atonement of Christ. (2) That it was *a work of surpassing difficulty.* "By thy *great power* and by thy *strong hand.*" The redemption from Egypt was difficult because of the waywardness of the Israelites, and the opposition of Pharaoh The ransom of the race from the penalty of sin still more difficult, on account of the depravity of fallen humanity, and on account of the claims of God's inviolable law. The provision and subsequent government of Israel a work of gigantic and humanly insurmountable difficulty Yet as Jehovah fed and led, and settled his people not only in the wilderness but in Canaan, so will he supply all the need of all his children   "He is able to save them *to the uttermost*, that come unto God by him" (Heb vii 25) (3) That it was a work *accomplished through human agency.* Moses was the leader and deliverer of Israel under God's direction   "*Thy strong hand*" may refer to his agency, as "thy great power" indicates the source of his strength. The second redemption required a human agent Christ came as God's "strong hand" to lift up and lead out of captivity the enslaved human race

Illustrations —A senator related to his son the account of the book containing the names of illustrious members of the commonwealth. The son desired to see the outside. It was glorious to look upon. " Oh ! let me open it," said the son. "Nay," said the father, "'tis known only to the Council" "Then," said the son, "tell me if my name is there." "And that," said the father, "is a secret known only to the Council, and it cannot be divulged." Then he desired to know for what achievements the names were inscribed in that book. So the father told him, and related to him the achievements and noble deeds by which they had eternized their names. "Such," said he, "are written, and only such are written in this book " "And will my name be there," asked the son   "I cannot tell thee," said the father ; "if thy deeds are like theirs, thou shalt be written in the book ; if not, thou shalt not be written." And then the son consulted with himself ; and he found that his whole deeds were playing, and singing, and drinking, and amusing himself, and he found that this was not noble, nor temperate, nor valiant And as he could not read as yet his name he determined to make "his calling and election sure."

We may adopt Archbishop Leighton's beautiful illustration of a chain, which he describes is having its first and last link,—election and final salvation,—in heaven, in God's own hands, the middle one—effectual calling—being let down to the earth into the hearts of his children, and they laying hold of it, have sure hold of the other two, for no power can sever them.

"Though the mariner see not the pole-star, yet the needle of the compass that points to it, tells him which way he sails Thus, the heart that is touched by the loadstone of Divine love, trembling with godly fear, and looking towards God in fixed believing, points at the love of election, and tells the soul that its course is heavenward, towards the haven of eternal rest. *He that loves may be sure that he was loved first,* and he that chooses God for his delight and portion, may conclude confidently that God hath chosen him to be one of those that shall enjoy him for ever, for that our love, and electing of him, is but the return and re-percussion of the beams of his love shining upon us."—*Salter.*

Suppose a rope cast down into the sea for the relief of a company of poor shipwrecked men ready to perish, and that the people in the ship, or on the shore, should cry out unto them to lay hold on the rope that they may be saved ; were it not unreasonable and foolish curiosity for any of those poor distressed creatures, now at the point of death, to dispute whether the man who cast the rope did intend and purpose to save them or not, and so minding that which helpeth not, neglect the means of safety offered ? Thus it is that Christ holdeth forth, as it were, a rope of mercy to poor drowned and lost sinners. It is our duty then, without any further dispute, to look upon it as a principle afterwards to be made good, that Christ hath gracious thoughts towards us *but for the present to lay hold on the rope.—Rutherford.*

MODEST GOODNESS.

i. 11.   *Thy servants, who desire to fear thy name.*

I. It counts it an honour to serve God in any capacity. "Thy servants." 1. *It regards God as Master as well as Father.* Dutiful obedience to explicit commands, required no less than filial to devotion. It surrenders not only affection, but will. 2. *It regards the meanest task in God's service as an unspeakable honour.* The lowest office in the court of an earthly monarch is a post of honour; how much more so the lowest footstool in the house of the King eternal. The service not a task, because offspring of love (a)

II. It makes very humble professions before God. "Who desire to fear thy name." 1. *It dares not mention faultless conduct.* With Abraham it says, "I, that am but dust and ashes, have taken upon me to speak unto the living God" (Gen. xviii. 27); with Jacob, "I am not worthy of the least of all the mercies" (Gen. xxxii. 10); with Asaph, "So foolish was I, and ignorant, I was as a beast before thee" (Ps. lxxiii. 22); and with Paul, "I am less than the least of all saints" (Eph. iii. 8). The Pharisee appealed to his virtuous conduct, and was rejected; the publican, to his unworthiness, and was accepted. This, a sphere of action and of trial, rather than of rapture and triumph. "Blessed is the man that feareth always." 2. *It makes profession only of good intentions.* "Who desire to fear thy name." Even Nehemiah can boast of nothing higher. The whole life of a Christian is nothing else but *sanctum desiderium*, a holy desire; seeking that perfection which cannot be fully attained on earth (Phil. iii. 12). 3. *It does not remain satisfied with good desires.* Many there are who cannot speak with assurance of any higher experience than the presence of holy purposes and intentions. They cannot yet say they *do* fear, or love him, but that they desire to do so. Encouraging promise for all such :—"Blessed are they that do hunger and thirst after righteousness," &c. (Matt. v.). These desires are proofs of something good, and pledges of something better. They are evidences of grace, and forerunners of glory. They are the pulse of the soul, indicating the state of spiritual health. But these desires must be active ones, issuing in realized power and purity, and Christ-like gentleness. Desires which issue in no effort to attain them are like the vain prayer of Balaam, who could say, "Let me die the death of the righteous, and let my last end be like his" (Num. xxiii. 10), but who had no concern to live their life. Herod wished to see our Saviour work a miracle, but would not take a journey for the purpose. Pilate asked, "What is truth?" and would not wait for an answer. Desires are nothing without endeavours. (β)—*Jay.*

III. It cherishes a reverent fear of God. "Who desire to *fear* thy name." 1. *Not fear of punishment.* Such fear cast out by love. All fear that hath torment eradicated in the believer by the "expulsive power of a new affection." (γ) 2. *The filial fear of grieving an infinitely tender Father.* "God has three sorts of servants in the world; some are *slaves*, and serve him from a principle of fear; others are *hirelings*, and serve him for the sake of wages; and the last are *sons*, and serve him under the influence of love."—*Secker.*

Illustrations : (a) When Calvin was banished from ungrateful Geneva, he said, "Most assuredly if I had merely served man, this would have been a poor recompense; but it is my happiness that I have served Him who never fails to reward his servants to the full extent of his promise."

(β) Sir Joshua Reynolds, like many other distinguished persons, was never satisfied with his own efforts, however well they might satisfy others." When M. Mosnier, a French painter, was one day praising to him the excellence of one of his pictures, he replied, "Alas, Sir! I can only make sketches, sketches."

Virgil, who was called the prince of the Latin poets, was naturally modest, and of a timorous nature. When people crowded to gaze upon him, or pointed at him with the finger in raptures, the poet blushed, and stole away from them, and often hid himself in shops to escape the curiosity and admiration of the public The Christian is called upon to "let his light shine before men " but then it must be with all meekness, simplicity, and modesty.

(γ) Pagan nations have always stood in awe of deities, whose wrath they have deprecated, and whose love they have never hoped for. Their worship is one of slavish joy-killing dread. In the East India Museum, in London, there is an elaborately carved ivory idol from India, with twelve hands, and in every hand a different instrument of cruelty. On the door of the Cathedral of St. Nicholas, in Friburg, Switzerland, is a notice requesting the prayers of the charitable, for the souls of the departed, who are represented as being surrounded by purgatorial flames. Underneath is a contribution-box with this inscription, "Oh ! rescue us , you at least who are our friends."

UNANSWERED PRAYERS.

i. 11.   Prosper, I pray thee, thy servant this day, &c.

Here is help urgently needed, earnestly solicited, yet unaccountably delayed The prayer does not seem to have been answered until four months later, though offered continually.   Prayer may remain unanswered—

I Through some defect in the spirit of the suppliant. 1. Want of submission   The Lord's prayer is the model for all prayer. There we find three conditions preceding the only petition for temporal good, viz. "Hallowed be thy name , thy kingdom come ; thy will be done," &c.   These implicitly precede all true prayer. Unsubmissive prayers sometimes answered to teach men their folly in choosing their own way in preference to God's   Payson was asked, when under great bodily affliction, if he could see any particular reason for this dispensation   "No," he replied, "but I am as well satisfied as if I could see ten thousand , God's will is the very perfection of all reason." It is said that Dove, the Leeds murderer, was preserved from what appeared to be the certain fatal termination of an illness, by the passionately unsubmissive prayers of his mother, who lived to see her son led to the gallows. 2. *Weakness of faith* "He that cometh unto God must believe," &c. " Without faith it is impossible to please God" (Heb. xi. 6). This truth illustrated by most of Christ's miracles. 3. *Self-seeking motives.* God regards the spirit, and will grant nothing to gratify unhallowed and selfish ambition. We ask amiss if we seek for good that we may consume it on our lusts (Jas. iv. 3)   Thus did Simon Magus desire the gift of the Holy Ghost for the sake of personal gain and fame, but was detected and punished (Acts viii. 9—13). (*a*)

4. *An unforgiving spirit*   "Let us lift up holy hands, *without wrath*," &c. (1 Tim ii. 8). An uncharitable spirit condemns itself whenever it repeats the words, " Forgive us *our* trespasses *as we forgive* them that trespass against us " " If we regard iniquity in our *heart* God will not hear us" (Ps lxvi. 18). The importance of a forgiving spirit in approaching the throne of mercy is fully and clearly expressed in the opening sentences of the Communion Service. " Ye that do truly and earnestly repent of your sins, *and are in love and charity with your neighbours,* draw near," &c. 5. *A superficial sense of want.* God only promises to satisfy real, not fancied wants. Until we come to feel the *pain* of want, not able fully to value heavenly gifts   God bestows few blessings where not wanted, or not valued

II. Through some defect in the nature of the petition. 1. *It may be unsuitable.* This, not cause of delay in Nehemiah's case. The king's favour was necessary to the success of his enterprise. Good men err in judgment. God may answer prayer, but not as we expected. The means desired may not be the most suitable for the attainment of the end contemplated. 2. *It may be harmful* Child may ask for a razor to play with. Father refuses because life would be endangered. Our Father loves *his* children too well to grant them what he knows would ruin both body and soul. 3. *It may be impracticable.* Whilst true that nothing is impossible with God, also true that he has chosen to govern the moral and material universe by certain fixed laws, some of which he never interferes with, and others only for very momentous reasons. Our

D

prayers may require the over-riding of these laws on insufficient grounds ; hence their failure. This he will make known to the sincere suppliant by the inspiration and illumination of the Holy Ghost.

III. Through immaturity in the conditions required to give full value to the blessing sought. This probably the cause of the delay in Nehemiah's case. He was a good and upright man, and his petition was unimpeachable, for it was eventually granted. Circumstances were not ripe. Answers are sometimes delayed : 1. *Because God's agents are not yet in full sympathy with the work.* King not yet in favourable mind, people not yet driven to extremity. All God's agents are to be educated in his school for his work. When their training complete he brings them forth and uses them, not before. Thus Moses, David, Paul, &c. were educated. 2. *Circumstances are not yet congenial.* Every great enterprise needs favourable surroundings for its inception, as much as the seed requires good soil. Bury the acorn in the sand, and it remains barren. Cast the corn-seed into the ocean, and it produces no harvest. Even so, the most laudable enterprise, the most desirable reformation, planted in the midst of unfriendly circumstances will come to nought. Germany was ready for Luther, England for Wesley, Scotland for Moody, hence their success where others failed. 3. *Because the time was not opportune.* The hour had not yet come. God's times are in his own hands. Of the times and seasons knoweth no man. Having done all, it is our duty to wait the moving of the pillar. At the right moment God will manifest himself, and appear on behalf of his people.

Illustration —(a) It is recorded of an architect of the name of Cnidus, that having built a watch-tower for the king of Egypt, to warn mariners from certain dangerous rocks, he caused his own name to be engraved in large letters on a stone in the wall, and then having covered it with plaster, he inscribed on the outside, in golden letters, the name of the king of Egypt, as though the thing were done for his glory. He was cunning enough to know that the waves would ere long wear away the coat of plastering, and that then his own name would appear, and his memory be handed down to successive generations. How many are there who, whilst affecting to seek only the glory of God and His Church, are really seeking whatever is calculated to gratify self-love. Could the outer coat of their pretences be removed, we should see them as they really are, desirous not of God's glory, but of their own.— *Trench.*

MAN'S EQUALITY BEFORE GOD.

i. 11. *In the sight of this man.*

The familiar way in which Nehemiah speaks of the king before God suggests—

I. That the greatest earthly potentates are themselves subjects of a higher King. They equally under his laws and subject to his will (a) They and their meanest subjects on a perfect level in the heavenly court. God no respecter of persons. This thought should enable us to conquer the fear of man. This thought should make us satisfied with our lot. Their Master and Judge and ours the same. (β)

II. That the most powerful monarchs are but men. " *This man* " 1. *Fallen men.* "*All* we like sheep," &c. "There is no difference," &c. "None righteous, no not one" (Ps. xiv. 2 , Rom. iii 9 , Isa. liii 6 , Ps. cxliii. 2. All needing the same mercy; all requiring to seek it in the same way (humbly), and on the same terms (repentance and faith). "All stand before judgment-seat of Christ" (Rom. xiv. 10 ; 2 Cor. v. 10). 2 *Suffering men.* Liable to same pains, infirmities, bereavements, accidents, &c. One touch of nature makes all the world akin. One pang of suffering too. 3. *Dying men.* All amenable to king of terrors. He enters the palace as well as poorhouse. Queen Elizabeth begged for another hour to live, but death was inexorable. It lays the monarch low with the same stroke that smites his meanest subject. Honours thus fleeting not to be compared with the everlasting joys which are at God's right hand.

III. That God is no respecter of human distinctions. 1. *Not that he disapproves of the ordinary distinctions of social position* This inevitable. If all men made equal to-day, some would have risen and others have fallen by to-morrow Masters and servants, monarchs and subjects, teachers and taught, there must of necessity be as long as human society exists. The ideas of the socialist contrary alike to Divine law and practical utility. Only before God are men in any sense equal. 2. *But that he regards character as everything; the accidentals of social position as nothing.* What a man *is*, not what he *has*, commends him to God. (γ)

IV. That the best means of influencing earthly monarchs is to secure the aid of Jehovah. So did Nehemiah. The propriety of this act seen in his management of the undertaking. Intercourse with God will best prepare for dealings with men. When we thus address ourselves to God, difficulties vanish. "His kingdom ruleth over all" Every event under his direction; every character under his control. When Herod imprisoned Peter, the Church assembled together, not to draw up a petition and address it to the king; but to seek God's interposition. They applied, not to the servant, but the master; to one who had Herod completely under check: "Prayer was made, without ceasing, of the Church unto God for

him." What was the consequence? "When Herod would have brought him forth," &c. (Acts xii. 6) Solomon says, "'The king's heart is in the hands of the Lord, as the rivers of water: he turneth it whithersoever he will" (Prov. xxi. 1). Eastern monarchs were absolute; yet God had them more under his command than the husbandman has a direction of the water in a meadow. There is a two-fold dominion which God exercises over the mind of man 1. *By the agency of his grace,* as in the case of Saul of Tarsus. From a furious persecutor, he becomes at once an apostle. 2. *By the agency of his providence.* History is full of this.— *Jay.*

Illustrations ·—(a) What are they when they stand upon the highest pinnacles of worldly dignities, but bladders swelled up with the breath of popularity? nothings set astrut; chessmen, that on the board play the kings and nobles, but in the bag are of the same material, and rank with others.—*Bp. Hopkins.*

(β) King Canute was one day flattered by his courtiers on account of his power. Then he ordered his throne to be placed by the sea-side. The tide was rolling in, and threatened to drown him. He commanded the waves to stop. Of course they did not. Then he said to his flatterers, " Behold how small is the might of kings."

(γ) With God there is no freeman but his servant, though in the galleys; no slave but the sinner, though in a palace; none noble but the virtuous, if never so basely descended; none rich but he that possesseth God, even in rags; none wise but he that is a fool to the world and himself; none happy but he whom the world pities. Let me be free, noble, rich, wise, happy to God. —*Bp. Hall.*

ADDENDA TO CHAPTER I.

i. 3. SIN RUINS A KINGDOM.

I. If there be a moral governor of the universe, sin must provoke him. A righteous God must love righteousness; a holy God, holiness; a God of order, order; a God of benevolence, benevolence, and accordingly he must abhor all that is opposite to these. Hence, it is said, that "God is angry with the wicked every day; the wicked

shall not stand in his sight; he hateth all workers of iniquity." And this is essential to every lovely and reverential view we can take of God. For who could adore a being who professed to govern the world, and suffered the wicked to go on with impunity.

II. If sin provoke God, he is able to punish it. He is " the Lord of Hosts, the Lord strong and mighty, the Lord mighty in battle." All the elements are his Every creature obeys his nod, from an archangel to a worm How idle therefore to talk of armies, navies, and alliances, and say after comparing force with force, "Oh ! the enemy cannot come !" He cannot come unless God send him , but he can come easily enough if he should Is anything too hard for the Lord, when he would either show mercy or execute wrath.

III Bodies of men are punishable in this world only. In eternity there are no families, churches, nations. If therefore a country is to be destroyed, it is tried, condemned, and executed here. When we see an individual sinner prospering in the world, and not immediately punished, our faith is not staggered ; for we know that "his day is coming." But if a wicked people were allowed to escape, we should be confounded, we should ask, "Where is the God of Judgment ?" For in this case they *are* not punished now ; and they *cannot* be punished hereafter.

IV. There is a tendency in the very nature of sin to injure and ruin a country It violates all the duties of relative life It destroys subordination. It relaxes the ties which bind mankind together, and makes them selfish and mean It renders men enemies to each other. Social welfare cannot survive the death of morals and virtue.

V. God's dealings with guilty nations are confirmed both by his word and all human history. He has invariably punished them in due time. Witness the state of Nineveh, Babylon, and others. Thus the nation Samuel addressed put his declaration to the trial and found it true. A succession of severe judgments befell them, till at last wrath came upon them to the uttermost, and "the Romans came and took away both their place and nation "

VI. God always gives previous intimation of his coming to judge a nation So that were men not blind and deaf, they must see and hear his coming. When you see the body wasting away by disease, and every complaint growing more inveterate, you suspect that death will be the consequence ; it is already begun. Christ said, "When ye see a cloud rise out of the west, straightway ye say, There cometh a shower ; and so it is . . Ye hypocrites ! ye can discern the face of the sky, and of the earth ; but how is it that ye do not discern this time ?"

VII. If God has favoured a nation with the revelation of his will, their sins are aggravated by means of this light "Where much is given, much will be required." "He that knew his Lord's will, and did it not, shall be beaten with many stripes." Thus, a heathen country committing the very same sins with a country enlightened with the Gospel, is far less criminal. A country overspread with superstition, where the Bible is scarcely known, would be far less guilty than a country favoured with a purer worship, and where evangelical instruction is open to all.

VIII. When God has distinguished a people by singular instances of his favour, that people will be proportionally criminal, unless they distinguish themselves by their devotedness to him Thus God from time to time aggravated the sins of the Jews. "He made them ride upon the high places of the earth," &c "But Jeshurun waxed fat, and kicked," &c.

IX. When a nation is under the corrections of the Almighty, they are eminently sinful if they disregard the tokens of his wrath. Hence Isaiah says, "In that day did the Lord God of Hosts call to weeping and to mourning, &c., and behold joy and gladness , let us eat and drink, for to-morrow we die." Jeremiah also says, "Thou hast stricken them, but they have not grieved ; thou hast consumed them, but they have refused to receive correction ; they have made their faces harder than a rock ; they have refused to return."

X. Shameless sinning is a sure proof of general corruption. And where is there a man who is not more ashamed of a threadbare coat than a dishonest action ? To fail in business, and defraud innocent sufferers of their lawful property, is no longer scandalous.

Impurity is tolerated. Behold the experiments which fashion has tried upon the reserve, the decency, the purity of woman ! Learn—1 Who is the worst enemy of his country—*the sinner.*

2. Who is the best friend—*the Christian.* "By the blessing of the upright the city is exalted but it is overthrown by the mouth of the wicked."—*Jay, abridged.*

i. 7. FORGOTTEN SINS REMEMBERED.

I. We are all chargeable with faults Testimony of Scripture and conscience are both against us "There is not a just man upon earth, that doeth good and sinneth not." "They are all gone out of the way : there is none that doeth good, no, not one." (Eccl. vii. 20 ; Rom iii 12). David feared God, and hated evil, yet needed to pray, " Cleanse thou me from secret faults " (Ps. xix. 12) James, though an apostle, affirms, " In many things we offend all." John was beloved above all the apostles, and bore most of his Master's image, yet he declares, " If we say that we have no sin, we deceive ourselves " (1 Jno i 8). " All have sinned, and come short of the glory of God." This fact is confirmed by everything we feel within us, and observe without us. What faults ? We have forgotten the Son of God, the Lord of life and glory. We are chargeable with ingratitude, not against an earthly benefactor, but a heavenly one. Every forbidden action that we have done, every sinful word that we have spoken, every irregular thought that we have entertained, or unhallowed wish that we have harboured in our breast, accumulates our load of guilt

II We are liable to forget our faults. Men have convictions of sin, but they stifle them Amidst the pleasures or employments of time, they lose even the recollection of their guilt , and go forward in the same course, suspecting no danger, till utter destruction overtakes them 1. *Through ignorance of the true nature of sin* Its malignity is not properly understood. Men think of sin as a light matter if it inconvenience them, they exclaim against it ; if not, they practise it with little compunction or concern They do not reflect on what sin is in the sight of God, nor think as they ought of its result in a future world ; and hence

they forget it. 2 *Through self-love.* Self-love when regulated is laudable and useful , because it leads to the hatred of what is evil, and to the pursuit of what is good But that love of self which possesses and actuates thousands, is little different from the love of sin , they love indolence, sensual gratification, and ease ; they resemble a man with a diseased limb, who chooses death by fatal degrees, rather than amputation 3 *Through hurry of business.* 4. *Through elevation in worldly circumstances.* Great numbers, from the pressing importunity of their secular concerns, from the eager desire of getting forward in the world, forget their souls, forget their sins, forget the Saviour, and abide in the most dangerous state of folly and insensibility.

III. Various circumstances are adapted to remind us of our faults. 1. *Providential occurrences.* These regard ourselves, the affliction of our persons, or our immediate connections The case of the widow of Zarephath an illustration. She had one son ; the prophet Elijah resided in her house , no affluence was there . but by him, the Lord made her barrel of meal not to waste, and her cruse of oil not to fail. Suddenly her son was taken from her by the stroke of death ; hear what she said to the prophet, " Art thou come unto me to call my sin to remembrance, and to slay my son ?" (1 Kings xvii. 18). Had her son lived, and Providence continued to smile, probably her convictions would have remained asleep. Other providential occurrences regard the condition of those about us, and thus strike our observation. We witness sometimes the difficulties in which others are involved ; we think of what occasioned such difficulties, and are reminded of similar causes in ourselves, which might have produced similar effects An idle man sees in another the effects of indolence,—that he is reduced to poverty, and clothed in rags ; a drunkard observes in another the effects of intemperance,—that his health is impaired his circumstances embarrassed, and his character ruined. These things are adapted to awaken conviction, to bring a man's own faults to remembrance. Illustration furnished by the account of "the woman taken in adultery" (Jno. viii. 7—9); Joseph's interview with his brethren (Gen. xlii. 21), and Belshazzar's feast (Dan. v. 1—7). In each case the men remembered their faults. 2 *The ministry of God's word.* This word is profitable not only for "doctrine and instruction," but also for "correction and reproof." See this in the case of the Jews who stoned Stephen. "They were cut to the heart" (Acts vii. 45). The case of Felix also another illustration in point. Whilst Paul "reasoned of righteousness, temperance, and judgment to come, Felix trembled" (Acts xxiv. 25). When Peter preached on the day of Pentecost, "they were pricked in their hearts, and said unto Peter, and to the rest of the apostles, Men and brethren, what shall we do?" (Acts ii. 37). David and Nathan (2 Sam. xii. 7—12). "By the *law* is the knowledge of sin" (Rom. iii. 20).

IV. When we are reminded of our faults we should be ready to confess them. "Confess your faults one to another" (Jas. v. 16). This gives no countenance to the arbitrary practice of popish confessions ; for according to this passage the people have as much right to demand confession from the priests, as the priests have from the people. It enjoins candour, and open confession of blame, when professing Christians have offended one another. Confession also must be made to God.

"He that covereth his sins shall not prosper ; but whoso confesseth and forsaketh them shall have mercy" (Prov. xxviii. 13). This clearly implies that they can have no mercy who do not confess their sins. Let a man proudly persist in maintaining his innocency ; let him think highly of what he calls his moral rectitude ; let him vainly imagine that his good deeds outweigh his bad ones ; or let him sink into a state of obstinate indifference—that man is certainly not in the way of mercy. "If we say that we have no sin, we deceive ourselves." "If we confess our sins, God is faithful and just to forgive us our sins" (1 Jno. i 8, 9). What sins? Lament before God a hard heart, a proud heart, a corrupt heart Lament before him a fretful temper, a peevish, a passionate temper. Lament the weakness of your faith, the deadness of your hope, the languor of your love, the coldness of your zeal, the inefficiency of all your desires and resolutions.

V. Confession of faults should always be attended with real amendment. This is an incumbent duty ; for what is repentance? It includes a disposition to undo all the evil which we have done. Zaccheus' repentance was of the right kind, for he offered to make restitution. "Lord, the half of my goods I give to the poor; and if I have taken anything from any man by false accusation I restore him fourfold" (Luke xix. 8). Repentance is nothing without reformation, and reformation, in many instances, is a mere name without restitution . "Surely it is meet to be said unto God, I have borne chastisement, *I will not offend any more.* If I have done iniquity, I will do no more" (Job xxxiv. 31, 32).—*Kidd, abridged.*

i. 10.   A<small>N</small> E<small>LECT</small> P<small>EOPLE</small>.

I. True believers are the objects of a special choice Note—1. *Its author* "God hath from the beginning chosen you to salvation." We cannot, without contradicting Scripture, dispute the fact that God's people are a *chosen people*— chosen of God Do not object to the

term ; remember where you find it ; seek rather to understand the subject, and objections will subside Whilst God *injures* none, surely he may confer special benefits on some. Let it be granted that the choice of some implies that others are not chosen ; yet who can gainsay the language of St. Paul, " Nay but, O man, who art thou that repliest against God ? " &c. (Rom ix 20). " Shall not the Judge of all the earth do right ? " Doubtless he shall !—of this we may rest assured : " The Lord is righteous in all his ways, and holy in all his works." 2 *The date of this choice.* " From the beginning " This expression must be explained by similar passages which relate to the same subject St. Peter says, " Ye are a chosen generation, elect according to the foreknowledge of God " (1 Pet. ii. 9 ; i 2). St Paul, " whom he did foreknow, he also did predestinate." Foreknowledge leads us back to some period previous to the existence of those persons, and there is no text more explicit than that which occurs in the Epistle to the Ephesians, " According as he hath chosen us in him (Christ), *before the foundation of the world.*" Now, what was before the foundation of the world must have been in eternity; for we cannot conceive a point of time, before time commenced. Time is a parenthesis in eternity ; a limited duration which regards creatures Here then is taught the *freeness* of this choice. If it was from the beginning, it was before man had his being : consequently there could be no worthiness in us, or any of our race, influencing the Most High to such a choice 3. *The end of this choice* " To salvation." The Israelites as a nation were chosen of God, but not all of them to salvation, for many fell , and we are admonished to take heed lest we " fall after the same example of unbelief" (Heb iv. 11) The twelve were chosen to the office of apostleship, but not all of them to salvation, for Judas was of their number " Have not I chosen you twelve, and one of you is a devil ? " (Jo vi. 70) Do you ask, " What is salvation ? " It is heaven. It includes the complete deliverance from all evil, and the full possession of all good, it includes an entire freedom from sin, and the constant enjoyment of purity and peace ; it includes an everlasting release from all that is painful and distressing, and the endless fruition of whatever can satisfy and exalt the immortal mind, the eternal fruition of God himself.

II True believers are persons of a peculiar character The people of God are " predestinated to be conformed to the image of his Son." They are chosen in Christ before the foundation of the world, " that they should be holy and without blame before him in love" (Ephes. i. 4) 1. *They are believers of the truth.* Chosen to salvation, " through belief of the truth " Not possible to give a more concise definition of faith than here—*"the truth,"* hence our Lord said, " Ye shall know the truth, and the truth shall make you free." *Believing* the truth is receiving it as the record of God, in such a way as to feel affected and influenced by it according to the nature of the things which it regards Are *we* believers of the truth ? If not, we have no Scriptural evidence of our election of God to salvation. 2. *They are partakers of the Spirit.* " If any man have not the Spirit of Christ he is none of his " (Rom viii. 9). A man is not born again but of the Spirit , and the new birth or regeneration is the commencement of the new life " Know ye not that ye are the temple of God, and that the Spirit of God dwelleth in you " (1 Cor. iii. 16). Not without reason are we admonished, " Quench not the Spirit." 3. *They are the subjects of sanctification.* The Holy Spirit produces it, and gradually promotes it ; they are chosen to salvation " through sanctification of the Spirit." Sanctification is holiness, and there is no way of attaining holiness but by " the Spirit of Holiness " Sanctification is the best evidence of faith ; it is also the best possible mark of election to salvation We have proof that we are " of God," only so far as we are *like* God. Is he our Father ? Where then is resemblance to him ? If multitudes of professors examine themselves by this test, it is to be feared they will have little hope left of their interest in everlasting love. —*Kidd.*

ILLUSTRATIONS.

Benevolence. 1 It is said of Lord Chief Justice Hale, that he frequently invited his poor neighbours to dinner, and made them sit at table with himself. If any of them were sick, so that they could not come, he would send provisions to them from his own table He did not confine his bounties to the poor of his own parish, but diffused supplies to the neighbouring parishes as occasion required. He always treated the old, the needy, and the sick with the tenderness and familiarity that became one who considered they were of the same nature with himself, and were reduced to no other necessities but such as he himself might be brought to. Common beggars he considered in another view If any of these met him in his walks, or came to his door, he would ask such as were capable of working, why they went about so idly. If they answered, it was because they could not get employment, he would send them to some field, to gather all the stones in it, and lay them in a heap, and then paid them liberally for their trouble. This being done, he used to send his carts, and cause the stones to be carried to such places of the highway as needed repair 2. "I often think," says Coleridge, "with pleasure, of the active *practical* benevolence of Salter. His rides were often sixty, averaging more than thirty miles a day, over bad roads, and in dark nights; yet not once was he known to refuse a summons, though quite sure that he would receive no remuneration, nay, not sure that it would not be necessary to supply wine, or cordials, which, in the absence of the landlord of his village, must be at his own expense This man was generally pitied by the affluent and the idle, on the score of his constant labours, and the drudgery which he almost seemed to court , yet with little reason, for I never knew a man more to be envied, or more cheerful, more invariably kind, or more patient , he was always kind from real kindness and delicacy of feeling, never being even for a moment angry

Prayer must be submissive 1. A Christian widow in London saw, with great alarm, her only child taken dangerously ill As the illness increased she became almost distracted from a dread of losing her child ; at length, it became so extremely ill, and so convulsed, that she kneeled down by the bed, deeply affected, and in prayer said, "Now, Lord, thy will be done" From that hour the child began to recover, till health was perfectly restored. 2. Lord Bolingbroke once asked Lady Huntingdon how she reconciled prayer to God for particular blessings, with absolute resignation to the Divine will. "Very easily," answered her ladyship, "just as if I were to offer a petition to a monarch, of whose kindness and wisdom I had the highest opinion In such a case my language would be, —I wish you to bestow on me such or such a favour , but your Majesty knows better than I, how far it would be agreeable to you, or right in itself, to grant my desire. I therefore content myself with humbly presenting my petition, and leave the event of it entirely to you " 3 The late Mr. Kilpin of Exeter writes, "I knew a case in which the minister praying over a child apparently dying, said, " If it be thy will spare——' " The poor mother's soul, yearning for her beloved, exclaimed, "It *must* be his will, I cannot bear *ifs.*" The minister stopped. To the surprise of many the child recovered ; and the mother, after almost suffering martyrdom by him while a stripling, lived to see him hanged before he was twenty-two ' It is good to say, "Not my will, but thine be done."

Modest goodness 1. Two or three years before the death of John Newton, when his sight was so dim that he was no longer able to read, an aged friend and brother in the ministry called on him to breakfast Family prayer succeeded. It was the good man's custom to make a few remarks upon the passage read. After the reading of the text, " By the grace of God I am what I am," he paused for some moments, and then uttered the following affecting soliloquy .—" I am not what I *ought* to be! Ah, how imperfect and deficient. I am not what I *wish* to be. I am not what I *hope* to be. Soon, soon, I shall put off mortality, and with mortality, all sin and imperfection. Yet though I am not what I ought to be, nor what I wish to be, nor what I hope to be, I can truly say I am not what I once was, a slave to sin and Satan, and I can heartily join with the apostle and acknowledge, ' By the grace of God I am what I am ' Let us pray " 2. "An individual," says a missionary, " employed in the translation of the Scriptures at a station where I resided, on arriving at the passage, ' Now are we the sons of God ' (1 Jno. iii 2), came running to me in great haste, exclaiming, No, no, it is too much ; allow me to render it, ' Now are we permitted to kiss his feet.' A simple and beautiful representation of those feelings with which Christians should ever contemplate the dignity of their character, and the honour conferred upon them " 3 Dr Lathrop was a man of generous piety, but much opposed to the noisy zeal that seeketh the praise of men A young divine, who was much given to enthusiastic cant, one day said to him, " Do you suppose you have any *real religion* ? " " None to *speak* of," was the excellent reply.

CHAPTER II.

EXPLANATORY NOTES.] 1. Nisan] Called Abib in Exod. xiii. 4, first month in Hebrew national year. Corresponds to parts of our March and April. **3 Let the king live for ever]** (Heb hammelek l'olam yihyeh.) (Comp. 1 Kings i. 31, Dan. ii. 4; vi 6—21.) The mere formula of address, like our "God save the Queen." Even Daniel used it without compunction. **The place of my fathers' sepulchres]** The Persians regarded their burial-places as peculiarly sacred. **6. The queen also sitting by him]** Some have thought this was Esther, but "Shegal" refers to the principal wife of the king. Damaspia was the name of the chief wife according to Ctesias. **7 The governors]** (Heb. pahawoth, modern pacha.) Oriental name for viceroy. **Beyond the river]** i. e. Euphrates. **8 Asaph, the keeper of the king's forest]** may have been a Jew. Name, Hebrew. Word translated "*forest*" is "*pardes*," our "paradise." It signifies a *walled round place*, a preserve of trees. Probably a royal park of which Asaph was keeper. **The palace which appertained to the house]** Probably Solomon's palace, situated at the south-east corner of the temple-area, was next to *the* house; i. e., the temple as the house of God (2 Chron. xxiii 12—15). **The house that I shall enter into]** Some think this refers also to the temple, which Nehemiah would enter into to inspect, more probably the house where he would dwell during his stay in Jerusalem. **10 Sanballat the Horonite]** (Beth-horon, in full.) Two Horons in Palestine, a few miles north of Jerusalem; also Horonaim in Moab. Sanballat, probably a native of the last mentioned, was a Moabite; and satrap of Samaria under the Persians. Tobiah, his vizier or chief adviser. Origin of name Sanballat uncertain. **Tobiah, the servant, the Ammonite]** Tobiah, a Jewish name (Ezra ii. 60, Zech. vi 10). Probably a renegade Jew, who had become a slave, and had risen by his talents and cunning to be Sanballat's chief officer, hence the epithet, "Tobiah, the slave." **13. The gate of the valley]** (Heb Sha'ar haggai.) Probably overlooking valley of Hinnom, called in Jer. ii. 23 simply "the valley." It was about 1200 feet south of the present Jaffa gate. The Septuagint calls it Portam Galilæ; the gate of dead men's skulls, because that way they went to Golgotha. **The dragon well]** So called either because some venomous serpent had been found there, or because the waters ran out of the mouth of a brazen serpent (Heb. Fountain of the sea-monster.) **The dung port]** (Rather, *Rubbish-gate*.) The gate near which the refuse of the city was cast, and burned. Directly before that part of Hinnom known as Tophet (Jer. vii 31, 32; xix. 6—14). **14 The gate of the fountain]** A gate in front of the pool of Siloam (ch. iii. 15). **The king's pool]** (Berechath hammelek.) The pool of Siloam, so called because it watered the king's garden. **There was no place for the beast that was under me to pass]** The ruin was great, and the rubbish so accumulated, that Nehemiah could not pursue his course along the wall any further, but was obliged to go down into the valley of the brook Kidron (Nachal, *the brook*.) **15 And viewed the wall]** That which was left of it. **16. The rulers]** A Persian word (Seganim) signifying the executive officers of the colony. **Nor to the nobles]** (Heb. white ones.) Among the Jews great men robed in white, as among the Romans in scarlet or purple. Herod and Christ (Luke xxiii. 11; Matt. xxvii. 28). **19 Geshem the Arabian]** Lieutenant of Arabia under the king of Persia, or chief of those Arabs whom Sargon had settled in Samaria (Rawlinson's Anc Mon., vol. ii. p. 146).

HOMILETIC CONTENTS OF CHAPTER II.

DIVINE INTERPOSITION

ii. 1—8. *And it came to pass in the month Nisan, &c.*

THE first chapter occupied with account of state of Jerusalem and Nehemiah's grief and prayer. This opens with the relation of those circumstances which led to the fulfilment of his desires, and the accomplishment of his purposes. We learn from text—

I. That God's interposition was opportune. "It came to pass *in the month Nisan*" (v. 1) The best month, because the one chosen by God. Chosen by God because the best. Note—1. *That God's plans are worked out with the utmost precision.* Trace this in Bible. Often find expressions such as—"In due time," "Fulness of time," "Appointed time," "Mine hour is not yet come," "A set time," &c. God's timepiece never gains or loses. All his plans carried out with unfailing accuracy. He is neither slack, "as some men count slackness," in fulfilling his threats or his promises. Many details, apparently insignificant, combine to work out the most magnificent plans. A loop is a small thing, yet most gorgeous tapestry woven in single loops. A link a small thing, yet chain depends on support of every link. Trifles are links in the chain of God's providential government, or rather there are no trifles Illustrate by complex machinery of Lancashire cotton, or Coventry silk, or Kidderminster carpet machinery, which whilst wonderfully intricate, works out the appointed pattern with utmost precision and accuracy. Yet all human exactness fails in comparison with God's perfect accuracy. 2. *That God often interferes on his people's behalf when they least expect it.* Through not discerning God's methods of working, they get discouraged, and think themselves overlooked. Whilst we look for him to appear in one way he comes in another, and whilst we mournfully strain our eyes down one path, lo, he comes by another. Our most unlikely times are God's most favourable ones. 3. *That God generally interferes on his people's behalf in their most urgent extremity* It was so here. Nehemiah so distressed that his countenance was sad for first time. The case of the Jews was' becoming desperate. God interferes in their extremity as he had done on the shores of the Red Sea—(1) To try their faith, (2) To elicit their gratitude, (3) To impress upon them their dependence upon him The text suggests—

II. That God's interposition required human co-operation. God's agents are of two kinds, willing and unwilling, allied and non-allied. Both of these found in this history. 1. *Allied.* As Esther came to the kingdom, so Nehemiah to his office, for such a time as this (Esth. iv. 14). Though he was a prisoner, a stranger, of an alien religion, yet is he God's agent as well as the king's servant. Note concerning him,—(1) That he was *duly qualified* for his appointed work. *Mentally* he possessed forethought (ch. ii 5), tact (ch v. 5), and ingenuity (ch. iii.). His address to Artaxerxes a marvel of clever pleading. Words carefully chosen, respect humbly paid to rank, superstitious reverence for burial-grounds introduced No argument more powerful with an Eastern monarch. *Spiritually*, he was richly endowed with every grace required in so difficult a work. Courage, sympathy, generosity, and profound piety all combined to make him an eminently spiritual man. Such agents God chooses for important enterprises, utilizing great endowments for arduous tasks. Note, (2) That he was *favourably situated.* When God has work for his servants to do, he by his providence places them where they can do it. Nehemiah evidently a favourite with Artaxerxes, from fact of his having chosen him to this important office, over the heads of the Persian nobles. Had he been otherwise situated, or appointed to any other office, he would not so readily have found access to the king's ear. God appoints our lot and circumstances, and requires us to make the best of them, and not seek to leave them, with the idea that we can best serve him elsewhere. Note, (3) That he was *rightly actuated.* No personal ambition inspired his petition, but pure, unalloyed, unselfish desire for the prosperity of God's Church, and the holy City. No desire for gain, for he used his fortune in feeding the poor, and entertaining the returning exiles in his own house at Jerusalem. They who are engaged in God's work must lay aside all thoughts of worldly gain or personal honour. Reward there is, but not usually of a worldly sort. 2. *Unallied* God employs unconscious agents as well as willing ones "As he put small thoughts into the heart of Ahasuerus for great purposes" (Esth. vi. 1), so here he caused a heathen prince to favour a hostile religion, and to defend a people whom his subjects hated. God even employs his enemies (though not in the same sense in which he employs his friends), to carry out his purposes. Pharaoh, Philistines, Chaldeans, Romans, &c.

III. **That God's interposition was accompanied by providential coincidences.** All these known to Divine omniscience and taken into account. 1. *Nehemiah was unusually sad.* "I had not been beforetime sad in his presence." No mourner might be seen in Ahasuerus' court (Esth. iv. 4). Momus wished that men had windows in their breasts, that their thoughts might be seen. This not necessary, for "a merry heart maketh a glad countenance; but by sorrow of heart the spirit is broken" (Prov. xv. 13). Nehemiah had been afflicting his soul for four months. No wonder he betrayed it in his countenance. The Hebrews say that a man's inside is turned out, and discovered in oculis, in loculis, in poculis, in his eyes, purse, and cup. 2. *The king was unusually friendly.* Most Eastern monarchs would have condemned him at once either to banishment or death. Artaxerxes might have done so at another time. Sad looks were, in their eyes, bad looks, and savoured of assassination but love thinketh no evil, and the king had confidence in his servant. 3. *The queen also was present.* Not Esther, the queen-mother, for Hebrew word signifies wife. "Because 'the queen sat by,' it is probable that there was some solemn feast that day; for the queens of Persia used not to come into the king's presence, but when they were called by name, as it is written in the book of Esther." This might be the cause of Nehemiah's great fear: but would also be in his favour. The presence of a woman, even without her personal intercession, would temper any harshness the king might feel, and thus aid the suppliant's suit.

DISINTERESTED LOVE FOR A SUFFERING CHURCH.

ii. 1—8. *And it came to pass, &c.*

I. **Its sorrow.** "Why is thy countenance sad?" &c. (v. 2). 1. *In spite of personal prosperity.* This often hardens heart and deadens sympathies. So long as their own homes are flourishing many care little how God's house fares. This cannot satisfy a truly good man who has the welfare of God's cause at heart. No measure of personal prosperity will compensate for spiritual dearth and deadness in the Church. 2. *In the very midst of social festivities.* The revelry of the banquet could not repress the wretchedness of his heart, for whilst he was in the midst of rejoicing and mirth his spirit was not there. The inward grief was stronger than outward surroundings, and broke through all restraint. The wound of a broken heart cannot be healed by any outward gaiety of circumstance.

II. **Its confession.** "Why should not my countenance be sad?" (v. 3). 1. *It is not ashamed of the people of God.* "The city the place of my father's sepulchres." Surrounded by Persian nobles not an easy matter to thus avow friendship for an alien and oppressed people. Many temptations to expedient silence would have to be overcome. Much was risked by this avowal. Much probably to be gained by ignoring them. True piety is courageous. It says, "Thy people shall be my people" (Ruth i.), for richer for poorer, for better for worse, at all hazards and in all times. "A friend loveth at all times, and a brother is born for adversity" (Prov. xvii. 17). "There is a friend that sticketh closer than a brother" (Prov. xviii. 24). 2. *Not ashamed of poor relations.* When men rise from a low estate into high circles they readily forget those who once were equals, unwilling to betray their humble origin. Such pride always despicable as useless. No disgrace to have poor relations. The disgrace is in disowning them. Nehemiah not guilty of such folly or cowardice. He not only acknowledges, but pleads for them. 3. *Not afraid of personal danger.* Royal displeasure no trifle under the sway of Oriental despots. Witness recent events in Turkey. Thrones overturned by plots and intrigues continually. The nearer the throne, the more likely to incur suspicion. Artaxerxes had come to the kingdom through intrigue and bloodshed. Would be naturally vigilant and wary on this account. Hence the danger incurred by one even so favoured as Nehemiah, when he dared to avow sympathy with a captive and recently conquered people inhabiting a neighbouring province. Fervent love always self-forgetful It confers not with flesh and blood, but willingly incurs danger for sake of its object. This, type of Christ's love for his Church.

III Its petition " And I said unto the king," &c. (v. 5). 1. *It seeks help from God.* " I prayed unto the God of heaven " (v. 5). This, first step God has more interest in his Church than any other, and can do more If his aid be secured, it matters little who else fails. If his denied, none can do much. 2. *It craves human assistance.* " If it please the king, let letters be given me," &c. (v 7) Recognizes the principle that God always works by human agency, and helps man by man, to teach him lessons of mutual sympathy and mutual dependence 3. *It asks permission to give its own aid, and that with self-denial.* Nehemiah not one who would only work at others' expense No bargain for costs or travelling expenses He asks that he may be permitted to engage in an enterprise that will considerably diminish his private resources, and involve constant and heavy personal sacrifices. If we desire success in great reformations we must be prepared to make great sacrifices. Our gifts joined with God's, will accomplish almost anything. We have no right to expect God to render his assistance where we withhold our own

IV. Its joy. " So it pleased the king to send me " (v. 6) 1. *Its prayer is granted.* Both Jehovah and Artaxerxes looked favourably upon his request. When prayer is thus graciously answered, men should rejoice and speak good of the name of the Lord. Thus did the royal Psalmist often extol Jehovah's name. 2. *Its way is providentially opened* And this more prosperously than he could have anticipated. Not only permission granted to leave Persia for a time, but also to take with him an escort , and full authority to build, and command supplies, when he arrived at Jerusalem (v. 7, 8) Thus does God cause our cup to overflow with mercy, giving us far more than we deserve, and more than we either asked or had reason to expect. Not only *out of,* but *according to,* his riches in glory, does he supply his children's wants. A millionnaire might give a penny *out of* his abundance ; but not if he gave *according to* (in proportion to) his riches. Then must he give what would be a fortune to a poor man. Even so, God gives not grudgingly, or stintedly, but royally. " It was but ask, and have ; and so it is betwixt God and his people. When there was a discussion amongst some holy men as to which was the most profitable trade, one answered, beggary ; it is the hardest, and the richest trade. Common beggary is the commonest and easiest, but he meant prayer. A courtier gets more by one suit often than a tradesman or merchant haply with twenty years' labour ; so doth a faithful prayer."—*Trapp.*

SUBJECT AND SOVEREIGN.

ii 1, 2. *And I took up wine, and gave it to the king, &c.*

I He did not allow his duty to God to clash with his duty to his sovereign His religion not diminish his civility. " If it please the king." " Fear God, and honour the king," both enjoined in apostolic precept. He had been taken from his native land and placed under another king, whom it was his duty to serve and obey, in all quietness and meekness, until God ordered his lot otherwise. So lived Pharaoh, Daniel, Mardocheus, Ezra, and others. Jeremiah and Baruch taught the Jews thus to pray for those under whose sway they were living as captives, " Pray for the life of Nebuchadnezzar, and Belshazzar his son , seek the peace of that country whither ye be carried away captives " (Jer. xxix , Baruch i.). St. Peter taught the Christians that servants should not forsake their masters, though they did not believe (1 Pet. ii.). Both St. Peter and St. Paul command the faithful wife to abide by her unfaithful husband (1 Cor. vii. ; 1 Pet. iii.). The Scriptures enjoin faithfulness, duty, and obedience toward all men, so far as we offend not God thereby. Duty to God and duty to man two aspects of same life. One requires the other. Each incomplete, being alone. The more efficiently we discharge one, the more perfectly do the other. Neither may be made a substitute for the other. "This ought ye to have done, and not to leave the other undone."

II. He did not allow spiritual exercises to interfere with the discharge of secular duties. He prayed incessantly, yet failed not in discharge of duties as cupbearer. The believer should be "diligent in business," as well as "fervent in spirit," lest he bring reproach upon religion Spiritual activity no excuse for neglecting secular duty To be slothful in business will quench devotion as fatally as to pursue business with inordinate affection. The hardiest devotion healthiest. The devotion of the cloister, for the most part, like the ghastly light that hovers over decomposition and decay ; the devotion which characterizes the diligent, spiritually-minded man of business, resembles the star which shines on in the storm as in the calm, when the sky is clouded as when it is serene.

III He regarded the path of duty as the path of providential blessing. Not forsaking the common duties of his daily calling, he waited for the opening of his providential path. The faithful

discharge of duty itself a blessing. This, the channel through which special grace most likely to flow. Men need not leave the world to find the secret of holiness ; or their ordinary sphere of work to find the secret of blessing. The patient, conscientious discharge of life's ordinary tasks, always the safest path to pursue (a)

IV. He found the favour of his sovereign of great service in carrying out the work of God. His civility and humble demeanour had won the confidence and esteem of his royal master. This friendship now stood him in good stead Yet he presumes not upon this regard, but approaches the throne tremblingly, as a subject should, even the most favoured. Monarchs like not presumption even in their courtiers Diogenes says, "A man should use his prince or peer, as he would do the fire. The fire if he stand too near it will burn him ; and if he be too far off he will be cold. So to be over-bold, without blushing or reverence, bringeth into discredit of both sides ; for the king will think him too saucy, and the subject will forget his duty." Courteous and kindly behaviour has nothing to lose, and much to gain. Civility costs little, and is often worth much.

Illustration :—(a) Mr. Carter, a pious minister, once coming softly behind a religious man of his own acquaintance, who was busily engaged in tanning a hide, and giving him a tap on the shoulder, the man started, looked up, and with a blushing countenance said, " Sir, I am ashamed that you should find me thus." To whom Mr. Carter replied, "Let Christ, when he cometh, find me so doing." "What!" said the man, "doing thus?" "Yes," said Mr. Carter, "faithfully performing the duties of my calling."

SPIRITUAL RECOLLECTEDNESS.

ii. 4. So I prayed to the God of heaven.

This, a remarkable illustration of religious presence of mind.

I. The outcome of a consecrated life Unless he had been in the habit of making everything a matter of prayer, would not have been able thus to collect himself whilst trembling with excitement, fear, and suspense before the king

Having formed the habit of doing nothing without consulting God, had no difficulty in acting upon it. Agitated and affrighted, it would have been perfectly *natural* for him to have stammered forth his appeal in some incoherent manner. But here the irrepressible spirit of devotion, which permeated his whole life, revealed itself. If a man never prays anywhere save at stated times, and on public occasions, there is reason to fear that he never prays at all. If a man lives in the spirit of prayer, sudden emergency will spontaneously summon the familiar habit to his aid. Special prayer should be the outcome of constant prayerfulness. The way to have the heart in harmony with the worship of the sanctuary, is never to suffer its chords to be jarred. It was said of a distinguished Christian that he lived on the steps of the mercy-seat. It was said of a recent Bishop, who was sent to Western Africa, that "he lived upon his knees." This is to live safely. This is to live in the porch of heaven. Hence it was said of a dying saint, "I am changing my place, but not my company." Like Enoch, he had walked with God, and death was to him only like passing out of the vestibule into the inner sanctuary.

II. The result of long habit. Holy recollectedness not come naturally, nor easily, even to good men. Repeated action becomes habit. Practice makes perfect in this, as in other things.

III. A mark of self-distrusting humility. He dared not ask, without seeking wisdom higher than his own, in matter of such momentous issues. Self-diffidence impelled him to cast the burden of his responsibility upon one who was an unerring counsellor. "Travellers make mention of a bird so timid in disposition, and so liable to the assaults of unnumbered enemies, that she almost lives in the sky, scarcely ever venturing to rest her wings; and even when forced through very weariness to repose, she seeks the loftiest rock, and there still keeps her eyes only half shut, and her pinions only half folded, in readiness, on the first sign of danger, to spread her wings, and soar away to the heavens for safety." True emblem of how the child of God should "pass the time of his sojourning here in fear." Seldom should the wing of his devotion droop, or the eye of his watchfulness close; and even when he must repose it should ever be in an attitude of vigilance and prayerfulness."—*Stowell.*

IV. A source of incalculable blessing. 1. *It imparts confidence.* "He that believeth shall not make haste" (Isa. xxviii. 16). He shall not be afraid of evil tidings, whose heart is fixed, trusting in the Lord. "Thou wilt keep him in perfect peace, whose mind is stayed upon thee," &c. The calmness which comes from reliance upon a wisdom that is superhuman; the consciousness of Divine support. 2. *It preserves from missing the providential path.* The God of providence will direct those who cast themselves upon his care. Such "shall not full direction need; nor miss their providential way." 3. *It conduces to the accomplishment of God's will.* When everything is submitted to that will, and the stumbling-blocks of *self-will, pride, ambition,* &c. are removed, nothing can hinder the fulfilment of the purposes of Jehovah.

Ejaculatory Prayer.

ii. 4. *So I prayed to the God of heaven.*

I. It was suddenly required. A question addressed to Nehemiah by the king, point-blank, upon which hung, possibly, not only issues of life and death, but the success or failure of his long-prayed-for object. Great emergency. Great benefit to be able to seek aid of Omnipotence. Long formula impossible. No audible petition could be offered. Quick as thought the silent prayer of the heart flew to the ear of God, and not in vain. "He will fulfil the *desire* of them that fear him" (Ps. cxlv. 19). "The devout spirit, like the well-strung Eolian harp, not only gives out sweet sounds when woke by the gentler breathings that steal over its chords, but when vibrating under the ruder blasts that sweep across its strings." "On many occasions the servant of God requires special assistance, care, and counsel. Men of business are frequently called upon to decide summarily on questions big with importance, to make up their judgment *at once* on measures the issues of which they can neither over-estimate nor foresee. How commonly is the physician forced to form his conclusions in a moment; yea, to form them on uncertain grounds, and indeterminate symptoms. Yet a mistaken conclusion may endanger the life of his patient. Now if in such circumstances the medical man, or the merchant, rely simply on his own skill, and confer simply with his own judgment, to the neglect of calling in the wisdom and blessing of the Almighty, what a fearful risk and burden does he bring upon himself! But let his heart breathe forth the aspiration to God — 'Lord, direct me.' Will he not then, having cast his burden on the Lord, having invoked unerring skill, be able to act with faith, and nerve, and calmness? Call ye this fanaticism? The grossest fanaticism is that which leaves out God."—*Stowell*. (*a*)

II It was silently offered. No opportunity for audible vocal prayer This, good when alone, or in public assembly for worship, but not possible now. A sudden and secret desire darted up to heaven. Thus Moses cried unto God, yet said nothing (Exod. xiv. 15). Hannah was not heard, yet she prayed (1 Sam. i.). Austin reports it to be the custom of the Egyptian Churches to pray frequently and fervently, but briefly and by ejaculation, lest their fervour should abate It is the praying and crying of the heart that God delights in. Let no man then excuse himself and say he cannot pray; for in all places he may lift up his heart to God, though in the market, or on the mountain. (*β*)

III. It was suitably addressed "To the God of heaven." Ezra had previously used this expression. (See explanatory notes). It recognized the supremacy of Jehovah, and his power over human hearts and events. Thus calculated to impart confidence, and destroy the fear of man. The expression is similar in meaning to "Lord of Sabaoth," or "Lord of Hosts." "All power is given," &c.

IV. It was very brief Yet quite long enough. Not time for much. A question had been asked and an answer was required. Yet, between question and answer, was ample time for sending prayer to heaven, and receiving a reply. Length no virtue in prayer. Faith and fervour the two principal elements of success St. Augustine says, "He that carrieth his own temple about with him, may go to prayer when he pleaseth." How quickly thought can fly! many thousands of miles in a minute Prayer can travel as rapidly as thought towards heaven.

V. It was completely successful. 1. *In that wisdom to ask aright was given.* Nehemiah's petition was marked by—(1) Becoming *humility*. "If it please the king." (2) *Tact* "The place of my fathers' sepulchres." (3) *Forethought.* "Let letters be given me." 2 *In that the king's heart was favourably disposed towards him.* "And the king granted me," &c. This, God's doing, in direct answer to prayer. Nehemiah confesses this when he adds, "according to the good hand of my God upon me."

Illustrations : — (*a*) "Sudden extremity is a notable trial of faith, or any other disposition of the soul For as, in a sudden fear, the blood gathers suddenly to the heart, for guarding of that part which is principal, so the powers of the soul combine themselves in a hard exigent, that they may be easily judged of."—*Bp Hall.*

(*β*) "As the tender dew that falls during the silent night makes the grass, and herbs, and flowers to flourish and grow more abundantly than great showers of rain that fall in the day, so secret prayer will more abundantly cause the sweet herbs of grace and holiness to flourish and grow in the soul, than all those more public and open duties of religion, which too often are mingled with the sun and wind of pride and hypocrisy."—*Brooks.*

RELIGIOUS PRUDENCE.

ii. 7. *Moreover, I said unto the king, &c.*

Not satisfied with bare permission to go to the relief of his co-religionists at Jerusalem, he makes provision for all contingencies, and anticipates every difficulty that is likely to arise. From this learn :—

I. That prudent forethought is essential to success in spiritual as in secular enterprises. For, 1 *God has nowhere commended rashness.* The reverse of this enjoined and approved in word of God. "He will guide his affairs with discretion" (Ps. cxii. 5). "The fool shall be servant to the *wise of heart*," (Prov xi 29). "A prudent man," &c (Prov. xii. 23 ; xiv. 15). "He that handleth a matter wisely shall find good" (Prov. xvi. 20). "Give not that which is holy" (Matt vii 6). "Which of you intending to build," &c. (Luke xiv. 28). Examples.—Jacob (Gen. xxxii) Joseph (Gen xli.) Jethro (Exod xviii.) David (1 Sam. xvii.). Abigail (1 Sam. xxv). Paul (Acts xvi.). Town-clerk of Ephesus (Acts xix.) 2. *Pains-taking effort is at the foundation of all human success.* "By the sweat of thy face shalt thou eat thy bread" (Gen. iii. 19), is the curse pronounced upon all human labour. Even the curse turned into blessing, for labour is not necessarily an evil. "No gains without pains," under present social laws. No reaping without sowing. No permanent and substantial success in business, or art, or literature, or religion, without earnest, patient, unremitting diligence (2 Pet i. 10). This inexorable law reigns in the spiritual realm as in the secular, for—3 *Spiritual work as well as secular is amenable to natural law* Miracles wrought now in the moral rather than in the physical universe. Not obsolete in the latter, more frequent in the former. Natural law is no respecter of persons. It demands allegiance from the saint and sinner alike Errors in spiritual work are as surely followed by penalties as in secular. Sloth and senility undermine the success of religious as certainly as profane enterprises Here, as elsewhere, "whatsoever a man soweth, *that* shall he also reap"

II. That prudent forethought is not opposed, but helpful, to spiritual faith 1. *It furnishes a rational basis for expecting success* No right to expect success, merely because we hope for and earnestly desire it. "We are saved by hope ;" but it must rest on a solid foundation Hope without faith is dead. If there is a *living*, there is a *dead*, hope (1 Pet i. 3). The one stimulates, the other seduces. Faith must have a rational basis to distinguish it from credulity The basis may appear irrational to men who do not acknowledge God or the supernatural. 2. *It acts upon the supposition that mental powers were given to be employed in the service of God.* The use of this faculty no more opposed to strong faith and intense spirituality, than the use of other mental powers, as memory, imagination, perception, &c. All powers are to be consecrated to holy purposes, and diligently employed in assisting faith. 3. *It takes no step without seeking Divine guidance and approval.* Nehemiah used every precaution to ensure success, and made every needful arrangement beforehand, but not without previous thought and earnest prayer. Even so must we take each step, in religious work especially, depending on the Holy Ghost for direction He committed himself to God ; yet petitions the king for a convoy ; teaching that in all our enterprises God is so to be trusted as if we had used no means ; and yet the means are so to be used as if we had no God to trust in.

Illustrations —As the hermits were communing together, there arose a question as to which of all the virtues was most necessary to perfection. One said, chastity ; another, humility ; a third, justice St. Anthony remained silent until all had given their opinion and then he spoke. "Ye have all said well, but none of you have said aright. The virtue most necessary to perfection is *prudence ;* for the most virtuous actions of men, unless governed and directed by prudence, are neither pleasing to God, nor serviceable to others, nor profitable to ourselves." Juvenal speaks to the same effect · "No other protection is wanting, provided you are under the guidance of prudence." Bishop Hacket bears similar testimony —"He that loves to walk dangerous ways shall perish in them. Even king Josiah, one of the most lovely darlings of God's favour among all the kings of Judah, fell under the sword for pressing further against his enemies than the word of the Lord did permit him. The ancient Eliberitan Council enacted, that all those who plucked down the idols or temples of the heathen should not be accounted martyrs, though they died for the faith of Christ, because they plucked persecution upon themselves, and provoked their own martyrdom."

THE HAND OF GOD.

ii. 8.   *According to the good hand of my God upon me.*

The hand sometimes used in an ill sense, for inflicting punishments (Ruth i. 13; Jer. xv. 17), for we *strike* with the hand. Sometimes in a good sense, for helping others, for we *bestow favours* with the hand. In Psalm lxxxviii. 6, "Cut off from thy hand," means fallen from thy favour. Pindar uses the expression, "Θεῶ σὺν παλάμᾳ," in the sense of "by the aid of God." Thus Nehemiah is to be understood. By the Divine favour, which inclined the king to do what he desired, his suit had prevailed.

I. The hand of God is with his people for protection. Nehemiah's life was in jeopardy in God's service. Hence God's special protection. 1. *He was protected from the wrath of the king.* Had the king been in an angry mood Nehemiah might have paid for his temerity with his life. "The wrath of man" doth he restrain. David delivered from the outburst of Saul's murderous anger. Nehemiah saved from the outbursting of Artaxerxes'. God will ever defend those who trust him and seek his glory, from the malice of evil oppressors. 2. *He was protected from the hostility of his enemies.* The Samaritans and surrounding heathen would have not only hindered his work, but probably taken his life, but for the military guard which the king granted, through God's gracious influence. Thus will the Lord "make a hedge about his people" (Job ii.), for "the angel of the Lord encampeth round about them that fear him" (Ps. xxxiv.).

II. The hand of God is with his people for providential guidance. 1. *The hand of God guided Nehemiah to the Persian court* 2. *To the official position which brought him into the presence of the king.* 3. The providence of God directed him *when to speak,* and 4. *what to say.* "If it please the king," &c. "Silken words must be given to kings, as the mother of Darius said (ἡ διοία, ἡ ἥκιστα); neither must they be rudely and roughly dealt with, as Joab

dealt with David (2 Sam. xix. 5), who therefore could never well brook him afterward, but set another in his place."— *Trapp.*

III. God's servants should thankfully acknowledge the good which they receive from him. Nehemiah does not take any credit to himself, but gives all glory to God. This conduct requires— 1. *Genuine humility.* He might have boasted of his services to the king, of his place and authority in the Persian Court, and arrogated to himself the credit of success; but he was of another spirit, and ascribed all to the "good hand of his God." Ingratitude is the child of pride; thankfulness the offspring of humility. A proud man will never be truly grateful, a humble man possesses the first element of gratitude. Benefit a vain man, and he will ascribe the service to his own desert, he will regard it as no more than a just tribute to his excellence; but serve a lowly man, and he will attribute the service to the kindness of his benefactor. A proud child thinks that he has laid his parents under obligation; a lowly child feels that he can never liquidate the debt of gratitude he owes to them. The same holds good in relation to God. We must be lowly to be grateful The lark hides her nest in the grass, but her flight is far up in the heavens. This spirit continually exclaims, "It is of the Lord's mercies that we are not consumed," &c.; and, "I am less than the least of all his mercies" (Lam. iii 22) Paul a striking illustration of it: "To me, who am less than the least of all saints, is this *grace* given," &c. David also exclaims when the splendid offerings had been collected for the erection of God's house. "Thine, O Lord, is the greatness," &c. (1 Chron. xxix. 11). 2. *True faith* The believer in chance who ascribes everything to fortune, or fatality, cannot own a Divine hand. Faith, discerning the Almighty hand within the machinery of second causes, actuating, controlling, determining all, is the parent of sincere gratitude.

E

Men of business, from the very nature of their occupations, specially liable to lose the lively exercise of this practical faith. "Hard by the altar of incense in the ancient temple, stood the altar of burnt-offering As the one signified the atonement to be made by Christ, and the other the fragrant merits of that atonement; so did the latter represent also the offering of prayer to God through Christ's mediation by his faithful people, and the former the oblation of praise, presented through the same intercession, as a sweet-smelling savour to God Prayer and praise are twin services. They should always go hand in hand Praise is the fragrance breathed from the flower of joy. He is happiest who is thankfullest. This lesson taught by the brute creation Morose and unkindly animals express as little of enjoyment as they do of gratefulness by their snarling and growling sounds. The beasts and birds of night are rarely gladsome. But the lambs which sport and gambol in their green pastures, and the birds which in the early morning wake the echoes of the woodland with their songs, all tell most unmistakeably that they are happy How much more then must it be the blessedness of man 'to look through nature, up to nature's God,' and glorify the giver in all his varied gifts "—*Stowell* (See Addenda.)

Illustrations ·—" Your father had a battle with Apollyon," said Great-heart to Samuel, "at a place yonder before us, in a narrow passage, just beyond Forgetful Green. And indeed the place is the most dreadful place in all these parts, for if at any time pilgrims meet with any brunt, it is when they forget what favours they have received, and how unworthy they are of them This is the place, also, where others have been hard put to it."—*Bunyan.*

Luther said when he heard a little bird sing, when he was out in the fields one morning, "The bird had no storehouse or barn, and did not know of any provision for the future, and yet it seemed to sing, 'Mortal, cease from toil and sorrow, God provideth for the morrow.' We do not find any sparrows with large storehouses, or any swallows with a great quantity of grain laid by for the morrow, yet never find a sparrow starved to death, or a swallow that has perished from cold God 'careth for them, and are ye not much better than they?'"

THE INITIAL STAGES OF A GREAT REFORMATION.

ii 9—20.   *Then I came to the governors, &c*

I. Great reformations often have an insignificant commencement, and are slow in developing their true proportions Who would have expected such great things to spring from that interview in the palace, and now from the visit of this one man to Jerusalem? Yet who dare "despise the day of small things"? How slight the first streak of dawn! How minute the grain of mustard-seed! Some of the noblest exploits of the Church have had the feeblest beginnings. A few Christian men met together in the vestry of a plain chapel ; they pondered and prayed over the state of the heathen world ; they conceived and planned the glorious enterprise of evangelizing all pagan lands They arose and built The Church Missionary Society is the result. Not only small at beginning but *slow* in *developing*. May travel rapidly on land or by sea, but in morals must be content to proceed gradually Deep-rooted evils, profligate and abandoned habits, not to be eradicated in a moment ; nor are excellent characters manufactured in a moment, as a piece of work from the loom The restoration of God's image rather resembles the growing likeness to its beautiful original in the canvas of the artist. At first the outline, and slowly the form and features, of the human face appear ; gradually they assume more distinctness and expression, and the likeness stands confessed. So does the Holy Ghost restore the waste places of Christ's Church, and the moral deformities of his children.

II. Reformation work requires a vigorous leader Nehemiah eminently qualified for the post, for—1. *He occupied a commanding social position* The office of cupbearer a very honourable one with the Persians. A son of Prexaspes, a distinguished person, was made cupbearer to Cambyses. The poets make Ganymedes to be cupbearer to Jupiter, and even Vulcan himself is put into this office. It gave him influence with king and court, and status amongst even Persian nobles. 2. *He was inspired with intense enthusiasm.* Without this fire no hearts melt, no great work accomplished. It burns up all evil sordid desires, and kindles all goodness. Jeremiah was influenced by it. Kept silence for a time, but was constrained to break out again, saying the word within him was like burning fire (Jer. xx.). To the same effect Elijah cries out. " I am very zealous for the Lord of Hosts " (1 Kings xix.). Moses prayed to be blotted out of God's book, rather than his people should be destroyed (Exod. xxxii.). St. Paul " counted not his life dear unto him," &c. (Acts xx.). Phineas, when none else would take the sword to vindi- cate the outraged laws of Jehovah, himself slew the offenders (Numb. xxv.). Our Lord himself, moved with indignation, drove out the profaners of his sanctuary (John ii.). Such holy enthusiasm glowed in Nehemiah's heart, and urged him to undertake this difficult and dangerous work. 3. *He possessed unwearied energy and perseverance.* His enthusiasm not fitful, but patient. He had calculated the difficulties of his undertaking, and was prepared to carry it through. No great work will succeed without plodding. A great statesman once answered a friend who inquired to what he attributed his great success in life, thus—" *I know how to plod.*" Without this virtue Nehemiah must have succumbed to the almost over- whelming difficulties that beset his path.

III. Reformation work should not be undertaken without a deliberate estimate of its magnitude and difficulty. Blind courage that counts no costs always short-lived. This stood the tests which it had to endure because founded upon intelligent and mature conviction. 1. *Nehemiah forestalled opposition.* An escort had been asked for and granted (v. 10). Forewarned is forearmed. Thus did he fortify himself against failure from this quarter. Christian soldiers " must put on the whole armour of God " (Eph. vi. 11), and expect to be assailed. No mistake greater than presumption. To despise or ignore an enemy sure sign of weakness. 2. *He carefully examined the work to be done.* " And I arose in the night," &c. (v. 12). Wise proceeding before engaging in a work that might prove to be impracticable. Accurate knowledge helps the judgment and stimulates courage. 3. *He weighed the matter before proceeding to action.* " So I came to Jerusalem, and was there three days " (v. 11). Days spent in seclusion not spent in vain, if time be occupied in thought and prayer. (See outline on " Preparatory Retirement.")

IV. Reformation work in its initial stages is almost certain to provoke opposition. " When Sanballat the Horonite," &c. (v. 10). 1. *This often proceeds from a misconstruction of the nature of the work.* " Will ye rebel ? " (v. 19). Bad men always ready to attribute evil motives. Sometimes springs from ignorance, more often from wilful malice. Charges of treason more frequently brought against reformation work than any other. Insinuation often more deadly in its operation than open calumny. 2. *This often springs from aversion to self-sacrifice.* For this reason the men of Jabesh-Gilead stood aloof when Benjamin was to be punished; and were afterwards destroyed for their neutrality (Judges xxi.). Work that requires self-denial and hard toil cannot be good in the eyes of those who have no love for any but themselves.

V. Reformation work cannot be carried on without mutual co-operation. " So they strengthened their hands for this good work " (v. 18). *Necessary as a security against discouragement.* Individual workers labouring in isolation always liable to discouragement. " Not good for man to be alone." Christ recognized this principle in religious work, when he sent his disciples by twos. Mutual sym- pathy and counsel will often cheer faltering courage, and strengthen failing hope. 2. *Necessary as a safeguard against combined opposition.* Good men must combine, and present a united front to the combined forces of wickedness and opposition. Unity is strength in all work, and in all conflict.

VI. Reformation work cannot succeed without the Divine blessing. " The

God of heaven, he will prosper us" (v 20) When every precaution has been taken, and all available human aid enlisted, still all depends on God for success. 1 *Because the forces of evil are too strong for the unaided powers of man* Melancthon found this by experience, when he thought to convert the world to Christianity in a very short time "Without me ye can do nothing." "Not by might, nor by power," &c. 2 *The blessing of God will compensate for any amount of opposition.* "If God be for us," &c "Greater is he that is in you," &c

Illustrations —(a) The artist Correggio, when young, saw a painting by Raphael Long and ardently did the thoughtful boy gaze on that picture His soul drank in its beauty as flowers drink moisture from the mist He waked to the consciousness of artistic power Burning with the enthusiasm of enkindled genius, the blood rushing to his brow, and the fire flashing from his eyes, he cried out, " I also am a painter !" That conviction carried him through his initial studies, it blended the colours on his palette, it guided his pencil, it shone on his canvas, until the glorious Titian, on witnessing his productions, exclaimed, "Were I not Titian, I would wish to be Correggio "

(β) In the museum at Rotterdam is the first piece painted by the renowned Rembrandt It is rough, without marks of genius or skill, and uninteresting, except to show that he began as low down as the lowest In the same gallery is the masterpiece of the artist, counted of immense value What years of patient study and practice intervene between the two pieces ! If all have not genius, all have the power to work, and this is greater than genius.

(γ) Coleridge, one day when some one was enlarging on the tendency of some good scheme to regenerate the world, threw a little thistle-down into the air, which he happened to see by the roadside, and said, "The tendency of this thistle-down is towards China! but I know, with assured certainty, it will never get there, nay, it is more than probable, that after sundry eddyings and gyrations up and down, backwards and forwards, it will be found somewhere near the place where it grew" Such is the history of grand schemes of reformation apart from Divine power and benediction

(δ) William Rufus, having seen the coast of Ireland from some rocks in North Wales, is reported to have said, " I will summon hither all the ships of my realm, and with them make bridge to attack that country " This threat being reported to Murchard, Prince of Leinster, he paused a moment, and then said, " Did the king add to this mighty threat, *if God please ?* " and being assured he made no mention of God in his speech, he replied, rejoicing in such a prognostic, " Sure, that man puts his trust in human, not in Divine power, I fear not his coming."

SECULAR AID FOR SPIRITUAL WORK.

ii 9   *Now the king had sent captains of the army, &c.*

This martial escort granted to Nehemiah in response to his own request. As an official dignitary, had right to public honour and body-guard Learn—
I That the Church may employ secular power for purposes of protection When one has suitable means at hand for avoiding danger, he must not despise them (Josh ii. 15 ; 2 Cor. xi. 33) .1 *Every law-abiding subject has a right to claim the law's protection.* This holds good except in the case of conduct which is likely to provoke a breach of the peace 2 *It is a good man's duty to seek the protection of secular power rather than rashly to expose himself to danger.* Paul sought the shield of the law when certain men had taken an oath to kill him (Acts xxiii) 3. *When secular aid is denied, or granted only on terms inconsistent*

with righteousness, the believer may confidently cast himself upon the protection of Jehovah "When my father and mother forsake me," &c Under such circumstances the three Hebrews and Daniel committed their case to God. "This poor man cried, and the Lord heard him " (Ps xxxiv)
II That the Church may not employ secular power in matters of faith Ezra's work had been more purely spiritual than Nehemiah's now was, hence he sought no such aid as this Both sought the religious reformation of the people, but Nehemiah's chief mission was to restore the city of Jerusalem and rebuild the walls. 1. *God has never authorized the use of any but moral means in spiritual work* All coercion inadmissible "My kingdom is not of this world." "Go ye into all

the world," is the commission which follows upon the proclamation of Divine sovereignty "All power," &c "He that *winneth* souls is wise" The fire and the rack may command submission, but will never win the heart, or convince the conscience (β) 2. *The employment of secular power in matters of faith has always been productive of disastrous results.* This method predominated over all others in the dark or mediæval ages. Hence the war and bloodshed, strife and controversy, hatred and heresy that prevailed. A notable exception was Stephen, king of Poland, who when urged by some of his subjects to constrain certain who were of a different religion to embrace his creed, nobly answered, "I am king of men, and not of conscience The dominion of conscience belongs exclusively to God."

Illustrations :—(a) An old lady taking a long railway journey, prayed almost all the time that God would protect her from harm When she reached the last platform, and was but a few minutes walk from her home, she felt that now she could take care of herself; but just here she fell, and received an injury from which she was a long time recovering We must trust in God at all times

(β) The missionaries to the Fiji islands were threatened with destruction by the enraged natives, and had no means of defence except prayer Their enemies heard them praying, became fearful, and fled. The reason was given by one of themselves "They found you were praying to your God, and they know your God is a strong God, and they are gone" St. Augustine was saved from death by a mistake of his guide, who lost the usual road, in which the Donatists had laid wait to murder him.

FIRST HINDRANCE.—SECRET JEALOUSY

ii 10.   *When Sanballat the Horonite, and Tobiah, &c*

The name Sanballat signifies a pure enemy; for he belonged to a spiteful people who had always been troublesome to the children of Israel, and did constantly vex and provoke them to evil (Numb xxii. 3, 4)

I **Here is jealousy tyrannical in its spirit** The Hebrews in Palestine had been hitherto poor and helpless They were anxious to improve their condition, but these enemies were eager to keep them poor that they might be able to oppress and plunder them Jealousy naturally cruel, inasmuch as it feeds upon the poverty and destitution of others, and fears their prosperity, lest it should lose its food They probably heard of this new enterprise through their wives, who might be Jewesses Among the Turks every vizier used to keep a Jew as private counsellor, whose malice was thought to have had much to do with the Turks' bitter persecution of Christianity

II **Here is jealousy anti-religious in its attitude** Grieved that any should "seek the welfare of the children of Israel" (v. 10) Their opposition doubled by the fact that this was God's work, and these were his people They hated the name and worship of Jehovah.

The malice of unbelievers and scoffers against the kingdom of God can never be satisfied If envy had not blinded these men, they might have seen that they meant them no harm. As the building of this Jerusalem had many enemies, so the repairing of the spiritual Jerusalem (the Church) by the preaching of the gospel hath many more.—*Pilkington.*

III. **Here is jealousy covetously selfish in its motives** Samaria had become the leading state west of Jordan, and any restoration of Jerusalem might interfere with this predominance The fear of losing their gains had much to do with the acrimony of their opposition. Hippocrates in his epistle to Crateva gives him this good counsel; that if it were possible, amongst other herbs, he cut up that weed covetousness by the roots, that there be no remainder left; and then know certainly that together with the bodies, he would be able to cure the diseases of the mind.

IV. **Here is jealousy self-torturing in its effects.** "It *grieved* them *exceedingly*" (v. 10). The expression a very strong one (Compare Ps. cxii) "The wicked shall see it, and be *grieved, he shall gnash with his teeth*." Keen mental torture implied Envy compared to a poisonous serpent. Because it cannot feed upon other men's hearts it feedeth upon its own, drinking up the most part of its own venom, and is therefore like the serpent Porphyrus, which was full of poison, but wanting teeth, hurt none but itself. Austin describes it as a "madness of the soul;" Gregory, as "a torture;" Chrysostom, "an insatiableness;" Cyprian, "blindness, a plague subverting kingdoms and families, an incurable disease." A disease that neither Esculapius nor Plutus could cure; a continual plague and vexation of spirit, an earthly hell.

Illustrations:—The poets imagined that Envy dwelt in a dark cave; being pale and lean, looking asquint, abounding with gall, her teeth black, never rejoicing but in the misfortunes of others, ever unquiet and careful, and continually tormenting herself. (See Addenda.)

"The Bible abounds with instances of this sin

We find it in Cain, the proto-murderer, who slew his brother in a fit of jealousy. We find it in the dark and gloomy and revengeful spirit of Saul, who under the influence of jealousy plotted for years the slaughter of David. We find it in the king of Israel when he pined for the vineyard of Naboth, and shed his blood to gain it. Yea, it was envy that perpetrated that most atrocious crime ever planned in hell or executed on earth, on which the sun refused to look, and at which nature gave signs of abhorrence by rending the rocks; I mean the crucifixion of Christ, for the Evangelist tells us, that for envy the Jews delivered our Lord."—*J. A. James*

The infatuated Caligula slew his brother, because he was a beautiful young man. Mutius, a citizen of Rome, was reputed to be of such an envious and malevolent disposition, that Publius, one day observing him to be very sad, said, "Either some great evil hath happened to Mutius, or some great good to another." "Dionysius the Tyrant," says Plutarch, "out of envy punished Philoxenius the musician, because he could sing; and Plato, the philosopher, because he could dispute better than himself." Cambyses killed his brother Smerdis, because he could draw a stronger bow than himself or any of his party.

PREPARATORY RETIREMENT.

ii. 11. *So I came to Jerusalem, and was there three days.*

God's servants frequently thus retired for deliberation before entering upon arduous tasks. Moses had a forty-years half-involuntary preparation for his life work, in the wilderness of Midian. Paul spent three years in Arabia before commencing his career as a missionary. The disciples were commanded "to tarry at Jerusalem until," &c. Our Lord himself, at the commencement of his public ministry, was "led of the spirit into the wilderness to be tempted." And here we see Nehemiah spending three days in retirement, before entering upon a work that would tax all his powers and graces to the very utmost. Consider the reason of this—

I. It gave him time to look round. Jerusalem altogether strange to him. Unacquainted with the exact state of affairs or parties in the city. To have rushed headlong without premeditation into so gigantic an enterprise would have been madness. Probably made secret inquiries as to vigilance of foes, and spirit of people, as well as their numbers, character, and wealth. Knowledge always source of power to workers

and leaders. Knowledge of human nature, human history, and character, of great service in Christian work.

II. It gave him time to look forward. Evidently a man of wise foresight. Could see both difficulties and the way to meet and overcome them. Careful, yet not over-anxious, because made God his counsellor and guide. Neither optimist nor pessimist. By anticipating difficulties we may obviate them, and so make them comparatively harmless when they do come. Guard against other extreme, of making them when there are none, and magnifying them when they are insignificant. Such pre-vision not inspiriting, but disheartening.

III. It gave him time to look within. Now was the time for self examination. Motives tested, heart probed. Trying moment to faith. Looking at self alone drives to despair. "Who is sufficient for these things?" the cry of one burdened with such tremendous responsibility. Luther spent the night before the Diet of Worms on the floor of his little chamber, humbling himself before God, and laying hold on Divine strength. No wonder he triumphed

IV. It gave him time to look up-ward. The contemplation of his own faults and frailty alone would have completely unnerved him for the work he had come to accomplish His eye would turn from personal demerit to infinite perfection, from personal impotence to infinite strength. From penitence to prayer a single step, thence to confidence and hope. Such preparation necessary for all who would achieve great works for God. Careless self-confidence as sure to meet with failure as humble and contrite faith to be crowned with success. (See Addenda.)

Illustrations.—" Domitian, about the beginning of his reign, usually sequestered himself from company an hour every day; but did nothing the while but catch flies, and kill them with a penknife. God's people can better employ their solitariness, and do never want company, as having God and themselves to talk with. And these secret meals are those that make the soul fat. It was a wise speech of Bernard, that "Christ, the soul's spouse, is bashful, neither willingly cometh to his bride in the presence of a multitude."—*Trapp*

The noblest works, like the temple of Solomon, are brought to perfection in silence.—*Sir A. Helps.*

Solitude hath been the custom not only of holy men, but of heathen men Thus did Tully, and Anthony, and Crassus, make way to that honour and renown which they afterwards obtained by their eloquence; thus did they pass *a solitudine in scholas, a scholis in forum,* "from their secret retirement into the schools, and from the schools into the pleading place."—*Farindon.*

THE WALLS INSPECTED.

ii. 12. *And I arose in the night, &c.*

I. A work involving considerable danger. 1. *From the ruined state of the walls* (v 13—15). No safe path Stones scattered along road made travelling dangerous God's servants often required to traverse perilous roads. Missionaries often wonderfully preserved when journeying. 2. *From the enmity of the Samaritans.* Had they known would probably have waylaid so small and defenceless a company. Exposed to the midnight marauders who lurked about the city, taking advantage of its open condition. This danger did not deter. God often protected his servants from malice and bloodthirstiness of hostile nations. Missionary annals of Church furnish many instances of sublimest heroism and hair-breadth escapes from threatened destruction

II A work requiring personal sacrifice 1. *He gave up his much-needed rest.* The physician will watch by his patient all night. The captain will not think of sleep if his vessel be in danger. So should the Christian forego his rest in times of danger, that he may call upon God in faithful prayer. David ' rose at midnight to give praise " unto the name of the Lord (Ps. cxix.). Our mortal enemy, Satan, sleepeth not night or day, but continually "goeth about like a roaring lion, seeking whom he may devour;" and had we not an equally vigilant watchman we should be destroyed. "Behold, he neither slumbereth nor sleepeth, that is the watchman of Israel" (Ps. cxxi) Christ himself set us an example of self-denying vigilance, prayed the whole night before sending forth his disciples (Luke vi.). Joshua marched all night to conquer the Amorites (Josh. x). Gideon arose in the night to pull down the altar of Baal (Judg vi.). 2. *He laid aside his official dignity.* Might have sent a deputy, or gone attended by strong escort, or numerous retinue, but preferred to go himself, to teach us that nothing should be painful or degrading to any man, however exalted his station, which concerns the prosperity of God's City and Church David, when the ark was brought out of Abinadab's house, played on instruments, and after casting off his kingly apparel, danced before the ark in his ephod. Michal mocked, and was punished; but David declared that he would yet "more lowly cast himself down," and was blessed of the Lord (2 Sam. vi.). Moses forsook the dignity and pleasure of Pharaoh's court to become a tender of sheep, that he might serve the cause of God (Heb. xi.).

Christ washed the disciples' feet, and humbled himself to the death of the cross, that he might effect our redemption. Such humble self-abasement is the greatest honour that can come to a man. Pride has its own reward, and a paltry one it is ; but humility shall be rewarded by the great Father in heaven.

III. A work requiring great moral courage. The view of such a wreck likely to dishearten. The magnitude of the task would appear all but overwhelming. Would serve to impress him with a sense of personal insufficiency for so gigantic a work. Ezekiel, surrounded by the valley of bleached bones, when suddenly asked, " Son of man, can these bones live ?" in despair could only reply, " O Lord God, thou knowest." Nehemiah, surrounded by a ruin equally hopeless, can only cast himself and his work upon the strength of the Omnipotent. (*a*)

IV. A work which had an important bearing upon subsequent operations. 1. *It furnished accurate information of the work to be done.* Some render the words, " viewed the *walls*," " *broke the walls* " (*i.e.* broke off a piece of the wall), to try the soundness of it, that he might know whether it required to be pulled down entirely, or might be repaired on the same foundation. Must have been moonlight, or could not have seen to do this ; as, to have carried torches or lamps would have betrayed their presence. Knowledge obtained by personal investigation always most valuable. Illustrate this in the case of pastors, sick visitors, and Sunday School

teachers. They who come into personal contact with human nature in its varied phases know best how to remedy its ills, repair its losses, and alleviate its woes. In all religious work knowledge is power. 2. *It kindled his enthusiasm for the performance of the work.* The greater the ruin, the greater the work of restoration. Small works require commonplace zeal ; but great enterprises demand extraordinary grace. Two truths brought home to him by sight of ruins. (1) *How faithful God is.* He threatened that Jerusalem should become a heap (Isa. xxv. 2). Here was the manifest fulfilment of the threat. Surely, if God be faithful in punishing, he will not be less faithful in healing. (2) *How vile sin is.* This desolation the result of Israel's disobedience. The restoration of the city should be a sign of Israel's return to obedience ; these thoughts would serve to inflame Nehemiah's zeal. The same thoughts are calculated to stimulate all Christian effort.

Illustration :—(*a*) As Luther drew near to the door which was about to admit him to the Diet of Worms, he met a valiant knight, the celebrated George of Freundsberg, who four years later drove the French into the Ticino. The brave general, seeing Luther pass, tapped him on the shoulder, and shaking his head, blanched in many battles, said kindly : " Poor monk, poor monk ! thou art now going to make a nobler stand than I or any other captain have ever made in the bloodiest of our battles. But if thy cause is just, and thou art sure of it, go forward in God's name, and fear nothing. God will not forsake thee." He went forward and won a glorious victory.

A TIME FOR SILENCE.

ii. 12. *Neither told I any man what God, &c.*

There is a time to keep silence, and a time to speak (Eccl. iii. 7). Taciturnity in some cases an eminent virtue. He is a wise man who can discern the proper season for its exercise. Jerome says, " Let us first learn *not* to speak, that we may afterwards open our minds with discretion." Solomon puts silence before speech, as a virtue rarer and more precious. Learn—

I. Good intentions are best kept

secret until they are ascertained to be practicable. Nehemiah would only have marred his work by disclosing his intention before he was sure it was worth disclosing. Ideas are prolific as insects, but few of them are fit to live. When Nehemiah had viewed the walls, he was able to render a reason, and expound his plan for their restoration. A good rule for all who contemplate any work of importance. They should first consider, then speak. Rashly to enter upon a crude enterprise is to court failure. A wise man will not open his mouth to others until he has formed some plan for the accomplishment of his purpose. Guard against other extreme of obstinate persistence in a course condemned by others as unpractical.

II Good intentions are best kept secret until they can be carried out with decisive energy. Great enterprises demand great faith, and intense enthusiasm. Many a grand reform has prematurely failed through the half-heartedness of its chief supporters Had Luther been less bold he would have been unfit for the work which God entrusted to him. Courage is contagious, and cowardice too

III. Good intentions are best kept secret from those who are likely to oppose them Nehemiah aware of the vigilance and enmity of Sanballat and his party Careful to avoid betraying his purpose to those who were related to them by inter-marriage. Herein we see the prudence of this great man. In this, worthy of our imitation, who are engaged

in good works for God Take no counsel with scoffers, nor give them any advantage in their profane opposition. Caution and forethought as necessary in this warfare as in carnal. We must not cast pearls before swine.

IV Good intentions are best kept secret until the co-operation essential to success can be relied on. This work impossible without co-operation Useless to attempt it until this secured. By personal effort and interview we prepare the way for united action and ultimate success The soldiers must be enlisted one by one, then the battle-cry may be sounded Workers in the Church must be secured one by one, then the work may be openly announced. This preparatory work done in silence and secrecy, afterwards declared openly.

Illustration — "When Homer makes his heroes to march, he gives them silence for their guide; on the contrary, he makes cowards to babble and chatter like cranes. The one pass along like great rivers, letting their streams glide softly with silent majesty; the others only murmur like bubbling brooks A sign of not being valiant is to strive to seem valiant."

AN APPEAL FOR HELP.

ii. 17. *Then said I unto them, &c.*

I The ground of the appeal "Ye see the distress that we are in" (v. 17) An appeal to their *patriotism*, their *pity*, and their *piety*. God's city is desolate *your* city is in ruins. "We (putting himself along with them) are in distress." A reproach to the Church, an object of derision to the world, shall we rest satisfied where we are? "*Ye* see." The fact is patent, it cannot be concealed. No need to expatiate on this point, for you are mourning on account of it every day See here model for all Christian appeals Shame a powerful motive To this Nehemiah appealed What inconsistency in their conduct!—that they who boasted of the greatness and goodness of their God should be living in this miserable plight, as though he could not or would not deliver them! For very shame we should arise and build the waste places of Zion; strengthen her

stakes, and lengthen her cords; then shall her converts be multiplied.

II The nature of the appeal. "Come, and let us build." 1 *It solicited personal effort,* "let us build" Time for debating and discussing past. Time for work had come. Nehemiah not satisfied with their good wishes, or money, or prayers; but sought their personal assistance. Every Christian is called upon to take his share of work in the Church. Not all adapted for same kind of work. All kinds of work, intellectual and manual, may be sanctified to the cause of God In Israel's battle with Midian, when Sisera was defeated and slain, we find all kinds of work recorded and commended (Judges v. 14) Meroz was cursed for its cowardly neutrality We may not substitute money, or prayers, or good wishes for *work* "Every man's *work* shall be tried," &c. "Let your light so shine before men, that they may see your *good works*" "Well *done*, good and faithful servant." The child and the invalid, the school-girl and maidservant, the merchant and his errand-boy, have all some work to do for God. To every believer he says, "*Go work* to-day in my vineyard." At our peril do we say "I go," and go not   2 *It promised personal aid*   "Let *us* build" Not *go*, but "*come* :" not go *ye*, but come, "*let us* build" An example as noble as rare, to see a courtier leave that wealth, and ease, and authority in the midst of which he was living, and go to dwell so far from court in an old, torn, and decayed city, where he should not live quietly, but toil and drudge like a day-labourer, in dread and danger of his life   Yet they who are earnest in God's work think not of ease, and bid none go where they are unwilling to go themselves, or do work which they are too proud to touch Personal example in workers, and soldiers especially, far more powerful than personal authority.   *Come*, always more successful than *go*.

III. The motive urged. "That we be no more a reproach" (v. 17). Here we see the misery they were in urged as a motive for action.   Several years had elapsed since Cyrus gave them permission to return, and yet hitherto they had been unable to rebuild the walls.   This plea often occurs in the Bible   "For thy great Name's sake," an argument often employed by eminent pleaders   (2 Kings xix. 4, Ps. xlii 10, lxxiv 18, lxxix 12, lxxxix 51, Prov. xiv. 31 ; 1 Kings viii 41, 42 , 1 Chron xvii. 24 , Ps xxv 11; Ps. lxxiv 10 ; Jer xiv. 7)   Jehovah jealous for his name, and will vindicate his character   When his Church is reproached and scorned he is assailed, and in jealousy for his honour will defend his own   Christ said to Saul of Tarsus, "Why persecutest thou me ?" The wounds inflicted upon the members of his body on earth, were felt by him, the living head, in heaven.

IV. The encouragement offered "Then I told them of the hand of my God," &c (v 18)   The time for silence now past, and the time for speech come The walls inspected, the work carefully

planned and thoroughly resolved upon, it only remained to make a bold appeal for immediate help, and commence forthwith, before the enemy could muster their forces or mature their plans Note, promptness in religious work will often sweep away like a tornado all obstacles, and baffle all opponents.   He assured his co-patriots—1 *That God was the instigator of the work.* "I told them of the hand of my God, which *was good* upon me" (v 18)   In previous verse the *law* was preached, here the *gospel*   First, he set forth their misery, then encouraged them by the promise of God's mercy This order the true one for all teachers and ministers.   They are the best scholars who will work without the rod   yet none so good but need the rod sometimes.   A wise schoolmaster will make such use of both gentleness and severity as to gain his point with the least possible friction   2 *That the king approved of the work.* "Also the king's words that he had spoken unto me." God had given him such favour in the king's sight, that as soon as he asked licence to go and build the city, where his fathers lay buried, it was granted , and the liberality and goodwill of the king were so great that he granted him soldiers to conduct him safely to Jerusalem, and commission to his officers for timber to build with   Why should they mistrust or doubt ?   With both God and the king on their side, what needed they more ?   God's servants should always seek to make themselves agreeable to those in high station, that they may receive their help in doing his work Learn to be thankful for wise and benevolent rulers, and pray for their conversion (1 Tim. ii. 2)

V The success of the appeal "And they said, Let us rise and build " (v. 18) 1 *The response was prompt*   Without delay or discussion they entered with spirit upon the work there and then Would that all congregations were equally prompt in accepting the invitations of the Gospel! "Now is the accepted time, behold, now is the day of salvation" (2 Cor. vi. 2)   Would that all Christians were as ready to work ! 2 *The response was practical*   "Let us rise and *build.*" Not propose substitute, or alternative, but undertook *the work required* of them Example for all Christian workers, not to go round difficulties, but meet them in the face. *Practical work* must be done in a *practical way* Fancy and flimsy methods break down, whilst simple and personal effort accomplish great results

3. *The response was unanimous.* " Let us rise and build" Even the listless were stirred for the time (Eliashib for instance). All with one accord undertook to carry out the work by God's blessing, and the king's favour. Co-operation necessary to the success of any large undertaking. World never converted until the churches are united.

The Strength of Unity.

ii. 18. *So they strengthened their hands for this good work.*

I. Consists in its power to protect individual workers against discouragement 1 *Isolated workers are always liable to depression* This, the result of bearing alone the burden of care and duty incident to their work. Few men have the indomitable courage of a Nehemiah, a Paul, a Luther. Most spirits quail when unsupported by the aid and sympathy of kindred workers 2. *Mutual sympathy and conference relieve mental strain, and renew exhausted energy* "Iron sharpeneth iron, so a man sharpeneth the countenance of his friend" (Prov. xxvii. 17). Burdens confessed are half removed. Mutual counsel will cheer the drooping spirit, and stimulate to increased effort Christ recognized this when he sent out his disciples two and two It is not good for man to be alone "Where no counsel is the people fall" (Prov. xi. 14) "Two are better than one, for if they fall, the one will lift up his fellow ; but woe to him that is *alone when he falleth*" (Eccl iv. 9, 10).

Illustration —There are stragglers in the Church as well as in the army, who fall out of the ranks and are lost. Sometimes they manage to subsist for a while, living on the charity of the people and the scraps left by those in camp, but generally fall a prey to their isolation and exposure. One such found his way, during the American war, to the hospital at Sedalia. He was dying then, and could not give his name or regiment. He was a mere boy, and unequal to the toil of marching He was wet and cold and weary, and in a few hours died, and was buried in a nameless grave So do many fall out of the Church's ranks, and soon faint by the way Pliny writes of a stone in the island of Scyros, that if it be whole, though a large and heavy one, it swims above water, but being broken it sinks. So long as saints keep whole, nothing

shall sink them ; but if they break up, and divide, they are in danger of going down.

II Consists in its power of resisting combined opposition from without 1 *The full force of individual strength only awakened by the enthusiasm of united action.* Men are like the stone pyrites, which is cold and dull until well rubbed ; then it becomes so brilliant and hot as to burn the hand. Intense earnestness only kindled by the contagion of glowing spirits. Coals need to be pressed together to become thoroughly hot. So do souls require to be brought into very close contact, and inspired by one common impulse, to be fully roused to fervour and self-sacrificing devotion 2 *In unity, the full force of individual strength is directed against the common enemy.* Not as separate individuals, but as forming one combined and glowing mass. Such union is resistless as a stream of glowing lava

Illustrations —The sand-reed, which grows on the sandy shores of Europe, represents the influence of religion and the Church upon society. Its roots penetrate to a considerable depth, and spread in all directions, forming a net-work which binds together the loosest sands ; whilst its strong tall leaves protect the surface from drought, and afford shelter to small plants, which soon grow between the reeds, and gradually form a new green surface on the bed of sand. But for the sand-reed, the sea-wind would long since have wafted the drift-sand far into the interior of the country, and have converted many a fruitful acre into a waste ; but that invaluable grass opposes its stubborn resistance to the most furious gale. So does the united front of Church organization present an insuperable barrier to the aggressions of profanity and unbelief.

Standing one day before a beehive, Gotthold observed with delight how the little honey-birds departed and arrived, and from time to time returned home laden with the spoils of the flowers. Meanwhile a great yellow hornet, the wolf among bees, came buzzing up in eager quest of prey. As it was evening-tide, and the bees after the heat of the day had settled about the mouth of the hive to breathe the cool air, it was amusing to observe that their fierce adversary lacked courage to attack their combined host and serried ranks. True, he often advanced for the purpose, but seeing how densely and compactly they were sitting, was forced to retreat empty-handed. At last, a bee, somewhat belated, arrived by itself, and on this straggler he instantly seized, fell with it to the earth, and instantly devoured it.

III. Consists in its power to cope with the inherent difficulties of the work, which otherwise would be insurmountable. 1. *Work which cannot be done by few may be accomplished by many.* This true of the wall-building. A small company of workers, however willing, would have been altogether inadequate for the work to be done. True of many other large Christian undertakings. Especially true of church or chapel building where the workers are mostly poor. 2. *Work which cannot be done by many acting separately, may be accomplished by the same acting in unison.* Unity is strength. It doubles the capacity of each individual worker. A hundred separate links or threads will accomplish nothing, but join into a chain or a cable, and they may save a hundred lives.

Illustrations.—"Separate the atoms which make the hammer, and each would fall on the stone as a snow-flake, but welded into *one*, and wielded by the firm arm of the quarryman, it will break the massive rocks asunder. Divide the waters of Niagara into distinct and individual drops, and they would be no more than the falling rain; but their united body would quench the fires of Vesuvius, and have some to spare for other volcanoes."—*Guthrie.*

"Union is power. The most attenuated thread when sufficiently multiplied will form the strongest cable. A single drop of water is a weak and powerless thing; but an infinite number of drops united by the force of attraction will form a stream, and many streams combined will form a river, till rivers pour their water into the mighty oceans, whose proud waves, defying the power of man, none can stay but he who formed them. And thus, forces which, acting singly, are utterly impotent, are, when acting in combination, resistless in their energies and mighty in power."—*Salter.*

"A thousand grains of powder, or a thousand barrels, scattered, a grain in a place, and fired at intervals, would burn, it is true, but would produce no concussion. Placed together in effective position, they would lift a mountain, and cast it into the sea. Even so, the whole Church, filled with faith, and fired by the Holy One who gave the tongues of fire on the Day of Pentecost, will remove every mountain, fill up every valley, east up the highway of the Lord, and usher in the jubilee of redemption."—*Boardman.*

SECOND HINDRANCE—OPEN DERISION.

ii. 19.   *They laughed us to scorn, and despised us.*

I. Here is an attempt to stop the work of God by the combined opposition of wicked men. "When Sanballat the Horonite, and Tobiah," &c. 1. *The work of God is sure to meet with opposition from wicked men.* They *must* hate and hinder it, because they are opposed to *all that is good* or godly. The triumph of good means the overthrow of evil. They will find some excuse for their oppression, and thus endeavour to make their conduct appear reasonable. 2. *The work of God will often provoke the combined hostility of those who have nothing else in common.* Thus did the Canaanites, Hittites, Hivites, Perizzites, &c., combine for the destruction of Israel, but in vain, for Jehovah brought to nought their evil counsels. Such opposition Luther met with when he began to reform. The pope excommunicated him, the emperor proscribed him; Henry, king of England, and Lewis, king of Hungary, wrote against him; but the work prospered, because it was of God.

II. Here is an attempt to stop the work of God by pouring contempt upon it. "They laughed us to scorn." 1. *They despised the workers.* "As a company of fools, who could never effect what they attempted. So Erasmus and Sir Thomas More thought to ridicule the Lutherans out of their religion. This the Scripture calls cruel mocking (Heb. xi. 36), and ranks it with bloody persecution. The bitterest persecution which man can inflict is that of cruel taunts and scurrilous invectives : but the least harmful also. · Jude, Peter, and Paul, all foretold that in the last days there should come mockers (2 Pet. iii. ; 2 Tim. iii. ; Jude) Christ thus spitefully treated by Herod, Pilate, the priests, and the people. Solomon says, " He that mocketh shall be mocked" (Prov. iii.). David thus describes the reward of mockers, " He that dwelleth in the heavens shall mock them, and the Lord shall have them in derision " (Ps. ii.). Michal was childless all her life as a punishment for mocking David (2 Sam. vi.). The children that mocked Elisha were devoured by bears (2 Kings ii.). Belshazzar, king of Babylon, was destroyed with his kingdom when he despised the warnings of God (Dan v.) 2. *They ridiculed the work.* " What is this thing that ye do ? " Scoffingly they asked the question, as Pilate asked, "What is truth ? " Wicked men will never be fast for a taunt. If the Church's character be above reproach, the Church's work is ridiculed as impossible or useless.

III. **Here is an attempt to stop the work of God by insinuating an evil design.** " Will ye rebel against the king ? " 1. *When a good work cannot otherwise be hindered an evil motive is sure to be suggested.* The *work* is open, the *motive* secret. More easy to explain and defend former than latter. Men fear what is secret. Wicked men employ this dread for their own ends. 2 *Disloyalty to the State has always been a favourite charge with the Church's enemies.* Elijah is accused by Ahab of being a troubler of Israel (1 Kings xviii.). David was persecuted by Saul because the people sung, " Saul hath slain his thousands, and David his ten thousands " (1 Sam xviii.). Daniel was accused of disobedience, and consigned to the lions' den, because he prayed to the God of heaven (Dan vi.). The Israelites were persecuted in Egypt lest they should rebel against Pharaoh (Exod. i.). Herod sought to slay the infant Christ, lest He should dethrone him (Matt. ii.). Christ was accused and executed as a malefactor guilty of treason (Jno. xviii.). The Apostles were accused of teaching sedi-

tion, and subverting the commonwealth (Acts v.). St. Paul was charged with the same crime at Athens (Acts xvii.). Luther was called a "trumpeter of rebellion." To excuse the shameful massacre of St. Bartholomew, a medal was struck with the inscription, *Valour against the rebels,* on one side, and on the reverse, *Piety hath excited Justice.*

IV. **Here is an attempt to stop the work of God utterly frustrated.** " Then answered I them, and said," &c. (v. 20). The boastful arrogance of Sanballat nothing daunted Nehemiah ; and as they were not ashamed to charge him and his people unjustly, so he is not ashamed to step forth boldly in defence of the work they had undertaken. Thus Moses bearded Pharaoh ; thus Jephthah withstood the Ammonites (Judg. xi.); thus Hezekiah defended the Jews from the blasphemies of Rabshakeh ; thus David stood up against Goliath (1 Sam. xvii.); thus did Moses and Aaron withstand the reviling and calumny of Korah, Dathan, and Abiram (Numb. xvi.). Nehemiah here in the same spirit appeals to God as the ground of his hope, and the source of his confidence. Balak, the king of Moab, hated the camp of Israel, and bribed Balaam, a prophet, to curse them Just so does the world hate the Church, and is never happier than when it can hire the ministers of the Church to turn against it, and betray its interests. But it can no more succeed by its curses than the wicked Balak could ; it must seduce Christians to sin, and then it prevails ; not by its own power, but by tempting the Church to provoke the anger of God. (See Addenda.)

Illustrations .—(a) Pliny, governor of Pontus, under the emperor Trajan, was appointed to punish the Christians, but seeing their great number he doubted what he should do, and eventually wrote to the emperor that "he found no wickedness in them, but that they would not worship images, and that they would sing psalms before day-light unto Christ as God, and did forbid all sins to be used among them." The emperor hearing this became a great deal more gentle to them (Euseb. Lib. iii cap. 33). Sallust, tormenting Theodorus, a Christian, in various ways, and for a long time, to make him forsake his faith, but all in vain, went to the emperor Julian, and told him what he had done, counselling him that " he should prove that way no more by cruelty, for they got glory by suffering patiently,

and he got shame in punishing so sharply," because they would not yield to him.

CONFIDENCE IN GOD AN INCENTIVE TO WORK.

ii. 20. *The God of heaven, he will prosper us, therefore, &c.*

"Knowledge is power," says the philosopher ; " faith is power," says the saint And what is faith ? Confidence in God, in his almighty power and faithfulness, a confidence which nerves the soul for every task. No principle can brace a man like the principle of implicit trust in God. It leads not to indolence, but to effort, because—

I It suggests almighty protection. " The God of heaven." 1 *It regards Jehovah as King of the celestial universe.* " Lord of Hosts," one of God's most frequent names (Ps. xlvi. 7 , Isa i 24 ; Jer. xlvi. 18 ; Zech i. 6 ; Mal. i. 14) " All power is given unto me in *heaven*" (Matt. xxviii.) When the God " who rolls the stars along," and " upholdeth all things by his word ; " the God who doeth according to his will amongst the armies of heaven, and controls the hidden forces of the universe , the God who is Almighty, and Omniscient, and Eternal, to whom every celestial knee bows in willing homage and adoration ; when this God is on our side, who can be afraid ?—what can hinder ? 2. *It regards Jehovah as the providential ruler of the terrestrial universe.* This implied rather than expressed. " All power is given to me in heaven *and in earth*." In earth because in heaven. All destinies in his hand, all events under his control.

II. It suggests providential direction. " He will prosper us." 1. *The way may be dark, but God will unfold it.* When we have, like Nehemiah, done our best, and given our utmost, then we may safely commit our cause to God and patiently await the issue. Thus Abraham followed the leadings of Providence (Gen. xii). Thus confidingly did he place his son Isaac on the altar (Gen. xxii), saying, " God will provide himself a sacrifice." Thus the apostles went at the Saviour's bidding without scrip, &c. (Luke xxii) In this spirit let all who fear God boldly begin his work,

and continue it steadfastly, looking for his guidance, and they shall not be disappointed

Illustration .—A Swiss chamois hunter, crossing the Mer de Glace, fell into one of the enormous crevasses that rend the ice in many places. He fell a hundred yards without serious injury ; but his situation seemed hopeless He could not climb out , and the cold would soon freeze him to death. A stream of water ran down the crevasse; he followed it, wading, stooping, crawling, or floating as best he could At length he reached a vaulted chamber from which there was no visible outlet. The water heaved threateningly. Retreat was impossible Delay was death. Commending himself to God the hunter plunged into the whirling flood. Then followed a moment of darkness and terror; then he was thrown up amid the flowers and hay-fields of the vale of Chamouni. Thus mysteriously are we led by a gracious Providence to safety and success.

2. *The way may be crowded with difficulties, but God will remove them.* " He *will* prosper us." Difficulties as many as Nehemiah encountered may beset our path and work, but not more or mightier than God can remove. *How* deliverance shall come we know not, and must leave to God. All we know is that *it will come in due time* On one occasion Luther was very importunate at the throne of grace to know the mind of God, and it seemed to him as if God spoke aloud and said : " *I am not to be traced.*" We can *trust* where we cannot trace The Almighty has his " times and seasons." An eminent saint thus wrote to a friend : " It has frequently been with my hopes and desires in regard to providence, as with my watch and the sun My watch has often been ahead of true time ; I have gone faster than providence, and have been forced to *stand still and wait*, or I have been *set painfully back* " Flavel says, " some providences are like Hebrew letters, they must be read backwards "

III. It suggests Divine benediction. " *He* will prosper us." 1. *It matters not how men may hinder if God prosper* *the work.* "If God be for us, who can be against us ?" 2 *It matters not how the king's favour may fluctuate if Jehovah's remain the same.* He is the Unchangeable One Man's favour may be fickle, and therefore little to be relied upon. God's never fails, therefore with confidence his saints may say, "He *will* prosper us."

IV It anticipates ultimate success. "He will *prosper* us." 1. *It concludes that what God initiates he intends to complete.* A good beginning is a strong reason to persuade a man that God will grant good success in the end. David comforted himself when he met Goliath by the thought that he who had delivered him from the lion and the bear, would now continue his gracious interposition God's plans never fail. 2. *It concludes that what God commences he is able to consummate.* When God said to Paul that all the souls with him should be safe, there were various means used ; all were not able to swim to the shore, and the ship was not able to bring them all to shore, but yet by broken boards and by

one means or other, all got to shore So the Lord brings things to pass in a strange, but a sure manner, sometimes by one way, sometimes by another. He breaks in pieces many ships, that we think should bring us to shore, but then he casts us on such planks as will eventually bring us there

Illustration —" I looked upon the wrong side of a piece of tapestry and it seemed to me a continued nonsense. There was neither head nor foot therein, a company of thrums and threads, with many pieces and patches of several sorts, sizes, and colours, all which signified nothing to my understanding But then looking on the reverse, or right side, all put together did spell excellent proportions, and figures of men and cities ; so that indeed it was a history, not wrote with a pen, but wrought with a needle. So, if men look upon some of God's providential dealings with a mere eye of reason, they will hardly find any sense therein. But alas! the *wrong side* is before our eyes, whilst the *right side* is presented to the God of heaven, who knoweth that an admirable order doth result out of this confusion ; and what is presented to him at present, may hereafter be so showed to us as to convince our judgments of the truth thereof."— *T Fuller.*

THE MISERABLE CONDITION OF THE CHURCH'S ENEMIES.

ii. 20. *Ye have no portion, nor right, nor memorial, &c.*

I. They are excluded from the Church's pale. 1. *Jerusalem a type of the Church militant and the Church triumphant.* There God's name recorded 2. *From which sinners are self-excluded.* By their country, creed, and conduct Sanballat and his friends were excluded from communion with the true Israelites Scoffers by their own conduct condemn themselves to separation from the true spiritual Church of God. Idolaters can have no part with those who worship the true God, for he will be worshipped in "spirit and in truth."

II. They are cut off from the Church's privileges. 1. *The privilege of Church membership.* "No portion." This a privilege which many ignore If the Church is the Body and the Bride of Christ, surely it must be an honour to belong to it. 2 *Privilege of Church support.* "Nor right." To the poor and afflicted this a great boon. As in the

Apostles' days, so now the Church undertakes to care for its poor 3. *Privilege of ancestral reputation.* "Nor memorial " The Samaritans endeavoured to claim Jewish ancestry, but unsuccessfully. Saints are held in sweet remembrance in the Church. Their name is often "as ointment poured forth " This honour denied to the families of those who have no fellowship with the Church.

III. They are forbidden to participate in the Church's work. As they feared not their threats, so now they would have none of their help. "Be ye not unequally yoked," &c. God's servants are knit together by two bonds ; the one is Christ their head , the other, brotherly love. Neither of these exist amongst idolaters. This work is—1 *The most exalted in which any human being can engage.* Work for God, for human souls, for the Church which Christ has redeemed by his own blood, for all eternity, cannot but exalt and ennoble those who take part in it   2 *The most remunerative in which any human being can engage.* All is pure gain without any loss. The gain is not temporal, but eternal The reward is found in the glory that is brought to Christ, the salvation that is brought to men, and the reflex benefit which descends upon the soul of the worker   3. *Work which requires moral qualifications possessed only by the true servants of God.* Hence the unfitness of the Samaritan unbelievers God never sends men out into the world as apostles until they have become true disciples in heart and life.

ADDENDA TO CHAPTER II.

ii. 8. THE HAND OF GOD,—THANKSGIVING.

I **The duty of thanksgiving.** "Giving thanks," a duty commanded (Eph. v. 20). When thanks are given thankfulness is implied, or it is mere formality. The seat of thankfulness is the heart ; there it ought to be cherished with the utmost care, and every motive remembered by which it is enlivened and increased. If the heart be thankful, it is perfectly reasonable and proper that its feelings be expressed. The most powerful arguments enforce this duty. 1. *Its antiquity.* It is as old as the creation.   No sooner did intelligent beings exist than gratitude was expressed "the morning stars sang together, and all the sons of God shouted for joy" (Job xxxviii. 7). Paradise was the seat of thanksgiving before man fell ; and consequently before the voice of prayer was heard, or the sigh of penitence was known 2. *Its perpetuity.* It not only commenced sooner, but will continue longer than other duties ; it will survive most other acts of service. Prayer will cease ; repentance will be no more ; faith and hope, as to their present use, will terminate ; but thanksgiving will be the delightful business of the upper world, and will extend to the countless ages of eternity.   3. *Express injunctions* to give thanks are numerous in Holy Scripture. "O give thanks unto the Lord, for he is good" (Ps. cvii 1). "Praise ye the Lord, for it is good to sing praises unto our God " (Ps. cxlvii. 1) 4. *Example of the best men.* What good men have lived without gratitude?

What eminent characters are recorded in the Bible who abound not in thanksgiving?   Nature conspires to engage us in this employment. " All thy works praise thee, O Lord, and thy saints shall bless thee " "Bless the Lord, all his works, in all places of his dominion ; bless the Lord, O my soul."

II. To whom thanksgiving is to be offered. 1. *To men.* We ought to give thanks to men for the favours we receive from them. So far as they are our benefactors they are entitled to grateful acknowledgments, and ingratitude is justly marked as one of the worst of crimes, and as evidencing the basest disposition of heart. 2. *To God.* He is our greatest benefactor : every other is but his instrument and agent. The Most High is our best Friend ; for other friends we are indebted to him, and they are all of his sending. Hence the injunction, " Offer unto *God* thanksgiving, and pay thy vows unto the Most High" (Ps. l. 14). "Giving thanks unto God, even the Father " Here we are reminded of his paternal character. He has the heart of a father, the tenderest feeling, the kindest affection. "Like as a father," &c. Such is the God to whom our thanksgivings are offered.

III. The time when thanksgiving is seasonable. 1. *When we enter the sanctuary.* "Enter his gates with thanksgiving, and his courts with praise." 2. *When we are the recipients of abounding mercies.* And who is not? He *daily* loadeth us with benefits. 3. *When we have received some special favour*, or been delivered from some great calamity. Hannah prayed and wept, and returned to offer thanksgiving in the place where she had prayed (1 Sam. i.) The lepers were reproached by Christ for not returning thanks for their miraculous cure. Nehemiah acknowledged "the good hand of God," which had been over him for good, opening alike the king's heart, and his own providential path. 4. *Always* "Giving thanks *always*" "I thank my God *alway*, on your behalf" "I will bless the Lord *always*, his praise shall continually be in my mouth" (Ps. xxxiv. 1). Saints are not to be always singing praises, or with their lips expressing gratitude; yet there is a sense in which they are always to be "giving thanks." They ought to cherish a thankful heart, a disposition of gratitude, and should frequently take occasion, by every suitable means, to manifest and express it. Thanksgiving should therefore be offered *to the end* of life, and in every *changing circumstance* of life "In everything by prayer and supplication with thanksgiving," &c. (Phil. iv. 6). This service is never unseasonable, and sometimes it is peculiarly appropriate.—*Kidd*

ii. 11.   PREPARATORY RETIREMENT.

The pleasures and advantages of solitude have been often admired, and recommended All love the world, yet all complain of it; and whatever schemes of happiness are devised, the scene is always laid in a withdrawment from it. It is there the warrior feeds his courage, and arranges the materials of victory. It is there the statesman forms and weighs his plans of policy There the philosopher pursues his theories and experiments. There the man of genius feels the power of thought, and the glow of fancy And retirement is friendly to communion with God. Consider—

I The duty of retirement. Premise two things—1. The *place* is indifferent It matters not whether it be a private room, or an open field. 2 It is not a state of *absolute retirement.* Man was made for society as well as solitude A great part of our religion regards our fellow-creatures, and can only be discharged by intermixing with them What our Saviour thought of hiding in woods and cells, appears obviously from his words, "Ye are the light of the world. Let your light so shine before men," &c It is therefore possible for a Christian to be alone, when he *ought to* be abroad. It may be much more pleasing often to sit alone, reading or reflecting, than to be called forth to give advice or to visit the afflicted What God requires is *comparative* and occa-*sional* secession for moral and spiritual purposes "Stand in awe, and sin not; commune with your own heart upon your bed, and be still" "Enter into thy closet, and when thou hast shut thy door, pray to thy Father which is in secret" This duty enjoined by *example* as well as by precept. "Isaac went out into the field at eventide to meditate" "Jacob was left alone, and there wrestled with him a man, until the dawning of the day." "Then went king David in, and sat before the Lord, and he said, Who am I, O Lord God, and what is my house," &c Daniel retired three times a day Peter went up to the house-top to pray about the sixth hour, and received a Divine communication. Of our Saviour, whose life has the force of a law, it is said, "In the morning, rising up a great while before day, he went out, and departed into a solitary place, and there prayed." At another time, "he went out into a mountain to pray, and continued all night in prayer to God." *The Sabbath* brings us immediately into the presence of God, and gives us an opportunity to examine our character and condition, such as cannot be obtained during the six days of toil. It renews those pious impressions, which our intercourse with the things of time and sense is continually wearing off. This retirement often enforced by the *dispensations of Providence.* Affliction

F

both disinclines us to social circles, and disqualifies us for them. Sickness separates a man from the crowd, and confines him to his bed that he may ask, "Where is God my maker, who giveth songs in the night?" *A reduced condition* will diminish your associates. It will drive away the selfish herd, who think that a friend is born for prosperity. This retirement produces—1. *A devotional temper.* There we can divulge what we could not in the presence of the dearest earthly friend. 2. *A desire to rise above the world.* This will induce a man to retire. Where is the world conquered? In a crowd? No—but alone. In the midst of its active pursuits? No—but viewed in the presence of Jehovah, and in the remembrances of eternity. Then its emptiness appears. Then the fascination is dissolved. Then we look upward, and say, "Now what wait I for? my hope is in thee." 3. *A wish to obtain self-knowledge.* Only when alone can he examine his state, estimate his attainments, explore his defects, discern the source of past danger, or set a watch against future temptations. 4. *Love to God.* When we are supremely attached to a person, his presence is all we want; he will be the chief attraction, even in company. Friendship deals much in secrecy; kindred souls have a thousand things to hear and to utter that are not for a common ear. This pre-eminently the case with the intimacy subsisting between God and the believer. "The heart knoweth his own bitterness, and a stranger intermeddleth not with his joy." "Behold, I will allure her, and bring her into the wilderness, and there will I speak comfortably unto her."

II The advantages of retirement
1. *It furnishes opportunity for communion with God.* "Arise, go forth into the plain, and I will there talk with thee" (Ezek. iii. 22). We admire the nobleman that kindly notices a peasant, and the sovereign who deigns to converse with one of his poorer subjects. But

here is the Creator talking with his creature. Some of us cannot aspire after intercourse with many of our fellow-creatures by reason of our condition, and our talents. But whatever be our condition, or our talents, we have a free and invited access to God. The *subject* of this communion is variously called "his secret," and "his covenant." "The secret of the Lord is with them that fear him, and he will show them his covenant." "He will speak peace unto his people." "The meek will he teach his way." The *mode* of this communion is not supernatural, as of old. God talked with Moses, as a man talketh with his friend. It is mere fanaticism to expect God to commune with us in dreams, visions, sudden impulses, and audible sounds. He opens our understandings in the Scriptures. He leads us into all truth. He applies the doctrines and promises of his word by his Spirit. The *result* and *evidence* of this communion will be that our hearts will burn within us. Other effects produced by this communion are—1. *A deep and solemn sense of our vanity and vileness.* Fellowship with God, instead of encouraging unhallowed presumption, gives a man such intimate views of the peculiar glory of God as fill him with godly fear. Thus was it with Jacob, Moses, Elijah, Job, Isaiah, and Peter. 2. *An unquenchable desire for closer communion.* That which contents the believer makes him insatiable. He desires no more than God; but he desires more of him. 3. *An ever-increasing likeness to God.* "He that walketh with wise men shall be wise." Some boast of being much with God; but so censurable are their conduct and temper, that few of their fellow-creatures would like to have much to do with them. "The wisdom that is from above is first pure, then peaceable, gentle, and easy to be entreated, full of mercy and good fruits, without partiality, and without hypocrisy."—*Jay.*

II 19. OPEN DERISION

I The sin of mocking weakens every virtuous restraint. There are restraints of education, of example, of regard to reputation But when a man becomes a mocker, such restraints are relaxed ; they gradually lose their hold With every advance in levity and jesting, a sense of shame subsides, the fear of incurring censure abates, respect for the authority of parents and for the opinion and expostulation of friends declines, custom degenerates into habit, and habit becomes settled and easy

II The sin of mocking strengthens vicious propensities This naturally results from the preceding As the one declines the other gains ground Let a man become indifferent to what is right, and he will practise what is wrong, let him cease to do good, and he learns to do evil. Is a bad temper, for instance, which is never repressed, no worse after years of indulgence? Does harmless mirth never proceed to profaneness? Does the habit of loose talking never lead to falsehood, nor settle in deceit? You cannot mock at the Bible without your regard for the sacred Book sinking in proportion You cannot mock at sin but your aversion to sin dies and your love to sin revives

III The sin of mocking gives great advantage to your worst enemies Such are improper companions Go with them one mile, and they will easily induce you to go two Every compliance only emboldens their demands, and facilitates their conquest ; and every victory they gain only throws you more completely into their power Walk in the counsel of the ungodly, and stand in the way of sinners, and ere long you will

sit " in the seat of the scornful." But there is a worse enemy than these , " the spirit which now worketh in the children of disobedience," " that old serpent, called the Devil, and Satan, which deceiveth the whole world " Resist him, and he will flee from you ; but invite his attacks, and you inevitably fall into his hands. We read of those " who are taken captive by him at his will " These are they who indulge the tempers he would have them indulge, who practise the works which he instigates and approves

IV The sin of mocking exposes to peculiar marks of God's displeasure. Witness the destruction of the youths who mocked Elisha (2 Kings II 23) Some who have scoffed at the Bible and blasphemed its author have been struck dead in a moment Persistence in sin has more often been followed by judicial hardness. Men who have begun with jesting at the things of God, and sporting with their own iniquity, have been given up to strong delusions and final impenitence

V The sin of mocking terminates in remediless ruin There is a world beyond the present There mockers of every class have their full recompense " They have chosen their own ways, and their soul delighteth in their abominations, I also will choose their delusions, and will bring their fears upon them " " Ye have set at nought my counsels, and would none of my reproof, I also will *laugh* at your calamity, I will *mock* when your fear cometh " " Behold, ye despisers, and wonder, and perish " (Isa. lxvi 3, 4 ; Prov i 25, 26).—*Kidd.*

ILLUSTRATIONS

The hand of God *Protection* 1. John Knox, the celebrated Scotch reformer, had many remarkable escapes from the malicious designs of his enemies. He was accustomed to sit at the head of the table in his own house, with his back to the window, but on one particular evening he would neither himself sit in his chair, nor allow any one else to do so. That very evening a bullet was shot through the window, purposely to kill him; it grazed the chair in which he usually sat, and made a hole in the foot of the candlestick 2 Posidonius, in the Life of Augustine, relates that this good man, going on one occasion to preach at a distant town, took with him a guide to direct him in the way. This man, by some unaccountable means, mistook the usual road, and fell into a by-path. It afterwards proved that in this way the preacher's life had been saved, as his enemies, aware of his journey, had placed themselves in the proper road with a design to kill him.

Envy. "Dionysius the tyrant," says Plutarch, "out of envy, punished Philoxenius the musician, because he could sing, and Plato the philosopher, because he could dispute better than himself." Cambyses, king of Persia, slew his brother Smerdis, out of envy, because he could draw a stronger bow than himself or any of his followers, and the monster Caligula slew his brother because he was a beautiful young man.

> "Base envy withers at another's joy,
> And hates that excellence it cannot reach"

Derision A poor man who had heard the preaching of the gospel, and to whom it had been greatly blessed, was the subject of much profane ridicule and jesting amongst his neighbours. On being asked if these persecutions did not sometimes make him ready to give up his profession of religion, he replied, "No. I recollect that our good minister once said in his sermon, that if we were so foolish as to permit such people to laugh us out of our religion, till at last we dropped into hell, *they could not laugh us out again.*" Admiral Colpoys relates that when he first left his lodgings to join his ship as a midshipman, his landlady presented him with a Bible and a guinea, saying, "God bless you, and prosper you, my lad, and as long as you live never suffer yourself to be laughed out of your money or your prayers." The young sailor carefully followed this advice through life, and had reason to rejoice that he had done so.

CHAPTER III.

EXPLANATORY NOTES] **1** Eliashib] The grandson of Jeshua, and the first high priest after the return from Babylon No reason to doubt that the same Eliashib is referred to in Ezra x. 6 **The sheep gate**] In regard to the gates of ancient Jerusalem much uncertainty prevails The sheep gate probably the προβατική of John v. 2, translated in E. V. "sheep market" Modern topographers seek it near the present St. Stephen's gate, through which the Bedouins to this day drive sheep into the town for sale. Near the temple area. **Sanctified**] Consecrated it by special ceremonies. "It was the first-fruits, and therefore, in the sanctification of it, the whole lump and building was sanctified "—*Poole.* **The tower of Meah, the tower of Hananeel**] Meah is the Hebrew word for "a hundred." Fuerst translates it the giant tower Whence the names of these towers were derived is unknown **2. And next unto him**] Lit *And at his hand.* The wall was divided into portions, one of which was assigned to each of the great families. **3. The sons of Hassenaah**] Rather, *the sons of Senaah* (see Ezra ii. 35) Senaah was a city or perhaps a district **6 The old gate**] Keil reads, "gate of the old wall," as referring to the old wall in distinction from "the broad wall," which was newer **8. The broad wall**] "or double wall, formerly broken down by Joash, afterwards rebuilt by Uzziah, who made it so strong Chaldeans left it standing" —*Jamieson* **9. The ruler of the half part**] A half district, the district being divided into two that it might be managed more easily (comp vers 12, 14, 15, 16, 17, 18) **13** Zanoah] The name of two towns in the territory of Judah **14** Beth-haccerem] From Jeremiah vi. 1 we find that it was used as a beacon-station, and that it was near Tekoa Supposed to be now occupied by Bethulia on the hill called by Europeans "The Frank Mountain" **16** The sepulchres of David, &c] i e along the precipitous cliffs of Zion —*Barclay* **19** At the turning of the wall] i e the wall across the Tyropœon being a continuation of the first wall, connecting Mount Zion with the temple wall —*Barclay* **25** The tower which lieth out from the king's high house] Solomon's palace doubtless occupied the south-east corner of the present Haram **26** The Nethinims] The Nethinim were a servile and subject caste "Not only the priests and the Levites, but the meanest persons that belonged to the house of God contributed to the work."—*Bishop Patrick*

HOMILETIC CONTENTS OF CHAPTER III.

THE MORAL SIGNIFICANCE OF NAMES.

A CHAPTER of names. To be passed over by the bulk of Bible readers. But the names are biblical. The chapters of names are a noticeable part of the Book of Nehemiah, as they are of the Bible.

I. The meaning of individual names. The origin of language is mysterious. But in earliest times amongst all nations—our own not excepted—names meant things. Specially true of the Jewish nation. Names were not given from caprice or because others bore them. They shadowed forth the character, or commemorated a circumstance, or prophesied a future.

Abel signified breath, vapour—a sign of the transitoriness of his life. David meant dearly-beloved. Enoch, disciplined. Elijah, God the Lord, or the strong Lord. Elisha, "to whom God is salvation." Abraham, "the father of a multitude," and Moses, "drawn out of the water," were commemorative. Sometimes the name was a protest. Amittai, a veracious man living in a time of laxity.

Eliashib's name (ver. 1) perpetually reminded him that "God was in heaven, and governed the world he created." Nehemiah could not have borne a name better adapted for a work so arduous as his. Nehemiah means, "whom God comforts." Meremoth (ver. 4), if true to his name, should be a firm man. Jehoiada (ver. 6) needed no priest to remind him that he was known of God. Uzziel (ver. 8) might work fearlessly, for, said his name, "God is my strength." Malchijah (ver. 11) would hardly be afraid of Sanballat's anger or Tobiah's scorn. "Am not I Malchijah," he would say, "and does not that tell me that God is my king?" The Nethinims (ver 26) were the dedicated ones.

In other languages the same law prevailed. A man bearing the name of Andrew was courageous, and an Augusta majestic. Arthur was a strong man. She who was honoured with the name Agnes was chaste. An Alice was noble, and a Louisa modest.

In more artificial times names lost their meaning. When the mother of John Baptist declared that he should be called John, her friends said, "There is none of thy kindred that is called by this name." Names were losing their meaning. Here was a man born into the world filled with the grace of God—what shall his name be? "Zacharias," they say; "that is his father's name." They ask the dumb father, and he writes "John." Now-a-days a man may have the name of John and be graceless enough. We have no proof that Charles will be noble. We give our children fancy names. Family names are reasonable; fancy names are foolish. Except that they are given thoughtlessly, their morality would be doubtful. Our true name is our Christian name.

II The solemn significance of names. A name is a key to the nature or history of the thing which bears it. In the history of the creation we read that "God formed every beast of the field, and every fowl of the air, and brought them unto Adam to see what he would call them : and whatsoever Adam called every living creature, that was the name thereof." And so it has been well said by Carlyle that not only all common speech, but science, poetry itself, is no other than a right *naming.* Some languages have the same expression for WORD and THING. Jesus Christ said, " Out of the abundance of the heart the mouth speaketh " (Matt. xii. 34). " As a man thinketh in his heart, so is he " (Prov. xxiii. 7). " Lie not one to another "—not because you will not be trusted, but because— " ye have put off the old man with his deeds " (Coloss. iii. 9). Wise men say that you can tell the character of any nation by its language. " There was a time in the history of Europe when the controversy about what a name represents involved issues so grave that men were burnt for taking what was considered the heretical side of this controversy."—*R. W. Dale* " Our general terms, man, tree, insect, flower, are the names of particular or single specimens extended, on the ground of a perceived similarity, to kinds or species They come in this manner to stand for millions of particular men, trees, insects, flowers that we do not and never can know. They are, to just this extent, WORDS OF IGNORANCE ; only we are able, in the use, to hold right judgments of innumerable particulars we do not know, and have the words so far as WORDS OF WISDOM."—*Horace Bushnell* Reality is a cardinal virtue Speech is not given us to hide our thoughts. What is truth but the correspondence of words with things, of life with speech ? " By thy words thou shalt be justified, and by thy words thou shalt be condemned " (Matt xii 37).

III. The relation of the individual to the race. Names perpetuate memories William is named to-day after a William of sixty years ago Of this latter there is only a name " One generation passeth away, and another generation cometh " (Eccles. i. 4). THE DAY OF JUDGMENT will harmonize names and things. " Then shall the King say," &c. (Matt. xxv. 34—46).

ILLUSTRATIONS.

Hebrew names. " The Hebrew names were nearly all significant Sometimes commemoration was in a name. Sometimes it uttered a testimony. Sometimes a prophecy stirred in it. The very name of a man sometimes shone like a burning lamp in the darkness of an evil time When need was, a new name was taken or given, in addition to, or in place of, the original one, and borne as men bear a banner or speak a watchword."—*Alexander Raleigh, D.D*

Names and periods in Hebrew history. " What signifies a name ? In these days, when names are only epithets, it signifies nothing. ' Jehovah, Jove, or Lord,' as the ' Universal Prayer' insinuates, are all the same Now, to assert that it matters not whether God be called Jehovah, Jove, or Lord is true, if it mean this, that a devout and earnest heart is accepted by God, let the name be what it will by which he is addressed. But it it mean that Jove and Jehovah express the same Being— that the character of him whom the pagan worshipped was the same as the character of him whom Israel adored under the name of Jehovah—that they refer to the same group of ideas—or that ALWAYS names are but names, then we must look much deeper

" In the Hebrew history are discernible three periods distinctly marked, in which names and words bore very different characters. These three, it has been observed by acute philologists, correspond to the periods in which the nation bore the three different appellations of Hebrews, Israelites, Jews.

" In the first of these periods names meant truths, and words were the symbols of realities. The characteristics of the names given then were simplicity and sincerity. They were drawn from a few simple sources . either from some characteristic of the individual, as Jacob, the supplanter; or Moses, drawn from the water; or from the idea of family, as Ben-jamin, the son of my right hand; or from the conception of the tribe or nation, then gradually consolidating itself, or, lastly, from the religious idea of God. But in this case not the highest notion of God ; not Jah, or Jehovah, but simply the earlier and simpler idea of Deity: El—Israel, the prince of El; Peniel, the face of El. In these days names were real, but the conceptions they contained were not the loftiest.

" The second period begins about the time of the departure from Egypt, and it is characterized by unabated simplicity, with the addition of sublimer thought and feeling more intensely religious. The heart of the nation was big with mighty and new religious truth, and the feelings with which the national heart was swelling found vent in the names which were given abundantly. God, under his name Jah, the noblest assemblage of spiritual truths yet conceived, became the adjunct to names of places and persons. Oshea's name is changed into Je-hoshua.

" Observe, moreover, that in this period there was no fastidious, over-refined chariness in the use of that name. Men conscious of deep and real reverence are not fearful of the appearance of irreverence. The word became a common word, as it always may, so long as it is FELT, and awe is REAL. A mighty cedar was called a cedar of Jehovah ; a lofty mountain, a mountain of Jehovah.

Human beauty even was praised by such an epithet. Moses was divinely fair, beautiful to God. The eternal name became an adjunct. No beauty, no greatness, no goodness was conceivable except as emanating from him : therefore his name was freely but most devoutly used.

"Like the earlier period, in this too words meant realities ; but, unlike the earlier period, they are impregnated with deeper religious thought.

"The third period was at its zenith in the time of Christ. words had lost their meaning, and shared the hollow, unreal state of all things. A man's name might be Judas, and still he might be a traitor. A man might be called Pharisee, exclusively religious, and yet the name might only cover the hollowness of hypocrisy, or he might be called most noble Festus, and be the meanest tyrant that ever sat upon a pro-consular chair. This is the period in which every keen and wise observer knows that the decay of national religious feeling has begun. That decay in the meaning of words, that lowering of the standard of the ideas for which they stand, is a certain mark of this. The debasement of a language is a sure mark of the debasement of a nation. The insincerity of a language is a proof of the insincerity of a nation : for a time comes in the history of a nation when words no longer stand for things, when names are given for the sake of an euphonious sound ; and when titles are but the epithets of unmeaning courtesy, a time when Majesty, Defender of the Faith, Most Noble, Worshipful, and Honourable not only mean nothing, but do not flush the cheek with the shame of convicted falsehood when they are worn as empty ornaments."—*F. W. Robertson*

Origin of language. "The opinions about the origin of language may be divided into three classes, as follows :—

"(a) The belief that man at his creation was endowed with a full, perfect, and copious language, and that as his faculties were called forth by observation and experience, this language supplied him at every step with names for the various objects he encountered. In this view, which has found many able advocates, speech is separated from and precedes thought ; for as there must have been a variety of phenomena, both outward and in his mind, to which the first man was a stranger, until long experience gradually unfolded them, their names must have been intrusted to him long before the thoughts or images which they were destined ultimately to represent were excited in his mind.

' (b) The belief that the different families of men, impelled by necessity, invented and settled by agreement the names that should represent the ideas they possessed. In this view language is a human invention, grounded on convenience. But to say that man has invented language would be no better than to assert that he has invented law. To make laws, there must be a law obliging all to keep them ; to form a compact to observe certain institutes, there must be already a government protecting this compact. To invent language presupposes language already, for how could men agree to name different objects without communicating by words their designs ? In proof of this opinion, appeal is made to the great diversity of languages. Here it is supposed again that thought and language were separate, and that the former had made some progress before the latter was annexed to it.

"(c) The third view is, that as the Divine Being did not give man at his creation actual knowledge, but the power to learn and to know, so he did not confer a language, but the power to name and describe. The gift of reason, once conveyed to man, was the common root from which both thought and speech proceeded, like the pith and the rind of the tree, to be developed in inseparable union. With the first inspection of each natural object the first imposition of a name took place (Gen. ii. 19). In the fullest sense language is a Divine gift, but the power, and not the results of its exercise, the germ, and not the tree, was imparted. A man can teach names to another man, but nothing less than Divine power can plant in another's mind the far higher gift, the faculty of naming. From the first we have reason to believe that the functions of thought and language went together. A conception received a name ; a name recalled a conception ; and every accession to the knowledge of things expanded the treasures of expression. And we are entangled in absurdities by any theory which assumes that either element existed in a separate state antecedently to the other."—*Archbishop of York*.

"We do not make words, they are given to us by One higher than ourselves. Wise men say that you can tell the character of any nation by its language, by watching the words they use, the names they give to things, for out of the abundance of the heart the mouth speaks. It is God, and Christ, the Word of God, who gives words to men, who puts it into the hearts of men to call certain things by certain names ; and according to a nation's godliness, and wisdom, and purity of heart will be its power of using words discreetly and reverently. That miracle of the gift of tongues, of which we read in the New Testament, would have been still most precious and full of meaning if it had had no other use than this—to teach men from whom words come. When men found themselves all of a sudden inspired to talk in foreign languages which they had never learnt, to utter words of which they themselves did not know the meaning, do you not see how it must have made them feel that all language is God's making and God's giving ? Do you not see how it must have made them feel what awful, mysterious things words were, like those cloven tongues of fire which fell on the apostles ? The tongues of fire signified the difficult foreign languages which they suddenly began to speak as the Spirit gave them utterance. And where did the tongues of fire come from ? Not out of themselves, not out of the earth beneath, but down from the heaven above, to signify that it is not from man's flesh or brain, or the earthly part of him, that words are bred, but that they come down from Christ, the Word of God, and are breathed into the minds of men by the Spirit of God."—*Charles Kingsley*.

LIFE'S MASONRY.

INTRODUCTION — The Scriptural figures of life's work as a building. St Peter's description of God as building up a fabric of "lively stones" (1 Peter ii 4, 5) It is his remembrance of the Saviour's own use of the figure in Matt xvi 18 "Upon this rock I will build my Church" St Paul's description of his own apostolic life as that of a "wise master-builder"—a spiritual Nehemiah (1 Cor. iii. 10—15).

I. **Every one to contribute his life-toil to the building up of the city of God.** 1 *True of the individual character*—the fallen, ruined "city of Mansoul" Not what we rake together of earthly things, but what we rear in the edifice of our personal character, our true work. 2 *True of society* The history of the world a history of the restless reconstructions of society The reformers and teachers of every age, scanning the desolations of their time, have said, "Let us arise and build !" and with none of Babel's profanity have said in hope, "Go to, let us build a tower whose top shall reach to heaven !" That is what the piled-up fruit of generations of toil shall be

II **Every man has his own appointed sphere and kind of work.** 1 *The manifold division of labour in the erection of a great edifice may become to us a parable of the various uses of human character and ability* To some the strong work—the foundations and buttresses—plain, practical usefulness. To others there is given work at the gates of knowledge and intercourse To some it is the task to beautify and embellish life and its surroundings, to sculpture bright things and thoughts To the sagacity of others is committed the towers of outlook and defence for human society. 2 *Every man to find his own task* Providential circumstances and the bent of wise inclination point us to our share of the wall. The ruin lying nearest our feet, the weak place nearest our own home, is our task-work. 3 *Every man to be content with his own task* Who does not at times sigh in envy of his brother's portion in life's great enterprise ! We think we could work with less moiling, and get the lines truer, if we were working on some other piece of ground. It's better as it is "To every man his work" (Mark xiii. 34)

III **Every man contributes but a fragment to the great whole** All each builder does is to contribute so many feet of the great girdle of masonry, but it is the multiplication of these small piles which completes the circumference. 1 *Individual life* Do not judge of experiences singly and alone. Life is a complex and mingled process, and that which seems to have no uses of edification may be one of many powers which uplift the character. Our life is a great whole WE "walk to-day and to-morrow, and the THIRD day WE are perfected"

> "If sad thy present, fancy not
> The *whole* of life is in to-day,
> To past and future look away;
> Thy *life* is *not* thy *present lot* "

2 *Socially* Do not judge a life with regard to society in its mere isolation or as a disconnected unit; it is a length of fabric to join on with some one else's work.

Moses bursts out of Egypt, Joshua leads through Jordan into Canaan, David prepares for a consolidated nation, Solomon ushers in the rest and magnificence of peace · each builds his own layer and length of the history.

One man toils to feed the people, another gives them garments, another settles their quarrels, another tells them the story of the day's life; another teaches them knowledge; another pleads with them for God, another heals their sickness; another goes out to sea for their merchandise, another gives them a book of cheering song ; and each contributes to the walls and gates and towers of man's life below.

EACH is but a small length, but ALL make the mighty ring

IV. Every man to work in harmonious aim with his fellow builders 1. *Recognizing the one reigning purpose*—the edification of a city of God ; to make Jerusalem a praise in the earth and a city of the great King. 2. *Recognizing the worth of his brother's work.* He has his own task, and has not to work by our piece of the plan. 3. *Eccentric people who will pile their stones in other people's way,* and blind other people with their chippings and the bespatterings of their mortar. Do not hinder your "brother mason."

V. The united work is superintended by the great Architect. 1. *He only understands the whole of the great intricate plan of life.* He has surveyed the whole field, and has appointed each one his place. To understand our own section and task, and to trust to the great unifying power above, is all we can do. These broken, incomplete piles rising in their fragmentariness will, under his direction, circle into the order of his great will. The full plan of life is only seen and understood in heaven, but it IS understood THERE. 2. *He is near us with directions.* In their straits these amateur masons must have often summoned Nehemiah as he rode round among the workers. In all perplexities we can call in Divine direction. "If any man lack wisdom, let him ask of God" (James i 5). 3. *Let the thought "THOU GOD SEEST ME" animate us at our toil.* (a) *It is a cheering thought.* No eye can look so indulgently as his. "He knoweth our frame," &c (Ps. ciii 14). (b) *It is an admonitory thought.* He WILL have true work, and all the wrong that we pile up he will push down.

> "As ever in my great Taskmaster's eye"

CONCLUSION.—What this finished work shall be we read in the closing chapters of the Bible. The New Jerusalem is man's work transfigured by the glory of God.

The rude foundations we have put in with weariness and toil shall show themselves "garnished with all manner of precious stones." The gates so clumsily made will shine "every several gate of one pearl." The building of the wall shall be "as jasper," and the shapeless, disjointed masses shall be all joined and balanced "the length of it, and the breadth of it, and the height of it equal."

"And the throne of God and of the Lamb shall be in it. And there shall be no night there; for the Lord God giveth them light and they shall reign for ever and ever."

ILLUSTRATIONS

Sacredness of labour. "Two men I honour, and no third. First, the toil-worn craftsman that with earth-made implement laboriously conquers the earth, and makes her man's. Venerable to me is the hard hand—crooked, coarse ; wherein notwithstanding lies a cunning virtue, indefeasibly royal, as of the sceptre of this planet. Venerable too is the rugged face, all weather-tanned, besoiled, with its rude intelligence ; for it is the face of a man living man-like. O, but the more venerable for thy rudeness, and even because we must pity as well as love thee! Hardly entreated brother! for us was thy back so bent, for us were thy straight limbs and fingers so deformed: thou wert our conscript, on whom the lot fell, and fighting our battles wert so marred. For in thee too lay a God-created form, but it was not to be unfolded; encrusted must it stand with the thick adhesions and defacements of labour ; and thy body, like thy soul, was not to know freedom. Yet toil on, toil on; THOU art in thy duty, be out of it who may ; thou toilest for the altogether indispensable, for daily bread.

"A second man I honour, and still more highly ; him who is seen toiling for the spiritually indispensable; not daily bread, but the bread of life. Is not he too in his duty, endeavouring towards inward harmony ; revealing this, by act or by word, through all his outward endeavours, be they high or low? Highest of all when his outward and inward endeavours are one ; when we can name him artist ; not earthly craftsman only, but inspired thinker, who with heaven-made implement conquers heaven for us! If the poor and humble toil that we have food, must not the high and glorious toil for him in return, that he have light, have guidance, freedom, immortality? These two, in all their degrees, I honour: all else is chaff and dust, which let the wind blow whither it listeth.

"Unspeakably touching is it, however, when I find both dignities united, and he that must toil outwardly for the lowest of man's wants is also toiling inwardly for the highest. Sublimer in this world know I nothing than a peasant saint, could such now anywhere be met with. Such a one will take thee back to Nazareth itself; thou wilt see the splendour of heaven spring forth from the humblest depths of earth, like a light shining in great darkness."—*Carlyle.*

Work is the common duty of all. "It would be very strange if it were not so. The first thing we read of God doing for man when he made him was to assign him work. Before he gave him a right to eat of the fruit of the trees, 'he put him into the garden of Eden to dress it and to keep it' (Gen. ii. 15). When man is translated to the heavenly Eden it is not to idleness: 'they serve him day and night in his temple.' The wise man when he looked abroad on the world made this deep reflection : 'All things are full of labour.' The calm stars are in ceaseless motion, and every leaf is a world with its busy inhabitants, and the sap coursing through its veins as the life-blood through our own. He who made all worlds has said, 'My Father worketh hitherto, and I work.'"—*John Ker, D.D.*

All the workers shall be rewarded. "Each shall find that he has a share in the completed results, where the labours of all are represented. What does it matter in which stage of the great process our co-operation has been enlisted ? Every man that has had a part in the building shall have a share in the glory. What does it matter whether we have been set to dig out the foundation, working amongst mud and wet, or have laid the lowermost courses, which are all covered up and forgotten, or happen to have been amongst those who bring forth the head-stone with shoutings ? We are all builders all the same. The main thing is that we have some work there. Never mind whereabouts it is. Never mind whether it be visible or no. Never mind whether your name is associated with it. You may never see the issues of your toils. If you can see them they will generally not be worth looking at. We work for eternity. We may well wait for the scaffolding to be taken away. Then we shall find that preparatory work is all represented in the final issue; even as the first film of alluvium, deposited in its delta by some mighty stream, is the real foundation for the last, which, long ages after, rise above the surface and bear waving corn and the homes of men."—*Alexander Maclaren, D.D.*

A SUGGESTIVE CHURCH RECORD.

I. The potency of personal influence. Nehemiah created a spirit of enthusiasm which set all this train of exertion in motion.

II. The force of example. The priests took the lead in the common labour.

III. Advantages of systematic organization. Each volunteer made responsible for some limited portion of work.

IV. The gigantic results achievable by individual action. Like coral insects at work, the multitude of builders each did his part of the whole.

V. The diversity of disposition revealed by a great emergency. 1. Enthusiastic work. 2. Refusal to put the neck to the yoke.

VI. The consentaneity of purpose and effort which a great emergency demands and is calculated to bring about. All rivalries forgotten in the great aim—to again rebuild Jerusalem.

VII. The diversity of gifts which a great emergency calls into requisition.

Illustrations :—

"No life is waste in the great Worker's hand
  The gem too poor to polish in itself
  Is ground to brighten others."—*P. J. Bailey.*

"Do your work, and I shall know you. Do your work, and you shall reinforce yourself."—*Emerson.*

"The body is not one member, but many" (1 Cor. xii. 4—27).

"Clouds when full pour down, and the presses overflow, and the aromatical trees sweat out their precious and sovereign oils, and every learned scribe must bring out his treasure for the Church's behoof and benefit."—*John Trapp.*

PRIESTHOOD.

III. 1. *Then Eliashib the high priest rose up with his brethren the priests, and they builded the sheep gate; they sanctified it, and set up the doors of it; even unto the tower of Meah they sanctified it, unto the tower of Hananeel.*

INTRODUCTION. — Priest and king amongst the most terrible words in language. War, oppression, rapine have come at their call. 1. *Elevation is dangerous.* Separateness from sympathies and ways of common men a misfortune. Men easily enslave those whom they see to be lower than themselves 2. *Privilege and responsibility are co-extensive* Shepherd feeds and guards flock. King lives for subjects. Priest must think, speak, and act for his fellows. *Noblesse oblige.* What is true priesthood?

I A true priest identifies himself with men Institution and consecration (Exod. xxviii., xxix.). Interpretation (Heb.).

1. *Called from amongst men* (Heb. v. 1).
2. *Offers gifts and sacrifices* (v. 1).
3. *Compassionates weakness and ignorance* (v. 2).
4. *Comes between men and God.* (*a*) To present intercessions (*b*) To reveal God's will.

A priesthood is necessary "You tell me, my sceptical friend, that religion is the contrivance of the priest How came the priest into being? What gave him his power?"—*Channing* [*See illustration below, "Christian worship."*]

Priest's dress, robes, &c. stand for a NEEDED and SUPPOSED sanctity. If not sacred, all the worse for the priest. Must come to his work from a higher ground Of the people, but above the people. More thoughtful, not less saintly. MANHOOD first, PRIESTHOOD afterwards.

II. A true priest identifies thought with life. The wall-building was Nehemiah's THOUGHT. Eliashib and his brothers helped to make it REALITY.

Priest makes God's thoughts man's life. "Be ye holy" (Lev. xi. 44, 1 Pet. i. 15), God's thought. How to become holy, priest's life-work. A sinless and sorrowless world, God's thought. How to approximate to this a priest's work. Obedience to Divine laws, God's purpose; enunciations of these and incitements to keep them, priest's work.

1 *Harmonizes ideal and actual*
2 *Harmonizes thought and practice*
3 *Harmonizes inclination and conscience.*

III A true priest identifies the lower with the higher, the common with the sacred, earth with heaven. Priests "sanctified the wall;" built near the temple. God's house and city wall both SACRED. Sanctity is relative or real The temple; the temple utensils Churches (e. g Corinth) with unholy members in them are sanctified or holy relatively Only individual believers really sanctified. Broad distinctions between sacred and secular not well. Sabbath sacred; make all days. God's house is sacred; so is your own. Bible sacred; read nothing impure.

Illustrations —Christian worship "There have been those who have sought to disparage worship by representing it as an arbitrary, unnatural service, a human contrivance, an invention for selfish ends I will meet the objection by a few remarks drawn from history There have been, indeed, periods of history in which the influence of the religious principle seems to have been overwhelmed; but in this it agrees with other great principles of our nature, which in certain stages of the race disappear There are certain conditions of society in which the desire of knowledge seems almost extinct among men, and they abandon themselves for centuries to brutish ignorance There are communities in which the natural desire of reaching a better lot gives not a sign of its existence, and society remains stationary for ages There are some in which even the parental affection is so far dead that the new-born child is cast into the stream or exposed to the storm. So the religious principle is in some periods hardly to be discerned; but it is never lost No principle is more universally manifested In the darkest ages there are some recognitions of a superior Power. Man feels that there is a Being above himself, and he clothes that Being in what to his rude conceptions is great and venerable. In countries where architecture was unknown men chose the solemn wood or the mountain-top for worship; and when this art appeared its monuments were temples to God. Before the invention of letters hymns were composed to the Divinity, and music, we have reason to think, was the offspring of religion. Music in its infancy was the breathing of man's fears, wants, hopes, thanks, praises to an unseen power. You tell me, my sceptical friend, that religion is the contrivance of the priest. How came the priest into being? What gave him his power? Why was it that the ancient legislator professed to receive his laws from the gods? The fact is a striking one, that the earliest guides and leaders of the human race looked to the heavens for security and strength to earthly institutions, that they were compelled to speak to men in a higher name than man's. Religion was an earlier bond and a deeper foundation of society than government. It was the root of civilization. It has founded the mightiest empires; and yet men question whether religion be an element, a principle of human nature!

"In the earliest ages, before the dawn of science, man recognized an immediate interference of the Divinity in whatever powerfully struck his senses. . . . Every unusual event was a miracle, a prodigy, a promise of good or a menace of evil from heaven . . . The heavens, the earth, the plant, the human frame, now that they are explored by science, speak of God as they never did before. His handwriting is brought out where former ages saw but a blank. . . . The profoundest of all human wants is the want of God. Mind, spirit must tend to its source. It cannot find happiness but in the perfect Mind, the infinite Spirit. Worship has survived all revolutions. Corrupted, dishonoured, opposed, it yet lives. It is immortal as its object, immortal as the soul from which it ascends."—*W. E. Channing, D.D.*

The origin of the Christian clergy. "Amongst the gifts which our blessed Lord gave to mankind during his life on earth, the Christian ministry as we now possess it was not one of them. The twelve apostles whom he chose had no successors like them. The seventy disciples also, who went forth at the Lord's command to preach the gospel, they, too, were soon buried in their graves, but no order of the same kind, or of the same number, came in their stead.

"Yet there was another sense in which the Christian ministry was the gift of their Divine Master, and it was that which St. Paul so well expresses. 'When he ascended up on high he gave gifts unto men. And he gave some, apostles; and some, prophets; and some, evangelists; and some, pastors and teachers.' Now what was it that was meant by this statement—this very pointed statement—that it was only after his ascension, after his withdrawal from earth, that he gave those gifts to men, and amongst those gifts were the various offices, of which the two last named contained the germ of all the future clergy of Christendom? What was meant was surely this, that not in his earthly life, not in his direct communication with man, not as a part of the original manifestation of Christianity, but as the result of the complex influences which were showered down to the earth after its Founder had left, as part of the vast machinery of Christian civilization, created by the spirit of Christ for filling up the void of his absence, were the various gifts and professions of Christian forms, and amongst these were the great vocation, the sacred profession of the Christian ministry. Look at the gradual growth of the Christian ministry. In no single instance did the order of clergy now resemble what it was in the first century or even the second. The deacons of every existing Church were very different from the seven deacons of the apostolic age. The presbyters of every Church were either in themselves or in their relations to their brethren very different to the presbyters of the first or second century. Take the bishops, in many important respects they differed essentially from those who bore that title seventeen hundred years ago. They all varied in each age and country, according to the varieties of the age and country; according to the civil constitutions under which they lived, according to the geographical area; according to the climates and customs of east, west, north, and south, in regard to their election, whether by breathing, by popular election, by internal election, by ministerial election, by ordination, by sacred relics, by the elevation of hands, by the imposition of hands; spheres more or less limited, a humble country village, a vast town population, or a province as large as a kingdom. These variations were not a condemnation, but a justification rather, of their existence. They showed that the order of the Christian clergy, instead of remaining a stiff and useless relic of the past, had grown with the growth and varied with the variations of Christian society. This, therefore, was at once the Divine and the human origin of the Christian ministry; Divine, because it belonged to and formed an important link in the inevitable growth of all Christian communities, of Christian aspirations, and of Christian sympathies; human, because it arose out of and was subject to the necessities and vicissitudes of human passions and human infirmities, and in so far as it was of a permanent and Divine character, having a pledge of an immortal existence so long as Christian society exists; in so far as it was of human character, needing to accommodate itself to the want of each successive age, and needing the support, the sympathy, and the favour of all the other elements of social intercourse by which it was surrounded."—*Dean Stanley.*

MINISTERIAL ADAPTABILITY.

iii. 1 *Then Eliashib the high priest rose up, &c.*

I. The priests sharing the interests and toils of common manhood. A minister's power lies not in that in which he differs from others, but in that in which he is like them — "*brotherhood.*" He shares their weaknesses. He knows headache and heartache, weariness and worry, trouble and temptation; and just in proportion as he is a man will his ministry be sometimes powerful and sometimes powerless. At times he will wish himself in the most distant seat in the Church; at other times speech will be like the upliftings of angels, and the declaration of the gospel as admission into the paradise of God. A white tie, a black coat, and conventional manners do not make a minister; let him come and say, "Brethren, I am as ye are."

II. The priests an example to the people. The high priest and his subordinates were the first to build. Then common people tied on their aprons and took trowel in hand.

There must be leaders; then there will be followers. Simon Peter said, "I go a fishing." The rest say unto him, "We also go with thee" (John xxi.) The rank and file will ride into any valley of death if the officers say, "Comrades, come on." When he "put-teth forth his own sheep he goeth before them" (John x. 4).

III. Sacredness of work depends not on its nature, but on its purpose and spirit. "They sanctified" a *common* wall. They were toiling for hearth and home, for the city of their fathers and the temple of their God. Our work in the world not important; the spirit in which we do it the main consideration. A mother who represents Christ to her children, who becomes to them their idea of what God must be, is as sacredly engaged as some woman of genius whose fame fills a hemisphere. The blood and bones of the man who digs out the foundation are as necessary as the architect's skill. In building Solomon's temple the noise and dust of cutting and polishing the stones were confined to the quarry; in the temple all was calm.

In this world of striving and unattainment, of sin and sorrow, we do not see the plan. That is in the mind of the great Architect. Out of confusion he will educe order. "Whatsoever thy hand findeth to do, do it" (Eccles. ix. 10).

Illustration.—"Man, it is not thy works, which are all mortal, infinitely little, and the greatest no greater than the least, but only the spirit thou workest in, that can have worth or continuance."—*Carlyle.*

SYSTEM AND DETAIL IN WORK.

iii. 2, 3. *And next unto Eliashib builded the men of Jericho. And next to them builded Zaccur the son of Imri. But the fish gate did the sons of Hassenaah build, who also laid the beams thereof, and set up the doors thereof, the locks thereof, and the bars thereof.*

> " We live not to ourselves, our work is life;
> In bright and ceaseless labour as a star
> Which shineth unto all worlds but itself."

Then life is A VOCATION. "I beseech you that ye walk worthy of the vocation wherewith ye are called" (Ephes. iv. 1). "Your calling" (Ephes. iv. 1). "Let every man abide in the same calling wherein he was called" (1 Cor. vii. 20). In modern phrase, a man's trade or profession is *his calling.* This gives work dignity. Labourer, carpenter, mason, sailor, surgeon, preacher, schoolmaster, newspaper editor, thou art called. A hand not thine own placed thee where thou art. Every man's work should have a Pentecost. Manual labour is honourable. It must be redeemed from a spurious disregard. Indolence is degrading; dishonesty is ruinous; honest toil need fear no shame.

"None of us liveth to himself" (Rom. xiv. 7). Then life is a MINISTRY. This redeems it from selfishness. "My servants" (John xviii. 36). "Let a man so account of us as of the ministers of Christ, and stewards of the mysteries of God" (1 Cor. iv. 1). Not Paul, Peter, and Apollos only. Judgment-day decisions turn on this—"Inasmuch as ye have done," or, "Inasmuch as ye did not to the brethren" (Matt. xxv.). Ban or blessing each man carries in himself. Influence is conscious, direct, and intentional; then it is occasional, and often fails. Influence is unconscious, indirect, and streams on, like light from the heavens; then it is constant and all-pervasive. Life is more solemn than death. A man's daily work is not only religious, it is his religion. There he fights and conquers, or fights and falls. Well for him if he

> "be up and doing,
> With a heart for any fate;
> Still achieving, still pursuing,
> Learn to labour and to wait."

On the work of life let Nehemiah and his noble band teach us somewhat.

I. A great work can only be planned by a great mind. Many saw the desolations of the city; some wept over them. Nehemiah only had a vocation and talents to "build the old wastes and repair the desolations of many generations" (Isa. lxi. 4). An equality is impossible. In any circle of twelve there will be a Peter to lead. These are Kings by Divine right. The laureate's wreath is only green on the brows of him who utters nothing base. Nehemiahs have comprehensive minds, like some insects that put out "feelers" on all sides. Insight is a dangerous gift, hence granted only to the elect ones. Nehemiah rebuilds Jerusalem; Augustine governs a period, Wesley organizes a society; Shakespeare Shakespearizes a language.—they are "born to command."

II. A great work can only be carried out by division of labour. Nehemiah's organizing brain needed the hands of the men of Jericho. Farmer requires ploughman, horsekeeper, diggers, and delvers. Architect, clerk of works, mason, carpenter, stone-cutter, hod-man. Writer, an amanuensis, a printer, binder, bookseller. How long it would take one man to make a pin; by dividing the work they are counted by millions. Miner, sailor, soldier hazard their lives for the general good. One goes abroad, another stays at home; this man works with the hand, that with the brain; the husband rules without, the wife rules within; all obeying the same law, the needs be that into the world's mill each one casts some corn.

III. A great work can only be accomplished by attention to details. "Bars and locks." Gates and doors without bars and locks useless. "There must be detail in every great work. It is an element of effectiveness which no reach of plan, no enthusiasm of purpose, can dispense with. Thus, if a man conceives the idea of becoming eminent in learning, but cannot toil through the million of little drudgeries necessary to carry him on, his learning will be soon told. Or, if a man undertakes to become rich, but despises the small and gradual advances by which wealth is ordinarily accumulated, his expectations will, of course, be the sum of his riches. Accurate and careful detail, the minding of common occasions and small things, combined with general scope and vigour, is the secret of all the efficiency and success in the world"—*Bushnell*. 1. *Young man carving out his fortunes.* "By little and little." "Take care of the pence," &c. Trifling delinquencies; white lies are the unlocked gates through which "seven spirits worse" than these enter. Regard to minor courtesies, use of spare moments, buying up opportunities, lead on to honour always, to fortune sometimes. 2. *Church work.* Sunday schools, mission bands, tract distributors, missionary collectors are needed. Churchwardens, sidesmen, deacons, stewards, let each fill his place and attend to the duty specially allotted him. Hast thou a contracted sphere? Thou mayest fill it better. Is thy work humble? It is not of necessity mean.

> " Forth in thy name, O Lord, I go,
> My daily labour to pursue;
> Thee, only thee, resolved to know
> In all I think, or speak, or do."

IV. A great work brings out special adaptations. The men of Jericho built the wall. But the fish gate with its locks and bars did the sons of Hassenaah build.

The disciples of Christ. Prophecy-reading Philip finds prophecy-reading Nathaniel (John i. 43—51). Peter speaks and acts impetuously, and dies courageously (John xxi.). John, with a piercing insight, writes the angelic Gospel, and waits to see and war against rising error (John xxi.; Epistles of John, Revelation).

Does the hero mould the age, or the age mould the hero? Partly both.

In the Church " every man hath his proper gift of God, one after this manner, and another after that" (1 Cor. vii. 7). The eloquent Apollos expounds the Scriptures; the deft-handed Dorcas clothes the naked; the man of wealth sustains the charities, the strong minister to weakness; the wise enlighten the ignorant. "There is a different colour of beauty in different stones that are all of them precious. One man may be burnishing to the sparkle of the diamond, while another is deepening to the glow of the ruby. For this reason there are such different temperaments in Christian character and varying circumstances in Christian life, that the foundations of the wall of the city may be garnished with all manner of precious stones. Each Christian has his own place and lustre in that temple, and therefore there is no ground to disparage our neighbour, and none to despair of ourselves, if we are both in the hand of Christ."—*Ker*.

V. A great work must have regard to practical utility. The fish gate as necessary as the repairing of temple wall. Began at the temple, but did not stop there. What is it for? to be asked of every man's work. Does it begin and end in itself. True work should brighten somebody's dark life, cast out the stones from the rugged road along which some brother's stumbling feet must go, expel some one of the legion of demons that possess men.

VI. A great work must be inspired by a lofty purpose. Nehemiah and his fellows were rebuilding the city of David (ver. 15). Milton chose 'Paradise Lost,' and aimed to justify the ways of God to men. The painters find the sufferings of Christ an inexhaustible subject. A great religious reformer desired to spread holiness throughout the land. Man, art thou moved by a lofty motive inspired by God's good Spirit to take unto thee thy office in the world and Church?

VII. A great work must look on to the future. *It must have in it the element of permanence.* They were rebuilding the chosen city—the city of the future, as they fondly hoped.

CONCLUSION.—In heaven "they have no rest day nor night" (Rev. iv. 8). Two worlds, but only one law. Here from grace to grace, there from glory to glory. Here "faithful in that which is least" (Luke xvi. 10), there " ruler over many things " (Matt. xxv. 23). The first word is, Be faithful; and the second, Be faithful; and the third, Be faithful.

ILLUSTRATIONS.

Verse 3. "If a man would stand on figures and allegories, this gate may well signify Christ, who made his apostles and preachers fishers of men, who by him brought and daily bring them into this spiritual Jerusalem; for he is only the door whereby all must enter into the Lord's city. These men, like good builders, leave nothing undone that might fortify that gate; for they set on not only the doors, but also bolts and locks. So must God's Church be made strong by laws, discipline, and authority, that ravening lions and filthy swine rush not in and disquiet or devour God's people, and the wholesome doctrine must be confirmed with strong arguments and reasons against false teachers."—*Pilkington*

Working for the unknown future. "An old tattered volume found among his father's books, Bunny's 'Resolutions,' aroused Richard Baxter to concern, and Sibb's 'Bruised Reed' led him to the Saviour. From Baxter's pen proceeded 'The Call to the Unconverted,' which, in addition to its most extensive circulation elsewhere, was given by a beggar at the door where Philip Doddridge lived. It was the voice of God to the youthful reader, who became the author of 'The Rise and Progress of Religion in the Soul'—a book which gave the first impression to William Wilberforce. He became the author of 'A Practical View of Christianity,' which was blessed to the conversion of Leigh Richmond, a successful minister, and author of 'The Dairyman's Daughter' and 'Young Cottager,' little works that have had many seals in souls won to God. The 'Practical View' was also instrumental in the saving change of Dr. Chalmers, whose works are world-wide, and whose labours were so eminently owned for the revival of religion in the ministry and people of Scotland."—*Dr. Steel.*

RIVAL CLASSES.

iii. 5. *And next unto them the Tekoites repaired; but their nobles put not their necks to the work of their Lord.*

The rivalry of classes in all history. 1. *Use of this rivalry.* The mutual suspicion and watchfulness of classes serves to put all on their best behaviour; one is as a goad to the other for exertion in industry and excellence. 2. *Abuse of this rivalry.* All the hatreds and bigotries and wars of mankind.

I Rival classes. 1. *A noble peasantry.* "The Tekoites." (1) Simplicity. Lowly life is favourable to simplicity of aim and endeavour. Among the poor you find the most faithful servants; among the poor the Church finds her most diligent workers. Men who have been grinding at the tread-mill of hard labour all the week are the men who work the wheels of Christian service on a Sunday. Among the "better people" of religious communions "the labourers are few." (2) Devotion. Steady adherence to great principles is more often found amongst the poor. There is something in the saying about ignorance being the mother of devotion. Not in the cynical sense. But those who see only the hard realities of life are often capable of deep attachment to friends and to God and to a great cause, while the *dilettante* "feels no interest" in anything human or Divine. *Enthusiasm* is a *popular* quality. 2. *An effeminate aristocracy.* (1) Selfishness. Not confined to one class, but in its hardest manifestations to be found among the gay and worldly, who have multiplied their natural wants by a thousand artificial needs. To expect a burst of noble-hearted, generous enthusiasm from the frozen circle of worldly society is to look for grapes on thorns and figs from the thistle-stalk. [Of course in all this contrast we are only keeping in mind the really worldly circle, and are not forgetting the fact that in Jerusalem's rebuilding and in the reconstructions of English history the noble have nobly stood to the front.] (2) Pride. Beautiful is the way in which modern society is returning in many respects to humility in regard to practical things. A Prince of Wales sends his boys to the routine of a sailor apprenticeship; a Duke of Argyle sends his son to a house of business; a gentleman's son doffs his neat coat and stoops down, hammer in hand, in the engineer's yard. In this there is a more hopeful sight than when the proud nobles of Jerusalem disdained the rough work which the God-inspired Nehemiah designed.

II Rival views. 1. *Popular desire for reform.* (1) Politically. Trace course of national history. Instance the case of the Corn Laws, with its mechanic poet Ebenezer Elliott. (2) Ecclesiastically. Nothing is so fatal to a Church as for the people to let Church government alone and leave it to professional men. The sheep are for the sake of the shepherd in farming, but Christ's shepherds are for the sake of the flock. In our Lord's time "the common people heard him gladly" (Mark xii. 37); but it was asked as an incredible thing, "Have any of the rulers or of the Pharisees believed on him?" (John vii. 48)   The Reformation was a reply to *the people*, who groaned by reason of the afflictions wherewith the task-masters afflicted them   (3) Theologically.   The popular sentiment is the curb of theological opinion.   What men, *as men*, think and feel are the governor-halls of the great logic-engine of systematic theology.   The mother's heart in the theologian adjusts his harsh, cold views of God   2   *Reform cried down by the nobles.*   The doctrine of standing still is only preached by the few who find the place comfortable; the "noble discontent" which spurs on the needy and oppressed is the animation of all reform in State or Church

> "Ill fares the land, to hastening ills a prey,
> Where wealth accumulates, and men decay:
> Princes and lords may flourish or may fade,
> A breath can make them, as a breath has made;
> But a bold peasantry, their country's pride,
> When once destroyed, can never be supplied."
>   *Goldsmith's 'Deserted Village.'*

Application.   1. *Beware of luxurious aspirations.*   Think not merely of the pleasures of greatness, but of its enervating perils.   2. *Remember that the duties of individual manhood and the sources of happiness in the individual character remain the same under all changes of costume and title*   A man is never more or less than a servant of the great Taskmaster, and a fellow-labourer with others in the ruined city of Mansoul.   3. *Beware of indolence and pride, and do thy task for God and man.*

ILLUSTRATIONS.

A life of idleness. "And who art thou that braggest of thy life of idleness; complacently showest thy bright gilt equipages, sumptuous cushions, appliances for folding of the hands to mere sleep? Looking up, looking down, around, behind, or before, discernest thou, if it be not in Mayfair alone, any *idle* hero, saint, god, or even devil? Not a vestige of one. In the heavens, in the earth, in the waters under the earth is none like unto thee   Thou art an original figure in this creation, a denizen in Mayfair alone, in this extraordinary century or half-century alone! One monster there is in the world—the idle man."—*Carlyle.*

Rich and poor   "Let not the rich mislead the signs of the times, or mistake their brethren, they have less and less respect for titles and riches, for vestments and ecclesiastical pretensions; but they have a real respect for superior knowledge and superior goodness; they listen like children to those whom they believe to know a subject better than themselves.   Let those who know it say whether there is not something inexpressibly touching and even humbling in the large, hearty, manly English reverence and love which the working-men show towards those who love and serve them truly, and save them from themselves and from doing wrong. Alas! we have been very ready to preach submission.   For three long centuries we have taught submission to the powers that be, as if that were the only text in Scripture bearing on the relations between the ruler and the ruled. Rarely have we dared to demand of the powers that be *justice;* of the wealthy man and the titled *duties*   We have produced folios of slavish flattery upon the Divine right of power   Shame on us! we have not denounced the wrongs done to weakness, and yet for one text in the Bible which requires submission and patience from the poor, you will find a hundred which denounce the vices of the rich, in the writings of the noble old Jewish prophets, *that*, and almost that only, *that* in the Old Testament, with a deep roll of words that sound like Sinai thunders; and *that* in the New Testament in words less impassioned and more calmly terrible from the apostles and their Master; and woe to us, in the great day of God, if we have been the sycophants of the rich instead of the redressers of the poor man's wrongs."—*F. W. Robertson*

What the poor have done. "Thomas Cranfield, a tailor, established a prayer-meeting among the brickmakers in Kingsland, which was held *every morning at five o'clock*. He established schools at Rotherhithe, Tottenham, Kent Street, Southwark, the Mint, Garden Row, St. George's, Rosemary Lane, and Kennington   John Pounds, a Portsmouth cobbler, was the founder of *ragged schools.* Harlan Page consecrated *letter-writing* to the highest end—the salvation of souls."—*Dr. Steel.*

Handicraft   "It is not a mean thing to labour with the hand   There is a dignity in every duty, and especially in this.   Since the *Carpenter of Nazareth* toiled at his bench and made tools for Galilean peasants, labour has had a dignity, and artisans an elevation, and workshops a consecration. After this, the lantern-making of King Æropus, the ship-building of the Czar Peter, or the watch making of the Emperor Charles V., could do little to exalt it "—*Dr. Steel.*

G

" Let not ambition mock their useful toil,
Their homely joys, and destiny obscure,
Nor grandeir hear with a disdainful smile
The short and simple annals of the poor."
Gray's Elegy.

THE OLD GATE.

iii 6. *Moreover the old gate repaired Jehoiada, &c*

Memory needs to be awakened. *Forgetting* may be impossible, but we cannot always *recollect.*

Illustration.—" I am convinced that the dread book of account which the Scriptures speak of is, in fact, the mind itself of each individual Of this at least I feel assured, that there is no such thing as *forgetting* possible to the mind ; a thousand accidents may and will interpose a veil between our present consciousness and the secret inscriptions on the mind , accidents of the same sort will also rend away this veil ; but alike, whether veiled or unveiled, the inscription remains for ever, just as the stars seem to withdraw before the common light of day, whereas, in fact, we all know that it is the light which is drawn over them as a veil, and that they are waiting to be revealed when the obscuring daylight shall have withdrawn."— *De Quincey.*

I. The old gate brought up memories of the PAST. The past is valuable. God does.. not work *instantaneously.* Instance the seasons. Jewish law that the land should rest (Lev. xxv.). *Our fathers* made the roads, built the churches, founded schools, started commerce. Art, science, mechanical inventions are *improvements.* We build upon the past as on a bed of rock. " Custom passes into law *from precedent to precedent.*" Civilization does not grow up *in a night,* like Jonah's gourd. Right and wrong are *as old as the creation.*

Illustration :—" Every master has found his materials collected. What an economy of power! and what a compensation for the shortness of life ! All is done to his hand The world has brought him thus far on his way. The human race has gone out before him, sunk the hills, filled the hollows, and bridged the rivers. Men, nations, poets, artisans, women, all have worked for him, and he enters into their labours."— *Emerson.*

II. The old gate was an incentive to exertion in the PRESENT. *Our fathers' gate.* Patriotism fired their blood.

III. The old gate was a dumb prophet of the FUTURE. The builders were gone, but their work abode So would theirs. So will ours.

Application. 1. *Work, for Heaven so wills 2 Work, under the recollection that you are treading in the steps of the true nobility of the past 3. Work, because the day is passing. 4. Work, and eternity shall reward you*

THE BROAD WALL.

iii. 8. *The broad wall.*

Around Jerusalem in her days of splendour there was a broad wall, her defence and glory. *Jerusalem is a type of the Church.*

A broad wall suggests SEPARATION, SECURITY, and ENJOYMENT.

I. Separation. 1. *Every Christian should be more scrupulous than other men in his dealings. 2. By his pleasures the Christian should be distinguished. 3. In everything that affects the Christian; e. g. home business, going in and coming out; staying a night in a friend's house. 4. Most conspicuously in the spirit of his mind.*

The wall should be VERY BROAD. 1. *There should be a broad distinction between you Christians and unconverted people. 2. Our Lord Christ had a broad wall between him and the ungodly. 3. A broad wall is abundantly good for yourselves. 4. You will do more good to the world thereby.*

II. Safety 1. *The Christian is surrounded by the broad wall of God's power. 2. By the broad wall of God's love.* 3. By the broad wall of *God's law and justice* 4. By the broad wall of *God's immutability.* 5. By the broad wall of *God's electing love.* 6. By the broad wall of *God's redeeming love.* 7. *The work of the Holy Spirit* is a broad wall. 8. *Every doctrine of grace* is a broad wall.

9. *The honour of Christ* is a broad wall.

III. Enjoyment. On the walls of Nineveh and Babylon men drove, walked, chatted at sunset. Broad walls at York. 1. *Rest.* 2. *Communion.* 3. *Prospects and outlook.* The godless !—*Spurgeon, abridged.*

FAMILY ZEAL.

iii. 12. *Shallum repaired—he and his daughters.*

Women building stone walls. Perhaps they were heiresses or rich widows, who undertook to defray the expense of a portion of the wall. Perhaps! perhaps not. In crises women have donned armour — why may not these have wrought at the wall? When men have shown the white feather, women have turned bold. " Women's rights " The story of women's wrongs has not yet been told. Woman's influence a practical, ever-pressing question.

I. Notable women. 1 *Within the circle of Biblical story.* " In redemption's history we have Sarah's faith, Ruth's devotion, Abigail's humility, Shunammite's hospitality, Esther's patriotism, penitence of her anointing Christ, Canaanite's importunity, Mary of Bethany's love, Lydia's confidence, Dorcas' benevolence, Phœbe's kindness, Priscilla's courage, Tryphena and Tryphosa's diligence, and Persis' affection—*honoured of God.*"—*Van Doren.*

Most books of the Bible canonize women. *Genesis,* Eve, Rebekah, Rachel. *Exodus,* Miriam. *Judges,* Jephthah's daughter and the poetess Deborah. *Solomon* sings the praises of a good woman ; and *the Gospels of Jesus* contain Marys, Martha, and the unnamed who ministered to him. *The Epistles* teach women their duties, and reveal the depth of their influence and the width of their power.

2. *In history.* The mother of the Gracchi ; the mother of the Wesleys ; the mother of St. Augustine ; the mother of George Washington. Martyred women ; songstresses. Elizabeth Fry, who never forgot the mother in the philanthropist. Madame Guyon, whose faith she thus expressed :

" To me remains nor place nor time,—
  My country is in every clime ;
  I can be calm and free from care
On any shore, since God is there."

Countess of Huntingdon ; Lady Mary Wortley Montagu ; and time would fail us to tell of "*the nameless,*" whose records are on high.

II. Woman's influence. 1. *For evil.* Jezebel ; Solomon's wives, devotees of fashion ; women who spend their all at the gin-palace, and leave their children in dirt and destitution. A man must toil without ; a woman must guard within. 2. *For good.*

Application. 1 *Influence is not measurable by its circumference.* May be no larger than a house, no wider than a workshop. 2. *Every mother should be a missionary to her children.* She may save her husband (1 Cor. vii. 16). She has her children before teachers and ministers can influence them. To them she should represent God's care and Christ's mind, not by her words only, but in her life. Nothing can supersede *the religion of the hearth.*

Illustrations : — " One third more females church-members than males."—*Edwards.*

" The commonest and the least remembered of all great-little heroisms is the heroism of an average mother. Ah, when I think of that last broad fact I gather hope again for poor humanity, and this dark world looks bright, this diseased world looks wholesome to me once more, because, whatever it is or is not full of, it is at least full of mothers."—*Charles Kingsley.*

" Be good, sweet maid, and ' let who can be clever.
  Do lovely things, not dream them, all day long ;
And so make life, death, and that vast for ever
  One grand, sweet song "
        Charles Kingsley to his niece.

HIGH MEN AT LOWLY TASKS.

iii. 13—19. *The valley gate repaired Hanun, &c.*

The *fusion* of classes. Ordinarily society builds a broad wall betwixt class and class. But in the presence of a common danger, or under the inspiration of a common resolve, men break down all barriers, and stand side by side. Too often "the kings of the earth and the rulers take counsel together against the cause of the Lord" (Ps ii.); but the word of God standeth for ever. "Kings shall see and arise, princes also shall worship. . . . Kings shall be thy nursing fathers, and queens thy nursing mothers" (Isa. xlix.).

I. The differences and unities of the race. We make too much of distinctions; *e. g.* rich and poor, learned and ignorant, toilers and thinkers, manufacturers and hands, up-town and down-town, West-end and East-end One God created us, one cross redeems us, one Spirit inspires us; the same book teaches us, similar demons tempt us, similar sorrows confront us, a common grave awaits us, the same heaven is open to us. Society rings itself round. The aristocracy of birth says of the aristocracy of money, "Only a merchant." Better that emperor's wife who often said to her husband, "Remember what you were, and what you now are, and then you will be always thankful to God."

II Historical illustrations. The Romans called rulers "*fathers of their country.*" The Greeks styled them "*shepherds of their people.*" Most revolutions in Church and State have ranged high and low side by side. Paul was aided by "Erastus, the city chamberlain" (Rom xvi. 23), "and they of Cæsar's household" (Phil. iv. 22). The Reformation was indebted to the Elector Frederick. Lord Cobham's castle afforded shelter to Lollard preachers. England owes a debt of gratitude to "Albert the Good" for his devotion to science and art, and whatever would ameliorate the people's conditions.

III. **Practical purport.** 1. *With honour comes responsibility.* May I not do what I will with mine own? No; thou art only a steward. Hast thou wealth? The poor shall never cease out of the land, they are lawful claimants on thy sympathy. Hast thou wisdom? Teach the ignorant, guide the perplexed. Art thou elevated? Stoop to those who are low, lift down a helping hand to those who have stumbled and fallen.

> "Heaven does with us as we with torches do;
>   Not light them for themselves; for if our virtues
>   Did not go forth of us, 'twere all alike
>   As if we had them not. Spirits are not finely
>   touch'd
>   But to fine issues ; nor Nature never lends
>   The smallest scruple of her excellence,
>   But, like a thrifty goddess, she determines
>   Herself the glory of a creditor—
>   Both thanks and use."

2. *Be not deceived by appearances.* Not what a man *hath*, but what a man *is*, determines his worth It is the cause, not the suffering, makes the martyr. The motive decides the action. Pierce beneath the surface, plant thy foot on the rock of reality. 3. *Gather courage and patience from the thought of the future.* Look unto Jesus, who for the joy that was set before him endured, &c. (Heb. xii. 2). Remember Moses (Heb. xi. 26). Whose *names* were in the foundations of the city of vision? Not the leaders only (Peter, James, and John), but "the *twelve* apostles" (Rev. xxi. 14). "The Holy Ghost hath registered unto us the names and diligence of the builders of this earthly city Jerusalem, by the pen of his faithful servant Nehemiah, for our comfort, and to teach us that much more he hath registered the names of the builders of the spiritual Jerusalem in the book of life, where no devil can scrape them out, but shall be the dear children of the Lord God, defended by him from all ill. Let us therefore cast away this slothful sluggishness wherein we have lain so long, rise up quickly, work lustily, spit on our

hands and take good hold, that we fall not back again from our Lord God. It is more honour to be a workman in this house than to live the easiest life that the world can give."—*Pilkington.*

DAVID THE NATIONAL HERO.

iii. 15. *The city of David.* iii. 16. *The sepulchres of David.*

They were working on sacred ground. Hence their enthusiasm. Effort must have inspiration. This city David conquered; he beautified it; here he reigned; here he sleeps. They did not stay to shape such thoughts as these. They were instincts. Patriotism lives not by bread only, but by sentiments, by every word that proceedeth out of the mouth of good king and wise teacher in the ages past. *Theme,* DAVID'S LIFE-WORK the basis of national hero-worship.

I. Preparing for a throne. "He that is born is listed; life is war" "The foundation of David's character is a firm, unshaken trust in Jehovah, a bright and most spiritual view of creation and the government of the world, a sensitive awe of the Holy One of Israel, a striving ever to be true to him, and a strong desire to return after errors and transgressions"—*Ewald.* Ps. lxxviii. 70 tells how David was God's elected king. The prophet Samuel shaped the character of the period. His work was long developing. Takes months for common seed to grow. Samuel cast seed into God's world-field; David and Solomon put in the sickle and reaped. What of that? Sower and reaper equally indispensable (John iv. 36—38). David had a creative faculty—he was the poet of song. We have "the book of the chronicles" of King David; we have, too, the books of psalms, hymns, and spiritual songs he sang and wrote. Saul's FATAL DAY not the day of the battle of Gilboa, but the day of the battle with Amalek; not the day when Saul died, but the day when Saul disobeyed, led to David's election and anointing. The story is told in the Book of Samuel (I xvi.). Eliab is rejected The height of a man's stature and the beauty of his countenance shall not henceforth be signs infallible that God has endowed that man with kingly qualities. God-elected shall be God-endowed. *That day* David anointed, but God's hand had been upon him in the pastures of Bethlehem. There he *thought out,* if he did not *write,* Ps. xxiii. There he discerned a presence which beset him behind and before (Ps. cxxxix.). To him the heavens declared God. How perfect God's law was, and what God's fear meant, he was being taught by the order of God in nature; how guilty and feeble he was, he was being taught by the voice of God in his own conscience (Ps. xix). David's God was a living, ever-present, helping God (Ps. xxvii.). *From the sheepfolds David came to encounter Goliath. From the sheepfolds he was summoned to be harp-player to King Saul.* He was anointed, but not enthroned. He must learn to wait. God never extemporizes. "Soon ripe, soon rot." Moses eighty years of preparation. Elijah a full-grown man before he appears in sacred history. Jesus Christ eighteen quiet, uneventful years after seeing the holy city, and afterwards forty days in wilderness. The harvest of God in human souls ripens slowly. As David thought of his great work, and felt himself a child with a giant's task, he said, "O Lord, our Lord, how excellent is thy name in all the earth! who hast set thy glory above the heavens. Out of the mouth of babes and sucklings hast thou ordained strength" (Ps. viii.). He recollected the storms he had witnessed as he watched the sheep when he wrote Ps xxix. But after the longest night the morning breaks. *David was called to the court as harp-player to King Saul.* Saul's servants described David to the king as "a son of Jesse the Bethlehemite, that is cunning in playing" (1 Sam xvi 18). David was an *artist,* as we now speak. In Eastern lands shepherd-life and songs have always gone together. The elected king is harpist to the enthroned king. How slowly David ascended the steps to the throne. We, who *look back,* see some reasons why ascent was gradual. In the pastures he had time to *think;* in the court he had opportunity to *observe.*

David's harp quieted Saul's excitement (1 Sam. xvi. 23) ; David's harp helped him
to compose his Psalms for the song-life of the Church universal His chequered life
fore-shadowed in Saul's court. To-day the king's bosom friend, to-morrow the butt
for the king's javelin The love of David and Jonathan the one bright and beautiful thing. Purer and more constant friendship was never known. With his
escape from Saul's court began—

II. The work and warfare of David's life. 1. As a freebooter. 2. As king.
1 *As a freebooter.* Cave of Adullam (1 Sam. xxii. 1, 2). Wild wilderness life.
Hunted by Saul (1 Sam xxiii. 25—29 ; xxiv 8—22) Saul's hope failed him
in the hour of need, and he fell on Gilboa's fatal field. 2. *David was king.* First
over Judah, then over all Israel David's reign was one of creation ; Solomon's
was one of consolidation. A brilliant reign of a great and good man ; but, like
all things human, not without fault (2 Sam. xi ; 1 Chron xxi.). The fifty-first
Psalm the cry of this kingly penitent. But did "the free spirit" ever come back
again as in the earlier days ? However, Carlyle's words are both wise and charitable. "Who is called 'the man after God's own heart' ? David, the Hebrew
king, had fallen into sins enough—blackest crimes—there was no want of sin ;
and therefore the unbelievers sneer, and ask, ' Is this your man according to God's
heart ? ' The sneer, I must say, seems to me but a shallow one What are faults,
what are the outward details of a life, if the inner secret of it, the remorse, temptations, the often-baffled, never-ended struggle of it be forgotten ? David's life and
history, as written for us in those Psalms of his, I consider to be the truest emblem
ever given us of a man's moral progress and warfare here below. All earnest souls
will ever discern in it the faithful struggle of an earnest human soul towards what
is good and best Struggle often baffled, sore baffled, driven as into entire wreck ;
yet a struggle never ended, ever with tears, repentance, true, unconquerable purpose
begun anew." He died full of age and honours, and his sepulchre Nehemiah looked
upon with reverence, Peter the apostle spoke of with exultation, and to it the feet
of countless thousands of weary pilgrims have been directed.

ILLUSTRATIONS.

A true man — " Every true man is a cause, a country, and an age , requires infinite spaces and
numbers and time fully to accomplish his design ; and posterity seem to follow his steps as a train
of clients A man Cæsar is born, and for ages after we have a Roman empire An institution is
the lengthened shadow of one man as monachism of the hermit Antony , the Reformation, of
Luther , Quakerism, of Fox ; Methodism, of Wesley, Abolition, of Clarkson Scipio, Milton called
'the height of Rome ,' and all history resolves itself very easily into the biography of a few
stout and earnest persons "—*Emerson*

Sepulchres.—" Next to the wells of Syria, the most authentic memorials of past times are the
sepulchres, and partly for the same reason. The tombs of ancient Greece and Rome lined the
public roads with funeral pillars or towers. Grassy graves and marble monuments fill the church-
yards and churches of Christian Europe But the sepulchres of Palestine were like the habitations of its earliest inhabitants, hewn out of the living limestone rock, and therefore indestructible as the rock itself In this respect they resembled, though on a smaller scale, the
tombs of Upper Egypt , and as there the traveller of the nineteenth century is confronted with
the names and records of men who lived thousands of years ago, so also in the excavations of the
valleys which surround or approach Shiloh, Shechem, Bethel, and Jerusalem he knows that he
sees what were the last resting-places of the generations contemporary with Joshua, Samuel, and
David And the example of Egypt shows that the identification of these sepulchres even with their
individual occupants is not so improbable as might be otherwise supposed. If the graves of
Rameses and Osirei can still be ascertained, there is nothing improbable in the thought that the
tombs of the patriarchs may have survived the lapse of twenty or thirty centuries. The rocky cave
on Mount Hor must be at least the spot believed by Josephus to mark the grave of Aaron The
tomb of Joseph must be near one of the two monuments pointed out as such in the opening of the
vale of Shechem. The sepulchre which is called the tomb of Rachel exactly agrees with the
spot described as ' a little way ' from Bethlehem The tomb of David, which was known with
certainty at the time of the Christian era, may perhaps still be found under the mosque which bears
his name in the modern Zion Above all, the cave of Machpelah is concealed, beyond all reasonable
doubt, by the mosque at Hebron But, with these exceptions, we must rest satisfied rather with the
general than the particular interest of the tombs of Palestine."—*Stanley's ' Sinai and Palestine.'*

THE WORKMEN'S DAY-BOOK.

iii. 20—32.   *After him Baruch the son of Zabbai, &c.*

I. Every man is carefully credited with his own tasks and achievements. Rulers, priests, slaves (Nethinims), men, women (ver. 12). Nobody is forgotten. The humblest not passed by in contemptuous silence.

II. Special honour is accorded special work. Levites and priests began at the temple, but did not stop there (vers. 22, 28). Zabbai, who earnestly repaired a second piece, having completed his task did not fold his arms, but went with open eyes and willing hands to seek another task. The goldsmiths and the temple traders came down to the wall not to inspect, but labour (vers. 31, 32).

III. Regard is had to the men of practical wisdom. Benjamin and others built over against their house (vers. 23, 28, 29). Meshullam built over against his chamber (ver. 30). Perhaps he was a lodger. (*a*) *They were men of practical sense.* Work was near at hand; why go abroad? "There are many Christians who can never find a place large enough to do their duty. Some Churches seem to feel that if anything is to be done some great operation must be started. They cannot even repent without concert and a general ado." — *Bushnell.* (*b*) *These men found here an inspiration for effort—the defence of home.* With practical enthusiasm, Hananiah and others built "*another piece.*" *All cannot keep the same pace, but all can build.*

Let us hear the conclusion of the whole matter. "The Son of man shall come . . . and then he shall reward every man according to his works" (Matt. xvi. 27). "Be thou faithful unto death, and I will give thee a crown of life" (Rev. ii. 10).

ADDENDA TO CHAPTER III.

TOPOGRAPHY OF THE BOOK OF NEHEMIAH.

THE only description of the ancient city of Jerusalem which exists in the Bible so extensive in form as to enable us to follow it as a topographical description is that found in the Book of

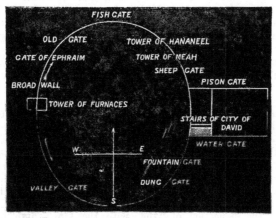

Nehemiah, and although it is hardly sufficiently distinct to enable us to settle all the moot points, it contains such valuable indications that it is well worthy of the most attentive examination. The easiest way to arrive at any correct conclusion regarding it, is to take first the description of the dedication of the walls in ch. xii. (31—40), and, drawing such a diagram as this, we easily get at the main features of the old wall at least.

The order of procession was that the princes of Judah went up upon the wall at some point as nearly as possible opposite to the temple, and one half of them turning to the right went towards the dung gate, "and at the fountain gate, which was *over against them*" (or, in other words, on the opposite or temple side of the city), "went up by the stairs of the city of David at the going up of the wall, above the house of David, even unto the water gate eastward." The water gate, therefore, was one of the southern gates of the temple, and the stairs that led up to it are here identified with those of the city of David, and consequently with Zion.

The other party turned to the left, or northwards, and passed from beyond the tower of the furnaces even "unto the broad wall," and passing the gate of Ephraim, the old gate, the fish gate, the towers of Hananeel and Meah, to the sheep gate, "stood still in the prison gate," as the other party had in the water gate. "So stood the two companies of them that gave thanks in the house of God."

If from this we turn to the third chapter, which gives a description of the repairs of the wall, we have no difficulty in identifying all the places mentioned in the first sixteen verses with those enumerated in the twelfth chapter. The repairs began at the sheep gate on the north side, and in immediate proximity with the temple, and all the places named in the dedication are again named, but in the reverse order, till we come to the tower of the furnaces, which, if not identical with the tower in the citadel, so often mistaken for the Hippicus, must at least have stood very near to it. Mention is then made, but now in the direct order of the dedication, of "the valley gate," the "dung gate," the "fountain gate," and lastly, the "stairs that go down from the city of David."

Between these last two places we find mention made of the pool of Siloah and the king's garden, so that we have long passed the so-called sepulchre of David on the modern Zion, and are in the immediate proximity of the temple; most probably in the valley between the city of David and the city of Jerusalem. What follows is most important (ver. 16): "After him repaired Nehemiah the son of Azbuk, the ruler of the half part of Bethzur, unto the place over against the sepulchres of David, and to the pool that was made, and unto the house of the mighty." This passage, when taken with the context, seems in itself quite sufficient to set at rest the question of the position of the city of David, of the sepulchres of the kings, and consequently of Zion, all which could not be mentioned after Siloah if placed where modern tradition has located them.

If the chapter ended with the sixteenth verse there would be no difficulty in determining the sites mentioned above, but unfortunately we have, according to this view, retraced our steps very nearly to the point from which we started, and have got through only half the places enumerated. Two hypotheses may be suggested to account for this difficulty: the one, that there was then, as in the time of Josephus, a second wall, and that the remaining names refer to it; the other, that the first sixteen verses refer to the walls of Jerusalem, and the remaining sixteen to those of the city of David. An attentive consideration of the subject renders it almost certain that the latter is the true explanation of the case. In the enumeration of the places repaired, in the last part of the chapter, we have two which we know, from the description of the dedication, really belonged to the temple. The prison court (iii. 25), which must have been connected with the prison gate, and, as shown by the order of the dedication, to have been on the north side of the temple, is here also connected with the king's high house; all this clearly referring, as shown above, to the castle of David, which originally occupied the site of the Turris Antonia. We have on the opposite side the "water gate," mentioned in the next verse to Ophel, and consequently as clearly identified with the southern gate of the temple. We have also the horse gate, that by which Athaliah was taken out of the temple (2 Kings xi. 16, 2 Chron. xxii 15), which Josephus states led to the Kedron, and which is here mentioned as connected with the priests' houses, and probably, therefore, a part of the temple. Mention is also made of the house of Eliashib the high priest, and of the eastern gate, probably that of the temple. In fact, no place is mentioned in these last verses which cannot be more or less directly identified with the localities on the temple hill, and not one which can be located in Jerusalem. The whole of the city of David, however, was so completely rebuilt and remodelled by Herod that there are no local indications to assist us in ascertaining

whether the order of description of the places mentioned after ver. 16 proceeds along the northern face, and round by Ophel, and up behind the temple back to the sheep gate, or whether, after crossing the causeway to the armoury and prison, it does not proceed along the western face of the temple to Ophel in the south, and then, along the eastern face, back along the northern, to the place from which the description started. The latter seems the more probable hypothesis, but the determination of the point is not of very great consequence. It is enough to know that the description in the first sixteen verses applies to Jerusalem, and in the last sixteen to Zion, or the city of David, as this is sufficient to explain almost all the difficult passages in the Old Testament which refer to the ancient topography of the city.—*Fergusson in Smith's ' Bible Dictionary.'*

MODERN JERUSALEM.

The first sight of Jerusalem as seen from the south, the first moment when from the ridge of hills which divide the valley of Rephaim from the valley of Bethlehem one sees the white line crowning the horizon, and knows that it is Jerusalem, is a moment never to be forgotten. But there is nothing in the view itself to excite your feelings Nor is there even when the Mount of Olives heaves in sight, nor when "the horses' hoofs ring on the stones of the streets of Jerusalem" Nor is there in the surrounding outline of hills on the distant horizon. Nebi-Samuel is indeed a high and distinguished point, and Ramah and Gibeah both stand out, but they and all the rest in some degree partake of that featureless character which belongs to all the hills of Judæa

In one respect no one need quarrel with this first aspect of Jerusalem. So far as localities have any concern with religion, it is well to feel that Christianity, even in its first origin, was nurtured in no romantic scenery; that the discourses in the walks to and from Bethany, and in earlier times the psalms and prophecies

of David and Isaiah, were not, as in Greece, the offspring of oracular cliffs and grottos, but the simple outpouring of souls which thought of nothing but God and man. It is not, however, inconsistent with this view to add, that though not romantic, though at first sight bare and prosaic in the extreme, there does at last grow up about Jerusalem a beauty as poetical as that which hangs over Athens and Rome. First, it is in the highest degree *venerable.* Modern houses it is true there are; the interiors of the streets are modern The old city itself (and I felt a constant satisfaction in the thought) lies buried twenty, thirty, forty feet below these wretched shops and receptacles for Anglo-Oriental conveniences. But still, as you look at it from any commanding point, within or without the walls, you are struck by the gray ruinous masses of which it is made up; it is the ruin, in fact, of the old Jerusalem on which you look—the stones, the columns, the very soil on which you tread is the accumulation of nearly three thousand years. And as with the city, so it is with the

work, to encourage them in their labour, and in case of attack to lead them against the enemy   17
They which builded, &c] The burden-bearers worked with one hand and held a weapon with the
other.   **18 The builders, &c]** Needing both hands for their work had swords girt to their sides
22 Lodge within Jerusalem] Those that had their homes in the villages and distant towns should
now continue night and day in the city   **23. Saving that every one put them off for washing]**
A puzzling sentence. Conjectures and emendations have been resorted to   The idea of the whole
verse is clear—unceasing watchfulness.

HOMILETICAL CONTENTS OF CHAPTER IV.

AN UNDAUNTED HEART.

Chap iv

THE childlike piety and the white integrity of Nehemiah not more marked than his
heroic undauntedness   Recapitulate his progress from the first resolution —silent
cherishing of his purpose ; maturing of his plans ; organized schemes and allotments
of labour, vigilant precautions ; cheery " FEAR NOT !"   " Be not ye afraid " (ver.
14)   A model to the Christian workman and soldier.

I. Reasons for fear. 1. *Ridicule* (vers. 1—3) " Mocked " Jesus Christ
mocked and spitted on   And it is enough for the disciple that he be *as* his Master
(John ix 28). " Foolishness " of apostolic preaching   Greek philosophy and
Roman civilization, scorn and reviling of the Nazarenes. Religion not the only
department in which the right has been reviled by the wrong   Science has always
begun to climb upward amid the laughter of circling ignorance. Most great
principles have had a point in their history when they were believed in by one and
ridiculed by all the rest   Instance—George Stephenson and the railway enterprise.
(*a*) Don't be ashamed of your Christian faith, let Sanballat and Tobiah laugh
themselves hoarse, follow *thou* after life ! (*b*) Don't be ashamed of your Christian
work   It is easy for a keen witling to pull out his cigar and point to a humorous
element in your little tasks. " What do these feeble Christians ? Will they revive
the stony hearts of fallen men, and rear a dwelling-place for truth and peace amid
the rubbish of the world ?" They will, God being their helper ! 2. *Guile* In
chap. vi are accounts of strategy adopted by Nehemiah's opponents where it required
a wise head to keep the heart firm   Plausible pretences of enemies and feigned
friendship were of no avail to bend the iron purpose of the Jewish liberator.
Nehemiah's enemies bade him join them for a conference in order to trap and
hinder him (vi 2, 3) ; they warned him to beware of his reputation (vi 6) ;
they urged him to " show the white feather " (vi. 11)   " Satan is transformed into
an angel of light " (2 Cor. xi 14)   (*a*) How many plausible excuses a treacherous
heart and a worldly friend can coin for postponement of religious decision and
devotion   (*b*) How many reasons might not every one find in the world's opinion
for leaving his Christian work undone   " Be ye wise as serpents " (Matt x. 16).
3 *Force* (iv 8)   The conspiring rabble around the rebuilders of Jerusalem but an
emblem of the circling forces which press upon the servant of God. Our way is
like the way of Paul's mariners, against " contrary winds " Our progress is
disputed ' inch by inch." (1) The oppositions to the culture of the Christian
character are manifold. A false heart within, a sin-maimed world without ;
break-downs and discouragements in experience   (2) So of the oppositions to
Christian work You must rebuild your fallen fellows into society not because
you are invited to do it, but in face of oppositions ; nay, " the very stones will cry

out ; " the people you want to lift up will try in this to throw you down, or at least will " conspire to hinder " " But consider him ! " (Heb. xii. 3)

II Motives for courage. 1. *The power of God* (iv. 14, 15)   The courage of Moses based on the " Certainly I will be with thee " of God (Exod iii 12). David's fearlessness rested on the " Some trust in chariots, and some in horses · but we will remember the name of the Lord our God " (Ps xx 7)   The three Hebrew children were firm because " our God is able to deliver us " (Dan iii. 17).   The undaunted apostles were fixed on the same centre (Acts iv. 29, 30).

> " And were this world all devils o'er,
>   And watching to devour us,
> We lay it not to heart so sore ,
>   Not they can overpower us
> And let the prince of ill
>   Look grim as e'er he will,
> He harms us not a whit
>   For why ? His doom is writ ;
>   word shall quickly slay him."

2. *The strength of right.*   " Thrice is he armed who hath his quarrel just."

> " My strength is as the strength of ten,
>   Because my heart is pure "

" Great is truth, and shall prevail "   All such maxims of the ancient and the modern world bear the popular faith that RIGHT IS MIGHT.   " The world passeth away, and the lust thereof · but he that doeth the will of God abideth for ever " (1 John ii. 17).   To have " this testimony, that we please God," is to be clad in triple steel.

III. Expedients of the imperilled. 1. *Prayer* (vers 4, 9)   " *We made our prayer unto God.*"   " I cried unto the Lord " is the Christian's explanation of many a hairbreadth escape.   2. *Vigilance* (ver 9)   " *We set a watch against them day and night.*"

> " Hear the victors that o'ercame,
>   Still they mark each warrior's way,
> All with one sweet voice exclaim,
>   Watch and pray."

3 *Hope* (ver. 20)   " *Our God shall fight for us.*"   Giant Despair is a sad foe of Christian souls.   The stroke of despondency stuns us like a blow on the head ; therefore " take the *helmet of hope* " (1 Thess. v. 8).   4. *Perseverance* (ver. 21 and ver. 23).

Application   In Christian life and in Christian work take as a motto Polycarp's words to his pupil—" *Stand thou firm as an anvil that is beaten.*"

> " Write on thy heart this holy principle,
>   Nobly resolve and *do* as thou resolvest,
>   Thou shalt not die till victory crown thy brows."

ACTIVE HOSTILITY FRUSTRATED.

Chap. iv.

Various forms of active hostility frustrated through the combined vigilance and prayer of the Church   " The adversaries of the Lord shall be broken to pieces " (1 Sam ii. 10)   Whenever a door of usefulness is opened there are many adversaries (1 Cor. xvi. 9).   Stand firm and fearless, " in nothing terrified by your adversaries " (Phil i. 28)   " Be not ye afraid of them : remember the Lord ! "   (a) Remember the Lord God, who has been described as *All-eye*.   Let this encourage.   He knows all the details of individual lives.   Let this warn.   He scrutinizes all thoughts and deeds. (*b*) Remember the Lord Christ. " All his adversaries were ashamed " (Luke xiii. 17)

I. Hostility to the work of God assuming phases of growing intensity. 1. *Rage.* Sanballat had laughed (ii. 19), now he is enraged (ver. 1). 2 *Mockery* (ver. 2). Tobiah was only Sanballat's echo (ver. 3). 3. *Conspiracy* (vers. 7, 8). This opposition a sign of success ; an honour paid to truth. When Dr Johnson wrote anything that was not vilified he said, " I did not strike hard enough, or the blow would rebound." " Woe unto you when all men shall speak well of you ! " (Luke vi 26).

II. The Church fortifying herself against expected assault. 1. *By appealing to God* (vers. 4, 5). " Eight times in this book Nehemiah interjects a prayer. They are prayers while writing, not while acting. The grounds of this prayer are—(1) God's people are despised ; (2) excited to fear by the enemy."—*Crosby.* " Prayer is a sure anchor in all storms ; and they never perish that humbly fly unto it and cleave unto it. Prayer is a salve for all sores ; yea, it healeth not only body and soul, but even hard stony walls. No kind of earthly physic that God hath made is good for all kind of folk at all times, and all kind of diseases ; but this heavenly physic of prayer, in wealth and woe, in plenty and poverty, in prosperity and adversity, in sickness and in health, in war and peace, in youth and age, in life and death. in mirth and sadness, yea, in all things and times, in the beginning, midst, and ending, prayer is most necessary and comfortable. Happy is that man that diligently useth it at all times."—*Pilkington.* 2. *By redoubled activity in prosecuting the work* " So built we the wall," &c. (ver. 6). " Prayer did not slacken the energy of the Jews. They experienced the redoubled zeal and activity which all true prayer produces. They made their prayer to God, and set a watch against their foes day and night All the natural means, whether of mind or matter, form channels through which God conveys his grace in answer to prayer. To stop these channels is to cancel prayer. Prayer was never intended to foster idleness or diminish responsibility."—*Crosby* 3. *By organized vigilance* (ver. 9). 4. *By defensive preparations* (ver. 13) " The Lord said unto Moses, Wherefore criest thou unto me? speak unto the children of Israel, that they go forward " (Exod. xiv 15) There is a time to pray and a time to prepare to fight. Let the farmer sow his seed, and then pray for rain and sunshine. 5. *By mutual encouragement* (ver. 14). Workers tire ; warriors flee when hope dies. 6. *By self-denying assiduity* (vers. 16, 21—23).

III. The evil counsels of the Church's adversaries frustrated by Divine interposition. " God brought their counsel to nought " (ver. 15) " Our God shall fight for us." There are laws ; is there not a law-giver ? There are agencies ; point they not to an agent ? Will our modern magicians never say, like those of Egypt (Exod viii 19), " This is the finger of God."

> " Oft in danger, oft in woe,
> Onward, Christians, onward go ;
> Fight the fight, maintain the strife,
> Strengthened with the bread of life.
>
> Onward, then, to glory move,
> More than conquerors ye shall prove :
> Though opposed by many a foe,
> Christian soldiers, onward go."

THE SOLDIER BUILDERS

Chap. iv.

Energy, unity, and perseverance (chap iii.) give way to discouragement within and conspiracy without.

I. Combination of prayer and watchfulness (ver. 9). Prayer without watchfulness is hypocrisy; watchfulness without prayer is presumption. An old writer, speaking of men as stewards, urges wise trading. Their WAREHOUSE (*i. e.* heart and memory) must store up precious things—holy affections, grateful remembrances, celestial preparations. Their WORKHOUSE (or their actions), wherein they retail to others. Their CLOCK-HOUSE (*e. g.* their speech), which must speak the truth. Their COUNTING-HOUSE (or conscience), which should be scrupulously kept, or everything else will fail.

II. Combination of precept and example. Nehemiah "looked, and rose up, and said unto the nobles, and to the rulers, and to the rest of the people, Be not ye afraid," &c. (ver 14). But he was not content with that. "WE returned to the wall" (ver. 15). "He that sounded the trumpet was *by me*" (ver. 18).

III. Every builder was also a soldier. "They which builded on the wall, and they that bare burdens, with those that laded, every one with one of his hands wrought in the work, and with the other hand held a weapon. For *the builders*, *every one* had his sword girded by his side, and so builded" (vers. 17, 18).

IV. A mutual co-operation went hand in hand with personal work and responsibility. "*Every one unto his work*" (ver. 15).

(*Abridged from Rev. J. M. Randall's 'Nehemiah, his Times and Lessons.'*)

THE LAWS OF OPPOSITION.

iv. 3. *But it came to pass, &c.*

The unconscious working of men's minds is a servant of law. There is a reign of law. Distinguished Christian thinkers hold that the great scientific doctrine of evolution "ratifies all that is highest and holiest in the nature of man," and makes out a new "claim to reverent acceptance of supernatural truths." There is a Divine government of the passions of men. "Surely the wrath of men shall praise thee," &c. (Ps lxxvi 10). "The emotions excited by the passions in our senses are not *free.* An angry man is carried beyond himself in spite of himself. These emotions are not proportional. A timorous man turns as pale at the sight of a fanciful as of a real danger. These emotions do not obey the orders of our *will.* The movement is not a gentle stream, but a rapid flood." — *Saurin.* Sanballat was angry; Tobiah was scornful.

I. Men seek in others what they find in themselves. The old maxim of English law. Every man is to be deemed honest until he is proved to be a rogue; the dishonest the reverse. Cowards disbelieve in bravery. There is a moral obliquity of vision. The unjust cannot appreciate justice. Impure men suspect impurity everywhere. The compact of the wicked is not binding. Judas and the priests. "I have sinned." "What is that to us?" (Matt. xxvii. 4—6). They cast off Judas when he had served their purpose, and took back their own accursed coins. All wrong-doing is blunder as well as crime. Marvellously deep and philosophic are the prophet's words: "Wherefore do ye spend money for that which is not bread?" (Isa. lv. 2).

II. All the branches of opposition grow out of the great trunk of selfishness. Sanballat the Samaritan and Tobiah the Ammonite rejoiced in the laying waste of Jerusalem. Its loss was their gain. "*Our gain*" explains many facts of history in ancient and modern times. Selfish gain has entered temples, disgraced senate houses, tarnished otherwise fair reputations. Gain has been England's god. Speculation has been a species of madness. "Look not every man on his own things, but every man also on the things of others," is a peculiarly Christian injunction.

III. Great work is generally accomplished by a committee of one. There was *one Nehemiah* against Sanballat, Tobiah, men of Arabia, &c. (ver. 7); *one Luther* against Rome, the monks, and the schoolmen; *one Tindal* against

Bishop Tonstal and Sir Thomas More. *John Evangelist Gossner* was a solitary worker — " One - in - hand " somebody styled him. ' It's quite true," he said, laughing, when it came to his ears ; "and yet old ' One-in-hand ' carries more passengers than your Four." Organize, organize—that is well. But individuality is lost in the mass.

Application. 1. " *We mortal millions dwell alone.*" 2. *The way of sorrow leadeth to the city of God.* 3. *Whatever has value is bought at a high price.*

Illustrations :—The spirit of cynicism "The Cynics were a sect of philosophers among the Greeks, founded by Antisthenes, who, on account of his snappish, snarling propensities, was frequently called 'the dog ;' and probably enough it may have been on account of this that his school of philosophy was called the Cynic or Dog school. He was stern, proud, and unsympathetic. He taught that all human pleasure was to be despised. He was ostentatiously careless as to the opinions, the feelings, and the esteem of others. He used to appear in a threadbare dress, so that Socrates once exclaimed, 'I see your pride, Antisthenes, peeping through the holes in your cloak !' His temper was morose, and his language was coarse and indecent. It is from this old school of philosophy that we derive the term cynicism, and we commonly apply it now-a-days to that mood or habit of mind which looks out upon mankind with cold and bitter feeling, which finds little or nothing to admire in human character and action, which systematically depreciates human motives, which rejoices to catch men tripping, which sneers where others reverence, and dissects where others admire, and is hard where others pity, and suspects where others praise. Distinguish between *cynicism* and *satire.* No doubt the cynic is often satirical ; satire is just the kind of weapon that comes ready to his hand But the same weapon may be wielded by very different hands, and in very different causes, and satire may often be employed by men who are anything but cynical. There is such a thing as genial satire—the light and even humorous play of irony or sarcasm around some venial fault, or some peculiar excrescence of character. Then there is also the satire of moral indignation, which applies the stinging lash to manifest vices, or pours the vials of scorn on some detestable meanness, in order to make the shameless ashamed, or to infuse a healthy contempt of vice into the souls of those who are still uncontaminated by it. The old Hebrew prophets knew how to wield this weapon, and even in the pages of the New Testament it finds its fitting place. In fact, all such satire as this—whether of the genial or the vehement type—is often used by men who are passionate admirers of human excellence, and who are not only warmly attached to individuals, but also earnest lovers of their race. Whereas it is the very characteristic of cynicism that it lacks earnestness. It knows nothing of a noble scorn. Its satire is neither genial nor vehement. Even its humour is always sardonic. Its very bitterness, although intense, is unimpassioned. It is a kind of acrid gelatine. The fully-developed cynic prides himself on his indifferentism. Remorselessly he dissects and analyzes human character and action ; for, like Iago, he 'is nothing, if not critical ;' but his criticism has no useful end in view ; he is not seeking to make others wiser or better. He is scarcely earnest enough even to care about his success in stinging and wounding ? It is simply his ' way ' to pick faults and to sneer We find the culmination of this cynicism in Goethe's ' Mephistopheles ; ' and indeed the word ' devil ' itself means 'accuser' —the slanderer of God and man."—*Finlayson.*

" Let us keep our scorn for our own weaknesses, our blame for our own sins, certain that we shall gain more instruction, though not amusement, by hunting out the good which is in anything than by hunting out the evil."— *Kingsley.*

"Sarcasm I now see to be, in general, the language of the devil, for which reason I have long since as good as renounced it."—*Carlyle.*

ANGER.

iv. 1. *Sanballat was wroth, and took great indignation.*

It is not a sin to be angry, but hard not to sin when we are angry. Anger is a tender virtue, and such as by reason of our unskilfulness may be easily corrupted and made dangerous. He that in his anger would not sin, must not be angry at anything but sin. Our Saviour was angry with Peter, and angry with the Pharisees for the hardness of their hearts (Matt. xvi. 23, Mark iii 5). Moses was even blown up with holy anger at the people for the golden calf. " Do not I hate them that hate thee ? I hate them with a perfect hatred," saith David ; " I count them mine enemies " (Ps cxxxix. 21) This is the anger of zeal, found in Phinehas, Elijah, Elisha, our Saviour, John ii. 17 ; and should have been found in Adam towards his wife, in Eli towards his sons, in Lot towards his servants (Gen. xiii. 7). It must have a good rise and a good end, saith Bucer, else it becomes a mortal, not a venial, sin, as the Papists fondly conclude from Matt. v. 22 : " Whosoever is angry with his brother without a cause," &c. There is a just cause then of anger, sin, as an offence to God. And there must be a just measure observed, that our anger for sin render us not unfit either to pity the sinner (as our Saviour in his anger did the obstinate Pharisees) or to pray for him (as Moses for those idolaters he was so enraged at—Exod. xxxii. 31, 32). Anger that is not thus bounded is but a "momentary madness," saith the heathen; it resteth in the bosom of fools, saith Solomon, whether it be anger, wrath, or hatred (for into those three degrees Damascen distinguisheth it). The one, saith he, hath beginning and motion, but presently ceaseth; the other taketh deep hold in the memory; the third desisteth not without revenge. Clichtoveus compareth the first to fire in stubble, the second to fire in iron, the third to fire that is hid and never bewrayeth itself, but with the ruin of the matter wherein it hath caught. Some are sharp, some are bitter, a third kind are implacable, saith Aristotle. The first are the best, that, as children, are soon angry and as soon pleased again. "Be ye children in malice" (1 Cor. xiv. 20). Of Beza, his colleagues would often say that, like the dove, he was without a gall. Giles of Brussels, martyr, when the friars (sent to reduce him) did any time miscall him, he ever held his peace, insomuch that those blasphemers would say abroad that he had a dumb devil in him. Cassianus reports that when a certain Christian was held captive of infidels, tormented with divers pains and ignominious taunts, being demanded by way of scorn and reproach, "Tell us what miracle thy Christ hath done?" he answered, "He hath done what you see, that I am not moved at all the cruelties and contumelies you cast upon me." Christ did "not strive, nor cry, nor did any man hear his voice in the streets," who, "when he was reviled, reviled not again, when he suffered, he threatened not; but committed himself to him that judgeth righteously" (Matt. xii. 19; 1 Pet. ii. 23). So did Moses when murmured against by Aaron and Miriam. He was meek, and complained

not. The less any man strives for himself, the more is God his champion. Anger is a short devil, saith Chrysostom; the fury of the unclean spirit. "Wrath killeth the foolish man" (Job v. 2), delivers him to the destroyer, if it rest in his bosom especially, and lodge a night with him, which is the second degree above mentioned.

"Let not therefore the sun go down upon your wrath;" for that is all one as to give place to the devil, who hereby entereth the heart and takes possession. Many there are that suffer the sun not only to go down upon their anger, but to run his whole race, yea, many races, ere they can be reconciled; whereby their anger becomes inveterate, and turns into malice, for anger and malice differ but in age. Now "cursed be this anger, for it is fierce; and this wrath, for it is cruel" (Gen. xlix. 7). It is the murder of the heart (Matt. v. 21 *seq*), the fountain of the murder both of the tongue and hand. Hence it is said, "He that hateth his brother is a man-slayer" (1 John iii. 15). He is so in desire, he would be so in deed if he durst. There is a passion of hatred and there is the habit of it. The former is a kind of averseness and rising of the heart against a man when one sees him, so that he cannot away with him, nor speak to nor look courteously or peaceably upon him, but one's countenance falls when he sees him, and he even turns away, and by his good will would have nothing to do with him: this is the passion of hatred. The habit of it is when the heart is so settled in this alienation and estrangement that it grows to wish and desire and seek his hurt. This is that third and worst sort of anger. Are we mortal, and shall our anger be immortal? To be revenged is more honourable than to be reconciled, saith Aristotle. This is the voice of nature. Thus "the spirit that is in us lusteth to envy." But God giveth more grace. 1. *Cease therefore from anger and refrain strife.* "Fret not thyself in any wise to do evil" (Ps. xxxvii. 8). When thou findest thyself incensed and chafing ripe, presently lay a necessity of silence upon thyself; as Ahasuerus walked a while in his garden ere he would pass sentence upon Haman. Another repeated the Greek alphabet ere he would say or do anything in his anger. He doth better that repeateth some grave sentences of Scripture, such as these: "Be angry, but sin not; be slow to wrath, avenge not yourselves, but give place to wrath; submit to God; resist the devil, and he will fly from you." This devil of anger, if thus resisted by Scripture, will surely fly; he cannot bide by it; especially if we set ourselves to pray it down 2. *Get thy heart purified by faith, for faith makes patience.* When the disciples heard that they must forgive till seventy times seven times in a day, they prayed, "Lord, increase our faith" (Luke xvii. 5). The wisdom from above is first pure, then peaceable (James iii. 17). Unrepentant David was cruel to the Ammonites. The devils

are most impure, and therefore most malicious; Christ, on the other side, most pure, and therefore most gentle. 3. *Study to be quiet and do your own business.* Seldom is a patient man inquisitive, or an inquisitive man patient. It doth require much study to live quietly. 4. *Consider the deformity, disgrace, and danger of anger.* Plato and Seneca have advised the angry man to look at his face in a glass. Anger hurteth not great minds. 5. *Consider wisely of God's providence, presence, patience.* Set God before thy passions, and they will be soon hushed 6. *Add a constant endeavour to be lowly.* Keep the strict watch of the Lord over your heart; pray down your passions. Your labour will not be in vain.

(*From Trapp's 'Marrow of many good Authors.'*)

THE DAY OF SMALL THINGS.

iv. 2.   *What do these feeble Jews?*

Two great events in the history of the returned captives from Babylon: building the second temple; rebuilding and fortifying the city. Subject—*That God produces great events by comparatively feeble means.*

I. As it relates to the objects of personal religion. "What do these feeble Jews?" Zechariah said, Who hath despised the day of small things? (iv. 10). We may ask, *Who has not?* All do. It is quite to the taste of human nature in its search after that which is great to overlook that which is small. The captives did so as well as their heathen persecutors; they wept when they saw the foundation (Ezra iii. 12). Zerubbabel and Zechariah probably did too. "Not by might!" (Zech. iv. 6). Good men do, both in judging of their own religion and that of other people. It is possible to err on the side of despondency as well as on that of presumption. We dishonour God as much by denying the grace we have as by boasting of the grace we have not. We ought not to despise it because *it is day.* (*a*) A day which God originates; (*β*) the day of Christ's power; (*γ*) a day

which must advance to its perfection, and shall never know a night. Though man despises it, God does not. He sees the flower in the bud, the pearl in the shell, the man in the infant, the heir of glory in the child of grace. He sees not only what they are, but what they shall be. Remember that God accomplishes his greatest designs by apparently slight and inconsiderable means. (*a*) In nature. (*b*) In providence. (*c*) In grace. The birth of an infant child in the manger at Bethlehem seemed a very ordinary occurrence, but it was an event on which the salvation of the world was made to turn. The cross of Christ is to them that perish foolishness; to the saved it is the power of God (1 Cor. i. 18). The rod of Moses; Gideon's lamps, pitchers, and trumpets; the rams' horns at Jericho; David's sling and stone, worked wonders. Pharaoh's dreams were made the means of Joseph's advancement. The ark, though small, saved the heirs of a shipwrecked world. Zoar, a little city, saved Lot from the shower of fire. The mantle of Elijah divided the waters of Jordan. The kingdom of heaven is like a grain of mustard seed (Matt xiii 31, 32). The stone which the builders rejected was made the head of the corner. This is the Lord's doing! (Matt. xxi 42)

II. That God accomplishes great events by small means encourages in all our efforts to promote the good of others 1. *To the preaching of the gospel at home and the diffusion of the gospel abroad* "We have this treasure in earthen vessels" (2 Cor iv. 7). We are often discouraged. The disproportion between the means and the end ; the slow progress of the renovating principle We would recognize the presence and advance of the kingdom of God. Where is the Lord God of

Elijah ? (2 Kings ii. 14) Where are the kings for nursing fathers ? (Isa xlix. 23). Where are the great masters of science and literature ? Where are the nations born in a day ? The confederacies of guilt are still powerful, and the enemies of the truth replete with confidence The answer to all this is, God's ways are not our ways. That we can clothe our exertions with a power not our own. Remember, the most weak and uninfluential may be made to effect great things, as Naaman's little maid. A mite cast into the treasury of God is not overlooked. It may produce ten talents 2. *The parent and Sunday school teacher.—Anonymous.*

PRAYING AND WORKING.

iv. 4—9 *Hear, O our God ; for we are despised, &c.*

The man-ward side of prayer
I. It narrows the conditions of the strife. Who are Sanballat and Tobiah ? Men of position, ranging under them Arabians, Ammonites, and Ashdodites— a crowd of warriors. Who is Nehemiah ? A chieftain of a handful of "feeble Jews." "Hear, O our God !" The cause is thine. "Let *thy work* appear unto thy servants, and thy glory unto their children Establish thou *the work of our hands* upon us" (Ps. xc. 16, 17). When, like "Moses the man of God," any man of God discovers that God's work and his work are one and the same thing, the aspect of affairs is changed. The contest is then spiritual. The forces arrayed are light and darkness, truth and error, God and the devil.

II. It inspires energy. "So built we the wall," &c. (ver. 6). "Nevertheless we made," &c. (ver 9). Nevertheless ! The foes were many, powerful, determined, bloodthirsty. Nevertheless God was approachable. Work was possible, pressing, needing earnest minds and willing hands.

III. It awakens faith. Prayer first, then work, in the assurance that the prayer will be answered and the work successful.

"Patience ! have faith, and thy prayer will be answered.
Look at this delicate plant that lifts its head from the meadow,
See how its leaves all point to the north as true as the magnet ;
It is the compass-flower, that the finger of God has suspended
Here on its fragile stalk, to direct the traveller's journey
Over the sea-like, pathless, limitless waste of the desert.
Such in the soul of man is faith "

Illustrations :—" '*Ora et labora*,' writes Dr. Wichern in one of his pleasant papers, 'is carved on a peasant's house in the Vierland. "It must be French," said a neighbour's wife, as I stood looking at the legend , "but you know it just means—

With this hand work, and with the other pray,
And God will bless them both from day to day." '

" *Ora et labora* is the legend of the Christian's faith, and the plan of his life His fervent prayer begets honest, manly, unshrinking work , his work, as it is faithful, and it is faithful in proportion as he realizes it is for God, throws him back upon prayer It is true that this connection is regarded with some suspicion. It is associated with the failure, and worse, of monastic life *Ora et labora* was the monkish watchword with which men went into the wilderness, and builded up their lonely cells, and toiled at their simple gardens, and knelt in solemn thought of the world behind them, through long fastings and wakeful nights But on their lips it was a profound mistake. They had cut themselves off from brotherly sympathies and social duties, from the entire sphere of

Christian work. They had thrown themselves upon the selfishness of lonely hours and solitary thoughts Their ora, earnest and well meant at first, became mechanical and unreal; their *labora* was a fiction. They had no right to their motto And remembering the hollowness and hypocrisy to which their system brought them, its utter worthlessness, its world-wide scandal, men have shrunk with fear from the truth they misused Nor are they alone guilty Those who by practice or speech arrogate to prayer the time and place of ordinary duties are in the same error Divorced from the common charities of life, prayer must become mechanical and untrue. If it be used to set some apart, on some sacred and haughty height above the rest and the ordinary obligations of society, if it only make them more rigid censors of others, while they themselves are less kindly, less helpful, less useful, who can wonder that the world revolts, or that the more thoughtful and reverent minds are carried to the other extreme, and boldly say that work is prayer? Work is no more prayer than prayer

is work, although the looseness of the expression is often forgiven for the deeper truth of the thought. Work is no more prayer than a walk in the fields is religious worship To the devout man both are devout, to the undevout man they are nothing Nay, work without prayer is as dangerous, ay, and more, than prayer without work. It is the practical ignoring of God, of a spiritual world and spiritual laws It is the start downwards to the grossest and most superstitious materialism It is a clear peril of our present time We do not want to be reminded of the need and dignity and sacredness of work, the whole century is preaching that, but we do want to be taught the need and sacredness of prayer, and that it is a force, of which though the world knows nothing, yet it establishes greater than the world's works"—*Stevenson*

"Prayer is a strong wall and fortress of the Church It is a godly Christian's weapon, which no man knows or finds but only he who has the spirit of grace and of prayer."—*Luther*.

IMPRECATIONS.

iv. 4, 5. *Hear, O our God; for we are despised, &c*

This prayer takes its tone, form, and expression from the imprecations in the Psalms — the "*Cursing Psalms*," as some have styled them Consider we then some specimens of such Psalms, that we may know where the difficulty lies, and in what way, if any, this difficulty may be solved.

I. The following are fair specimens :—

Ps v 10 "Destroy thou them, O God, let them fall by their own counsels, cast them out in the multitude of their transgressions, for they have rebelled against thee"

Ps. x. 15 "Break thou the arm of the wicked and the evil man seek out his wickedness till thou find none."

Ps. xxviii 4 "Give them according to their deeds, and according to the wickedness of their endeavours give them after the work of their hands, render to them their desert"

Ps. xl 14 "Let them be ashamed and confounded together that seek after my soul to destroy it, let them be driven backward and put to shame that wish me evil."

Ps lxviii 2 "As smoke is driven away, so drive them away as wax melteth before the fire, so let the wicked perish at the presence of God"

Ps lxxxiii 9—17. "Do unto them as unto the Midianites; as to Sisera, as to Jabin, at the brook of Kison which perished at Endor they became as dung for the earth Make their nobles like Oreb, and like Zeeb yea, all their princes as Zebah, and as Zalmunna O my God, make them like a wheel, as the stubble before the wind As the fire burneth a wood, and as the

flame setteth the mountains on fire, so persecute them with thy tempest and make them afraid with thy storm Fill their faces with shame, that they may seek thy name, O Lord. Let them be confounded and troubled for ever, yea, let them be put to shame, and perish."

Ps. cix 6—15 "Set thou a wicked man over him and let Satan stand at his right hand When he shall be judged, let him be condemned : and let his prayer become sin Let his days be few; and let another take his office Let his children be fatherless, and his wife a widow. Let his children be continually vagabonds, and beg; let them seek their bread also out of their desolate places Let the extortioner catch all that he hath; and let the strangers spoil his labour Let there be none to extend mercy unto him neither let there be any to favour his fatherless children. Let his posterity be cut off, and in the generation following let their name be blotted out Let the iniquity of his fathers be remembered with the Lord; and let not the sin of his mother be blotted out Let them be before the Lord continually, that he may cut off the memory of them from the earth"

Ps. cxxxvii. 7—9. "Remember, O Lord, the children of Edom in the day of Jerusalem, who said, Rase it, rase it, even to the foundation thereof. O daughter of Babylon, who art to be destroyed, happy shall he be, that rewardeth thee as thou hast served us Happy shall he be, that taketh and dasheth thy little ones against the stones"

These passages seem to breathe a vindictive spirit; they seem to be opposed to the spirit of the New Testament.

II In what way is the difficulty to be solved? 1. *Whatever difficulty there exists is created by the Bible itself.* It cannot be said that the writers indulged in feelings which they were unwilling to record. The Bible is thus a book of candour. There was some reason for making the record. 2 *It may be a fair subject of inquiry how much of what is charged as wrong, harsh, and vindictive belongs to the spirit of the age.* To know how much words express, we must understand the customs and habits of the times. The strong language used by a Covenanter or a Puritan may have expressed no other internal emotion than would be expressed by the milder language which we should use. 3. *Part of these passages may undoubtedly be regarded as prophetic : expressing what would be, rather than indicating any wish that such things should be.* Part— not all. 4 *Some of the expressions are a mere record of the feelings of others.* The inspired writer is only responsible for the fairness of the record; *e g.* cruelty of sons of Jacob (Gen xxxiv. 25—29 ; xlix. 6, 7), David (2 Sam xii. 31), Joab, Ahithophel, Ahab In Ps. cxxxvii. 8, 9 the pleasure which they would actually feel who should wreak vengeance on Babylon is described. 5. *Can such imprecations ever be right ?* (*a*) David was a magistrate, a king. As a magistrate, he represented the state, the majesty of the law, the interests of justice. (*b*) Punishment is right when properly inflicted. (*c*) Arrangements are made in every community for detecting and punishing crime. (*d*) A judge who prays that he may discharge his duty has no vindictive feeling. 6. *There is another solution of the difficulty. These expressions are a mere record of what actually occurred in the mind of the Psalmist, and are preserved to us as an illustration of human nature when partially sanctified.* If such is a just view of the matter, then all that inspiration is responsible for is the correctness of the record ; the authors of the Psalms actually recorded what was passing in their own minds. They gave vent to their internal emotions. They state feelings which men have actually had. They do not apologize for it ; they do not pause to vindicate it ; they offer no word in extenuation of it, any more than other sacred writers did when they recorded the facts about the errors in the lives of the patriarchs, of David, and of Peter. In some of these ways it is probable that all the difficulties with regard to " imprecations " in the Bible may be met. Those who deny the inspiration of the records that contain them should be able to show that these are *not* proper explanations of the difficulty ; or that they are *not* consistent with any just notions of inspiration —*Barnes, abridged.*

THE CRAFT AND CRUELTY OF THE CHURCH'S ADVERSARIES.

iv. 11. *And our adversaries said, They shall not know, neither see, till we come in the midst among them, and slay them, and cause the work to cease.*

Chapter gives view of Nehemiah's discouragements Like waves of the sea breaking upon him, he an unshaken rock. Like Job's messengers, one hardly gone before another comes Like Ezekiel's prophecy, mischief upon mischief.

First verse adversaries' rage. Second verse : venting itself in foam. But this is cool : it reaches blood-heat (vers. 7, 8).

I. **A strong combination against the Church of God.** " *Adversaries.* "

II **A wicked design they were** combined in " *To cause the work to cease.* "

III. **A bloody means propounded.** " *Slay them* "

IV. **A subtle way projected for the effecting of this** " *Secretly, suddenly.* "

Sum of the whole. The great design of the enemies of the Church is by craft or cruelty, or both, to hinder any work that tends to the establishment or promoting of the Church's good.—*Matthew Newcomen, 1642.*

SATANIC SUBTLETY.

iv. 11. *And our adversaries said, They shall not know, neither see, till we come in
the midst among them, and slay them, and cause the work to cease.*

The malice of Satan by his members
is so great against the building of God's
city, that by all means, inward enemies
and outward, fair words and foul, sword,
fire and faggot, war and peace, in teaching or holding their tongue, knowledge
or ignorance, undermining or conspir-
acies, and all other devices whatsoever,
they let none slip, but try all, that they
may overthrow all, and not so much to
do themselves good as to hinder others ;
to set up themselves in the sight of the
world, and to deface the glory of God ,
but in the end all is in vain, and our
God shall have the victory. They will
not yet use any open violence, but
cunningly come on them unawares.

1. *In this serpentine, crafty, and
malicious dealing of these wicked men
appeareth the old serpentine nature and
malice of Satan,* that old enemy of
God and man from the beginning. God
said to the serpent that the seed of the
woman should tread upon his head, and
the serpent should tread upon his heel
(Gen. iii). Crafty and subtle men,
when they will work a mischief, go
privily about it, to deceive the good
man. God endued man, when he made
him, with such a majesty in his face,
afore he fell to sin, that all creatures did
reverence and fear him ; and although
sin hath much defaced and blotted out
that noble majesty and grace that God
endued him with, yet it is not utterly
disgraced and taken away, but some
spark and relic remaineth at this day,
that no wild nor venomous beast dare
look a man in the face boldly and hurt
him, but will give place for the time,
and seek how he may privily wound or
hurt him when he seeth him not. These
crafty and subtle foxes, therefore, like
the seed of the serpent, would not openly
invade nor gather any great power of
men against them, but at unawares steal
on them privily, afore they should sus-

pect any such thing. This is the nature
of wicked men, so craftily to undermine
the godly.

2. *The next property of the serpent
that appeareth in these wicked men is,
that they mercilessly would murder
them* when they had once thus suddenly
invaded them Satan was " a murderer
from the beginning," as St. John saith ;
and therefore no marvel if his children
be bloodsuckers, like unto the father.
When he would not spare the innocent
Lamb of God, Jesus Christ, but most
cruelly crucified him, why should we
marvel to see him by his wicked children so greedily seek to shed innocent
blood still ?

3. *The last property of Satan appeareth
here most plainly in these wicked men, in
that they would so gladly overthrow this
building of Jerusalem, that it should
never be thought on any more.* Satan is
" the prince of this world," and therefore cannot abide another king to reign,
nor any kingdom to be set up but his
own ; and for maintaining of that he
will strive by his members unto death.
And as it falleth out thus generally in
the building of God's spiritual house
and city that all sorts of enemies most
diligently apply themselves, their labour,
wit, power, policy, and friendship to
overthrow the true worship of God, so
particularly " Satan goeth about like a
roaring lion, seeking whom he may
devour," and therefore every man hath
great need to be wary and circumspect,
that he be not suddenly overthrown, but
let him watch and put on " the whole
armour of God " (Ephes. vi. 13—18),
that he may stand stoutly in the day of
battle, and through the might of his
God get the victory. The devil never
ceaseth, for if he cannot overthrow the
whole Church, yet he would be glad to
catch any one that belongeth to the
Lord if he could.—*Bishop Pilkington.*

A Pause in the Work.

iv. 15. *We returned all of us to the wall, every one unto his work.*

A dangerous pause. Judah had become faint-hearted (ver. 10). The opponents were gaining strength (ver. 11). Terror had taken hold upon the neighbouring Jews (ver. 12). An armed outlook was necessary (ver. 13). Nehemiah encouraged the workers to wait the issue (ver. 14). The enemy noted the attitude and saw that God had brought their counsel to nought (ver. 15). The pause was over. Once again to the work. There is the truth of life in this parable.

I. A period of preparation is essential to successful work. Lightly begun means easily discontinued. Count the cost (Luke xiv. 28—33). Raw haste is sister to undue delay. Find thy task, calculate thy strength, and rest not until the evening. Impetuous natures need patience and perseverance; fearful and timid natures need courage and self-reliance; all need encouragement. Moses —"Who am I, that I should go unto Pharaoh?" (Exod iii. 11—22). Joshua —"Be strong" (Josh. i. 1—9). Jeremiah —"I am a child" (Jer. i. 4—10). Ezekiel — "Be not afraid of them" (Ezek. ii. 3—8). Nehemiah's workmen — "Be not ye afraid" (iv. 13, 14).

II. Joyous acceptance of the allotted task is a great element of strength. Duty as duty, or duty joyously done, how different! Love thy task. Do it for its own sake, and it will become easier. Such service is perfect freedom. Men see what most interests them. An artist on entering a room sees pictures; a student books; an architect decorations.

" The wide world
Is full of work, and everything therein
Finds in it its best blessedness The bee
Sings at his task throughout the summer day."

III. Earnest work is sure to provoke opposition. Ridicule (ver. 1), compromise (vi. 2), misrepresentation (vi. 7), attack (iv. 8).

IV. Work is instrumental in developing personal character. What canst thou do? Nehemiah proved his men by trial.

V. Fluctuation in the success of an undertaking is no reason for relinquishing it (vers. 10—15).

George Stephenson's motto was "PERSEVERE." "Go on, sir, go on," was D'Alembert's advice to a young discouraged student. John Wesley, interrogated as to the remarkable success of his followers, said, "They are all at it, and always at it."

VI. The power of combined action in meeting a common foe (vers. 13, 23). Nelson the day before Trafalgar took two officers who were at variance to the spot where they could see the fleet opposed to them. "Yonder," he said, "are your enemies; shake hands and be friends, like good Englishmen."

" Oh! ye the ministers of Christ, and stewards
    of his truth,
Lead ye the band, all vigorous in faith's immortal youth
    But not alone shall ye repair,
    For all must aid in toil and prayer.
Then let them say the work is nought, to scoff
    us into fear.
What is the answer we must make? Calmly
    the walls to rear;
Building with weapons girded on;
Warriors until the work is done."
    Enlarged from ' Scenes from the Life of Nehemiah.'

The Work and Warfare of Life.

iv. 17, 18. *They which builded on the wall, and they that bare burdens, with those that laded, every one, &c.*

Nehemiah iv. one of the Bible scenes that has indelibly impressed itself upon the popular imagination. Like the "lamps, pitchers, and trumpets" of Gideon's army, the "sword and trowel" of Nehemiah's army has passed into a proverb. Only scenes, books, pictures, sculptures become popular that present the elementary conditions of human life, that go down to the rock on which the structure of human society rests, *e. g.* the parables of Jesus, Bunyan's 'Pilgrim's Progress,' Nehemiah iv. a picture of the work and warfare of life.

I. The conditions of the conflict. 1. *Against the solicitations of self-indulgence.* "The people had a mind to work" (ver. 6). Not always so. The spirit is *not always* willing. And when the spirit is willing the flesh is often weak. True (*a*) of the cultivation of personal character. To conquer pride, subdue passion, root out evil dispositions, to "grow in grace," not an easy thing. In this sense "flesh and blood cannot inherit the kingdom of God." A Christian does not always "sail with a straight course," as did Paul on his first voyage to Europe (Acts xvi. 11). Oftener, like the same apostle on a later voyage, he "sails slowly" (Acts xxvii. 7), or the "ship sticks fast and remains unmoveable" (Acts xxvii. 41). Speak to the children of Israel that they go forward, is God's message to the inspired leaders of every age. What doest thou here? is his question to every dispirited and inactive Elijah. Jonah may sit for awhile under the shadow of the gourd, but when the morning calls him to his work and to his labour the gourd perishes. True (*b*) of working for one's fellows. Social and philanthropic work. How little response of gratitude from those to whom you give, from those whom you toil to raise. Religious teaching and influence. Manifold are difficulties and discouragements. Unless work be its own reward, who shall continue? No motive lower than the stars, no inspiration less stable than trust in God, will enable a man to war against the lust of self-indulgence. **2.** *Against foes.* (*a*) Foes may be violent and pronounced as Sanballat (ver. 1). With such as these a man can count. Rouse a lion, and the consequences are clear. The arch foe and many of his emissaries are not unwilling to show a bold front to a servant of God. Specially if it can be said of him—

> "Servant of God, well done!
> Well done! thy words are great and bold;
> At times they seem to me
> Like Luther's in the days of old,
> Half battles for the free!'"

Words for freedom, for brotherhood, against oppressors, against shams, must count the cost. Reformers, Covenanters, Puritans "resisted unto blood, striving against sin" (Heb. xii. 4). (*b*) Foes may be subtle and plot in secret (ver. 11). Against these we are comparatively defenceless. It is dastardly to stab in the dark. But the assassin is dastardly. Guilt makes cowards. (*c*) Foes have the advantage of numbers and possession (ver. 7). They were on the ground. Nehemiah and his compatriots' loss was their gain. "They conspired all of them together," &c. (ver. 8). The good have always been a minority. The great have too often been on the side of the majority. "Not many wise, not many mighty," &c. (1 Cor. i. 26—29). "We wrestle not against flesh and blood" only, "but against principalities," &c. (Ephes. vi. 12, 13). **3.** *Against friends.* (*a*) Half-hearted friends (ver. 12). They had patriotism enough to warn Nehemiah of danger. But they dwelt near the adversaries. A decided foe better than a doubtful friend. Gideon's 300, who had not time to kneel to drink, better than countless crowds of self-indulgent people (Judges vii.). "Art thou for us?" said Joshua to the angel-captain (Josh. v.). For or against is understood. But half-heartedness never won a battle, never gained a victory. (*b*) Dispirited friends (ver. 10). The wall was built somewhat, but they feared their strength would give out. Fear and faith are antagonists. Trust in thy cause, trust in the God of thy cause, cures for dispiritedness.

> "I know not what the future hath
>   Of marvel or surprise,
> Assured alone that life and death
>   His mercy underlies.
> And if my heart and flesh are weak
>   To bear an untried pain,
> The bruised reed he will not break,
>   But strengthen and sustain."

II. The conditions of victory. 1. *All at it* (ver. 13). Every man at work. Every man at his own work. Every man under discipline—under the rulers (ver. 14), under Nehemiah (vers 18—20). Generalize these particulars Nobody can do my work My task is my own. No man can lift responsibility off his own shoulders. There is a cry to every man from some helpless man, or mass of men, "Come over and help us" The unnamed disciple of John xx. did outrun Peter, and came first to the sepulchre; but Peter first went into the sepulchre. Had he more courage or less reverence? Never mind—each left the other scope to work. St. John has left a greater name than his brother James But James died for the truth In this holy war men call life the feeble cannot be dispensed with Nehemiah conferred with the nobles (ver. 14). Nehemiah needed the bearers of burdens (ver 17) 2 *Unslumbering vigilance.* We "set a watch" (ver 9). "I set the people," &c (ver 13). "And it came to pass," &c (ver 16). There is a lesson of life in the heading of this chapter in our Bibles—"Nehemiah prayeth and continueth the work." Patient waiting is a grace; perseverance is a virtue Men are sometimes enervated by success They become unwatchful. "Doctor," said his wife to Martin Luther one day, "how is it that, whilst subject to papacy, we prayed so often and with such fervour, whilst now we pray with the utmost coldness and very seldom?" "Every one with one hand held a weapon" (ver. 17) "He that sounded the trumpet was by me" (ver. 18) "In what place ye hear the sound of the trumpet, resort ye thither unto us" (ver. 20). These are only the dictates of worldly prudence. So true is it that "the children of this world are in their generation wiser than the children of light" (Luke xvi. 8). What said the greatest Christian Teacher? "The Son of man is as a man taking a far journey, who left his house, and gave to every man his work, and commanded the porter to watch. Watch ye therefore. What I say unto you, I say unto all, Watch" (Mark xiii. 34, 35, 37).

Illustration —"That man is happy who can combine work and watching in perfect harmony —who has Stephen's life of labour and Stephen's vision in the end. In every soul there should be the sisters of Bethany, active effort and quiet thought, and both agreeing in mutual love and help But Mary no longer sits at the feet of Christ and looks in his face, she stands at the door and gazes out into the open sky to watch the tokens of his coming, while in this hope her sister in the house still works In due time he will be here to crown every humble effort with overflowing grace, to satisfy the longing soul that looks for him, and to raise all the dead for whom we weep."—*Dr Ker.*

3 *Resort to the unseen Refuge.* "Hear, O our God" (ver. 4). "Be not ye afraid remember the Lord" (ver 14) "Our enemies heard that God had brought their counsel to nought" (ver 15). "Our God shall fight for us" (ver 20) Our God—the attestation of experience. "He shall deliver thee in six troubles yea, in seven there shall no evil touch thee" (Job v. 19). The Apostle Paul appealed from Festus unto Cæsar Nehemiah appealed from Sanballat to God. In the miracle of feeding our Lord turned an inward look upon the troubled, calculating thoughts of his disciples, though "he himself knew what he would do." He turned an outward look upon the hungry, trustful crowd : "Make the men sit down." He directed an upward look to God : "When he had taken the five loaves and the two fishes he looked up to heaven" The inward look revealed distrust; the outward look revealed need; the upward look revealed strength and supply A parable of life. Look abroad — the work is great; look within—calculate resources; look up—"Thy God hath commanded thy strength." "Not unto us, O Lord, not unto us, but unto thy name give glory, for thy mercy, and for thy truth's sake. The Lord hath been mindful of us : he will bless us. He will bless them that fear the Lord, both small and great We will bless the Lord from this time forth and for evermore. Praise the Lord" (Ps. cxv.).

ADDENDA TO CHAPTER IV.

SENTENCES FROM OLD WRITERS.

Sanballat's opposition (vers. 1, 2). "The devil and his servants have ever been utter enemies to reformation. Jabesh-gilead would send in none to help the Lord against the mighty (Judges xxi. 9), no more would Meroz (Judges v 23). Josiah met with much opposition; so did St. Paul wherever he came to set up evangelical and spiritual worship, which is called a reformation (Heb. ix. 10). All the world was against Athanasius in his generation, and Luther in his; rejecting what they attempted with scorn and slander. Nehemiah and his Jews were not more busy in building than the enemies active in deriding, conspiring, practising to hinder and overthrow them." "If thou hast not the favour of men, be not grieved at it; but take this to heart, that thou dost not behave thyself so warily and circumspectly as it becometh the servant of God and a devout, religious man." "Why art thou troubled when things succeed not as thou wouldest or desirest? For who is he that hath all things according to his mind?"

Tobiah's scorn (ver. 3). "Say not, 'Should I suffer these things from so contemptible a fellow as this?' Yes, truly; in consideration of that patient and meek spirit which was in Christ No man will ever be reconciled by wrath or revenge. Victory consists in virtue, not in vice." "One devil does not drive out another." "We chiefly seek God for our inward witness, when outwardly we be contemned by men, and when there is no credit given unto us." "Thou canst not have two paradises." "Christ was willing to suffer and be despised; and darest thou complain of any man?" "Let thy thought be on the Highest." "Whom God will keep no man's perverseness shall be able to hurt." "Have a good conscience, and God will well defend thee."

Nehemiah's prayers (vers. 4, 5, 9). "Nehemiah hateth not the men, but their wickedness; so we learn to put a difference betwixt the man and the sin of man, and pray for mercy to the one and justice to the other. Man is God's good creature, and to be beloved of all sorts; sin is of the devil, and to be fled of all sorts." "His prayer is not long, but full." "Faithful prayer is never ineffectual. So built we the wall. This followed upon Nehemiah's prayer as a gracious answer to it; the people were encouraged, and the wall finished." "Beware of hating the person whilst thou abhorrest his sin." "Prayer is the key of heaven; the pillar of the world; the fire of devotion; the light of knowledge; the repository of wisdom; the strength of the soul; the remedy against faint-heartedness; the forerunner of honour; the nurse of patience; the guardian of obedience; the fountain of quietness; the comfort of the sorrowful; the triumph of the just; the helper of the oppressed; the refreshment of this life; the sweetening of death; and the foretaste of the heavenly life." "God *prevents* our prayers, meets us (as it were) half-way, and courts our friendship, being a thousand times more ready to give than we are to receive."

Nehemiah's watchfulness (ver. 9). "It is not sufficient to pray and then to neglect such means as God hath appointed us to use for our defence and comfort, no more than it is to say, when he hath prayed, I will live without meat and drink, and God himself shall feed me. For as the Lord hath taught us to pray, 'Give us this day our daily bread,' so he hath commanded us to work for it, and saith, 'If any will not work, neither shall he eat.'" "Sin opens the door to the devil." "Awaken us, O God, that we may watch, draw us to thee, and we will run the straight way, through Jesus Christ our Lord."

Judah's defection (ver. 10) "It is an easy matter to begin a good work, but a special gift to stand in all storms and continue to the end." "Judah's escutcheon was a lion, but here he is unlike himself." " Nehemiah might well have said to these men of Judah, as Alexander once did to a faint-hearted soldier of his that was of his own name, ' Either leave off the name of Alexander, or be valiant.' So either hold out and bear up under your burdens, or be Judah no more. Never was anything too hard for Alexander, because he never had anything impossible to be effected."

Nehemiah's policy and appeal (vers. 11—14). " Their brethren from abroad gave the workmen intelligence ; and this was a friendly office, for premonition is the best means of prevention." " It was their duty to have come home, stood in storms, and help to build Jerusalem. But God, which turneth our negligence and foolishness to the setting forth of his wisdom and goodness, gave them a good will and boldness to further that building as they might." " Away with that cowardly passion which unmans a

man. Remember the Lord, whom he that feareth needs fear none else." " God and the world cannot be friends ; and that maketh so few courtiers to tread this road."

Soldier - builders (vers. 15 — 23). " Courage and strength without wisdom is foolish rashness, and wisdom without courage and strength is fearful cowardliness." " Nehemiah was an active man, trading every talent." " In the Christian's panoply there is no mention of armour for the back, though there is for the breast, because a Christian soldier should never fly." " In God's cause a man must be bold and blush not." " Fear of the enemy did not weaken them, but waken them." " Time was precious, and they redeemed and improved it. The common complaint is, We want time ; but the truth is, we do not so much want as waste it " " Nehemiah said not to his men, Go YE, but, Go WE."

CHAPTER V.

EXPLANATORY NOTES] **1. Against their brethren]** *i e* the richer portion (ver. 7). **2—4. There were that said**] Keil divides into three classes. (*a*) The workers, who had no property. (*b*) Those who had mortgaged their fields, vineyards, and houses. (*c*) Those who had borrowed money for the king's tribute upon their fields and vineyards. **2. We take up corn**] Not by force. The words mean, We desire that corn may be provided. **3. Because of the dearth**] Probably Sanballat and his army intercepted the supplies. **4. For the king's tribute**] We have made our fields and our vineyards answerable for money for the king's tribute (Bertheau), *i. e* We have borrowed money upon our fields for tribute. This they could only do by pledging the crops (comp. the law, Lev. xxv. 14, 17). **5. "Our brethren"**] The richer Jews. The sense of the first half of the verse is, We are of one flesh and blood with these rich men. The law not only allowed to lend to the poor on a pledge (Deut. xv. 8), but also permitted Israelites, if they were poor, to sell themselves (Lev. xxv. 39), and also their sons and daughters, to procure money. It required, however, that they who were thus sold should not be retained as slaves, but set at liberty without ransom, either after seven years or at the year of Jubilee (Lev. xxv. 39—41, Exod. xxi. 2 *seq*). It is set forth as a special hardship in this verse that some of their daughters were brought into bondage for maidservants.—*Keil.* **Neither is it in our power**] Lit. *Our hand is not to God* (Gen. xxxi. 29). Keil explains thus : The power to alter it is not in our hand. Our fields and our vineyards are in the hands of others. **7. I consulted with myself**] My heart took counsel upon it. **Ye exact usury**] Usury and injustice are closely allied. **8. We redeemed. Ye sell**] Strong contrast. The sale of their brethren for bondservants forbidden (Lev xxv 42). **11 Hundredth part**] Probably a monthly interest. **12 I called the priests**] To witness the oath. **13. I shook my lap**] A symbolical action. " The lap of the garment, in which things are carried (Isa. xlix. 22), where alone the word is again found."—*Keil* See for this significant action Acts xviii. 6. **14.**] Crosby says this verse and those which follow form an interruption of the narrative. They show that Nehemiah was for twelve years governor of Judah, and did not write this history till the expiration of that time. **The bread of the governor**] The food and wine with which the community had to furnish him. **15. Even their servants bare rule**] Arbitrary, oppressive rule. Abuse of power for extortions. **17. The rulers**] The heads of the different houses of Judah. **19. Think upon me**] (Comp. xiii. 14 and 31).

HOMILETICAL CONTENTS OF CHAPTER V.

GREED CORRECTED.

Chap. v.

THE chapter is complete in itself. It is not only a story, but a parable of everlasting suggestiveness. In the history of every generation we find some situation similar to the one recorded here. The great humanness of the Bible is not less striking than its divinity. *God's book* is sublimely crowded with pathetic interest in *man's life.* Here is a picture of the desolations of greed and their correction.

I. The desolations of greed. The cry of the people in the first verse is a note in the " still, sad music of humanity " which has rung out in every age. The cry of the people in the days of *Norman tyranny ;* the wail of nations in the priest-ridden *dark ages ,* the lamentations of the *negro race* in the slaveries of the last century ; the shriek of the despised people prior to the bloody struggle of the *French Revolution ,* the clamour of the English poor in the days of *the Corn Laws,*—are all re-echoes of this old cry. " So I returned, and considered all the oppressions that are done under the sun : and behold, the tears of such as were oppressed, and they had no comforter ; and on the side of their oppressors there was power; but they had no comforter " (Eccles. iv. 1). Such was the melancholy view which made Solomon praise the *dead,* whose eyes were shut upon the scene, and the *unborn,* who had the chance of coming to look upon a better spectacle. In this fifth chapter of Nehemiah we have the whole of the dark parable of poverty and oppression— *hunger, debt, mortgage, serfdom.* Jesus Christ redeemed poverty by himself becoming poor ; not to show that poverty is a good, but to show that the highest moral conditions of man's soul may co-exist with these hard conditions. He, Jesus of Nazareth, was (temporally speaking) a vassal of Rome, and had not where to lay his head. This story of the earthly sojourn of the mighty God is a golden ray which gilds the deep valley of humiliation, where millions walk all through their threescore years and ten ; but woe to those who help to deepen the gloom of that dreary place by their own narrow and damnable selfishness. " I was angry," says Nehemiah, " when I heard their cry " (ver. 6) ; and *he did well to be angry.* 1. WANT. *Bread! bread! bread! what a cry is that to be the chief cry of immortal creatures.* Yet such is and will yet be the wail of the hungry. " God deliver us," says Isaac Walton, " from pinching poverty." " Feed me with food convenient for me," meekly said the good man in olden days. By *industry* and *frugality* let us offer this prayer. 2. DEGRADATION *is the result of this want.* Great are thy temptations, O Poverty. What will not the poor man in the wilderness, with hunger in his body and the devil beside him, do to make stones into bread ? How can a man be a man while he is kept in slavery to his pinching need ? Again let the woe, woe, woe go forth upon those whose selfish greed breaks the staff of bread for the people. 3. HOPELESSNESS. Here is a picture from one of Thomas Carlyle's graphic books. "Passing by the workhouse of St. Ives in Huntingdonshire, on a bright day last autumn" (about 1840), "I saw sitting on wooden benches, in front of their Bastille, and within their ring-wall and its railings, some half hundred or more of these men. Tall, robust figures; young mostly, or of middle age; of honest countenance; many of them thoughtful and even intelligent-looking men. They sat there, near by one another; but in a kind of torpor, especially in a silence, which was very striking. In silence; for, alas, what word was to be said? An earth all lying round, crying, Come and till me, come and reap me;—yet we here sit enchanted! In the eyes and brows of these men hung the gloomiest expression, not of anger, but of grief, and shame, and manifold, inarticulate distress, and weariness. They returned my glance with a glance that seemed to say, 'Do not look at us. We sit enchanted here; we know not why.' There was something that reminded me of Dante's hell in the look of all this, and I rode swiftly away." What a dark outlook utter want has! what a dreary nightmare to lie on a human spirit! In the poor wretches whose condition stirred Nehemiah's anger with their want and their hopeless debt and their heart-breaking family separations, *as son and daughter went in pawn for bread*, there is a scene to smite the buried conscience of the grinding oppressor, and to call forth some natural tears from the eyes of onlooking philanthropists. "Man's inhumanity to man makes countless thousands mourn."

II. The corrections of philanthropy. Like a Howard moved with pity and shame for the *prisoner* as if he had been his own mother's son, or a Wilberforce making his vow to break the iron chain of the *negro*, Nehemiah rose up to mend the evil. It was a monster that would have frightened back to Persia a less dauntless man, *but fear and discouragement were his playmates.* Nehemiah proceeded to correct this evil by his *exhortation* and by his *example.* 1. *Exhortation.* He rebuked the greed of gain. In vers. 6 — 8 we have the grand outpouring of his aroused sympathies. "Then they held their peace, and found nothing to answer." Read from verse 12 to 13. Knowing how subtle is the devil of greed, Nehemiah called the priests to a religious solemnity, that the promise of the repentant oppressors might as it were *be written down in the great doom-book of God*, so that each man might go back to his money-bags with his own Amen! with the curse on greed ringing in his ears. *Here is an example.* What is good to be done should be done in the solemn name of God. Strike the iron of a good resolution while it is hot. *Second thoughts are selfish thoughts in all Divine things.* Bind the soul *while it is willing* fast to God's altar. Pledges, vows, oaths; let those mock these who will. Our evil nature is a Samson, who snaps cords like tow; nay, a demoniac whom no man can bind, no, not with chains. If the obligations of a solemn pledge to God can do it, let it be done. "I called the priests, and *took an oath of them*, that they should do according to this promise." You who are meditating surrender to Christ, or reformation from drunkenness, or abandonment of some evil thing or associate, *go and do likewise.* 2. *Example.* Grand as was Nehemiah's exhortation, his example is still grander. He enforced his sermon by *living it out before his congregation.* The perquisites of his office he abandoned for the sake of example (ver. 15); what he might have regarded as a right he surrendered in order to be himself a type of unselfishness. His chances of gain were many. He knew what his plans were, and could have invested well in the new city, but, says he, "Neither bought we any land," *a suggestion to public persons whose office gives them the chances of gain.* "I took no advantage of my opportunites." Besides his servants, he maintained himself. The men he had brought to do the noble work of renovation were men who had claim to reward; and what was needful Nehemiah gave them out of his own private means. He wanted to build Jerusalem as Michael Angelo said he would build St. Peter's—"for the glory of God."

Application. 1. *Have an ear for the cry of the poor and oppressed.* Keep a heart alive for such as be prostrate.   2. *Emulate Nehemiah's self-sacrifice.*   Do not say, " He was a hero."   His character made him a hero   His sublime fear of God and pity for man did not flow from his heroism so much as make it   He was but a cupbearer to the king, and had a snug birth and a good stipend and great expectations, but these were chaff when compared with an opportunity of making a good mark in his generation, and of writing his name in the book of life.   " By faith he obtained a good report ! "

Illustrations ·—" Every grain of riches hath a vermin of pride and ambition in it." " Oppression is a bony sin" (Amos v. 12, 13).   " As God hath enlarged any man in his outward estate, he must be answerably enlarged in works of mercy."   " It is one thing to be rich in this world, and another thing to be rich towards God, as our Saviour phraseth it ; to be rich in knowledge, as St. Paul hath it , rich in faith, as St James "   " Highmindedness, causing men to think great things of themselves, and to seek great things for themselves, is a blab that the devil will easily blow up in rich misers, to think themselves simply the better men because richer than others, which is all one as if the silly ant, the higher she gets upon her hillock, the greater she should conceit herself " —*Trapp*   " Poverty," it has been said, " has many wants ; but avarice is in want of everything."

> " The sense to value riches, with the art
> T'enjoy them, and the virtue to impart,
> Not meanly nor ambitiously pursued,
> Not sunk by sloth, nor raised by servitude ;
> To balance fortune by a just expense,
> Join with economy, magnificence ;
> With splendour, charity ; with plenty, health ;
> O teach us."—*Alexander Pope.*

GODLESS RICH MEN.

Chap. v.

This is not the only page of the Bible on which the sins of covetousness, oppression, and luxury are linked together and denounced.   Isaiah represents the Lord of Hosts looking for judgment, but behold oppression; for righteousness, but behold a cry , and then hurls a Divine woe against those that join house to house, that lay field to field, till there be no place, that they may be placed alone in the midst of the earth ; that rise up early in the morning that they may follow strong drink, &c. (Isa. v. 7—12).   Amos speaks of those who cause the seat of violence to come near, that lie upon beds of ivory (Amos vi. 3, 4).   Micah utters a woe against those who covet fields and houses, and take them by violence (Micah ii. 2).   *Even Christ takes up his parable* against those who devour widows' houses (Matt. xxiii. 14)   The apostles follow his example.   But they remind us that other gifts may be misused—power, beauty, any gift of God

I. **The value of wealth.**   The word of God does not despise wealth.   The references to riches and rich men are no fewer than one hundred and seventy— descriptive, regulative, corrective.   1. *Riches are God's gift.*   Not invariably.   He has not ordained that right and riches should be inseparable, or that wrong and want should be invariably cause and effect.   Still it is true that " the Lord maketh poor and maketh rich "   " Riches and honours come of him."   " The earth is full of his riches."   The virtuous he " maketh fat and flourishing."   He has not made poverty *the outward and visible sign* of his displeasure, nor wealth of his favour.   Had he done so the Church would have been sectional.   Large numbers would have been shut out by circumstances.   It would have been in antagonism to human weal. There is a working force and a conserving force.   2. *Wealth is man's glory.*   With it he can surround himself with all that is ennobling in science and art, the conveniences of life.   With it he can rule men.   It elevates.   Prosperous families and prosperous nations become refined.

II. **The responsibility of wealth.**   We take this responsibility to be personal and relative. 1. *A man owes a duty to himself.* The first contrast here is between getting and covetous hoarding. The Bible preaches no Crusade against getting. It does not say, "Take no care for the morrow." It does say, "Take not anxious, boding thought." Christianity is a system of prudence. It imposes restraint because license leads to ruin. It gives a premium to diligence. Idleness is treated with scorn by the inspired writers. The sun shines on no fairer prospect than a *diligent* person; whatever his station, whatever his aim, the first condition of success is toil, the second is toil, the third is toil. But the crucial test is, "Are we getting to live?" or, "Are we living to get?" Do we lay up or lay out? At every step in our inquiry we are upon the horns of a dilemma. The breakers are on every side. The vessel needs careful piloting. Laying up is not wrong, and nature as well as revelation teaches that he that does not provide for his own house is worse than an infidel. "Naked came we into this world, and naked shall we return thither;" but we do not read that *we must leave those naked whom we leave behind.* For the majority this must be so. The law of life for most is from hand to mouth. Very literally their prayer is answered, "Give us *this day* our *daily* bread." But for the middle and upper classes John Wesley's famous rules apply. "Get all you can, save all you can, give all you can." At eighty years of age he thus narrated his own experience. "Two-and-forty years ago I wrote many books Some of these had such a sale as I never thought of, and by this means I unawares became rich. I gain all I can without hurting either my soul or body. I save all I can, not willingly wasting anything, not a sheet of paper, or a cup of water. I do not lay out anything, not a shilling, unless as a sacrifice to God. Yet by giving all I can I am effectually secured from laying up 'treasures upon earth.' And I am secured from either desiring or endeavouring it as long as I give all I can. But my own hands will be my executors." Generally no better executors can be found. The Peabodys and Burdett-Coutts act on this principle, and their memorial remains in model cottages and Christian sanctuaries. Howard's rule was "that our superfluities give way to other men's conveniences, that our conveniences give way to other men's necessities; and that even our necessities sometimes give way to other men's extremities." "Charity," says Chrysostom, "is the scope of all God's commands." 2. *A man owes a duty to others.* "No man liveth to himself." (*a*) We have spoken of the kingly rule of wealth. A king's is a noble office. But sometimes kingship becomes kingcraft. Kingship rules for the good of the subject; kingcraft rules for personal ends, and then power becomes tyranny. To rule well is a difficult task. In most men the love of power is a ruling passion. In no form is it stronger than in ruling men. The pages of history are stained with the blood shed by the oppressor But there are other thrones than that on which the monarch sits. Every master is a king Let him never forget that kingly honours imply kingly responsibilities. "Read the indictment in Epistle of James v 1—6." The "*labourers*" are dependent on you—their masters. The *moral* claim is stronger than the *legal.* There are forms of oppression which are too subtle for the coarse instruments of law. But God has a special controversy with the oppressor. "He raiseth up the poor out of the dust." "The poor, and him that hath no helper," find a helper in God. One duty of a Queen's Counsel is to plead the cause of the queen's subject, who would otherwise be defenceless. The queen is the defender of the weak. "Now will I arise," saith the Lord, "for the oppression of the poor, for the sighing of the needy" (Ps. xii. 5); "He shall judge the poor of the people" (Ps lxxii. 4); and, not to quote passages, he is the Advocate of the poor, the Elevator of the poor, the Satisfier of the poor, the Deliverer of the poor. The sin of oppression is the child of covetousness Ye exact usury! Sins which are passed by because of the power of those who commit them, or passed by because of the poverty and powerlessness of those who suffer from them, are said to *cry to God.* There are many species of slavery below the actual thing. When we get from our servants more than they are well able to do, when remuneration is insufficient, when in any way we prey upon their necessities *we are slaveholders in all but the name.* Remember, "*the Lord of Hosts*" is the poor's Avenger. *What hosts he can send against us.* Wilt thou contend with God? " It is a fearful thing to fall into the hands of the living God " (Heb x 31) It is hard to possess riches without sin. They are called " the mammon of unrighteousness." They are often possessed by the wicked, much admired by them, and not seldom gained by fraud Many a fortune is built on wrong, and *wrong is a foundation of sand* It is not easy to have them and not be hindered by them. A ship that takes in too much cargo is liable to sink. Many rich men bend under their mountain of gold. A man who should bear this burden should be a very Atlas for moral strength. The beasts become fierce when well fed. And it is hard for the purse-full to be other than purse-proud God can best be served by a mean, " Give me not riches, lest I be full and deny thee, and say, Who is the Lord ? " " Give me not poverty, lest I take the name of God in vain " If riches increase, set not thine heart upon them " Possess them , let them not possess you " " God gives riches to the good lest they should be thought evil ; he gives them to the bad lest they should be thought the only good " It is not impossible for a rich man to be virtuous. Abraham and Job were the wealthiest men of the East In the highest circles the fair flower of piety flourishes. Those, however, who have so much to keep them *here* may well find it difficult to be absorbed in the contemplation of a *hereafter.* Prosperity begets security

III The punishment of misused wealth. Nehemiah cites them, as it were, to God's judgment-seat. They are called upon to plead their cause 1 *The punishment is self-caused* " Ye have heaped treasure together for the last days," as the New Testament apostle teaches (James v.) The punishment grows out of the gain. The wind shakes the tallest trees The willow bends under the storm and rises when the gust is over , the oak stands until endurance is no longer possible. Men fall from eminences. He who keeps on the ground has generally secure foothold. 2. *The punishment is self-inflicting.* All speech is translatable by God The young lions' cry for prey is an appeal to God, and he gives scent and swiftness. The parched ground speaks to him and pleads that the windows may be opened, and the rain-drops fall from the closed storehouse. There is something terribly suggestive in the RUST of wrongly-withheld gain, and the helpless CRIES of the defrauded poor passing up through distant space and taking their case to the highest tribunal, pleading with an earnestness akin to that of the woman who came to the unjust judge, but, unlike her, pleading with the Judge of the whole earth, the only absolutely righteous Judge, who will surely avenge his own elect Heard by God, it becomes the instrument of the punishment " The canker and rust shall witness against you " " Miseries shall come upon you " Calamities everywhere attended the Jews soon after the ascension of Christ. Proverbial for their wealth, they were ransacked and punished From then till now they have been a persecuted people, and mainly through their wealth Every one remembers Shakespeare's Shylock, and Sir Walter Scott's Isaac of York. Covetousness brings God's curse on our estates He sends putrefaction, the rust, and the moth Ill gains are equivalent to losses, because providence often scatters them There is a " withholding that tends to poverty." " He that will save must lose " is the gospel riddle The best way of bringing in is laying out What is given to the poor is lent to God, and he is a safe banker , he repays with interest. God can easily corrupt that which we lay up, and *make the worm breed in manna* God is in no lack of servants to carry information or effect his purposes. Corruption, canker, moth, all are at his beck and call. Some rise from within, as *corruption ,* some attack from without, as *the moth ; the rust* corrupts the substance, eats it away. He can arm the elements of fire, wind, and water. He can take the lightning into his hand. The stormy wind and vapour fulfil his word, and these he can bring at last as witnesses against us. Sealed volumes God breaks the seal, and each circumstance becomes an unbribed witness Many things now fair-seeming will show rottenness in the day of judgment. Vividly does the prophet tell us of the houses built by oppression coming as witnesses against the owners. "The stone shall cry out of the wall, and the beam out of the timber shall answer it." The stones will say, "We were hewn by violence," and the timbers, "We were inlaid by fraud." Many of the great works of ancient times, *i. e.* the pyramids, many colossal fortunes and magnificent mansions of modern times, were built with bones and cemented with blood—the blood and bones of the men who built them, or the men from whom the wealth was obtained. The circumstances of sin are so many memorials to put us in mind of guilt and to put God in mind of vengeance. Conscience writes when it does not speak. There is a book of remembrance. All conceptions of torment indicate a relation between sin and punishment not only in justice and duration, but in kind. In this world each sin has its own avenger; many sins are their own avengers. Anger—the agitation and unrest, are not they like whips whose lashes are weighted with lead?

Application. 1. *Let us learn to weep tears of penitence, that we may not have to shed tears of remorse.* After great showers the air is clear. It is better to weep in a way of duty than to weep in a way of judgment. 2. *Let us learn the secret of happiness.* The saint in the Old Testament commanded his soul to be merry because God was the light of his countenance; the fool in the gospel because he had much goods laid up for many years. 3. *Let us learn to provide ourselves bags which wax not old, a treasure in the heavens that faileth not, where no thief approacheth nor moth corrupteth.* For all that is in the world is not of the Father. And the world passeth away, but he that doeth the will of God abideth for ever.

ILLUSTRATIONS.

The rich man's empire.—"The empire which a rich man exercises finds no nation or tribe that wishes to resist it. It commands the services of man wherever man can be reached, because it offers to the desires of man the power of acquiring whatever objects of external enjoyment he is most eager to acquire. From the north to the south, from the east to the west, everything that can be rendered active is put in motion by him, who remains tranquilly at home, exciting the industry of those of whose very existence he is ignorant, and receiving the products of labour for his own use without knowing from whom he receives them. It is almost as in the magic stories of romance, in which the hero is represented as led from the castle-gate by hands that are invisible to him, ushered to a splendid banquet, where no one seems present, where wine is poured into the goblet before him at his very wish, and luxurious refreshment after refreshment appears upon the board, but appears as if no hand had brought it. To the rich man, in like manner, whatever he wishes seems to come merely because he wishes it to come. Without knowing who they are who are contributing to his idle luxury, he receives the gratification itself, and receives it from hands that operate as invisibly as the fairy hands at the banquet. He gathers around him the products of every sea and every soil. The sunshine of one climate, the snows of another, are made subsidiary to his artificial wants; and though it is impossible to discern the particular arms which he is every instant setting in motion, or the particular efforts of inventive thought which he is every instant stimulating, there can be no doubt that such a relation truly exists, which connects with his wishes and with his power the industry of those who labour on the remotest corner of the earth which the enterprising commerce of man can reach."—*Dr. Thomas Brown.*

Possessions.—Possessions distinguish man from the brute, and civilized man from the savage. Labour finds in possessions its normal fruit: possessions are labour as having become reality. The brute is possessionless because he does not labour. In property man ceases to be a mere isolated individual of his species; he creates for himself a world about himself which he can call his own; his property is the outward manifestation of his inward peculiarity. The fact that he who possesses much is also much regarded and esteemed in the world is indeed often very hollow and baseless, though in reality it springs from the correct consciousness that possessions are the fruit of labour, the result of moral effort. He who acquires nothing for himself passes in the world, not without reason, for unrespectable. Of a special virtue of possession-despising, as with the mendicant monks, there can, in the ante-sinful state, be no question; and even after the fall possessions are presented as a perfectly legitimate end of moral effort, and their being increased as a special Divine blessing. Cain and Abel possess already personal property; and the God-blessed possessions of the patriarchs occupy a very large place in their morally religious life [Gen. xii. 5, 16; xiii. 2; xiv. 14; xxiv. 22, 35, 53; xxvi. 13, 14; xxvii. 28; xxx. 27, 30, 43; xxxi. 42; xxxii. 5, 10, 13 *sqq.*; xxxiii. 11; xxxix. 5; xlix. 25; Exod. xiii. 25; Lev. xxv. 21; Deut. ii. 7; vii. 13; xv. 14 *sqq.*; xvi. 15, 17; xxviii. 3 *sqq.*; xxxiii. 13 *sqq.*; xxiv. 25: comp. 1 Kings iii. 13; Ps. cvii. 38; cxii. 2, 3; cxxxii. 15]. Property being the enlarged life-sphere of the moral person,—in some sense his enlarged personality itself,—

I

the moral phase thereof lies not merely in its antecedent ground, namely, labour, but also in its moral use and application. To its *enjoyment* man has a moral right, as such enjoyment is the reward of labour , but to the exclusive enjoyment of it for himself alone he has no moral right, seeing that he is bound to other men by love, and love manifests itself in communicative distribution."—*Wuttke's 'Christian Ethics.'*

A GREAT SCHISM AVERTED.

v. 1—13. *And there was a great cry of the people, &c.*

The paragraph teaches—

I. That social injustice may exist even amongst fellow-workers in a great and good cause (vers. 1—6) The complaint of the poor was forced from them. Wrong may be long endured ; but it will find a voice, a cry " not loud, but deep."

II. That social injustice, if not corrected, will undermine the stability of any cause, however righteous Sanballat's army less fatal than the nobles' avarice

III. That social injustice should be regarded by all good men with feelings of righteous indignation (ver. 6). From a realization of the brotherhood of men; of interdependence; of a Divine purpose in the elevation of the downtrodden.

V. That social injustice, whenever discovered, should be calmly yet promptly dealt with (ver. 7) The *prudent* Nehemiah brought a moral force to bear upon the offenders. "Set an assembly." The *courageous* Nehemiah rebuked the offenders, albeit they were highest in name and station. The *far-seeing* Nehemiah discerned ruin if internal wrongs remained unredressed

V. That conciliatory appeals are sometimes more efficacious than coercive measures in dealing with social injustice (vers. 8—13). Nehemiah used persuasive arguments 1. *The efforts already made to redeem their captive brethren* (ver. 8). 2. *The exposure of the national cause to reproach* (ver. 9) 3 *His own unblemished life and fit example* (ver. 10).

THE ACCUSING CRY OF HUMANITY.

v. 1. *There was a great cry of the people and of their wives against their brethren.*

THE ACCUSERS —"The many" who lack bread (ver 2) THE ACCUSED.— "Their" richer "brethren," "the nobles and the rulers" (vers. 1, 7). THE ACCUSATION —"Ye exact usury. Ye have our lands and vineyards" A story of the olden time of ever-new significance. A twice twenty-times told tale

I. The unending struggle. Wealth and poverty, knowledge and ignorance, brain and brawn, capital and labour— when in all the ages have not these come into collision ? Communists, Socialists, Nihilists—are not these to-day voices from many lands (whether rightly or wrongly) ; the "*great cry*" of the poor of many nationalities against their richer brethren ? The prayer of the philanthropists of every age has been expressed by a poet of our own :—

" Ring out the false, ring in the true ;
Ring out the darkness of the land ,
Ring out the feud of rich and poor ;
Ring in redress to all mankind ,
Ring out the want, the care, the sin,
The faithless coldness of the times ;
Ring in the love of truth and right ,
Ring in the common love of good."

THE HEBREW PROPHETS declare that they that be slain with the sword are better than they that be slain with hunger , for these pine away, stricken through for want of the fruits of the field (Lam. iv. 9). They tell how God's judgments came upon the land because the righteous were sold for silver, and the poor for a pair of shoes (Amos ii. 6). The scathing words of

JESUS CHRIST were reserved for those who used the pride of place to oppress the poor and him that hath no helper. The EARLY PERIOD of English history is associated with William *the Conqueror*. The DARK AGES had light enough to show the few how to prey upon the many. *Through much tribulation* NATIONS have emerged into the light, and CLASSES burst the shackles of slavery and proclaimed their freedom. *With a great sum* England obtained the freedom of the WEST INDIES The blood of AMERICA's sons wiped out the stain of slavery which disgraced the greatest republic the world has seen. *A great cry* has gone up to God as our poor world has struggled on towards knowledge and liberty.

II. **Elements of bitterness in this struggle.** 1. *On the side of the oppressors there is power.* They are "the nobles and the rulers" (ver 7). "The names of king and priest are the most appalling in history." So perverted have they become Anciently *to rule* was also *to feed* (Ps. lxxviii. 71, 72). A bishop is a shepherd. The pastoral staff is the shepherd's crook. 2. *The oppressed are the brethren of the oppressors.* "Our flesh is as the flesh of our brethren, our children as their children." Same blood, same love of children, same sensitiveness to pain. Hath not *a poor man* eyes, hands, organs, dimensions, senses, affections, passions? Is he not fed with the same food, hurt with the same weapons, subject to the same diseases, healed by the same means, warmed and cooled by the same winter and summer as *a rich man?* If you prick a poor man, will he not bleed? if you tickle him, will he not laugh? if you poison him, will he not die? 3. *They were engaged in a common caus —rebuilding God's chosen city.* To make this world a paradise; to compel all kings to recognize the King of kings; to set up a kingdom of righteousness and peace, is not this the task given to humanity, the goal toward which our world should move?

III. **Light in the darkness.** "Watchman, what of the night? The watchman said, *The morning cometh.*" 1. *Christ-*

came to proclaim the brotherhood of humanity. His Beatitudes direct men to look to character, not to position, for Divine approval. The strait gate must be passed through by rich and noble as well as by poor and unknown. Jesus spoke to the poor, felt for the degraded, raised hope in the oppressed. 2. *Signs of the times.* The "many" (ver. 2) are not unheard, their influence not unfelt. There is wrong, but society tends towards redress. Ignorance abounds, but the teacher is abroad. Many rich forget their duties—not all. Tennyson's Sir Walter Vivian is not the creation of a poet's fancy.

"Sir Walter Vivian all a summer's day
Gave his broad lawns until the set of sun
Up to the people : thither flocked at noon
His tenants, wife and child, and thither half
The neighbouring borough, with their Institute,
Of which he was the patron.
        Why should not these great Sirs
Give up their parks some dozen times a year
To let the people breathe? "

Tennyson's vision will one day be actualized.

" I dipt into the future, far as human eye could see,
Saw the vision of the world, and all the wonder that would be ;
Saw the havens fill with commerce, argosies of magic sails,
Pilots of the purple twilight, dropping down with costly bales ;
Heard the heavens fill with shouting, and there rain'd a ghastly dew
From the nations' airy navies grappling in the central blue ;
Far along the world-wide whisper of the south wind rushing warm,
With the standards of the peoples plunging through the thunder-storm ;
Till the war-drum throbb'd no longer, and the battle-flags were furl'd
In the parliament of man, the federation of the world
There the common sense of most shall hold a fretful realm in awe,
And the kindly earth shall slumber, lapt in universal law."

" *How long, O Lord ?* "

ILLUSTRATION.

The passion for power.—"Christianity has joined with all history in inspiring me with a peculiar dread and abhorrence of the passion for power, for dominion over men. There is nothing in the view of our Divine Teacher so hostile to his Divine spirit as the lust of domination. This we are accustomed to regard as eminently the sin of the arch-fiend ' By this sin fell the angels' It is the most Satanic of all human passions, and it has inflicted more terrible evils on the human family than all others It has made the names of king and priest the most appalling in history There is no crime which has not been perpetrated for the strange pleasure of treading men underfoot, of fastening chains on the body or mind The strongest ties of nature have been rent asunder, her holiest feelings smothered, parents, children, brothers murdered to secure dominion over man The people have now been robbed of the necessaries of life, and now driven to the field of slaughter like flocks of sheep to make one man the master of millions Through this passion government, ordained by God to defend the weak against the strong, to exalt right above might, has up to this time been the great wrong-doer Its crimes throw those of private men into the shade Its murders reduce to insignificance those of the bandits, pirates, highwaymen, assassins against whom it undertakes to protect society. Power trampling on right, whether in the person of king or priest, or in the shape of democracies or majorities, is the saddest sight to him who honours human nature and desires its enlargement and happiness."—*W. E. Channing.*

THE MISERIES OF DEBT.

v. 3—5. *Some also there were that said,* &c.

Dr. Jamieson, the Bible interpreter, thus writes on this passage :—" The poor made loud complaints against the rich for taking advantage of their necessities, and grinding them by usurious exactions. Numbers of them had, in consequence of these oppressions, been driven to such extremities that they had to mortgage their lands and houses to enable them to pay the taxes to the Persian Government, and ultimately even sell their children for slaves to procure the means of subsistence." Generalizing this particular instance, we have the subject of debt and its miseries.

I. **Mental unrest.** *Credit* is necessary. The world's business could not otherwise be carried on The every-day word trust is, like most every-day words, suggestive. It is confidence between man and man It supposes an honourable undertaking. Faith is not only a theological word , it is a force in this working-day world. No man ought to receive credit without a prospect of being able to pay The violation of this rule is dishonest. To take a man's purse is stealing. So is taking up goods without paying for them, and receiving wages for which the stipulated labour has not been given. Unless hardened through a long series of dishonesties, a man cannot be contented who does not obey the New Testament law, "Owe no man anything."

II. **Social degradation.** It is proverbial that to be in debt is to be in danger ; danger of detection and exposure. Do not pretend to be what you are not ; do not keep up a style and scale of cost beyond your means.

III. **Family ruin.** A man owes a first duty to his own house The helpless hang on him. He may bring ruin through extravagance

IV. **A disregard of a Divine command.** "THOU SHALT NOT STEAL" was written with the finger of God. This law has not been abrogated.

Application. 1. *Christians should set the world an example* 2 *Watch the beginnings of extravagance.* 3. *In small things as well as in greater act on Christian principle.* " He that is faithful in that which is least is faithful also in much ; and he that is unjust in the least is unjust also in much."

Illustrations :—" The Persians reckoned these two very great sins. 1 To be in debt. 2 To tell a lie , the latter being often the fruit of the former "

" By the twelve tables of Rome, he that owed much, and could not pay, was to be cut in pieces, and every creditor was to have a piece of him according to the debt."

" We read of a certain Italian gentleman who, being asked how old he was, answered that he was in health ; and to another that asked how rich he was, answered that he was not in debt. He is young enough that is in health, and rich enough that is not in debt."—*Trapp.*

Righteous Anger.

v. 6.   *And I was very angry when I heard their cry and these words.*

"Ezra and Nehemiah were both of them very wise, good, useful men, yet in cases not unlike theirs there is a great deal of difference between their management. When Ezra was told of the sin of the rulers in marrying strange wives he rent his clothes and wept, and prayed, and was hardly persuaded to attempt a reformation, fearing it impracticable; for he was a man of a mild, tender spirit When Nehemiah was told of as ill a thing he warmed presently, fell foul upon the delinquents, incensed the people against them and never rested till, by all the rough methods he could use, he forced them to reform, for he was a man of a hot and eager spirit. Very holy men may differ much from each other in their natural temper, and in other things that result from it. Again, God's work may be done, well done, and successfully, and yet different methods taken in doing it; which is a good reason why we should neither arraign others' management nor make our own a standard There are diversities of operation, but the same spirit."—*Matthew Henry.* Nehemiah's soul was stirred within him as he saw the oppression of his voiceless brethren. But they who were not able to help themselves were not therefore to remain unhelped

> "The voice of their indignation
> Rose up to the throne of God."

They bore long, until suffering was no longer endurable, and then they appealed from Festus unto Cæsar, from the nobles and rulers who were set over them to Nehemiah under whom they all served. The longer Nehemiah mused the more fiercely the fire of his anger burned. There cannot be supreme love of right without bitterest hatred of wrong Admiration of virtue and scorn of vice are correlative. There is such a thing as righteous anger.

I. The righteousness of anger depends upon its cause and occasion.

"What is anger? It is displeasure felt in a high degree; a feeling which is awakened when we think ourselves injured. It is usually attended with a restless uneasiness of mind, and frequently with something worse. But is anger in no case allowable? Perhaps it is. 'God is angry with the wicked every day' (Ps. vii. 11); that is, he is highly displeased with their sinful conduct, and resolved to punish them on its account, yet anger in God is infinitely remote from anything of turbulence and malevolence We read of our Lord Jesus looking round on the people, particularly on the Pharisees, 'with anger, being grieved for the hardness of their hearts' (Mark iii 5); but this anger was perfectly consistent with the purest benevolence, with the tenderest, the most disinterested kindness Anger in depraved creatures is certainly very different from what it is in God, and from what it was in Jesus Christ, and we should be cautious how we give the least allowance to so dangerous a passion. It has been judiciously remarked, when anger 'proceeds from pride, or from selfishness, when it rises high, or continues long; and when it is accompanied by anything like hatred or ill-will towards the person who is its object, then it is sinful and hurtful. But whatever we may think of the lawfulness or unlawfulness of anger in itself, and how difficult it may be to ascertain in what cases and in what degree it is allowable, one thing is evident—we cannot be too cautious of yielding to its influence. It is a passion so difficult to be regulated and so dreadful often in its effects; so destructive of that meekness, gentleness, and love which form the very essence of the Christian character; so expressly forbidden in various passages of the New Testament, and so carefully guarded even in those where it seems to be in some measure allowed, that we have much more reason to restrain than to encourage it even in the smallest degree.' There is one object against which anger may be innocently directed, and this object is sin, either sin in ourselves, or sin in others. Peter was angry, exceedingly displeased with himself, when, at the recollection of his sin in denying his blessed Lord, 'he went out and wept bitterly.' The brethren of Joseph were angry with themselves, displeased at their base behaviour, when convinced of their cruelty towards an unoffending brother; and doubtless the feeling was laudable. The soul of righteous Lot was 'vexed;' he was angry with the filthy conversation of the wicked among whom he dwelt, and as we dwell among a people of unclean lips and unholy conduct, our blame would be great if we felt not displeasure at what we hear and witness."—*Kidd.* We read of the fierce anger of the Lord when Israel joined himself unto Baal-Peor (Num. xxv. 1—9). Pronounced upon disobedience (Deut. xxix 20). When Jesus Christ looked upon his spying enemies with anger, being grieved for the hardness of their hearts, which predominated, the anger or the grief? Contrast the anger of Sanballat (chap. iv.) with the anger of Nehemiah (chap v.), how different the occasion, how unlike the cause. For a good work Sanballat was prepared to stone the Jews, for an evil act of oppression Nehemiah rose up to rebuke the nobles. Be ye angry and sin not in reference to cause.

II The righteousness of anger depends upon its spirit and limitations Note, especially, the anger of Jesus Christ had reference to the evil, the hardness of their hearts Righteous anger is against wrong, not against wrong-doers. Must have in it no personal malice, no spleen. Must not cross the line to revenge Anger is the basis of magistracy, the support of laws, and the pillar of decency and right conduct. "Magistrates are mortal gods, and God is an immortal magistrate, therefore, as the merciful God heareth in his holy habitation in heaven the cry of the miserable, oppressed people in faith, so should every godly ruler hear and relieve the pitiful cry of the oppressed, being his

brethren, seeing he is God's lieutenant, and hath the sword and law in his hand to bridle such ill-doers, and must not for favour, gifts, nor fear suffer it unamended; else he doeth not his duty unto the mighty Lord, who set him in that place, gave him the authority, and will ask a strait account how he hath used it to the relief of the oppressed Some be of opinion that a magistrate should not be moved with anger in doing his office, but give every man fair words, pass over matters slowly, please all men, though he do them little good, but, the truth being well considered, it may be judged otherwise. Lactantius writeth a book wherein he proveth that God himself is angry, and every anger is not sin. If God then be angry against sin, why may not a good man in God's cause then do the same? Hate not the man, but his ill-doing; be not angry without a just cause unadvisedly; keep not thy anger long, that it grow not into hatred; let it be no more nor no less than the fault deserveth, and let it be without raging, fuming, fretting, swelling, and raving and disquieting of body or mind; not for malice of revenging, but for pity or justice to correct and amend; and anger well qualified is not ill. This is not spoken to give liberty to anger, for we are too ready to it by nature, but rather to bridle it, seeing it standeth on so narrow a point to keep measure in. This qualifying of anger is declared in the Scripture as that it should not continue. St Paul saith, 'Let not the sun set upon your anger;' and that it should not be rashly, without cause, nor more than the cause requireth The gospel teacheth, saying, 'He that is angry with his brother without a just cause is guilty of judgment' This anger of Nehemiah was just in all circumstances, and kept the rule of St Paul, 'Be angry and sin not,' which is a hard point to keep."—*Pilkington.* He who hates sin will escape it An extreme sentimentalism would make all virtue consist in amiability. Men have proclaimed the love of God as if it denied his justice. "God is love." "Our God is a consuming fire." The two poles of the Divine character.

Application 1. *Temperamental anger to be subdued by holy thought, prayer, and effort.* Lay aside every weight, and the sin that doth so easily beset. 2. *Distinguish between the wrong and the wrong-doers.* Vengeance is mine ; I will repay, saith the Lord. 3. *Remember Christian doctrine of forgive-* ness. If thy brother trespass against thee and return, saying, Repent, forgive him. Let the daily prayer be, Forgive us our trespasses, and help us to forgive them that trespass against us. For this doctrine of forgiveness is one of the hard sayings of Jesus Christ.

INTROSPECTION.

v. 7.   *Then I consulted with myself.*

The position was perilous. The nobles and the rulers were powerful; their services were needed. The toilers were embittered ; the common cause endangered. Too little courage or too much prudence, cowardice or temporizing, would prove fatal. "Then I consulted with myself." His heart took counsel upon the injustice. From this instance of introspection or self-communion let us consider self-communion generally.

I. The value of self-communion. Thought comes in solitude. Character is formed by self - communings. A preacher must return sometimes to "fructifying silence." We are not enough alone. Our age is restless. It craves results—speedy and sure. Too much bustle and hurry. Duty treads upon the heels of duty. Moses, Elijah, John Baptist, Paul, yes, and Christ himself, lived in the wilderness alone with God. Cecil, Scott, Newton, Wesley, the spiritual giants, were men of solitary hours. Too much familiarity with men breeds contempt and distrust. Know thyself! "Come ye yourselves apart," said Jesus to disciples flushed with success (Mark vi). *Need of rest and self-communion evident in all spheres of life.* Restlessness characterizes most men. Space and time are nearly annihilated. Parliamentary speech spoken in the early hours of the morning is printed and transmitted to the breakfast-table. Markets of Odessa, Alexandria, New York, Calcutta, and Sydney hardly closed ere the electric current has flashed the quotations. Rest and time to think almost denied many commercial and professional men. It was the sin of Israel. "My people doth not consider." "Consider your ways"—there speaks a prophet. "Think on these things"—there speaks an apostle. "Hear ye the word of the Lord" ushers in the Old Testament. "He that hath ears to hear let him hear" introduces the New. He who pleads the pressure of business has too much business. Men must find *time* to prepare for *eternity.* *Too much religious work dangerous.* "They made me the keeper of the vineyards, but mine own vineyard have I not kept" (Song of Solomon). "I keep under my body, and bring it into subjection ; lest that by any means, when I have preached to others, I myself should be a castaway" (Paul). "Nothing is so important as to keep an exact proportion between the interior source of virtue and the external practice of it, else, like the foolish virgins, we shall find that the oil in our lamps is exhausted when the bridegroom comes" (Chrysostom). Is this the meaning of our Lord's solemn words, "Many will say to me," &c. (Matt. vii. 22, 23)? Christian charity begins at home. It is possible to build reformatories and be ourselves unreformed ; possible to send the Bible to others and ourselves forget to read it ; possible to lay costly gifts on God's altar and not bow in penitence at his footstool. *The Christian life a growth.* It is the burden of direct precept. "Grow in grace and in knowledge" (2 Pet. iii. 18). "Add to your faith" (2 Pet i. 5). It is variously illustrated. "The righteous shall hold on his way, and he that hath clean hands shall be stronger and stronger" (Job xvii. 9). "He shall be like a tree planted by the waters, and that spreadeth out its roots by the river" (Jer. xvii. 8). It is the subject of apostles' joy when Christians "stand fast in the Lord" (Phil. iv. 1). Can this be effected without time and thought? Does not the garden of the soul require culture? Do the flowers of humility and charity grow wild? Does business demand application, but the soul's commerce none? Must the children's minds be educated and their hearts remain untrained? Each must come into some desert place and rest awhile with Christ.

II The dangers of self-communion.
1. *Morbid religion* Don't be always a spiritual anatomist. Too frequent looking within brings depression. Religious depression arising from neglect of duty or commission of sin cannot co-exist with spiritual life. But very much depression is needless or self-induced. We may say sometimes, "Why art thou cast down, O my soul?" (Ps xlii. 11). A man feels forsaken, and, projecting his own feelings, imagines God has forsaken him. Do not rashly imagine that because you cannot every hour "read your title clear" that therefore your name is erased from the book of life.
2. *Out of undue self-communion arose asceticism of middle ages, arises some conventual tendencies of our own.* Dream not of becoming unworldly by escaping from duty. "I pray not that thou shouldest take them out of the world, but that thou shouldest keep them from the evil" (John xvii. 15)

III. The safe-guards of self-communion. 1. *Action.* From the temple to the city.

> "'Twixt the mount and multitude,
> Doing or receiving good."

Thought the basis of action. Acts become habits. "I must work the works of him that sent me" (John ix. 4). "As the Father hath sent me into the world, even so have I sent them into the world" (John xvii. 18 , xx. 21). Do not put asunder what God hath joined together Different temperaments will give varying prominence to contemplation and action; the inward and the outward But woe to those who neglect either. A pure heart the indispensable condition of a noble life 2. *God's word.* Make that the only guide.

AN ASSEMBLY CONVOKED AGAINST SINNERS

v. 7 And I set a great assembly against them.

Partly because persons implicated were numerous and powerful to show them that greater numbers disapproved, and partly to cause such shame and remorse as might lead them to renounce their criminal practices The measure was successful. Show impenitent sinners how great *an assembly* may be set against them Sinners rely on being a majority They are decidedly superior to the servants of God ; not only in number, but in wealth and power and influence. Were the great question What is truth? to be decided by numbers, they could easily determine it in their own favour. Show that those whose opinions and approbation are more important are against them.

I. The good men now in the world. Not necessarily professors of religion Many professors not good men. By good men is meant men whom God will acknowledge to be good.

II. All the good men who have ever lived. These compose an assembly far exceeding in number all the good men who are now alive. Abel, Enoch, Noah, Abraham, Moses, Elijah, John Baptist, disciples of Jesus, early Christians, martyrs, reformers, men of 'May-Flower.'

III All the writers of the Old and New Testaments They are *good* men ; they are more—they are *inspired* men. Being taught by the eternal Spirit of God, with one voice they cry, Woe to the wicked ; it shall be ill with him ! Heaven and earth shall pass away, but God's words never.

IV The holy angels Consider number, character, and intellectual rank.

Perhaps exceed in number the human race. "An innumerable company." In comparison with the least angel the wisest human philosopher is a child. Their holiness is perfect, spotless. They execute the will of God.

V. The Lord Jesus Christ. The Lord of angels and men, the appointed Judge, who will pronounce a sentence on both.

VI. God the Father. Sinners strive with their Maker. Survey the whole assembly which is arrayed against evil and evil-doers. Terrible to sinners; consolatory to Christians.—*Dr. Payson, abridged.*

INCONSISTENCY WITHOUT EXCUSE.

v. 8. *And I said unto them, We after our ability have redeemed our brethren the Jews, which were sold unto the heathen; and will ye even sell your brethren? or shall they be sold unto us? Then held they their peace, and found nothing to answer.*

They found nothing to answer. For what answer could be given? They which heard Nehemiah's accusation were convicted by their own conscience Brotherhood, memories of bondage, the great price at which they had redeemed their brethren from Persian masters, the inspiration of their journey to the decayed city, the work God had given them to do—these rose up like prophets of evil tidings to second the noble censures of Nehemiah. Their inconsistency was without excuse.

I. The admirableness of consistency. It is manly. Everybody reverences it. Even in an unworthy cause it extorts a momentary recognition. In a worthy cause all bow the knee and do it homage. The heroes of history by flood and field, the redressers of human wrongs at home and abroad, the characters of Bible story, were consistent. They had a purpose and stuck to it. Despised of men, mocked at by demons, are those whom the inspired apostle describes as "wavering like a wave of the sea driven with the wind and tossed; the double-minded, who are unstable in all their ways" (James i. 6—8) Dignity is robbed of its excellency and power of its strength in the Reubens who are "unstable as water" (Gen. xlix. 3, 4). Be persistent. Be consistent. Is it consistent for Christian men to enter into partnership with those who work without a conscience? Ought Christian parents to consult first and foremost the worldly convenience and advantage of their children? If religion be true, should it not decide the just weight and the true measure? In business, in pleasure, at home, abroad, through the week as well as on the Sabbath, be consistent.

II. The inexcusableness of inconsistency. Has nothing to recommend it. Nothing gained. Brings discredit upon any cause. The inconsistent man has no faith in his position. An inconsistent Christian may profess but does not possess a good creed. The creed which influences conduct is not that which a man holds, but that which holds him. Life is the expositor of doctrine. Nehemiah's nobles called the workmen brethren. But that was only a word of the lip. The deed of the life made them slaves and foreigners. For a time the nobles prospered. Success smiled upon oppression. But a reckoning day came. Summoned to Nehemiah's bar, they "found nothing to answer." A New Testament parable is recalled. The man who had not on a wedding garment was "speechless" (Matt. xxii. 1 — 14). Profession and possession, reality and hypocrisy, are not always distinguishable here and now. Parable of tares: "Let both grow together until the harvest" (Matt xiii. 24—30). In earlier times men strove for a pure visible Church. That impossible. Our eyes cannot distinguish true from false in every instance. By-and-by inconsistency will stand self-convicted. At heaven's judgment-seat every one must give an account.

Application. 1. *The supreme importance of character.* "As a man thinketh in his heart, so is he" (Prov. xxiii. 7). "Keep thy heart with all diligence;

for out of it are the issues of life"
(Prov. iv. 23). 2. *The value of self-
reliance.* Wrong-doing is contagious.
One noble imitated another in exacting
usury. Those who were half conscious
that they were doing wrong were encouraged by the evil example of others.
Trust thyself when thou hast the approval
of thy own conscience. 3 *Remember
the bar of God.* He who made Nehemiah upright "is a God all whose ways
are judgment: a God of truth and without iniquity" (Deut. xxxii. 4). "He
that planted the ear, shall he not hear?
he that formed the eye, shall he not
see?" (Ps. xciv. 9).

SAME THEME.

The marvellous *personal* power of
Nehemiah. Great individuality triumphs over all things. Napoleon
laughed away the pretensions of rank
by saying, "I am an ancestor." The
force of personal character makes all
other forces give way. Especially
when the individuality is a *good* individuality; when the strength of manhood is backed by the strength of right.
Illustration of this in the text, where
the dumbfounded nobles stand ashamed
before the challenge of the man who has
come to spy out their faults and to mend
them at all costs to himself Subject,
the inexcusableness of inconsistency.

I. **The inconsistency.** Define inconsistency. Want of harmony in the
parts of a man's life. The presence in a
man's being of two things which cannot
be together. A man who swears the
British oath of allegiance and takes the
pay of the English state would be an
inconsistent man if he betrayed state
secrets to a hostile country, or gave
guidance to an invading foe. That
would be treason. Religious inconsistency is treason against the King of
kings—treason and treachery against
the truth. 1. *Worldly inconsistency.*
Worldly men point sneeringly to any
little deviation from consistency in
Christian people; but if Christian charity
did not forbid the sneer might be returned. The cant and pretence and
selfish departure from avowed principles

which fills the life of the children of
this world may well creep a little into
the Church. A politician who loves
liberty, and is at the same time a tyrant
in his household and to his servants;
a man who loves to read and to talk
fine sentiment, and whose common life
runs along a low level of worldly meanness, are examples of inconsistency. The
world had need to pluck the beam out
of its own eye before meddling with the
mote in the eye of the Church. 2. *Religious inconsistency.* Example of
Balaam, who prayed, "Let me die the
death of the righteous," and who died
with a sword drawn against God; the
Puritan, who fought for liberty to worship God, and then would not grant
toleration to his brother's creed; the
professing Christian of even late years,
who bought and sold men, women, and
children as slaves, are glaring instances
of contradictions in character and conduct. Enumerate common forms of
inconsistency in the ordinary life of
professedly Christian people. 3. *Injurious effects of inconsistency.* (a) To self.
It blunts the conscience, and so damages
the finer spiritual perceptions as to
deprive the soul of the perfect peace of
those who are in perfect truth. (β) To
others. It seems a contradiction of
religion, a confession of its inadequacy
to master the sin in a man, and shakes
the faith of an onlooking world in the
power of the gospel.

II. **The inexcusableness.** With
heads hanging like bulrushes the dumbfounded men stood before Nehemiah, as
now the inconsistent stands before the
convictions of God's Spirit and the
reproach of the world. 1 *Infirmity is
often pleaded as an excuse* The fol-
lower of the meek and lowly Jesus so
excuses his outbursts of violent passion.
The man who hides his convictions in a
worldly circle so excuses his want of
religious courage. The man who grasps
at some questionable advantage of the
world so covers the selfishness which
has shown itself mightier than his
Christian self-denial. It is dangerous to
so shake hands with our own infirmity.
2. *Ignorance is another excuse.* Want
of true perception of God's law and lack

of thoughtfulness concerning the true significance of his own actions are a reason, but not an excuse, for much inconsistency among the professed servants of God. As some uninstructed persons are not sure of the difference between green and blue, and are not pained by want of harmony in colours that are joined but not reconciled to each other, so a blunt moral sense may not detect all the contradictions of his own religious character. 3. *But infirmity may be strengthened and ignorance may be instructed.* These are not excuses. "Truth in the inward parts" is the requirement of him "whose we are, and whom we serve." To be sanctified *wholly* (not one-sidedly or partially) is the Christian's prayer—body, soul, and spirit all penetrated through and through with holiness

Application. 1. *Do not leave to others the task of detecting your inconsistency.* Find it out yourself. 2. *Do not weakly reconcile yourself to things which can have no place in a complete Christian character.* 3. *Seek more of that freedom of the truth which liberates a man from these reproaching faults*

GOD'S PEOPLE UNDER THE EYE OF A CRITICAL WORLD.

v. 9. *Also I said, It is not good, &c.*

The world has a spleen against the Church. The Church is an incarnate condemnation of the world. "I have saved them *out of* the world." However full of charity the elect of God may be, they stand rank on rank, by their creed and their practice, witnessing with silent censure against all ungodliness. Hence in self-defence the world watches for the Church's faults, "rejoicing in iniquity"—the discovered iniquity of the professedly good. Our religious self-government is watched by a critical "opposition," ever ready with its "reproach." Nehemiah asks a fair question: "Ought ye not to walk in the fear of God because of the reproach of the heathen our enemies?"

I. The reproach of the enemy. The world's criticism of God's people is very merciless and very unfair. It makes no allowances. It does not "remember that we are dust." It has no place for the extenuations of charity. The world will not under-rate, but over-rate, the defects of the good. Malicious rumour makes a mountain out of a molehill; like photography, it exaggerates every freckle or scar on the countenance of a good man's life. Beware of the reproach of the world our enemy. 1. *Accept this condition of life.* It is useless to kick against the pricks. We may be moved to scorn by the mean carping of the foe; but it flings back its motto, "All's fair in war." If you contend with an uncivilized enemy you get ready for uncivilized deeds. Give mercy, but expect none. Do not call the world hard names; the world is simply the world, and no more. "Fret not thyself because of evil-doers," nor because of their evil tongues. 2. *Do not despise this power of enmity.* (a) There is a noble scorn of the evil-tongued society. Here is an old motto of an independent mind. "They say! What do they say? Let them say!" Do not be afraid to live. Let us not creep apologetically through the world. We owe no one an apology for our fear of God. It is *they* who are wrong, and most of them know it very well. If you carry the Christian flag as if ashamed of it the world will despise you all the more. It likes out and out manhood. Do not "liberalize" your creed, or conceal your conviction, or blush at your good deeds for fear of reproach. "Whosoever is ashamed of me and of my words, of him will I be ashamed." Be no "reed shaken with the wind." (β) But there is an unwise scorn of the world's opinion. A thing lawful for me as a man may be inexpedient for me as a Christian man. Many good men are doing hurt to Christ's cause by a reckless bravado, which flows out of an uncontrolled independence or out of an unthinking foolishness. A man in ambush may show he is no coward by exposing himself to danger before the enemy, but he may show that he is a fool by revealing the position of his comrades and involving them in peril. "Walk circumspectly, not as fools, but as wise" 3. *For the world's own sake have a care of the world's reproach.* (1) You may make the evil man doubt the God you fear. "Another saint unmasked," says the world, as it exults over the declared inconsistency of a Christian. "By one judge all," says the critic. You cast a veil over God's face, and put truth at the bar "on suspicion," when you do not walk before the enemy in the fear of God. (2) You may hurt the conscience of the worldly man. To let him see his own fault in you is to justify his fault to his pliant conscience. When you do an ill thing you endorse the ill things another does. (3) You cast away your influence for good. All things are possible to you if the world believes in you. You can cast out its devils and tread on its serpents and scorpions, and nothing shall by any means hurt you. But if you cast away the confidence of your unconverted brother you can do nothing with him because of his unbelief. We want to have faith in God and to make the world have faith in us.

II. The caution of the godly "Sanctify the Lord God in your hearts · . . . having a good conscience, that, whereas they speak evil of you, as of evil-doers, they may be ashamed that falsely accuse your good conversation in Christ." 1. *Elements of caution.* (a) Be strong in the fear of God. Let the solemn thought of his watchfulness guide your steps. Remember the one omnipresent Witness whose eye shines like a star over the darkest gloom of secrecy. "Fear him, ye saints, and ye shall then have nothing else to fear." Cultivate the sentiment of that ancient saying, "Thou God seest me!" If clear of his reproach, the reproach of the enemy shall be but as a hailstone against the flint. (β) Be rigorous in self-condemnation. Be *charitable* in judging others; be *just* in judging thyself. If you are lax, let it not be with self For your own sake *be* what you would seem. Above all fear of the world's reproach, fear the reproach of an indignant self "To thine own self be true, and it shall follow, as the night the day, thou canst not then be false to any man." 2. *Spheres of caution.* (a) Personal life. In all those elements of life which are "your own business," and not the world's affair, be on your guard. Reverent behaviour, amiable temper, truth and kindness of tone and speech in conversation, godly direction of your habits and your household—let these be above suspicion Your habits are the atmosphere and your home the environment of yourself; let them become you (β) Public life. Though in Rome, despise the ill-doer's motto. *In* the world, be not *of* it Where association makes you unable to prevent be no advocate of evil. Do the world's work and change the world's gold with Christian fingers. (γ) Church life. Remember that in all Church life higher maxims and nobler usages than those of the world should predominate. Do not blare out the faults of fellow Christians. For Christ's sake, for the world's sake, cast a cloak of charity over the misunderstandings and the misunderstandable doings of the household of faith. Do not tell your enemy how weak your own brother is. In private life, in public life, in Church life, walk in the fear of God because of the reproach of the heathen our enemies. Application. 1. *Pray.* "Who is sufficient for these things?" Draw deep inspirations of the Holy Spirit of God. 2. *Watch.* Keep open eyes on yourself and on your temptations

---

WHAT OTHERS DO NO EXCUSE FOR MY DOING.

v. 10.   *I likewise, and my brethren, and my servants, might, &c.*

Nehemiah's great strength of goodness and his nobleness of mind made him in his historic conduct a law unto himself. 1. *He rose above all example.*

The contrast between himself and the common run of his contemporaries is evident throughout the story. "He heard a voice they could not hear" 2. *He rose above all the bare requirements of law.* "Is it so nominated in the bond?" is never the question of a heroically good man. Not what I am required to do, but what I am able to do; not what I am commanded, but what I can, is his rule of action. 3. *His generous goodness made him a law unto himself.* See this illustrated in the text. What others do is no excuse for my doing the same. "I might exact of them"

I. **Common contravention of this rule.** 1. *A common reason for wrong-doing is that others do it.* Easy to find precedent and example for anything we wish to do. In the practices of the world and in the faults of good men we can find, if we are perverse enough, plenty of examples of evil. 2. *A more powerful reason still is the fact that it will be done, so I may as well do it, and have the benefit of it.* This will justify anything to a man. The schoolboy in

Cowper's story robs the orchard because his companions will go even if he should remain away. The business man contents himself with iniquitous action because others would do it in any case, and he may as well have the benefit as another. The legislator enacts an unrighteous statute or favours an unholy conquest because these things will be done.

II. **Vindication of this rule.** 1. *Not another's conscience, but his own conscience, is a man's guide.* If every one descended to the lower level of his neighbour, the world would go with swift slide into the bottomless pit. To stand faithful where others fail is the glory of the servant of the Lord. "They do it, and will do it —let them do it; I will not" 2. *The evil doings of others will not save a man from the doom of his own wrong-doing.* "Thou hast delivered thy soul." That surely is some consolation for the man who stands aloof from evil. "I likewise, and my brethren, and my servants, might exact of them money and corn," if this wrong exaction by others might justify it in us.

CLENCHING A GOOD RESOLUTION.

v. 12.   *Then said they, We will restore, &c.*

"In a time of danger we understand a general interest. Every one is called in to take a part in the struggles that we make for liberty. And yet when the toil was a little over some of them acted as if they thought that Providence was not a public friend, but only a sort of a factor to a few private families. It is a misrepresentation of him who gives us the mercy if we do not make it extensive. He accepts not the persons of princes nor regards the rich more than the poor, for they are all the work of his hands. You must not think he is so lavish of his bounty to the great men of the earth merely that they may glitter upon a throne, but be his ministers for good; and this they cannot be if they resolve to confine their influence. Princes love to be called God's representatives, but they usually understand it in no other attribute than his power;

whereas that is incommunicable; it is a glory that he never gives to another. The chief titles in which he would be represented by them are those of justice and mercy." These strong, brave, and true words were written by Thomas Bradbury more than a century and a half ago, and applied to his own times. The human heart is the same in all ages. It is treacherous. Nehemiah knew this. The words of the oppressors were fair-seeming. "We will restore." "We will require nothing of them." "We will do as thou sayest." But the very greatness of the promise constitutes its danger. It is too good to be true; needs binding force. The priest's presence will give the oath "legal validity for judicial decisions." It will also impart solemnity. If tempted to oppress again the awful oath will rise to recollection. There is the truth of life in this old-world scene. Men need all the helps they can get.

I. In the resistance of temptation. The balance of our lives has need of one scale of reason to poise another of passion. The proverbs of many peoples speak of the fragile nature of promises and vows. He who stands on his unaided resolution has insecure footing. Forgetting is easy. Self - interest is powerful. The present moment outweighs the future hour. Philosophy would teach us to forego a moment's rapture for lifelong peace; but we are not all philosophical. The now is here, the rapture is possible; the future is uncertain, the peace is contingent. All experience of life teaches that men will barter future blessedness for present happiness. "The things which are seen" bulk larger in the eyes of men than "the things which are not seen." We cannot afford to neglect (*a*) the daily reading of the word of God; (*b*) private and ejaculatory prayer; (*c*) covenant engagements with God. Many Christians have found it helpful to enter into a written covenant. The *signature* has had the same effect as Nehemiah's *oath.*

Any system of spiritual mnemonics is valuable. What is wanted is quickness to discover temptation, and firmness to resist it. "Thy word have I hid in mine heart, that I might not sin against thee" (Ps. cxix. 11). "It is written!" Jesus answered and said to the tempter (Matt. iv.). "Watch and pray, that ye enter not into temptation" (Matt. xxvi. 41). All inspirations that are available are needed.

II. In the performance of duty. Doing good is a more comprehensive phrase than easy task. "Virtue is its own reward." Possibly, but not always so regarded. A hard task trying to help those who hinder. He who will serve must suffer Let him despise not the smallest strength from any quarter. Bind thyself to God's altar with any cords thou mayest obtain Reliance on God will bring the only safe self-reliance. For each day's task God has promised daily strength. For rugged paths he has provided wear-resisting shoes. Lift up thy burden. Put thy foot forward along the path God has marked out. "Trust in the Lord and do good." "*Thy God hath commanded thy strength.*"

THE TERRORS OF THE LORD PERSUADING MEN.

v. 13.   *Also I shook my lap, and said, &c.*

This text describes a solemn scene. A reformer with a stern, hard nerve of righteousness arraigning a guilty band of fellow mortals before God The nobles feel the spell of Nehemiah's strong conscience and the still stronger spell of Jehovah's threatening, and have promised to reform their deeds. Their *ruthless friend*, having compelled them to swear to their resolves, turning upon them, exclaims, "*Now you are committed to your course.*" "I shook my lap, and said, So God shake out every man that performeth not this promise. *And all the congregation said, Amen*" A similar scene is recorded in Deut. xxvii., where the curses of God were read as the doom of those who broke the laws solemnly repeated before the people, and where, like the murmur of a surge on the coast, the deep Amen of the people

rolled back in acceptance of the stern alternative — *obedience or the curse.* Twelve times over from the slopes of Ebal rang the "Cursed be he" of the officiating Levite, and twelve times was flung back the united Amen of Israel. In a similar spirit Nehemiah extemporized this solemn binding ceremony of the text.

I. The doom of unrighteousness acknowledged. Amen in one significance means "verily," "truly," "so it is and shall be." The Lord will shake out from his lap the wicked like a man shaking the worthless dust from his garment. *It is even so. Amen!* Say to the wicked, It shall be ill with him. 1. *Natural instinct asserts this.* By natural instinct one holds no precise philosophical dogma. This is enough for our purpose *Every rational mind* *in a land of light and knowledge has the deep, inwrought conviction that doom must follow misdoing.* Fiery sentences asserting this are written in legends of the heathen world. Nemesis, like a bloodhound, follows the wrong-doer. Ancient poetry grows terrible in its tragic representations of this great belief. "Our *heart* condemns us." God's warning words are answered by the soul's *Amen! It is even so!* 2. *The operation of natural law exhibits this great principle, that God must one day shake away the worthless.* "Nature gives us a word and a blow, and the blow first." Excess or transgression of physical law threatens us as with fixed bayonets. Put a bound upon thy lust and appetite, or beware, is the voice of all experience. No less a human than a Divine proverb is the saying, "He that breaketh the hedge, the serpent shall bite him." The sensual, who has lost his health; the drunkard, who has pulled down the pillars of his home; the dishonest, who is cast out a despised and characterless thing, all point one way. It is nature's Amen to the Bible curse— *It is so.* 3. *History fills her picture-galleries with illustrations of this point.* The history of nations is a story of well-doing and its reward, prosperity, and of ill-doing and its sure-footed vengeance. History puts her brazen trumpet to her lips and blows out an assenting Amen! It is so. God will shake out as he has shaken out the wicked. You cannot argue with or alter this stable law of life. You may lay an unbelieving hand upon the letters of doom, you may cast doubt after doubt into the bottomless pit, but not one jot or tittle of the world's law which is God's law 'can be affected thereby. "Be sure your sin will find you out."

II. The doom of unrighteousness accepted Amen not only means "It is so," but, "*So let it be.*" By their Amen the people signed their agreement to the conditions, their acceptance of the pains and penalties of the transgressor. The repentant people said Amen to the curse. *They indignantly denounced their baser self.* "If I could be so base as to neglect my vow to God,

let it be even thus—let me be shaken out of God's lap of rest and blessedness." That is the significance of their Amen! 1. *Yet it is dangerous to misunderstand this* Many a struggling man, after being repeatedly vanquished by a bad habit, has in an hour of despair clutched at something like this *as if to frighten his own soul.* He has invoked a conditional curse upon his head "If I repeat this let me perish by it!" has gone from the half-maddened mind in the hour of self-disgust. Then there has come the repetition of the sin, "for the strongest oaths are straw to the fire in the blood," and the poor sinner has settled down with the thought that his doom is sealed. *There is not a little of this practical fatalism.* Avoid it! "That way madness lies!" 2. *But there is no need to pray for a curse.* If we sin the curse is sure; and the Amen of the repentant soul, whose only wish is for well-doing, is *merely a waking up of the conscience to this gloomy fact.* Let it sink into the soul. Our God is a consuming fire, therefore *know* "the terrors of the Lord." We may look at the mild glories of mercy until we forget the sterner side of life. Brace the soul by meditations on the deep, inexorable sternness of *offended law.* 3. *When engaging in formal covenant with God, when taking the pledge of conversion, when engaging in the solemnities of public or private worship, we virtually bind our souls with this curse. To give ourselves up to blessing is to denounce upon our backsliding self the curse.* When a soldier takes his oath he insures his fidelity of the reward and prospective promotion, and by that same act says Amen to the law, "Thou shalt be shot for desertion or for treachery!" It is the same in citizenship. All well-doing, right-loving citizens agree to the pains and penalties which await their possible malefactions It is thus that life is girdled with a deep gulf of doom. Evil to the evil-doer is the proposition. *It is so. Amen!* says every voice that can argue with man. *So be it. Amen!* says the soul that rises up to follow good.

III. The doom of unrighteousness

avoided. "And the people did according to their promise." 1. *The good man shuts himself up to his course.* Like Simon Peter, he can turn nowhere. "To whom shall we go" but unto *Thee.* No turning, like Lot's wife The fire of doom is the end of all backward steps. Paul-like, let us "leave the things that are behind." 2 *The good man must not depend upon the mere binding force of his oath.* Pledges and prisons are but geeen withes on the strong man of sin if there be no other bond. Goodness by the ROD is not safe or real or lasting.

The commandment often arouses the contrary desire. 3. "*My grace is sufficient for thee.*" The vow of the soul is its warrant of sincerity; the steadfast faith of the soul in the grace of Jesus Christ is its defence against temptations to desertion and disobedience.

Application 1 *Ponder the inevitable terrors of the Lord against all unrighteousness.* 2. *Vow solemnly the vow of repentance and reformation.* 3. *Pray for hourly strength to do according to this promise*

A MAN FOREGOING HIS RIGHTS FOR THE SAKE OF HIS DUTIES.

v. 14. *Moreover from the time that I was appointed, &c.*

Nehemiah was a law unto himself. Refused to be guided by others' example. "I might exact of them money and corn" (v. 10). Rose superior to insistence on his own rights "The former governors were chargeable unto the people" (v. 15) The principle is this: —A man must sometimes forego his rights for the sake of his duties.

I Rights must be asserted. It will not do to weakly allow selfishness to trample upon the too submissive soul. St Paul's insisting on his privileges as a Roman citizen an example.

II Rights must not be pressed too far. A man has prejudiced views of his own worth and deserts According to his self-importance will be the largeness of his views of his own rights. "The rights of man" is frequently a hollow cry of selfishness

III Rights must be tempered by considerations of duty. Duty is a grand governing word. It sways men more than we think. The holiday-maker is restless after a while to get back to the routine of his duties Duty is our home, pleasure is the place we take a trip to now and then. Our happiness is more bound up with our duties than with our rights We can survive being cheated of a right, but we cannot

escape if we have neglected our duties. It was such considerations as these which swayed the Jewish liberator.

IV. The due adherence to this principle is the self-sacrificing spirit of Christianity. "The Son of man came not to be ministered unto, but to minister." The crowning glory of the redemptive life of Jesus is, that though he was rich, yet for our sakes he became poor. In the second chapter of the Philippian Epistle we have the Christian setting of this doctrine. The example of Nehemiah, who came among the miserly, selfish Jews, and flung back to the people even the dues and monies which were properly his, in the greatness of his self-sacrifice shrinking from insistence on his own rights as he would from sin, was like an incarnation of nobleness for the fallen minds of his contemporaries to look at and emulate. In the sweet story of old this same grand law is carried higher. In the life of St. Paul it is repeated. In the story of missionaries and martyrs there is a prolongation of this line of light Blessed are they who reflect its blaze and join this glorious succession.

Application. 1. *Guard against the selfish spirit of the world.* 2. *Seek and show the unselfish spirit of Christ.*

A Motto for a Manly Life.

v. 15.   *So did not I, because of the fear of God.*

There is a motto for a manly life. The key-note of his character was not fear of the *crowd*, but fear of his own *conscience*. What a noble thing is *the iron sense of duty*. This was the strong sinew of the Duke of Wellington's great nature. Whether in the Church or the world, every circle feels the presence and reverences the career of one who bears this hall-mark of duty. *So will not I, for conscience' sake*. Briefly sketch the story of Nehemiah, as illustrating his adherence to his self-chosen motto. It was the banner of his whole life-battle, and he held it with a *clenched hand* in every high place of temptation.

I. The regulative power of a lofty motive. In manifold forms the firm and heroic have ruled their lives by a power superior to their own lower nature. 1. "*The fear of God*" is Nehemiah's phrase. That reverential, loving awe of the all-holy Father and Ruler of men. 2. "*The love of Christ*" is the warmer sentiment which corresponds to this in Paul's phraseology. Fuller light brought a deeper sentiment. The thought of Christ's love awakening love for Christ, and becoming in man an incarnation of heavenly inspiration. 3. "*Religious principle*" is another colder, broader, yet noble expression of the same animator of good men. 4. "*Conscience*," "*the sense of duty*," "*the instinct of right*" are less precise variations of the motives which sway all whose lives are redeemed from the ignoble.

II. The courage to be singular is implied in this motto of the Jewish liberator. 1. *Let there be no singularity for singularity's sake.* Opposition may be our *misfortune*, but must not be our *ambition*. To sing out of tune for the sake of having your voice heard is weakness, not strength. 2. *Yet this world has always rested as on granite pillars on men who could be singular.* Moses refusing to be identified with the godless nationality of Egypt. The three Hebrew children standing upright in

Babylon like watch-towers of truth. Peter and John giving their summary answer to the council: "We ought to obey God rather than man." Luther at Worms crying out, "It is not wise or safe for a man to do anything against his conscience." These men and their heroic brethren in resistance have all glorified their lives by this motto: "So did not I."

III. Applications of this principle in the commonplace life of all men. 1. To HIMSELF *a man must say* NO! "*Let him deny himself*" is a precept we must practise if we would even *live*. It is also a necessity of our *happiness*. "True quietness of heart is gotten not by obeying our passions, but by resisting them." It is essential to our *self-respect* in "the struggle of the instinct that enjoys with the more noble instinct which aspires." The mastery of *self* is the foundation-victory. "To thine own self be true, and it shall follow, as the night the day, thou canst not then be false to any man." 2. To THE WORLD *a man must say* NO! Prevalency of temptations for a man to let himself down, to barter purity for pleasure and honour for gold. How many poor men *sell their birthright of immortality* for some animal gratification! How many *sell their Lord for thirty pieces of silver, more or less.* 3. "*So did not I*" *is the* YOUTH'S *motto*. "If sinners entice thee, consent thou not." It is a manlier and a stronger thing to go right than to go wrong. "Stand thou firm as an anvil that is beaten."

IV. The simplicity and directness of this life-motto. Nehemiah's reason for his nonconformity was a very simple one. "In my view this practice is not right!" You cannot be always arguing a thing. You cannot be "*seeking truth*" (to quote *the world's cant expression for moral irresolution*) all your life. Find it quickly, and stick to it always. Providing a man's *heart* is bad enough, his *head* will usually be clever enough to

K

argue for his defence. *The devil is said to be the best of advocates, and can quote Scripture to his purpose.* But in plain matters of right and wrong "there is a spirit in man, and the inspiration of the Almighty giveth him understanding" Nehemiah's reason for not pocketing the money as others had done was *a very simple answer—" I fear God."*

V. This motto is our guide in doubtful matters. Many bad things are doubtful for want of a sensitive nerve in the soul. That which to one is "but a choleric word, to another is flat blasphemy." To Nehemiah's contemporaries and predecessors this practice of money-making had seemed a lawful one, but Nehemiah said that it was one in which a man could not keep clean hands. *The scrupulous has the solution of his difficulties in his own conscience.* Forego the doubtful for *God's* sake. Make your self-denial in that matter a sacrifice to God, and it shall be to him as the odour of incense.

Application 1 *Let us understand and acquire this great life-principle* The fear of God is not fear or dread of *a Being outside us,* but reverence and submission to *a holy Spirit within.* 2. *Let it be our strife, at whatever sacrifice, to reverence this powerful sentiment.* "Hear the conclusion of the whole matter: Fear God, and keep his commandments: for this is the whole duty of man."

ILLUSTRATIVE POEM :—

" Brother, up to the breach
For Christ's freedom and truth;
Let us act as we teach,
With the wisdom of age and the vigour of youth.
Heed not their cannon-balls,
Ask not who stands or falls,
    Grasp the sword
    Of the Lord,
    And forward !

Brother, strong in the faith
That " the right will come right,"
Never tremble at death,
Never think of thyself 'mid the roar of the fight.
Hark to the battle cry
Sounding from yonder sky !
    Grasp the sword
    Of the Lord,
    And forward !

Brother, sing a loud psalm ,
Our hope's not forlorn.
After storm comes the calm,
After darkness and twilight breaks forth the
    new morn.
Let the mad foe get madder ;
Never quail ! up the ladder
    Grasp the sword
    Of the Lord,
    And forward !

Brother, up to the breach
For Christ's freedom and truth ;
If we live we shall teach,
With the strong faith of age and the bright
    hope of youth.
If we perish, then o'er us
Will ring the loud chorus :
    Grasp the sword
    Of the Lord,
    And forward !—*Norman MacLeod.*

ILLUSTRATIONS.

Singularity.—"We must learn to say 'No' We must dare, if need be, to be singular. Like the young Joseph, when you are tempted astray by seducing voices, let your answer be, 'How can I do this great wickedness and sin against God?' Like the young Daniel, when forbidden pleasures and questionable delights are urged upon your appetites, be 'purposed in' your 'heart that' you 'will not defile' yourself with them, and choose pulse and water with the relish of a good conscience rather than such dainties. Like the same Daniel, when the crowd are flocking at the sound of the sackbut and psaltery to worship some golden image, keep your knees unbent amidst the madness, learn to stand erect though you alone are upright in the midst of a grovelling multitude, and protest, 'We will not serve thy gods nor worship the golden image which thou hast set up.' Like Nehemiah, dare to lose money rather than adopt sources of profit which others may use without a thought, but which your conscience shrinks from ; and to all the various enticements of pleasure, and gain, and ease, and popular loose maxims for the conduct oppose immovable resistance, founded on a higher law and a mightier motive. 'So did not I, because of the fear of God.'"—*A. Maclaren, D.D.*

The mighty motive. "So did not I, *because of the fear of God.*" "The heart cannot be prevailed upon to part with the world by a simple act of resignation. But may not the heart be prevailed upon to admit into its preference another, who shall subordinate the world, and bring it down from its wonted ascendancy ? If the throne which is placed there must have an occupier, and the tyrant that now reigns has occupied it wrongfully, he may not leave a bosom which would rather detain him than be left in desolation. But may he not give way to the lawful sovereign ?"—*Chalmers.*

"By his place Nehemiah had an advantage of oppressing his brethren, if he durst have been so wicked ; and from those that had before him been honoured with that office he had examples of such as could not only swallow the common allowance of the governor without rising in their consciences, which showed a digestion strong enough, considering the peeled state of the Jews at that time; but could, when themselves had sucked the milk, let their cruel servants suck the blood of this poor people also by illegal exactions, so that Nehemiah, coming after such oppressors, if he had taken his allowance, and but eased them of the other burdens which they groaned under, no doubt might have passed for merciful in their thoughts. But he durst not go so far. A man may possibly be an oppressor in exacting his own. Nehemiah knew they were not in a condition to pay, and therefore he durst not require it. But as one who comes after a bad husbandman, that hath driven his land and sucked out the heart of it, casts it up fallow for a time till it recovers its lost strength, so did Nehemiah spare this oppressed people. And what, I pray, was it that preserved him from doing as the rest had done? We have the answer in his own words: 'But so did not I, because of the fear of the Lord.' The man was honest, his heart touched with a sincere fear of God, and this kept him right."—*Gurnall.*

Conscious Integrity.

v. 19 *Think upon me, my God, for good, according to all that I have done for this people*

Nehemiah's appeal to God to deal with him according to the integrity of his life is several times repeated in this book (xiii 14, 22). "He fed the people in the integrity of his heart, and guided them by the skilfulness of his hands." God-fearing, faithful, and unselfish, in every step he could boldly look back upon his progress and take the satisfaction of an approving conscience. There is something *noble* and something *dangerous* in this sentiment

I. The habit of righteousness To some men it is given to possess great *accuracy of character,* to others it is given to be exposed constantly to a course of *honest blundering.* Illustrated in the sphere of intelligence. One man can never write a letter to satisfy him the first time—he must re-write it, while another lays a firm hand on the paper and never writes anything that he needs to erase or be sorry for. Among men of genius there are some who are dashing and brilliant in their thoughts and deeds, but now and then their work is weakened by the mistakes found therein; while there are others who seem never to be inaccurate in thought or blundering in deed. "The Duke of Wellington is, I believe (says Niebuhr), the only general in whose conduct of war we cannot discover any important mistake." The mind of such men is a chronometer as compared with the cheap clock-work of less careful and less certain minds. So it is in the moral sphere. One has a severely even and consistent nature,

another full of *moral eccentricities* Bursts of virtue and of faultiness alternate in these last-named so as to make them a continual perplexity to their friends. Goldsmith happily touches this in his pleasantry on a contemporary.

" Here lies Edmund Burke, whose genius was such
	We scarcely can praise it or blame it too much."

Yet when we consider how *an hour's fault* may undo *a week's virtue,* how by one error or sin you may put back your nature or your work more than you promote it by many excellences, it is wise to be severe upon "faults," *especially upon our own.* To be "without fault in the day of God is the mark of all Christian longing; to have "neither spot nor wrinkle nor any such thing " in his glorious vesture the Church is the desire of that Lord of whom it was said while he tabernacled among men, " I find in him no fault at all." 1 *Aim at a perfect walk with God.* " Search me, O God, and see if there be any wicked way in me" See ver. 9 . "Ought ye not to walk in the fear of our God because of the reproach of the heathen our enemies." " Ye are the temples of the Holy Ghost " is the restraining thought to keep us from fault. " The blood of Jesus Christ cleanseth us from all sin " is our refuge in our stumbles. 2. *Strive to remedy the faults of your brother* To mend his *character* is better than to mend his *fortune,* to perfect him is better than to perfect the surroundings

which he must leave behind him. 3.
*At the same time, cover with charity and
bear with patience the failures of weak
human nature.* You cannot measure
the greatness of his inward difficulties.

> "What's done you partly may compute,
> But never what's resisted."

Be severe on your own fault; be gentle
with the fault of your brother.

**II The noble refuge of the right-
eous.** A little poem, whose every line is
a thread of gold, speaks of the man
"whose conscience is his strong retreat."
In every circumstance and crisis of life
this is a safe place for the thoughts to
dwell. 1. *In prosperity.* It is a joy
to know that good has come by good
means. The rich man whose money-
bags are all witnesses of iniquity, whose
every gain signifies dishonour, must
have a wasp-sting in every fruit he
tastes. Accumulated wealth is but an
accumulation of doom to the man who
prospers wrongfully. But to have *a
good conscience as the companion of good
fortune* is to drink of the sweetest cup
of earthly happiness. 2. *In adversity.*
When other miseries are upon a man it
is glorious to be free from *that archangel of misery, a guilty conscience.* The
drunkard, who looks upon the desolation
of his family, and who knows that his
own trembling hands have pulled down
the pillars of his home, the extravagant
and reckless, who see in their ruin the
ripe harvest for which they sowed, sit
in the dark place with no consolatory
light at all. If I am bereft of my
integrity I am bereaved. Sweet it is in
adversity to sit without the whips and
scorns of self-accusation. 3. *In the
relationships of life.* To know I have
not wilfully hurt the health, or conscience, or happiness of my fellow is
an angel remembrance as life's evening
comes on. Guilty men have repented

and found a Saviour's mercy before now
whose after-thoughts have been gloomy
with remembrance of injuries done to
their fellows. So St. Paul meekly
sorrows over the madness which had in
former days damaged the flock of God.
4. *In death.* O death, where is thy
sting if the soul is found in Christ, and
the memory plays like a setting sun on a
well-spent life? "All that I have done
for this people." The good deeds of a
well-spent life are shining companions to
the soul as it goes through the windings
of the last dark valley. Contrast with
all this the guilty thoughts of the bad
king.

> "I have lived long enough; my way of life
> Is fallen into the sear, the yellow leaf,
> And that which should accompany old age
> I must not look to have; but in their stead
> Curses, not loud but deep, mouth-honour breath
> Which the poor heart would fain deny, but
>   dare not."

III. The dangers of the righteous.
To stand upon our righteous habits is
to select a wrong basis. Goodness is
rather the buttress of the wall than its
foundation.

> "Nor alms or deeds that I have done
>   Can for a single sin atone;
>   To Calvary alone I flee,
>   O God, be merciful to me."

Self-righteousness brings pride and
uncharitableness. When Archbishop
Whately lay dying some one said, "It
is the greatness of your lordship's mind
that supports you." "No, it is not" (he
said), "it is faith in Christ that supports me." That is the Rock of ages.

Application. 1. *Strive after such
integrity as will bring satisfaction to the
soul in the great review at the last.* 2.
*Let no thought of your own goodness
come as a shadow in front of the cross to
rob the Redeemer of the glory of his salvation.*

THE SAINT'S SUPPORT.

v 19. *Think upon me, my God, for good, according to all that I have done for
this people.*

Two motives induced Nehemiah to
pray thus. the many great and good
things he had done for Church and

state; the many great and desperate
dangers he had already met with, and
would still have to encounter. There

were three solemn comings of three
famous persons to Jerusalem—Zerubbabel, Ezra, and Nehemiah. The secret
of Nehemiah's courage—his heart was
on his God.

First, of the sense of the text. "Think,"
properly "remember." To remember is
(*a*) to keep and hold fast in memory,
opposed to forgetting. (*b*) To call to
mind forgotten things. A word derived
from this root is put for a memorial
(Exod. xxviii 12) and for records
(Esther vi 1). Remembering is in
Scripture applied to (1) God and (2)
man. To God properly in first signification. God never forgets. "Known
unto him are all his works" (Acts xv.
18) Remembrance is also applied to
God in the second signification (Job
vii 7; x 9; xiv. 3). He has a book
of remembrance (Mal. iii 16) These
are to be taken "tropically," by way of
similitude. Nehemiah's "remember"
means, "May I have assurance and
others' evidence." "*My* God," an ap-
propriating particle ("*God*" — Heb
Elohim), a plurality of persons, a unity

of nature. "For good," *i. e.* goodness.
The saint's support is God

1. *The person petitioned.* 2. *The
point prayed for.*
I. **The person** 1. General title.
"God." 2. Special relation. "My"
II **The point prayed for.** 1. The
kind of it. 2. The end of it. 1. The
kind. (1) An act desired of God.
"Think upon." (2) The special object
"Me." 2. The end. (1) Generally.
"For good." (2) Particularly. (*a*) The
ground—"that I have done." (*b*) The
rule—"according to." (*c*) The extent
—"all." (*d*) The limitation—"for this
people." Observations hence arising.
1. *God the support of his saints.* 2. *Peculiar God to believer.* "*My.*" 3 *God
hath remembrancers.* 4 *God is soonest
drawn to his own.* 5. *Prayer proper
for one's own good.* 6. *Works may be
pleaded before God* 7. *Man's works
are the rule of God's reward.* 8. *Everything well done shall be rewarded* 9
*Good done to God's people is most
acceptable.—Dr. Wm. Gouge, 1642.*

THE REMEMBRANCE OF GOOD DEEDS A PILLOW OF REST FOR A GOOD MAN.

v. 19.   *Think upon me, my God, for good, according to all that I have done for
this people.*

"Nehemiah's soul was frank with
God. There is freedom of access to a
throne of grace for every believer (Heb
iv. 16). 'Think upon me, my God, for
good, according to all that I have done
for this people,' is not a presumptuous
conceit, but a childlike simplicity. The
gross mind of the world would confound
the two Where we know that God
has led us in paths of righteousness,
we may well use that knowledge, and
encourage our souls by it. Nehemiah had but few around him who
could reach high enough to sympathize
fully with him; and it was thus his
great comfort to pour out his soul,
according to truth, before the God
whose good hand had guided him. God
wishes no mock modesty from us. His
grace in our hearts and lives should be
acknowledged (comp 1 Tim i. 12)."—
Crosby. The personal pronoun is very

prominent in David's autobiography.
"I have preached." "I have not refrained
my lips" (Ps xl) "My defence is of
God" (Ps. vii). "Thou hast tried me,
and shalt find nothing" (Ps. xvii.).
St. Paul boldly cites his own example.
Readers of his epistles note his self-
consciousness. "Whatsoever things ye
have learned, and received, and heard,
and seen in me, do" (Phil. iv. 9).
"Brethren, be followers together of me"
(Phil iii 17). "I beseech you be as I
am" (Gal. iv. 12) "These hands have
ministered to my necessities" (Acts xx
34). "I have fought a good fight" (2
Tim iv. 7).
I. **Life's review will be a review of
the whole of life.** Its good as well as
its evil. When "backward are our
glances bent" we shall need the recollection of every pure thought, guiding
word, kindly deed. When we lie down

in the long sleep men call death may no *pleasant dreams* come?

II. Life's reward will be rendered according to its deeds. God will "give every man according as his work shall be" (Rev. xxii. 12). We are saved by grace, "looking for the mercy of our Lord Jesus Christ unto eternal life" (Jude 21). But there is a rewardable-ness of works. "We must all appear before the judgment-seat of Christ; that every one may receive the things done in his body" (2 Cor. v. 10). "Blessed are the dead which die in the Lord; their works do follow them" (Rev. xiv. 13). "We carry nothing out of the world with us but the conscience and comfort of what we have done for God."

CHAPTER VI.

EXPLANATORY NOTES.] "When Sanballat and the enemies associated with him were unable to obstruct the building of the wall of Jerusalem by open violence, they endeavoured to ruin Nehemiah by secret snares. They invited him to meet them in the plain of Ono (vers. 1, 2); but Nehemiah, perceiving that they intended mischief, would not come. After receiving for the fourth time this refusal, Sanballat sent his servant to Nehemiah with an open letter, in which he accused him of rebellion against the king of Persia. Nehemiah repelled this accusation as the invention of Sanballat (vers. 3—9). Tobiah and Sanballat hired a false prophet to make Nehemiah flee into the temple from fear of the snares prepared for him, that they might then be able to calumniate him (vers. 10—14). The building of the wall was completed in fifty-two days, and the enemies were disheartened (vers. 15, 16), although at that time many nobles of Judah had entered into epistolary correspondence with Tobiah to obstruct the proceedings of Nehemiah (vers. 17—19)."—*Keil.*
1. **When Sanballat . . . . heard**] "In the indefinite sense of it came to his ears. The use of the passive is more frequent in later Hebrew, comp. vers 6, 7, xii. 27."—*Keil.* The rest of our enemies] See iv 7. 2. **Come, let us meet together**] for a discussion = Let us take counsel together (ver. 7). Ono] According to 1 Chron. viii. 12, situated in the neighbourhood of Lod (Lydda), and is therefore identified by Van de Velde and Bertheau with Kefr Anna, one and three-quarter leagues north of Ludd. Roediger compares it with Beit Unia, north-west of Jerusalem, not far from Bethel There may have been two places of the same name **They thought to do me mischief**] Probably they wanted to make him a prisoner, perhaps even to assassinate him. 3. **I am doing a great work : I cannot come down**] Could not undertake the journey because his presence in Jerusalem was necessary for the uninterrupted prosecution of the work of building. 4] They sent unto him four times in the same manner, and Nehemiah gave them the same answer. 5. **An open letter**] That its contents might alarm all the Jews and create opposition to Nehemiah. In Western Asia letters, after being rolled up like a map, are flattened, and, instead of being sealed, are pasted at the ends. In Eastern Asia the Persians make up their letters in form of a roll, with a bit of paper fastened round it Letters were and are still sent to persons of distinction in a bag or purse, and to equals inclosed, to inferiors, or to express contempt, open. 6. **It is reported**] Sanballat throughout makes no accusation, but refers to rumour Nehemiah's answer is, " There is not according to these words which thou sayest," *i. e.* there is no such rumour (ver 8). 7. **Thou hast appointed prophets to preach of thee**] To proclaim concerning thee in Jerusalem, saying, King of Judah. 8. **Thou feignest**] Nehemiah charges his enemy with devising a wicked slander. 9. "'**For'**—adds Nehemiah, when writing of these things—'they all desired to make us afraid, thinking, Their hands will cease from the work, that it be not done'"] *Keil.* **Strengthen my hands**] Taken from Nehemiah's journal kept at the time of building. Quotes to show where his dependence was at that trying time. 10. **Shemaiah**] "A false prophet hired by Tobiah and Sanballat, who sought by prophesying that the enemies of Nehemiah would kill him in the night to cause him to flee with him into the holy place of the temple, and to protect his life from the machinations of his enemies by closing the temple doors His purpose was, as Nehemiah subsequently learned, to seduce him into taking an illegal step, and so give occasion for speaking evil of him."—*Keil.* The gift of prophecy did not prevent a man from selling himself to lie for others (see 1 Kings xxii 22) **Shut up**] Perhaps in performance of a vow, or as a mere pretence. " Your foes are my foes Let us escape together." **In the house of God, within the temple**] Within the holy place, where no layman was allowed to enter. **And let us shut the doors, &c.**] "He seeks to corroborate his warning as a special revelation from God by making it appear that God had not only made known to him the design of the enemies, but also the precise time at which they intended to carry it into execution."—*Keil.* 11. **Should such a man as**

I flee ?] Nehemiah had anxiety and alarm, but no cowardice. **To save his life**] "'That he may live.' May mean 'to save his life,' or, 'and save his life.' Not expiate such a transgression of the law with his life."—*Keil.* **14 The prophetess Noadiah, and the rest of the prophets**] Vers. 10 —13 only a specimen case. Nothing more is known of Noadiah. **15. Elul**] The sixth month. Parts of August and September. **16. They perceived that this work was wrought of our God**] Accomplished in so short a space of time. **17—19**] A supplementary remark that in those days even nobles of Judah were in alliance and active correspondence with Tobiah because he had married into a respectable Jewish family. **19. His good deeds**] "Good qualities and intentions."—*Bertheau.* They were trying to effect an understanding, Bertheau and Keil think. Or were they not traitors ?

HOMILETICAL CONTENTS OF CHAPTER VI.

THE PERILS OF GREATNESS.

Chap. vi.

THE interest of the history centres in the *man.* All history is the biography of the most eminent men. "Men of the time" make the time We have met Nehemiah before, but under different conditions. The accidents of men's lives change ; the character remains. Not in what a man *does,* but in what a man *is,* look we for permanence. Nehemiah the Persian cup-bearer becomes the reformer of abuses and rebuilder of the decayed city of God. Nehemiah, to-day confronted by visible armies, is to-morrow confronting the unseen foes of stratagem and deception. "Sanballat and Geshem sent unto me, saying, Come, let us meet together But they thought to do me mischief" (ver. 2). "It is reported among the heathen that thou and the Jews think to rebel ; it is reported that thou hast appointed prophets to preach of thee at Jerusalem, saying, There is a king in Judah. Come, let us take counsel.—There are no such things done as thou sayest" (vers. 6—8) "Shemaiah was hired, that I should be afraid, and sin" (vers. 10—14). "The nobles of Judah reported Tobiah's good deeds before me, and uttered my words to him. And Tobiah sent letters to put me in fear" (vers. 17—19). The Book written by inspired men gives the teaching of observation and experience when it says in every variety of expression, and with all the cumulative force of its progressive teaching, "Be watchful. The conditions of the conflict of life change ; the conflict never ceases. In this battle there is no truce. He that endureth to the end shall be saved."

I. The perils of greatness. High places are dangerous places, as poets, moralists, and preachers have told us with perhaps wearisome iteration. That each man should do his duty in that state of life in which God has placed him used to be a favourite text with many. The laws of self-help are, if not of recent date, at least of recent definition That the battle be to the strong and the race to the swift ; that all be unhelped and all unhindered, is historically of recent date. We must not forget to proclaim that the powers that be are ordained of God. There may be insanity in hero-worship over-much ; but it is idiotic to refuse to recognize the hero. The celebrated valet sees no genius in his master. Is it because he is *too near,* or because he is *too ignorant?* That there be men of Nehemiah's stamp occupying Nehemiah's station is indispensable. The world must have leaders who can infuse their own courage into their followers Nehemiah's men were devoted—but only in his presence and under his inspiration. They were liable to panic and subject to craven fear In doing the world's work there must be some who have opportunities for clearer vision and deeper knowledge The general on the heights, not the private in the thick of the fight, gives the word of command. To the captain the charts are an alphabet employed without distinct consciousness, leave to him the steering, whilst you walk or sleep. Kings have committed acts of folly; but has King Mob been always a Solomon? There is a needs-be for the king on his throne, the senator in the council-room, the judge on the bench, the barrister at the bar, the poet in the study, the painter in the grove, the preacher in the pulpit, the teacher at his desk. But let none dream that these offices are sinecures, or that the men who hold them are free from the thousand ills to which flesh is heir. It is a fierce light that beats upon a throne No man yet climbed the heights without the dogs of envy, hatred, and malice barking at his heels. Not Nehemiah's labourers, but Nehemiah, was the object of Sanballat's force and fraud. Strike him, and all are struck. The most eminent men are the best-hated men. In any task the responsibility of the *second* man is proverbially easier than that of the *first.* It is not always needful to point out the moral that adorns the tale of human life.

II The deportment of the imperilled. The great thing to be desired for those who hold high office in our world is the conviction that God has appointed their station, set the bounds of their habitation, and allotted their task. In this conviction there is power, from it courage springs. This was Nehemiah's strength "*I am doing a great work.*" And he explains the "I." "*This work was wrought of our God*" Hence the sublime trust of Moses in the day of God's anger. "Let *thy work* appear unto thy servants" (Ps xc) When neither sun nor stars in many days appeared, and men's hearts failed them for fear, Paul strengthened himself in the recollection of his mission. "There stood by me this night the angel of God, *whose I am, and whom I serve*" (Acts xxvii.). In the darkest hour of Luther's life he lifted up his eyes to God and cried, "*It is not my cause, but thine.*" "Not unto us, O Lord, not unto us, but unto thy name be the glory of the strength and endurance we have manifested," is the substance of the impassioned utterances of the noble army of martyrs, workers, and warriors from the days of Abel down to the last hours of the sainted sufferer who but yesternight went home to God The truest self-reliance rests upon the rocky foundations of trust in God. That thousands of professedly Christian and Bible-reading people are little bettered, but rather grow worse in temper and character, needs no proof—it is evident to the all but blind; but that the Christian and Bible-reading nations are immeasurably superior to the peoples that sit in the darkness of nature and the shadow of heathenism is indisputable. Any man who would be in any measure faithful to himself and equal to his life-task must "*believe that God is, and that he is a rewarder of them that diligently seek him.*" This is not a blind, unreasoning trust; not a reliance on another to do what the man can do himself. Nehemiah threw all his soul into those two little words in the fourteenth verse, "MY GOD." But he did not neglect to be watchful. "They thought to do me mischief" (ver 2). He was anxious to discover the truth, and sought out the origin even of misrepresentation. "I perceived that God had not sent the prophet; Tobiah and Sanballat had hired him" (ver 12). He recognized the appointed channels of God's revelation. "I came unto Shemaiah the prophet" (ver. 10) He was fearless in denouncing wrong-doers, albeit they sat in high places "There are no such things done as thou sayest, but thou feignest them out of thine own heart" (ver 8). Above all, he renewed his strength by waiting upon God "Now therefore, O God, strengthen my hands" (ver. 9). From God came his task; from God must come the strength to accomplish it. A great historian, after telling the tale of the life of a king of France, adds,

"Let no meanest man lay flattering unction to his soul.   Louis was a ruler, but art not thou also one? His broad France looked at from the fixed stars is no wider than thy narrow brick-field, in which thou too didst faithfully or didst unfaithfully." Brother, thy task is not Nehemiah's, nor Paul's, nor Luther's, nor John Wesley's, nor Calvin's, but it is *thy* task; and if thou strivest faithfully thou wilt find it thy *task.*   The work of a man's life is no child's play.   Do not sport with everything. It is said that when Carlyle was shown a Comic History, he inquired when we were to have a Comic Bible.   To such a man the word of God and the life of man were terribly earnest.   To all earnest men their daily task is earnest.   The humblest is a witness to the power of his own convictions of what he is, where he is, and whom he serves.   Let him take care to bear a constant, unfaltering, and ever-growing testimony.   Let him be more anxious to be great than to do some great thing.   Let him be more concerned to work faithfully than to work successfully, and by and by to the question, "Is all well?" he shall give the answer, "All is well!"   "Let your light shine before men " (Matt. v. 16).

Illustration.—Grown great.

" Some divinely gifted man,
Whose life in low estate began,
And on a simple village green,
Who breaks his birth's invidious bar,
And grasps the skirts of happy chance,
And breasts the blows of circumstance,
And grapples with his evil star,
Who makes by force his merit known,
And lives to clutch the golden keys,
To mould a mighty state's decrees,
And shape the whisper of the throne;
And moving up from high to higher,
Becomes on fortune's crowning slope
The pillar of a people's hope,

The centre of a world's desire,
Yet feels, as in a pensive dream,
When all his active powers are still,
A distant dearness in the hill,
A secret sweetness in the stream,
The limit of his narrower fate,
While yet beside its vocal springs
He play'd at counsellors and kings,
With one that was his earliest mate;
Who ploughs with pain his native lea
And reaps the labour of his hands,
Or in the furrow musing stands;
' Does my old friend remember me?' "
Tennyson.

PERSISTENCY.

vi. 1—4. *Now it came to pass, when Sanballat, and Tobiah, and Geshem the Arabian, heard, &c.*

To do a thing and see it all frustrated, and to begin again coolly, calmly, quietly, and repeat the action, that is a very necessary power in this world.   In your summer idleness you break a spider's web with your stick or disturb an ant-hill, and the tiny operatives, without wasting one moment, steadily begin again and repair their damaged property. These illustrate a grand faculty of man. In life you want the power to begin again and to keep on in spite of whatsoever break-down or hindrance. Nehemiah gives grand example of this. *Our text is a text on persistency— persistency of opposition, persistency of endeavour.* The opponents of this Jewish Garibaldi try one move more to check-mate and hinder the great Liberator, and, like the moon when the watch-dog barks, he simply keeps on doing what he was doing, unterrified, unmoved.   I cannot meet you for conference (he said); I am too busy, and cannot stop the work for you or for any one or for anything.   He had no time to say this in person; he "sent messengers" "four times after this sort."

I. This principle of persistency is illustrated in all the circle of nature and life. 1. *Everywhere there is exhibition of hostile force.*   Universal life is a conflict.   The "*Peace Society*," who have the noblest of all objects, the suppression of strife, have but few clients in inferior nature.   All natural forces, all life, energy, creep to their goal as the wave creeps to the shore after many a rebuff and after many a spurning.   The seed struggling up from its grave, the sapling bending through the crevice in the ruin, the tree battling with the sweep of the tempest—all are persistent fighters of opposition. The insect striving with its mortal foe in the cup of a tiny flower, the bird with vigilant eye watching foes below and above, the beast of the forest amid its dangers, are all showing us on what terms a place is to be found on earth— *clinging pertinacity.* You must not be tempted or coerced from your aim by hostility. 2 *It is so with man in all social life.* The boy at school wrestling with competitors for his prizes or his juvenile influence, the man of business watching the mischances and the adversaries of his success, the popular character striving against the envious among his contemporaries and the changefulness of the people, show us under what tenure the prizes, noble and ignoble, of social life are held "To him that overcometh" the crown of life is given. 3. *Consistently with this analogy of nature, the Bible represents all moral victory as against deep and persistent hostility.* A legion of devils, from without, a legion of lusts within seek to snare and to frighten the soul from its work. The Bible moves and stirs in eagerness to warn and to inspirit the threatened soul.

II This principle of persistency is illustrated in the general history of the kingdom of God. 1. *The Bible is one long history of God's controversy with his opponents.* From one generation to another, through millenniums of history, the Almighty Sovereign of the world is battling with opposition. *Physically speaking,* God can do *whatever he will*, but *morally speaking, God must do what he can against the wills of moral creatures who "dare defy the Omnipotent to arms"* And our Bible is the Iliad of heaven against earth. The clash of battle rings through its mighty leaves. This is the value of Old Testament history—it is God saving men in spite of the resistance of the men he seeks to save. *Hence the history of one chosen people has become the world's parable of life and salvation.* Jewish history is an immortal text-book concerning this Divine controversy and conflict. 2. *Christian history is in the same tone.* (*a*) The Captain of our salvation is set forth in the gospel story as in warfare with the obstinate and prejudiced all the way to his transcendent triumph "*I would and ye would not*" is the burden of the solemn story (*b*) Apostolic history makes a harmony with what has gone before. The chosen apostles and all who took up their great *watchword, Christ,* were *gladiators* in the great arena of the world; "of all men most miserable" unless their cause were Divine and eternal And the closing words of God's Testament fade away in St John's Apocalyptic visions of *wars in heaven,* and the noise of him who goes forth conquering and to conquer (*c*) Nor have we seen the end *The Church is a "militant Church"— every saint a soldier;* and the world, the flesh, and the devil set in battle array. Heathen creeds, worldly maxims, carnal forces, all opposing the will of the redeeming Lord.

III. It is the same with regard to this principle of persistency in individual salvation and work. 1. *To save your own soul is "a great work" —a work that is hindered.* This is why the gate of life is strait, not that it is narrow in itself, but it is narrowed by the throng of foes that block it to the soul John Bunyan saw in his dream a gate leading to a beautiful palace. At the gate sat a man with a book to record the names of such as would enter. Around the gate stood armed foes to drive back all who came. At length a man with "a stout countenance" came, and said to the recorder, "Set down my name, sir!" and then, girding on his sword, he set to and fought his way in, "but not before he had given and received many wounds." It is thus that most of us enter into life. Persistent opposition beaten back by persistent determination. This is what the Saviour means by those who are *worthy of him,* those who *will* have him. The *elect* are the *select* spirits who *must* enter into life because the *must* is in their will. They *will* go in, though hell move from beneath to oppose If you are about this purpose, the *one purpose* of man, you are doing a great work, and cannot come down from that, or you fail. 2. *To be instruments of salvation to others is a great work that is hindered, but must not cease.* The parent lovingly battling with the wills of his children, the Sunday School teacher bearing with the waywardness of a circle of opposing spirits, the minister standing as God's watchman in his congregation, the man of business striving to live without damage to the soul of his brother, and to live with good influence upon those who meet him in life's conflict, are Nehemiahs all of them. He toiled on amid the stones of Jerusalem, they amid the living stones of a better city of God. But the story is one story—the world-wide story of good hindered and opposed, but triumphant.

Application *Helps to persistency.* 1. *Do not magnify your foes* Right is itself "a big battalion." Greater is he that is for us than all that can be against us. 2. *Do not under-estimate your work* All good work is "a great work." Let its loftiness fill and inflame you 3. *Do not fail in hope.* Hope on, hope ever "Hope thou in God." On this rock of Peter-courage and inflexibility Christ will build his Church, "and the gates of hell shall not prevail against it."

OLD FOES WITH NEW FACES.

vi. 1, 2. *Now it came to pass, when Sanballat, and Tobiah, and Geshem the Arabian, and the rest of our enemies, heard that I had builded the wall, and that there was no breach left therein; (though at that time I had not set up the doors upon the gates,) that Sanballat and Geshem sent unto me, saying, Come, let us meet together in some one of the villages in the plain of Ono. But they thought to do me mischief.*

The enemies of reformation in Nehemiah's day were fertile in resources as well as persistent in opposition. When mockery failed to dishearten, and threats to drive Nehemiah from his task, Sanballat, Tobiah, and Geshem tried the art of deception. The same men, with purpose unchanged, but masked faces. "The voice is Jacob's voice, but the hands are the hands of Esau."

"My son, thou art never secure in this life, but as long as thou livest thou shalt always need spiritual armour. Thou dwellest among enemies" This golden sentence from the lips of Thomas à Kempis contains the moral application we may make of this historical passage.

I. Faults of character. "The natural man" is in Biblical language distinguished from "the spiritual man." "The past of our life;"—"the rest of our time." The dividing line we popularly call conversion. "If any man be in Christ, he is a new creature: old things are passed away; behold, all things are become new." That is the ideal; does not become the actual in a day. The life religious is a growth. A man becomes a Christian; supposes that conversion makes all things new, is soon disabused. He was before an angry man, he blazes up again in an unwatchful moment. He was full of health and vigour, animalism ruled him; he discovers that he needs to lay a strong hand upon himself. Temptability remains. "The snake is scotched, not killed." The natural prayerlessness of men creeps insensibly upon an unwatchful Christian. A principal will connive at the doubtful deeds of an agent—deeds which he himself would not stoop to do. There is a moral obliquity of vision. "If the light that is in thee be darkness, how great is that darkness." "Can't see" is pitiable, "won't see" is criminal. An under-current is often fatal when a hurricane would have been harmless. Against the second the captain would provide; of the first he might have no knowledge. The signing of the pledge does not of itself quench the burning thirst. The Church roll does not make defection impossible. Every man has one great foe—himself.

"Worse than all my foes I find
 The enemy within,
The evil heart, the carnal mind,
 My own insidious sin .
My nature every moment waits
 To render me secure,
And all my paths with ease besets,
 To make my ruin sure."

Faults of character are foes to interest.
Nobody has a fault that is not injurious.
" There is a *but* in every man's fortunes,
because there is a *but* in every man's
character."—*Maclaren.* A good cause is
sometimes injured by the intemperance
of its advocates; more often by their inconsistency   Creed and conduct are not
always equal   Beware of little sins.

II. Foes to progress Nehemiah was
reforming, uplifting the nation   Sanballat, Tobiah, and Geshem were advocates
of things as they were   Indolence and
selfishness of individuals are aggregated.
In the movements of history there has
been presented the spectacle of men fleeing from persecution to become persecutors in their turn   Presbyter was
priest writ large.   Human nature is
much the same under all conditions.
Luther overthrew the Pope's infallibility
to meet claimed infallibility in his own
followers.   Only to patient faith is the
prize sure.   They who work for eternity
can afford to listen calmly to the bab-
blings of contemporary opinion.   Utter
no rebuking word, although the " meet-
ening for the inheritance" and the
unsuccess of your toils require you to
possess the patience of God.   " One day
is with the Lord as a thousand years,
and a thousand years as one day."

"Christian! seek not yet repose,
 Cast thy dreams of ease away ,
Thou art in the midst of foes ,
  Watch and pray.

Principalities and powers,
Mustering their unseen array,
Wait for thy unguarded hours;
  Watch and pray.

Gird thy heavenly armour on,
Wear it ever night and day ;
Ambushed lies the evil one ,
  Watch and pray.

Hear the victors who o'ercame ,
Still they mark each warrior's way;
All with one sweet voice exclaim,
  Watch and pray

Hear, above all, hear thy Lord,
Him thou lovest to obey,
Hide within thy heart his word ;
  Watch and pray.

Watch, as if on that alone
Hung the issue of the day ;
Pray that help may be sent down ,
  Watch and pray."

THE GREAT WORK.

vi. 3.   *And I sent messengers unto them, saying, I am doing a great work, so that*
I cannot come down . why should the work cease, whilst I leave it, and come down
to you ?

Religion the most momentous and important matter that can possibly engage
the attention.   Either the veriest dream of superstition, or the most stupendous as
well as the most interesting subject   This is *the great work.*
I. The great work in which Nehemiah was engaged.   Repairing the wall
and setting up the gates around the city of Jerusalem.   He had many powerful
enemies.   They first tried to ridicule him and his brethren out of the undertaking ;
and this failing, they endeavoured to terrify them ; and not succeeding in this, they
had recourse to craft and stratagem.   In the verse preceding Nehemiah says,
" Sanballat and Geshem sent unto me," &c   And in the verse following Nehemiah
tells us that they sent unto him four times, after the same sort, and he answered
them after the same manner.   What is fortifying, defending, and preserving a city
when compared with the salvation of our immortal soul ?   If we are really on the
Lord's side we shall assuredly be opposed as he was, and perhaps more strenuously,
by ridicule, stratagem, and force.   To all opposition let us reply, " I am doing a
great work."   Some say the business of salvation so far as we are concerned is no
work at all.   Surely *faith* and *love* have something to do with salvation; and

although these graces of the Spirit may apparently be the farthest removed from what may be termed a work, yet we read in Scripture of "the *work* of faith, and the labour of love." Yes, faith worketh by love. True, as far as merit is concerned, salvation is not of works; yet there is a sense in which we are to "work out our own salvation with fear and trembling, for it is God that worketh in us both to will and to do according to his good pleasure." The believer "fears the Lord and his goodness." He fears to offend against infinite holiness, or to "grieve the Holy Spirit." He fears to bring guilt upon his conscience. And he trembles to be found "an unprofitable servant." Faith enables the believer to see the path of obedience, and love constrains him cheerfully to walk therein. The work of Christ, so far from freeing us from obedience, lays us under greater obligations to devotedness.

II. The opposition Nehemiah had to encounter in his undertaking. 1. *He was assailed by ridicule* (see chap. ii. 19; iv. 1—3). You may profess what you please without molestation, but if you proceed to act up to your profession you will certainly not escape opposition. How did Nehemiah meet the scoffs of his enemies? He did not desist from his purpose, nor did he take the matter of revenge into his own hands. 2. *Nehemiah's enemies attempted also to assail him by force* (iv. 7, 8). We ought to give all due obedience, in things lawful, to those who in the providence of God may have control over us, but there is a point beyond which to yield would be sin. When human authority is exerted contrary to the Divine command we ought not a moment to hesitate to "obey God rather than man." 3. *Nehemiah's enemies assailed him also with craft and cunning.* "Sanballat and Tobiah sent unto me, saying," &c. More persons are enticed and allured into sinful compliances by plausible inducements than by any other means. Never expect any spiritual advantage from the proposal of a confederacy with worldly men. 4. *When Sanballat could not succeed by stratagem, he endeavoured to effect his purpose by putting Nehemiah in fear.* Raised false reports against him, representing that he was building the wall that he might set up himself as a king and rebel against his Persian master. Expect misrepresentation. It was said of the apostles of old, "These that have turned the world upside down are come hither also." Think it not strange if modern Christians be accused of being enemies to the peace of society. When we see Sanballat not only falsely accusing Nehemiah, but also hiring the professed prophets of God to endeavour to turn him from the work in which he was engaged, let us learn the great need of watchfulness, caution, and circumspection. "Be ye wise as serpents." If an angel from heaven should speak anything contrary to the doctrine of godliness, shun his counsel. Even Satan can transform himself into the appearance of an angel of light, and his angels imitate his example. "Prove all things, and hold fast that which is good." Nehemiah went to Shemaiah for godly counsel and advice, little expecting that he was in the service of his great enemy (vers. 10—14). God will expose the snares and bring to nought the devices planned against his faithful servants. "I perceived," saith Nehemiah, "that God had not sent him." And as before he answered the rumours of Sanballat by saying, "There are no such things done as thou sayest, but thou feignest them out of thine own heart;" so now he boldly answers the counsel of the lying prophet who would have him shamefully neglect his duty, and shut himself up in the temple to save his life, by saying, "Should such a man as I flee—I on whose presence at the building of the wall so much depends, and who believe and have professed that God will protect and defend me?" When we are tempted to make sinful compliance, let us call to mind the noble answer of Nehemiah, and adopt similar language; let us say to every temptation to evil, "Should such a man as I, who profess to be a disciple of, yea, a joint-heir with, Christ, a son of God, and an heir of immortality—should such an one as I condescend to bring disgrace upon my profession, and thus dishonour God and sin against my own soul?" Or with Joseph 'let us ask our own conscience, "How can I do this great wickedness and sin against God?"

III. The magnitude of the work required that Nehemiah should not cease. It was a *great* work, for the walls of Jerusalem extended some miles round the city; and it was a very *necessary* work to be completed for the defence of the inhabitants Of what momentous importance is the salvation of a man! The destruction of the temple and city of Jerusalem is said to have forced tears from the eyes of its heathen conqueror; but what is a flaming temple or the destruction of a city to the destruction of an immortal spirit! Let your careful and constant attention be given to the one thing needful "For it is not a light thing, because it is your life." Nehemiah succeeded in accomplishing the work he had in hand by prayer, watchfulness, and painstaking diligence (vers. 15, 16) So will all the enemies of God's truth be finally cast down in their own eyes, they will be utterly ashamed and confounded, while they will be constrained to confess that the salvation of the righteous is of the Lord. The wall was built in troublous times, and we often find Nehemiah supplicating help from the mighty God of Jacob, like Jehoshaphat, who said, "Lord, we know not what to do, but our eyes are toward thee;" and while he was unceasing and fervent in prayer, he was also watchful and diligent in the work.—*Rev. James Shore, M.A., abridged*

HINDRANCES TO REVIVALS.

VI. 3.   *I am doing a great work*, &c.

Sanballat's opposition — threatened; complained; insisted that Nehemiah's design was not pious, but political. Nehemiah went on.

I A revival of religion is a great work. It is a great work because in it great interests are involved. In a revival of religion are involved both the glory of God, so far as it respects the government of this world, and the salvation of men The greatness of a work is to be estimated by the greatness of the consequences depending on it. And this is the measure of its importance.

II Several things may put a stop to a revival A revival is the work of God, and so is a crop of wheat, and God is as much dependent on the use of means in one case as the other 1. *A revival will stop whenever the Church believe it is going to cease.* No matter what the enemies of the work may say about it, predicting that it will all run out and come to nothing, they cannot stop it in this way. But the friends must labour and pray in faith to carry it on 2. *A revival will cease when Christians consent that it should cease.* When Christians love the work of God and the salvation of souls so well that they are distressed at a mere apprehension of

a decline, it will drive them to agony and effort to prevent its ceasing. 3 *A revival will cease whenever Christians suppose the work will go on without their aid.* The Church are co-workers with God in promoting a revival, and the work can be carried on just as far as the Church will carry it on, and no farther 4 *A revival will cease when Christians begin to proselyte* Do not raise selfish strife, and drive Christians into parties. 5. *When the Church in any way grieve the Holy Spirit.* 6. *When Christians lose the spirit of brotherly love.* 7 *A revival will decline and cease unless Christians are frequently reconverted*

III. Things which ought to be done to continue a revival 1 *Ministerial humiliation.* Ministers must not only call upon the people to repent; they must be ensamples to the flock 2 *Churches which have opposed revivals must repent* 3. *Those who promote the work of revivals must repent their mistakes.* There is a constant tendency in Christians to backsliding and declension. Let us mind our work, and let the Lord take care of the rest; do our duty, and leave the issue to God.—*Finney, abridged.*

SLANDER.

vi. 5—8.   *Then sent Sanballat his servant unto me,* &c.

An attempt to frustrate Nehemiah by a false report concerning his intentions is described in these verses. This *petty wasp of slander* may sting the even-minded Reformer, and make him swerve from his steadiness. Sanballat sent to say that it was a "common report" that Nehemiah was meditating the ambitious project of becoming a king; and to make the matter circumstantial, Gashmu was quoted as the authority for this information. Nehemiah, with noble indifference, brushed away the wasp—sent a short, sharp answer back —and *then, dismissing the matter, went on with his work.*

I The slander. Isaac Barrow's biographer quaintly wishes he could find an enemy of his hero, that he might have the honour of defending the memory of the great divine. All men are not so fortunate. The faultless have some fault found with them, and the faulty have their faults exaggerated. Let the most blameless man in the town offer himself as *candidate for parliament,* and the organ of the rival political party will give a picture astounding to the friends of the good man. Shimei finds foul things to say about David, and Gashmu knows a damaging thing about Nehemiah. In this example of the text there are three stages of slander. 1. *The common report.* "It is commonly reported among the heathen that thou and the Jews think to rebel." Who got up *that* report? is a common question about similar matters now-a-days. Who was the man in the iron mask? Who executed Charles I.? Who invents the lie that sings in the air about some faultless man? These are conundrums to "give up." Where all the gnats come from that fill the window-pane was a puzzle to our childhood. Where all the lies come from that buzz round our neighbourhoods is a puzzle to our later life. "*It is commonly reported!*" Woe to the tongue ingenious in this art! For our own part, let us

beware of giving our jealousies and suspicions wings. Let them die in the egg. Keep the door of the lips, especially when conversing with a fool. And equally necessary is it to beware of eager listening to groundless suggestions, born of malice and envy and uncharitableness. The demand creates the supply. Send these hawkers of mischief away from the door. Keep the door of the ears. 2 *The authority for the "fact."* "Gashmu saith it." Who's Gashmu? A very common authority on these matters. He's very often a myth. There is no Gashmu at all. Try to find him, and he is always "removed." Tracking a slander is often like seeking a grasshopper. It chirps here and there and everywhere, except on the handful of grass you lay your hand on. Looking for Gashmu is like hunting the cuckoo —it's "a voice, a mystery." *Gashmu!* He is not, or you find him not. Sometimes Gashmu is real enough. If you hear the report, you need not be told where it came from. Gashmu "his mark" is on the forehead of the slander. He sits in his window blowing peas at all passers-by. There are human creatures who delight in this kind of cowardly damage of other men's reputations. For some wise end they were created—all things are. The nettle and the hornet and the slanderer—perhaps these have their part to play. "*Gashmu*" *might be carved on some of the graves—"Here rests one who never let any one else rest."* 3. *The informant.* Sanballat sent the letter. These are the three steps : "Common report" — "Gashmu"—"Sanballat." An illustration of the development theory! The slander is born out of nothing; it is generated in that inorganic matter of lies which fills the atmosphere of the globe, it takes form and organization in Gashmu, in him it becomes a real thing; then Sanballat conducts it to its goal. Sanballat, who writes the letter of information, or whispers the thing in confidence, is often the mischievous originator of the whole mystery of lies—the predecessors are but imaginary. Sometimes he is "not a *knave*, but a *fool*" merely, some one who means well, a friend who thinks it is a part of friendship to do things like this. But for him the slander would be unknown and harmless, it is his work to post up the information in the window. The ill that is wrought for want of thought! It is only *thinking* that can stop that.

II. Treatment of slander. 1. *Give it no foundation in yourself.* Such a thing is said of you! exclaimed a zealous friend once. Ah! coolly answered the victim, and *the worst of it, it's true.* "Be ye wise as serpents and harmless as doves." There is a spirit of slumbering fairness in society. Do not say in your "haste, all men are liars." It is not so. Do not be soured by the abundance of mischief and the superfluity of naughtiness among men. But at the same time beware! Avoid the appearance of evil. Like Caesar's wife, be "above suspicion." Do not be content with such integrity as will go with the average, *let your white be snow-white.* [Illustrate by the grand integrity of Nehemiah.] Not in fear of the slander, but in love of what is right and good, seek the lofty character of the righteous man. Whatsoever things are true and lovely and of good report take as the garb of your character. 2. *Take no notice of it.* As the children say, "Don't believe it!" See the grand style of verse 8: "Then I sent unto him, saying, There are no such things as thou sayest, but thou feignest them out of thine own heart"—a message for Sanballat to think about. To have his elaborate slander crumpled up and flung at his head with the label "LIES" on it would be disappointing to this officious person. Silence is the best reply as a rule. We cannot waste the day in explanations. "When I have written an angry reply to a letter, I never send it off at once. I read it over. I often re-write it, and put more sting into the sentences. Then I argue thus. This letter will do if I send it in twenty-four hours. It shall not go earlier on any

consideration. To reserve my reply will show I was not annoyed much, and that I am a tranquil master of myself. I consequently lock up my letter, all sealed and addressed. And at the end of the twenty-four hours I take out the letter, and without reading it throw it on the fire. That has always been my course since I once wrote and posted immediately one of those replies. It proved to be a mistake. Since then I have done as I have said. It always relieves me—serves as a waste-pipe—and I never have to repent of harsh correspondence." 3. *Go on with your work.* Slander as a rule does the good man no harm, unless it stop him in his work and make him lay down his enterprise in disgust. Many a man has given up *his Master's work of "doing good"* because his good was evil spoken of. [Illustrate from the life of Jesus.] When the Lord of the vineyard cometh and asks, "Why did you leave my work?" what can you say? At your peril keep to the good course. This sharp-shooting of criticism is to try the soldier. Endure as seeing Him who is invisible. "They say? What do they say? Let them say." Many a man has given up the *good work of his soul's salvation* for a similar reason. It sometimes falls to the lot of a minister to be sent for to some dying man, and this is the story which comes from the departing deserter. "I was once a member of such and such a church, and there I was not treated as, &c., &c.; I took offence, and have hardly been in a place of worship since. It is ten years ago." "My brother," *thinks* the minister though he takes care not to say it, "do you think *that* excuse will cover those ten wasted years?" *You* are responsible for the *effect* of the slander; *another* may have a heavy score to pay on account of its *origin*.

Application. 1. *Live for the approval of the Lord of all.* Do not root yourself on the shallow, changing opinion of man. Seek a higher basis for endeavour, animated by the solemn fear of God. 2. *Consider the importance of life and its work.* Do not suppose you may please yourself whether you keep your hand on the plough or not Woe to Jonah, whatever be the cause of his flight from his God-appointed task 3. *Accept criticism—as an instructive corrector; and slander—as a discipline of patience and firmness.*

> " Lord, I adore thy gracious will,
>   Through every instrument of ill
>   My Father's goodness see ;
>   Accept the complicated wrong
>   Of Shimei's hand and Shimei's tongue
>   As kind rebukes from thee."

RUMOUR.

vi. 6. *It is reported among the heathen, and Gashmu saith it, that thou and the Jews think to rebel · for which cause thou buildest the wall, that thou mayest be their king, according to these words*

Matthew Henry well expresses the historical sense of this passage " Sanballat endeavours to possess Nehemiah with an apprehension that his undertaking to build the walls of Jerusalem was generally represented as factious and seditious, and would be accordingly resented at court. The best men, even in their most innocent and excellent performances, have lain under this imputation. This is written to him in an open letter, as a thing generally known and talked of ; that it was reported among the nations, and Gashmu will aver it for truth, that Nehemiah was aiming to make himself king, and to shake off the Persian yoke. Observe, it is common for that which is the sense only of the malicious, to be falsely represented by them as the sense of the many." From this particular instance let us consider generally *the tongue, its use and abuse*

I. **Use of the tongue.** 1. *To express thought and emotion.* A word is the incarnation of a thought. It lay hidden and formless in the thinker's mind The word is the body prepared for it. The thought stands out clear to the gaze of others. There is a language understood by the animals. A child speaks because of the necessity it feels to express its thought. It understands before it can express itself. The first dawn of intelligence is in a child's *smile ,* it enters into a new world when it utters the *first word.* The fountains of the great deep of intelligence are broken up The child performs "the miracle of speech." Were thought pent up in our minds without the medium of expression which words give, each one would live in a world of his own. We

cannot conceive of a family, a social state, a nation without language. "Speak, that I may see thee," said one to a fair-haired youth. As " we know metals by their tinkling," so we know men by their speech Dumbness excites pity. Expression is the first and simplest use of the tongue 2. *To glorify God.* "Therewith bless we God." We are not alone in this. "The heavens declare the glory of God ; and the firmament showeth his handywork Day unto day uttereth speech, and night unto night showeth knowledge " God is known by the works of his hands. But it is our province explicitly to bless God. The glory of the heavens is the glory of inference ; our glory is the glory of reference. "The whole creation is as a well-tuned instrument, but man maketh the music." Men of science reduce the myriad things in nature to laws , and these to still fewer , until all causes resolve themselves into the Cause of causes—God. To him all things tend. From him, as a fountain, all streams flow , to him, as a sea, they all return 3 *To fan the flame of devotion in others* "Death and life are in the power of the tongue." Words have moved the world. Pulpits, senates, law courts are centres from which words proceed. Men of words as necessary as men of action. Armies, nations have been stirred by eloquent speech. Possibilities of speech should make us humble, if not make us tremble Words escape our lips big with eternal issues "By thy words thou shalt be justified, and by thy words thou shalt be condemned." "Foolish talking" is condemned as well as " filthy communication."

II. The abuse of the tongue. "Take heed," says an Arabian proverb, "thy tongue cut not thy throat." 1. *Self-misrepresentation.* (1) *Under-statement.* Half - truths; concealing some material thing. We are not bound to satisfy everybody's curiosity. Two legitimate times for speaking—when God would be glorified or man benefited. But having professed to tell and then conceal is deception. There are spoken lies and acted lies. (2) *Over-statement.* Speaking in superlatives. A habit easily contracted. "All his geese are swans." (3) *False statement.* God and men hate lying. You may be clever, amiable, attractive, but if you lie, the swift, sure, terrible Nemesis is, you will never again be trusted. For this there is no place of repentance, though you seek it carefully with tears. Lying is a sin of which it is peculiarly true—"Be sure your sin will find you out." 2. *Defamation of others.* Grosser forms—evil speaking with malice aforethought; bearing false witness, slander. A form of this punishable by law. But some of the keenest slanders elude law. "A good name is great riches." It is to be desired. We must not superciliously discard the good opinion of others; we need not fawningly seek it. To some a good name is all they have; e. g. domestic servants, professional men. Studied wickedness is worst of all. "I saw," said Augustine, "a little child pale with envy." How many town scandals would have been avoided, how many Church quarrels prevented, had men acted on that golden rule—"If thy brother shall trespass against thee, *go and tell him his fault between thee and him alone.*" Be patient under detraction. "Blessed are ye when men shall say all manner of evil against you *falsely.*"

ILLUSTRATIONS

Silence and speech. "Why tell me that a man is a fine speaker if it is not the truth that he is speaking? Phocion, who did not speak at all, was a great deal nearer hitting the mark than Demosthenes. He used to tell the Athenians, 'You can't fight Philip. You have not the slightest chance with him.' He is a man who holds his tongue, he has great disciplined armies; he can brag anybody you like in your cities here, and he is going on steadily with an unvarying aim towards his object; and he will infallibly beat any kind of men such as you, going on raging from shore to shore with all that rampant nonsense.' Demosthenes said to him one day, 'The Athenians will get mad some day and kill you.' 'Yes,' Phocion says, 'when they are mad; and you, as soon as they get sane again.' It is told about him going to Messina on some deputation that the Athenians wanted on some kind of matter of an intricate and contentious nature, that Phocion went with some story in his mouth to speak about. He was a man of few words—no unveracity; and after he had gone on telling the story a certain time, there was one burst of interruption. One man interrupted with something he tried to answer, and then another, and, finally, the people began bragging and brawling, and no end of debate, till it ended in the want of power in the people to say any more. Phocion drew back altogether, struck dumb, and would not speak another word to any man, and he left it to them to decide in any way they liked. It appears to me there is a kind of eloquence in that which is equal to anything Demosthenes ever said. 'Take your own way, and let me out altogether.'"—*Carlyle.*

Slander. "In St James's day, as now, it would appear that there were idle men and idle women, who went about from house to house, dropping slander as they went, and yet you could not take up that slander and detect the falsehood there. You could not evaporate the truth in the slow process of the crucible, and then show the residuum of falsehood glittering and visible. You could not fasten upon any word or sentence and say that it was calumny; for in order to constitute slander it is not necessary that the word spoken should be false—half truths are often more calumnious than whole falsehoods. It is not even necessary that a word should be distinctly uttered; a dropped lip, an arched eyebrow, a shrugged shoulder, a significant look, an incredulous expression of countenance, nay, even an emphatic silence, may do the work; and when the light and trifling thing which has done the mischief has fluttered off, the venom is left behind, to work and rankle, to inflame hearts, to fever human existence, and to poison human society at the fountain springs of life. Very emphatically was it said by one whose whole being had smarted under such affliction, 'Adders' poison is under their lips.'"—*F. W. Robertson.*

"We have no right to spread an injurious report merely because somebody brought it to us. It is a crime to pass bad money as well as to coin it. We are bound to consider whether the person from whom we heard the report had opportunities of knowing the truth, was likely to form a sound judgment of the facts which came under his knowledge, and whether we should have believed him if he had said the same thing to us about some person to whom we bore no ill-will. There would be very much less scandal manufactured if there were less disposition to circulate it."—*R. W. Dale.*

SAME THEME.

One great sin wherein the corruption of human nature bewrayeth itself is detraction, or depriving others of a good repute. Here I shall show—

I What is detraction. 1. *The nature of it in general.* It is an unjust violation of another's fame, reputation, or that good report which is due to him. God, that hath bidden me to love my neighbour as myself, doth therein bid me to be tender not only of his person and goods, but of his good name. And indeed one precept is a guard and fence to another. I cannot be tender of his person and goods unless I be tender of his fame ; for every man liveth by his credit. (1) It is a sin against God, who hath forbidden us to bear false witness against our neighbour, and to speak evil of others without a cause. Eph. iv. 31 : "Let all evil-speaking be far from you." By evil-speaking is meant there disgraceful and contumelious speeches, whereby we seek to stain the reputation of others. (2) It is a wrong to man, because it robbeth him of his good name, which is so deservedly esteemed by all that would do anything for God in the world. "A good name should rather be chosen than great riches" (Prov. xxii. 1). Therefore, as he himself should not prostitute his good name, so others should not blast it and blemish it ; for it is a greater sin than to steal the best goods which he hath, and it is such an evil as scarce admits any sound restitution ; for the imputation even of unjust crimes leaveth a scar though the wound be healed. (3) The causes it proceedeth from are these. (*a*) Malice and ill-will, which prompteth us to speak falsely of others, so to make them odious, or do them wrong or hurt. To hate our brother in our heart is no way consistent with that charity which the impression of the love of Christ should beget in us. The hatred of offence, which is opposite to the love of complacency, may be justified as to the wicked. Prov. xxix. 27 : "An unjust man is an abomination to the just, and he that is upright in the way is an abomination to the wicked." But then we should first and most abominate ourselves for sin ; this very hatred and abhorrence should begin at home, and we should be most odious to ourselves for sin, for we know more sin by ourselves than we can do by another. But for the hatred of enmity, which is opposite to the love of benevolence, that should be quite banished out of the heart of a Christian. (*β*) It comes from uncharitable credulity, whereby men easily believe a false report, and so propagate and convey it to others. Jer xx. 10 : "I have heard the defaming of many. Report, say they, and we will report it." If any will raise a report tending to the discredit of another, some will foster it ; and it loseth nothing in the carriage, till by additions and misconstructions it groweth to a downright and dangerous infamy. (*γ*) It comes through rashness and unruliness of tongue. Some men never learned to bridle their tongues, and the Apostle James telleth us that "therefore their religion is vain" (James i. 26). Till we make conscience of these evils, as well as others, we content ourselves with a partial obedience, and therefore cannot be sincere. Whisperers must be talking. (*δ*) It comes from carnal zeal, which is nothing else but passion for our different interests and opinions. Many lies walk under the disguise of religion. Is all speaking evil of another unlawful? I cannot say so, but yet it is hard to keep it from sin. 1. He that doth it without just cause is plainly a detractor, and so a grievous sinner before God. God doth not only reject the liars for hypocrites, but also the backbiters and slanderers. 2. He that doth but speak what he hath heard from others, without any assertion or asseveration of his own, as not knowing the truth of the report, can hardly be excused from sin. He reporteth those things which may induce the hearers to think ill of another, and if without just cause he is in part accessory. 3. He that doth speak that which is true, but tendeth to the infamy of another, may be guilty of sin if he have not a sufficient call and warrant. If it be a matter we have nothing to do with, but only speak of their faults for talk sake. If we aggravate things beyond their just size and proportion. If we urge their crimes and deny their graces. Is there no good amongst all this evil? 2. *The kinds of detraction.* (1) Whispering, which is privy defamation of our brother, to bring him into disfavour and disrespect with those that formerly had a better opinion of him. Herein whispering differeth from backbiting, because the whisperer stingeth secretly, but the other doth more openly attack our credit. Now this whispering is a great sin; it is reckoned among the sins which reigned among the heathen, and God hath expressly forbidden to his people. Lev. xix. 16: "Thou shalt not go up and down as a tale-bearer among thy people." It is against natural equity, because they do that to others which they would not have done to themselves. It is a grief to the party wronged, and a cause of much debate and strife. (2) Backbiting is a more public speaking evil of our absent brother, to the impairing of his credit. Now this may be done two ways. With respect to the good things found in him, and with respect to the evil supposed to be committed by him. With respect to the good things found in him :—When we deny those good things which we know to be in another. When we lessen the gifts and graces of others. When we own the good, but deprave it by supposing a sinister intention. When we have just occasion to speak of a man's due commendation, but enviously suppress it. As to evil supposed to be committed by them :—When we publish their secret slips, which in charity we ought to conceal. Prov. xi. 13: "A tale-bearer revealeth secrets." When a man intrudeth himself into the mention of things faulty, which he might with better manners and more honesty conceal, it is the effect of a base heart. When, in relating any evil action of another, we use harder terms than the quality of the fact requireth, and make evils worse than they are,

beams of motes, and mountains of mole-hills. We should lessen sins all that we can; I mean the sins and faults of others. By imposing false crimes. The most godly and innocent persons cannot escape the scourge of the tongue, and unjust calumnies.

II. The heinousness of the sin. 1. *In general,* that is evident from what is said already. Two arguments more I shall urge. (1) Men shall be called to an account for these sins as well as others. (2) It is the property of a citizen of Zion—one that shall be not only accepted with God now, but dwell with God for ever—not to be given to backbiting (Ps xv.). 2. *More particularly,* it is the more heinous, (1) Partly from the person against whom it is committed ; e. g. the godly; public persons. (2) From the persons before whom the slander is brought, as suppose kings and princes; so that they are deprived not only of private friendships, but the favour and countenance of those under whose protection they have their life and service. (3) From the end of it. If it be done with a direct intention of hurting another's fame, it is worse than if out of a rash levity and loquacity. Some men have no direct intention of mischief, but are given to talking; others sow discord. (4) From the great hurt that followeth, be it loss of estate or general trouble. When men's good names are buried, their persons cannot long subsist afterward with any degree of service. And all this may be the fruit of a deceitful tongue. The use is, to show how good-natured Christianity is, and befriendeth human societies, it condemneth not only sins against God, but sins against our neighbour. Let us not speak evil of others behind their backs, but tell them their faults. Remembering our own faults, looking at home, will not only divert us from slandering of others, but make us compassionate towards them, and breed comfort in our own souls.—*Manton, abridged.*

BOLDNESS.

vi. 8.   *Then I sent unto him, saying, There are no such things done as thou sayest, but thou feignest them out of thine own heart.*

A bold word this to fling in the teeth of authority.

I Men of courage are men of convictions. Nehemiah's consciousness that he was doing a great work made him bold. Physical courage is a thing of blood and nerve. The morally courageous man may be nervous, shrinking, fearful. He is self-reliant because reliant on God. The men without convictions, what have they done? Those who tell us it is doubtful if there be a God, religion is the poetry of conscience, the Bible is a fetish, whom have they blessed? for whom have they agonized? Has the world's suffering wrung from them any great sweat of blood? The world's hard work has never been done by the mealy-mouthed. Great reformations have not been accomplished by the nerveless souls without strong convictions for or against. Men of one idea have made mistakes, but not the mistake of leaving the work undone. This Jewish Reformer and Liberator reminds us of Martin Luther, the stories of whose boldness have passed into proverbs, and of John Knox, whom Scotland delights to honour. Of him Carlyle tells the following story in his own inimitable way:—"In the galleys of the river Loire, whither Knox and the others, after their castle of St. Andrew's was taken, had been sent as galley slaves, some officer or priest one day presented them an image of the Virgin Mother, requiring that they, the blasphemous heretics, should do it reverence. 'Mother! mother of God!' said Knox, when the turn came to him. 'This is no mother of God; this is "a pented bredd"—a piece of wood, I tell you, with paint on it. She is fitter for swimming, I think, than for being worshipped,' added Knox, and flung the thing into the river." Rather dangerous sport that! "The courage of his convictions" makes a man a hero. There was *a sacred must* in the highest life. "I must work the works of him that sent me." "He *steadfastly* set his face to go to Jerusalem." Another story which Carlyle tells of John Knox will illustrate how these elect spirits shrank from the tasks laid upon them. "In an entirely obscure way Knox had reached the age of forty, was with the small body of Reformers who were standing siege in St. Andrew's Castle, when one day in their chapel the preacher, after finishing his exhortation to these fighters in the forlorn hope, said suddenly, that there ought to be other speakers, that all men who had a priest's heart and gift in them ought now to speak,—which gifts and heart one of their own number, John Knox the name of him, had. Had he not? said the preacher, appealing to all the audience. What then is his duty? The people answered affirmatively; it was a criminal forsaking of his post if such a man held the word that was in him silent. Poor Knox was obliged to stand up, he attempted to reply, he could say no word; burst into a flood of tears, and ran out." "Carlstad," said Luther, "wanted to be the great man, and truly I would willingly have left the honour to him, so far as it had not been against God. For, I praise my God, I was never so presumptuous as to think myself wiser than another man. When at first I wrote against indulgences, I designed simply to have opposed them, thinking that, afterwards, others would come and accomplish what I had begun." To be out of the roll of common men is not desirable. But when self-will and God's will come into collision, the will of the Lord be done. Don't be a straw upon the stream. Get convictions. Hold them. Search the Scriptures. Be loyal to conscience. Obey God. Spheres are narrow or wide. What matters that? In the narrowest men may fail; in the widest they can but be faithful. *Reverence "the sacred must" in thy life and work.*

II. Applications of this principle. 1. *A man's real foe is himself.* "Nothing," says St. Bernard, "can work me damage except myself; the harm that I sustain I carry about with me, and never am a real sufferer but by my own fault." The powerful opposition or skilful deception of the Sanballats and Gashmus within my sphere may make my duty more difficult, but cannot wholly prevent my performance of it. There is such a thing as self-degradation. This position is not uncommon—to do our duty and suffer: to leave it undone and escape the suffering. But to do the latter is to degrade oneself. 2. *Not such boldness, but some boldness is required of us all.* We may have opportunities of *speaking the truth in love;* we must not shrink from the responsibility of *speaking the truth.* Force, fraud, falsehood were arrayed against Nehemiah, are arrayed against us. The holy war arises out of an enmity of long standing. 3. *Pay homage to thy convictions.* Honour the grey-headed truths in the faith of which apostles, martyrs, and saints have lived and died God's love, Christ's atonement, your pardon and need of renewal —hold fast these convictions. "Take unto you the whole armour of God, that ye may be able to withstand in the evil day"—the conquered soldier can do that; "and having done all to stand" —only the conquering soldier can do that. So thou soldier of God. 4. *Do the task allotted thee.* "Work, in every hour, paid or unpaid; see only that thou work, and thou canst not escape the reward; whether thy work be fine or coarse, planting corn or writing epics, so only it be honest work, done to thine own approbation, it shall earn a reward to the senses as well as to the thought; no matter how often defeated, you are born to victory. The reward of a thing well done is to have done it."—*Emerson.* Nehemiah sent his message, and then went on with his work. "So the wall was finished."

FEAR AND FAITH.

vi. 9. *For they all made us afraid, saying, Their hands shall be weakened from the work, that it be not done. Now therefore, O God, strengthen my hands.*

The words come after the story of a new *scare* to Nehemiah. [Describe his anxieties from various forms of enmity.] *Words suggest two companion topics, Fear and Faith.*

I. Fear. "*For they all made us afraid.*" Man is accompanied through life by *foes and fears.* In some cases the fears are more numerous than the foes. *Frequently the only thing to be afraid of is our own fear.* There are foes of us all, however, who "make us afraid." To have an iron spirit not easily quailed is a great gift, and to have a spirit like a sensitive plant, which curls at every touch and interrupts its functions, is a great misery. We may allow fears to grow upon us, until they become an atmosphere to the soul. 1. *Causes of fear.* With Nehemiah there were causes enough—real flesh and blood foes, who made his career in Jerusalem one long vigil, always listening for the loud alarum of strife. Similarly with most men in most of life's enterprises. The soul has its foes; "they are lively and they are strong." All religious work is done against obstacles which "make us afraid." (a) *The devil is a downright foe.* We are not so much alarmed at *him* now as in days of superstition. Luther threw his ink-pot at the arch-enemy of his soul, and we smile at the picture of the rough student rising from his Bible and casting such a very *material* defiance at such a very *immaterial* foe. We have refined the devil since then to a "*general expression for,*" &c But was not the mistaken Reformer nearer right than ourselves? "*Your adversary the devil*" is not a mere generalization. (β) *Foes hide themselves or show themselves in our fellow-men.* The man who hinders my work for God is my foe, whether he scare me by opposition, or interrupt me by an unprofitable friendship. The foe who pushes me down the precipice, and the foe who persuades me to go to sleep in the sun, are alike reasons for fear. (γ) *The sinful nature in myself is my enemy.* "No one's enemy but his own" is a common form of speech. Every man is a ship with a mutinous crew on board, and destruction is averted only by the masterful assertion of my better self against my lower self, of my conscience against my passions, of the grace of God against the sin that dwelleth in me.

> "Christian, seek not yet repose,
> Cast thy dreams of ease away ;
> Thou art in the midst of foes ;
> Watch and pray."

2. *Effects of fear.* (*a*) *Exaggeration of peril.* Life grows very gloomy when the soul is afraid. Fear is a fearful thing. The palpitating, perspiring rustic in the dark lane misinterprets every shadow, and hears a voice of threatening in every sound, when once anything like superstitous terror has seized him. When you are frightened you are not in a position to judge of your situation. *Allow for the enlargements of fear* Sometimes when we hear a sensational story we say, Ah, Mr. Superlative told you that ; take off ninety per cent. Now if we could ' so deal with the alarming suggestions of our own fears it would be well. They deceive us. When the disciples saw Jesus walking on the sea, they were troubled, and supposed that they had seen a spirit, but he said, "Be not afraid ; it is I !" (β) *Paralysis of strength.* "The hearts of the people melted and became as water" —not much lion-work of fighting for them. A child can take the sword of a frightened man. Be very courageous if you would be very strong.

II. Faith "*Now therefore, O God, strengthen my hands.*" "What time I am afraid I will trust in the Lord." The word of God is full of *presuppositions of man's timorousness and fear.* It speaks gently, and as to a child, and bids its organs be soft. "Speak ye comfortably to Jerusalem !" Fear not, Abraham, I am thy shield ! Fear not, Moses—Joshua—Daniel : all through the story of man's struggle God's ringing cry of Fear not ! falls upon him from heaven. Do not over-chide yourself if you are of a timorous make, for why should there be chapter after chapter of bugle-calls to courage, except that men never have been overstocked with that grace. After faith in St. Peter's teaching comes courage : "Add to your faith *virtue*" (*courage*). Now faith stands as the counterpart of fear. 1. *In causes of fear.* Against our array of foes it brings into view the presence of God. We should strive to *think God as real as our foes are*, whereas we commonly in our panic see only the peril, and not the Saviour. At Waterloo the French were ranged on one side of a valley in brilliant force, while on the other side of the valley waited the army that was to conquer—*an army mostly hidden.* It is thus in religious life 2 Kings vi. 15—17 gives a beautiful illustrative story. Those "horses and chariots of fire round about Elisha" were hidden to the servant, though seen by the clear-eyed faith of his master. "Elisha prayed, and said unto the Lord, I pray thee, open his eyes, that he may see." Look not on the foes only, but see God.

> "Hell is nigh, but God is nigher,
> Circling us with hosts of fire."

2. *Against the effect of fear (despair) let us set the spirit of hope.* "Take for a helmet the *hope* of salvation." That will prevent you being stunned by fear What incitements to hope we find. (1) In *the history* of God's help. Dealings with faithful in all generations. (2) In *experience* of God's help. Our own remembered deliverances Read St. Paul's grand defiance of all foes, visible and invisible, present and to come, in his glorious burst at end of the eighth of Romans : "Who shall separate us from the love of Christ" (Rom. viii. 35—39)?

Application. 1. *Be aware of your foes.* 2. *Do not make too much of them.* 3. *Remember that it is not your own strength that wins, but the God who strengthens your hands.* 4. *Never despair.*

FELT WEAKNESS.

vi 9. *O God, strengthen my hands.*

INTRODUCTION.—Outline Nehemiah's position :—fierceness of foes; fear of friends, work endangered, his own heart failing him for fear. A critical moment, requiring instantaneous decision. Felt weakness casting itself on God.

I. The habit of devotion This prayer not uttered whilst writing He recalls his experiences in that time of danger. Such a trial-hour would stamp itself in the memory. Nehemiah is remarkable for his ejaculatory prayers. They were the habit of his life. You cannot be always devotional, if you mean by that engaged in acts of devotion. Habit will make you ready for occasion. A school-boy cannot be all day long repeating his father's name; enough if when a temptation arises to do what would offend his father he refuses. Bible precepts cannot be always on the tongue's end, but a Christian man should be so under the influence of Biblical principles that he will shrink instinctively from wrong - being and wrong-doing

> " I want a principle within
> Of jealous, godly fear,
> A sensibility of sin,
> A pain to feel it near;
> I want the first approach to feel
> Of pride, or fond desire,
> To catch the wandering of my will,
> And quench the kindling fire.
>
> That I from thee no more may part,
> No more thy goodness grieve,
> The filial awe, the fleshy heart,   .
> The tender conscience give.
> Quick as the apple of an eye,
> O God, my conscience make !
> Awake my soul when sin is nigh,
> And keep it still awake "

Some ask only for a sentiment. That is insufficient. Devotion must reach the core of our being. We must be " throughout Christian " Habit implies *formation* Not by a sudden bound do men reach perfection. Halting and stumbling characterize a Christian's first efforts to walk alone. God regards the bent of the will, the direction of the

desires. " He knoweth our frame; he remembereth that we are dust." Don't be discouraged by failure, repeated failure. Begin again. Learn to pray. Habituate thyself to devotional exercises.

II The limits of solitariness. " O God, strengthen MY hands." The hands of the workers needed to be strengthened. But on Nehemiah rested the responsibility. He stood alone. If his strength should fail in the day of adversity, all would be lost. The tallest trees feel the stress of the blast. Highly-wrought natures are subject to influences unfelt by coarser minds. Christ is the great champion here—the loneliest man that ever lived. You cannot read the Gospels without feeling how far apart from him even the disciples were. The best of the outside world had so little in common with him. And through the ages men have had to thank God for the lonely spirits. The noblest work is achieved by personal and lonesome effort. Sunday schools, prison reforms, hospital management, religious revivals, revolutions in Church and State are the result of the genius and energy of individual men and women. They strike out the path along which the less gifted, but not less earnest, travel. Doubtless there are times when the terrible loneliness of their position startles such men. Such a time came to Nehemiah, and he cried unto God. And in the commonplace life of all of us there is solitariness. For the value of a life does not depend upon externals. To himself the life of a peasant is as important as is the life of a prince. No second life is given. Great and small are relative terms, be it remembered None is alone who has God with him. " Jesus said, Behold, the hour cometh, yea, is now come, that ye shall leave me alone : and yet *I am not alone, because the Father is with me* "

III The value of certitude. " O God, strengthen my hands."

> " I am weak, but thou art mighty,
> Hold me with thy powerful hand."

That was about all Nehemiah knew. His creed was short, but he held it firmly. Sanballat and Gashmu might gather fresh forces or bribe Nehemiah's body-guard; one thing was clear amid the haze of others, God was Almighty, and always approachable. We have a fuller creed; have we a sublimer trust? A motto of the Apostle Paul—"We know." Nor is St. John one whit behind his brother-apostle. The circle of religious knowledge might be almost completed from his First Epistle alone. "We know that the Son of God is come." "We know that we are of God." "We know that we know him." "We know that we are in him." "We know that he abideth in us." "We know the Spirit of truth and error." "We know that he heareth us." "We know that when he shall appear we shall be like him." That which we have experienced becomes certain. "We speak that we do know." "One thing I know, that whereas I was blind, now I see."

IV. The secret of steadiness "They all made us afraid, saying, Their hands shall be weakened from the work, that it be not done. Now therefore, O God, strengthen my hands. *So the wall was finished.*" "Unbelief," says Gurnall, "is a soul-enfeebling sin. It is to prayer as the moth is to the cloth; it wastes the soul's strength, so that it cannot look up to God with any hope. 'They made us afraid, saying, Their hands shall be weakened.' Resist, therefore, Satan; be steadfast in the faith. Never let thy heart suffer the power, mercy, or truth of God to be called in question; thou hadst as good question whether he can cease to be God."

Application 1. *In striving to attain personal excellence be patient.* Effort and failure mark much of our life. The task we have in hand is herculean; the opponents are numerous and powerful. 2. *In any form of Christian enterprise moderate your expectations* Opposition will arise when least expected. Those for whom you toil will seldom appreciate your motives. Success may linger 3. *Make the secular sacred by infusing into it a sacred spirit.* Refuse to call anything common and unclean.

ILLUSTRATIONS.

Ejaculatory prayer.—"Ejaculatory prayer is prayer darted up from the heart to God, not at stated intervals, but in the course of our daily occupations and amusements. The word 'ejaculatory' is derived from the Latin word for a dart or arrow, and there is an idea in it which one would be loath indeed to forfeit. Imagine an English archer, strolling through a forest in the old times of Crecy and Agincourt, when the yeomen of this island were trained to deliver their arrows with the same unfailing precision as 'a left-handed Gibeonite' discharging a stone bullet from his sling. A bird rises in the brush-wood under his feet, a bird of gorgeous plumage or savoury flesh. He takes an arrow from his quiver, draws his bow to its full stretch, and sends the shaft after the bird with the speed of lightning. Scarcely an instant elapses before his prey is at his feet. It has been struck with unerring aim in the critical part, and drops on the instant. Very similar in the spiritual world is the force of what is called ejaculatory prayer. The Christian catches suddenly a glimpse of some blessing, deliverance, relief, a longing after which is induced by the circumstances into which he is thrown. Presently it shall be his. As the archer first draws the bow in towards himself, so the Christian retires, by a momentary act of recollection, into his own mind, and there realizes the presence of God. Then he launches one short, fervent petition into the ear of that awful Presence, throwing his whole soul into the request. And lo! it is done! The blessing descends, prosecuted, overtaken, pierced, fetched down from the vault of heaven by the winged arrow of prayer."—*Goulburn.*

"Ejaculations take not up any room in the soul. They give liberty of callings, so that at the same instant one may follow his proper vocation. The husbandman may dart forth an ejaculation, and not make a balk the more. The seaman, nevertheless, steers his ship right in the darkest night. Yea, the soldier at the same time may shoot out his prayer to God, and aim his pistol at his enemy, the one better hitting the mark for the other. The field wherein bees feed is no whit the barer for their biting; when they have taken their full repast on flower or grass, the ox may feed, the sheep fatten on their reversions. The reason is, because those little chemists distil only the refined part of the flower, leaving the grosser substance thereof. So ejaculations bind not men to any bodily observance, only busy the spiritual half, which makes them consistent with the prosecution of any other employment."

"In hard havens, so choked up with the envious sands that great ships drawing many feet of water cannot come near, lighter and lesser pinnaces may freely and safely arrive. When we are time-bound, place-bound, so that we cannot compose ourselves to make a large, solemn prayer, this is the right instant for ejaculations, whether orally uttered or only poured forth inwardly in the heart."—*Fuller.*

PANIC.

vi. 10—13.   *Afterward I came unto the house of Shemaiah, &c.*

In the varying romance of Nehemiah's brave struggle with difficulties occurs an instance of *panic,* or of what might have been panic to a less steadfast soul   A man was shutting himself up in alarm—real or assumed—and endeavoured to persuade Nehemiah to do the like, to turn the temple into a fortress, and to make the open porch of God's house a shelter for merely *personal* fear.   But Nehemiah (as always) was "*steadfast, unmoveable.*"   His resolute, fearless "*I will not go in !*" settled the matter, which after all turned out to be a mere theatrical scare, got up to order in the interest of Tobiah and Sanballat   *Panic is our subject — its effect and its correctives*

I   **Panic.**   Originally suggestive of *Pan,* the god of the woods.   To ignorant men the deep solemn shades of the virgin forests were fraught with awe, and full of causes for sudden alarm.   *Unreasoning, helpless* FRIGHT *is the idea.* 1.   *National panic.*   A people suddenly exaggerating a state danger, and acting in a way to be sorry for afterwards.   2. *Business panic.*   A trading community or firm scared out of its even regularity into some wild action.   3   *Personal panic.*   Sudden trouble not bravely met with a breastplate of patience and a helmet of hope, but with helpless alarm. 4   *Spiritual panic.*   Those soul-shiverings which are like fits in religious life These are common familiar forms. *Panic is commonly groundless.*   That is, the wave is not so high as it seems to the retreating bather, who hears its hiss behind him   No man is so bad as sudden indignation paints him, and few crises in man's history are so alarming as to the alarmed they appear   The downfall of the state—the end of the world—the collapse of trade—the ruin of a house—the overthrow of good— *these are often only scares*

II   **The effect of panic.**   To gather all the selfishness of man to a focus or to substitute a brief madness for calm thoughtfulness   and   decision.   1.   *It makes a man behave unworthily of himself.*   The leader shows his flying form as a scoff to the after-judgment of men. "*Unsoldierly conduct in presence of the enemy*"   Shall that be said of the pillars of the state, or of the strong support of the home, or of the Christian soldier in his discouraging battle with sin ?   Shall Nehemiah be hidden in some corridor of God's temple, or peep in alarm from the shut window of Zion ? 2.   *It makes a man behave unworthily toward his fellows.*   The man who tramples upon the woman in a burning theatre ;   the craven who sinks the boat which might have saved "all hands" in his eagerness for personal security ; the soldier who deserts the companions whom he might have helped to conquest—these are all exhibitions of the *unlovely possibilities of human nature.* Is Nehemiah to imperil the Jews by scrambling for a place a sword-length away from danger ?   3.   *It makes a man behave unworthily of his God.   Is not God* FOR *the hour of peril ?*   Am I to trust in Providence *up* to the dangerous moment, and *then* become my own *providence ?*   Is God's house to be a robber's den for timorous culprits to shelter in ?   Let a man die *in* God's hands, not "fleeing from the presence of the Lord "

III.   The correctives of panic. "Prevention, not cure," is the motto. 1   *Remembrance of a man's own dignity.* "I said, *Should such a man as I flee ?* and who is there, that, being as I am, would go into the temple to save his life ?   I will not go in "   For a man's *self* to fall is worse than to fall before a foe   Let not the supreme fear be *personal* fear, "fear of them that can kill THE ·BODY."   *Moral degradation is worse than physical death*   2.   *Remembrance of others.*   Carry the alarms of others as corrective of your own.   Fear for *others,* lest your own fear become too great.   Nehemiah hears the cry of helpless Jews, and he will not fly and leave them. 3. *Remembrance of God.* Nehemiah's book shows how the idea of " *my God* " had become part of his mental habit. His " heart was fixed, trusting in the Lord." Read Ps. xlvi. at the first murmur of unworthy alarm— " God is our refuge," &c. The iron nerve of Luther's hymn is a cry to turn the tide of warring fears. Paul is serene in the danger of shipwreck—nay, in the certainty of it—because of the forewarning of the Angel of the Lord, " whose I am, and whom I serve." That " *Fear not, Paul !* " made him deaf to the roar of the threatening sea. Cultivate a habit of confidence in God. Man's extremity is God's opportunity.

Application. *Keep a short account with conscience, and you will be able to make small account of panic.*

LYING PROPHETS.

vi. 10.   *Afterward I came unto the house of Shemaiah, &c.*

"Shemaiah was such a common name among the Jews, that it is impossible to identify this prophet with any other person of his name. He must, however, have been a man of prominence, and one, too, who had been in Nehemiah's confidence, or else the attempt would never have been made by Tobiah and Sanballat through him. It may have been the high position and reputation, of Shemaiah that led the prophetess Noadiah and the rest of the prophets (ver. 14) into the false dealings with Nehemiah "—*Dr. Crosby.*

I. **Great gifts may be dissociated from pure life** Shemaiah lied The gift of God in Shemaiah, Noadiah, and the rest of the prophets had been sold for money. Two lists of prophets may be compiled from " the Book " — the true, the false. Of the latter—Balaam (Num. xxiii), the old prophet (1 Kings xiii.), Zedekiah and the rest who seduced Ahab to his destruction (1 Kings xxii), Hananiah (Jer. xxviii.) Character is primal element of a conception of true prophet. "A grace does not differ from a gift in this, that the former is from God, and the latter from nature As a creative power there is no such thing as nature ; all is God's. A grace is that which has in it some moral quality, whereas a gift does not necessarily share in this. Graces are what the man *is,* but enumerate his gifts, and you only know what he *has.*"— *F. W. Robertson.* Gifts are sacred We speak of gifted men as men of talent. That word talent was probably borrowed from our Saviour's parable of the man who was travelling into a far country, who called his servants and delivered unto them his goods. Unto one he gave five talents, to another two, and to another one . to every man according to his several ability, and straightway took his journey. Unfortunately gifts may be abused. They have been abused. They have been used as instruments of oppression. And, shuddering at their abuse, Christian people have often condemned them as if they were the devil's gifts, not God's. Now this course is unwise , it is dangerous. We rob ourselves of so much power by refusing to enlist into the service of God whatever is good In the early Church the gifts of prophecy, of healing, of miracles were abused. St Paul denounces the abuse, but not the gift. On the contrary, he enumerates them ; he states their relative importance , he calls them emphatically *spiritual* (1 Cor. xii , xiv.). The gifts of our age are spiritual , the talented men of our time are inspired. Knowledge is power, but it is not piety The poets of ethereal intellects have not always been men of etherealized lives

II **Great gifts may lead to deterioration of character.** Shemaiah had been a true prophet, whom Nehemiah had found trustworthy. The hypocrite pays unconscious homage to virtue. Prophets and prophetess had gone from bad to worse through Sanballat's gold. The qualifications which the Jewish doctors deemed indispensable to a prophet were "true probity and piety." "That God may choose of men whom he pleaseth, and send him, it matters not whether he be wise and learned, or unlearned and unskilful, old or young; only that this is required, that he be a virtuous, good, and honest man; for hitherto there was never any that could say that God did cause the Divine majesty to dwell in a vicious person, unless he had first reformed himself." —*Maimonides.* The "lying spirit" entered into them and they fell. "Now these things were our examples." Use your gifts, not display them. Be not vain of them Has God given thee a clear judgment, penetration, retentive memory, or an eloquent tongue, thank him by cultivating it Has he endowed thee with health, thank him for it by preserving it. Has he given thee mechanical skill or business aptitude, recognize the Giver by turning it to best advantage. As God has appointed to every man his work, so he has given to every man his gift The sacred call of duty is heard along all the ranks of existence. Let not the humblest amongst us imagine that his gifts are unnecessary or valueless—they are his. The drop of water in which the animalculæ live is to them what the sea is to behemoth. The falling leaf is as great a catastrophe to the insect that feeds upon it as is a burning world to an angel Dost thou scorn the lesser gifted? Bethink thyself. The God who endowed thee endowed them; the Spirit who inspired thee inspires them "Who maketh thee to differ from another? and what hast thou that thou didst not receive?" Are you discontented with your gifts, and envious of the more highly endowed? Forget not that God who lights the sun lights the stars. He does not disown the meanest flower that blows. The seraph nearest to his throne does not cause him to forget the humblest missionary toiling in some island of the Southern Seas. 1 *Accept thy position.* God, who has appointed the bounds of our habitation, has fixed the limits of our power 2. *Cultivate your gifts.* Be not contented. Do not repine 3. *Remember that gifts*

are not graces. "Though I speak with the tongues of men and of angels, and have not charity, I am become as sounding brass, or a tinkling cymbal. And though I have *the gift of prophecy*, and understand all mysteries, and all knowledge; and though I have all faith, so that I could remove mountains, and have not charity, I am nothing." The only undying faculties are the affections; the only permanent work is that we do for others.

ILLUSTRATIONS.

Ahab's lying prophets (1 Kings xxii.) "Ahab consulted all his false prophets as to whether or not he should go to attack the Syrians at Ramoth-Gilead They knew what to say; they knew that their business was to prophesy what would pay them—what would be pleasant to him. They did not care whether what was said was true or not; they lied for the sake of gain, for the Lord had put a lying spirit into their mouths. They were rogues and villains from the first. They had turned prophets, not to speak God's truth, but to make money, to flatter King Ahab, to get themselves a reputation. We do not hear that they were all heathens Many of them may have believed in the true God. But they were cheats and liars, and so they had given place to the devil, the father of lies; and now he had taken possession of them in spite of themselves, and they lied to Ahab, and told him that he would prosper in the battle at Ramoth-Gilead. It was a dangerous thing for them to say; for if he had been defeated, and returned disappointed, his rage would have most probably fallen on them for deceiving him. And as in those Eastern countries kings do whatever they like, without laws or parliaments, Ahab would have most likely put them all to a miserable death on the spot But however dangerous it might be for them to lie, they could not help lying. A spirit of lies had seized them, and they who began by lying because it paid them, now could not help doing so whether it paid them or not."

Prophets of to-day "Do not fancy that there are no prophets in our days, unless the gift of the Holy Spirit, which is promised to all who believe, be a dream and a lie There are prophets now-a-days—yea, I say unto you, and more than prophets Is not the Bible a prophet? Is not every holy and wise book, every holy and wise preacher and writer, a prophet, expounding to us God's laws, foretelling to us God's opinions of our deeds, both good and evil? Ay, is not every man a prophet to himself? That 'still small voice'—is not that a prophecy in a man's own heart? Truly it is. It is the voice of God within us, it is the Spirit of God striving with our spirits, whether we will hear, or whether we will forbear—setting before us what is righteous, and noble, and pure, and what is manly and godlike; to see whether we will obey that voice, or whether we will obey our own selfish lusts, which tempt us to please ourselves—to pamper ourselves, our greediness, covetousness, ambition, or self conceit And if you ask me how to try the spirits, how to know whether your own thoughts, whether the sermons which you hear, the books which you read, are speaking to you God's truth, or some lying spirit's falsehood, I can only answer you, 'To the law and to the testimony'—to the Bible, if they speak not according to that word, there is no truth in them. But how to understand the Bible? for the fleshly man understands not the things of God. The fleshly man, he who cares only about pleasing himself, he who goes to the Bible full of self-conceit and selfishness, wanting the Bible to tell him only just what he likes to hear, will only find it a sealed book to him, and will very likely wrest the Scriptures to his own destruction. Take up your Bible humbly, praying to God to show you its meaning, whether it be pleasant to you or not, and then you will find that God will show you a blessed meaning in it, he will open your eyes, that you may understand the wondrous things of his law, he will show you how to try the spirit of all you are taught, and to find out whether it comes from God."—*Charles Kingsley.*

PERSONAL RESPONSIBILITY

vi. 11.   *Should such a man as I flee?*

Character, position, recollection, Nehemiah opposed to Shemaiah's cowardly proposal Personal responsibility overpowered all considerations of expediency. Let the instance suggest the wider theme. "We mortal millions dwell alone" "Every one of us shall give account of himself to God."

I A law of the Divine procedure. God has not dealt with men in the mass. He is not far from any one of us. 1. *Law implies individual responsibility.* The word contains the idea of pointing out, directing, leading; hence a rule of conduct. National law does not treat men as a society, but as a mass of responsible units. All our jurisprudence is based on this The Bible axiom that every man shall give account of himself has been brought into the sphere of political life Moral law rests on the same foundation. Its violation is sin; its honour is righteousness. In this none can be surety for his brother. Laws are for the safe-conduct of individual lives The general good is contained in that of the individual. The true communism is not that which would adopt the impossible expedient of dividing to all alike, but that which shall secure to every individual the scope for working out his responsibility as a man, a citizen, and a Christian 2. *The history of God's dealings is in harmony with this.* Angels—so far as the Bible and analogy lead us to infer—are subject to a similar moral government They had their testing-time They stood in probation as individuals. The most exalted spirits in the universe are amenable to God. There can be only one Supreme. They fell as individuals. Satan is distinctive.

> "He, above the rest
> In shape and gesture proudly eminent,
> Stood like a tower, his form had not yet lost
> All her original brightness, nor appeared
> Less than archangel ruined "

But they were all "fellows of his crime." He only "led the embattled seraphim to war" "His angels were cast out with him." They are "the angels that sinned.' "By ambition fell the angels."

> "Of their names in heavenly records now
> Be no memorial, blotted out and razed
> By their rebellion from the book of life."

The rest stand as individuals having kept their first estate Their past faithfulness insures the future Michael, Gabriel, Uriel, the Prince, the Archangel, whether they are personal, or like thrones, dominions, principalities, and powers, representative of ranks, are distinctive. For if not individual in themselves, they represent the ministry and defence of the angels. *Nations.* The Israelites were elected as a nation; but they fell as individuals One terrible verse sums up all "Their carcases fell in the wilderness" History confirms this. When honour is lost in public men, when domestic ties are violated, nations fall. A man's great enemy is himself; a nation's great enemy is itself. Truth and justice, law and order, the bond of a nation. The enemy without does not knock at the gates for admission until the enemy within has prepared the way for conquest *Churches.* The Churches of the Revelation of St. John are typical. There is a common danger. "He that overcometh!" belongs to Smyrna and Pergamos, to Ephesus and Sardis, to Philadelphia, Thyatira, and Laodicea. But right and wrong are not massed. Declension, false doctrine, seduction, semblance, are severally condemned. Hatred of evil, whether in doctrine or conduct, endurance, adherence to truth, charity, undefiledness, are severally praised. So with individual lives. The stern-souled prophet and the confiding Mary; the martyr Stephen and the traitor Judas; the impressible Herod and the unmoved Baptist; the faithful James and the faithless Peter: each stood alone—alone in relation to God, alone in relation to duty. 3. *Christianity recognizes personal responsibility.* Christ dealt with men as individuals. In his teaching, miracles, sympathies. One woman elicited his best teaching; one family found his great love; one widow sufficient to move his miraculous arm. Acceptance of Christianity personal. Repentance, faith, forgiveness. Exhibition of Christianity personal. Cross-bearing, truth-speaking, forgiveness, humility, unselfishness, generosity, work. The Church is a body fitly joined together. Every man hath his proper gift of God.

II. **A fact in human experience.** As every leaf among the myriad leaves of the forest is governed by the laws of growth, and yet in its conformation is distinct, so every man is subject to the general laws of Divine procedure and the special which apply only to himself. No two men are exactly alike in character or circumstances. 1. *Responsibility* Each is required to work out his destiny. The foundation of a noble life is Christ, but every man must take heed how he buildeth thereupon. Alone each must return his Lord's money Every one will be brought unto him It will not be important how much we return, but what is the measure of increase. If to the two talents by wise use of opportunities we add other two, we shall receive the same commendation as those who to the five talents add other five 2. *Mystery.* There is a strange mixture of good and evil in us. Our feet stand on the earth and our head points toward heaven, as if significant of our heavenly aspirations and earthly tendencies We can talk of the beauty of virtue whilst deliberately indulging in vice. Pilate-like, we can wash our hands in affected innocency whilst the guilt of blood rests upon us. A business loss, a bereavement, a change in circumstances, and all a man's fine talk about superiority to circumstances, the vanity of riches, and futility of earthly things avails nothing The mystery of the future is sometimes agonizing. 3 *Guilt.* We cannot shift upon the first sinner the guilt of our iniquity. "*My sin* is ever before me" is the wail of every kingly soul. Nor can we cast our guilt upon circumstances. No man is forced to violate his conscience. Where there is no will there is no guilt. A man must rule his circumstances, not be ruled by them. 4. *Faith.* Creeds and Churches will not save us They presuppose our salvation. The reason why the faith of so many is feeble is that they have never tested it. It is an unproved armour, and when the hour comes to encounter Goliath they are afraid. Every man must come into contact with God. "O taste and see that the Lord is good." One real wrestle with God will teach more about prayer than a treatise on it. Faith in God in an hour of real danger better explains it than a sermon on its philosophy. "Search the Scriptures." "Prove all things," that you may "hold fast that which is good." 5 *Temptation.* From this there can be no escape. Were we able to say as Christ did, "The prince of this world cometh and hath nothing in me," temptation would be powerless. Not here, but yonder, will the sons of God present themselves before the Lord and Satan *not* come among them. 6. *Sorrow.* "The heart knoweth his own bitterness."

III. A prophecy of destiny. 1. *What a man is* NOW, *that he will be* HERE-AFTER. God will judge every man according to his works, as these are the evidences of the man. Heaven may be a change of locality and circumstances, but not character. This is indestructible. 2. *There is no injustice, because each man is judged.* To one he gives five talents, to another two, and to another one; to every man according to his several ability; and he will expect a proportionate return. The manifestation of the Spirit is given to every man to profit withal. Unto every one of us is given grace. God is *not* a hard master, reaping where he has not sown, and gathering where he has not strawed. 3. *We are now fuelling the revealing fire—a fire that shall try every man's work of what sort it is.* Nothing ends in this world. Thoughts become incarnated as soon as we express them. Words live in those who hear us. Deeds have an undying influence. God will gather up the fragments of our daily lives, that nothing be lost. And the day shall declare every man's work.

SELF-RESPECT.

vi. 11.   *Should such a man as I flee? and who is there, that, being as I am, would go into the temple to save his life? I will not go in.*

Nehemiah would not run away, because he *could not fancy himself* doing anything of that sort. "Should such a man as I flee?" Our theme then is *self-respect.* Religion, though it brings with it humility,—an *unnatural* grace of character, an exotic from the gardens of the skies planted on earth by Divine hands,—though religion induces humility, it promotes self-respect. The eighth Psalm teaches not merely the littleness of man, but his greatness. Throughout the book of Nehemiah the Jewish patriot is not wanting in manly self-respect.

I. The ground of self-respect. 1. *False grounds.* (a) *Money* The vulgarest form of human conceit. To be a money-bag, and nothing else! (b) *Birth.* A by no means contemptible ground, if the greatness from which a man is born is bred into his own character. (c) *Intelligence.* Too frequently a reason for the smallest vanity. Vanities of authors and pride of bookmen. (d) *Office and association.* These are no necessary reasons for self-pluming, but may be the merest accidents. 2. *True grounds* Moral worth. Personal nobleness and sincerity of character and life. Under the eye of God, and in view of a Christian relation to God, a man may stand upright before the world. (a) *Sonship with God.* "That we should be called the sons of God" is a ground for dignity—to be of the inner elect family of God. (b) *Brotherhood with* the good. To be in the bead-roll of that long line of Divine heroes of all ages — following, but not with equal steps—that stirs the blood. "Brothers, we are treading where the saints have trod." (c) *Service in righteousness.* The great cause of God gives dignity to the meanest servant. "I had rather be a doorkeeper," &c. (d) *Heirship with the skies.* The celestial expectations of the good give grandeur to their earthly being.

II. The influence of self-respect. 1. *Negatively.* (a) *Not petty, strutting pride.* "Not I, but Jesus Christ that dwelleth in me." The dignity of the child of God—in its possessions and honours and hopes—is too tremendous to be proud of. (b) *Not contempt of others.* "He that is greatest among you, let him be your servant." Jesus has a name above every name, because "he took on him the form of a servant." 2. *Positively.* (a) *The effect of self-respect in duty.* To exalt all duty into the sublime, and to do it, beyond all its temporal and transitory purposes, "as unto the Lord." (b) *In temptation.* To make sin *beneath* a man. "He *cannot* sin, because he is born of God" — as a spotless Washington "cannot lie." Joseph's indignant "How can I do this great wickedness, and sin against God?" (c) *In trouble.* It prevents a man becoming unworthy of himself. "I know how to be *abased.*" "If thou faint in the day of adversity, thy strength is small." In worldly scenes and senses pride is a great restrainer of weakness. "Burning pride and high disdain forbad the rising tear to flow." So in the spiritual life the man of God chides his trembling soul "Why art thou cast down, O my soul?"

Application. *Know thyself!* 1. *A child of God* Are you a child of God? 2. *Then rightly view the dignity of your being.* On the *human side*, a vessel of clay, brief in life, weak in powers, limited by worldly accidents; but on the *Godward side*, an heir of God and a joint heir with Christ.

CHRISTIAN FIRMNESS.

vi. 11. *And I said, Should such a man as I flee? and who is there, that, being as I am, would go into the temple to save his life? I will not go in.*

Whoever examines the character of the primitive saints will see how religion dignifies and ennobles the mind of man. Nehemiah had engaged in an arduous work. In this he was opposed. From Shemaiah, a prophet, he might have expected better things.

I. The subtlety with which our great adversary will assault us. How specious was the proposal made to Nehemiah. Our adversary will propose to us—1. *To neglect our social duties to further our spiritual welfare.* A common temptation and specious. Apprentice and servant neglecting duty to attend religious ordinances. "These ought ye to have done, and not to leave the other undone." 2. *To conform to the world, with a view to conciliate their regard.* By conforming to the world we shall confirm them in their persuasion, that religion does not require that measure of spirituality which the saints of old maintained. 3. *To use undue means with a view to obtain some desirable end.* Safety was desirable to Nehemiah, but secretion not a desirable way to obtain it. Many objects are desirable, but must not be sought by any sacrifice of

duty or conscience. The greater the subtlety of Satan is, the greater should be our vigilance, and the more immovable.

II. The firmness with which we should resist him "Shall such a man as I flee—a man invested with authority, a man engaged for the Lord, a man in whom any act of cowardice will be productive of injurious effects?" Thus should we set the Lord ever before us, bearing fully in mind—1 *Our relation to him.* A servant of the living God. A child of the Father in heaven. My calling. 2. *Our obligations to him.* Shall I offend God? I will render unto the Lord according to the benefits he has conferred upon me. 3. *Our expectations from him.* For eternity I have been redeemed, sanctified; and for eternity alone will I both live and die. 4. *The interest which God himself has in the whole of our conduct.* God's enemies endeavour to beguile us, in order that they may triumph over us and exult in our shame. On review of the subject—1 *Expect temptation.* 2. *In every circumstance place your entire confidence in God.—Simeon, abridged.*

HUMAN PRESCIENCE

vi. 12. *And, lo, I perceived that God had not sent him*

"Because," says Gill, "he advised to that which was against the cause of God and true religion." That helped Nehemiah to discern Shemaiah's treachery; but was that all? The treachery was not yet discovered. Afterwards

Nehemiah learned that "Tobiah and Sanballat had hired him." Is there not a spirit in man—a spirit of divination? What do observation and experience teach? Are not men and women continually sitting in judgment upon one another? "To two states of soul it is given to detect the presence of evil, states the opposite of each other— innocence and guilt. It was predicted of the Saviour while yet a child that by him the thoughts of many hearts should be revealed; the fulfilment of this was the history of his life. He went through the world, by his innate purity detecting the presence of evil, as he detected the touch of her who touched his garment in the crowd. Men, supposed spotless before, fell down before him crying, 'Depart from me, for I am a sinful man, O Lord!' This in a lower degree is true of all innocence. You would think that one who can deeply read the human heart and track its windings must be himself deeply experienced in evil. But it is not so — at least not always. Purity can detect the presence of the evil which it does not understand. Just as the dove which has never seen a hawk trembles at its presence, and just as a horse rears uneasily when the wild beast unknown and new to it is near, so innocence understands, yet understands not, the meaning of the unholy look, the guilty tone, the sinful manner. It shudders and shrinks from it by a power given to it, like that which God has conferred on the unreasoning mimosa. Sin gives the same power, but differently. Innocence apprehends the approach of evil by the instinctive tact of contrast; guilt, by the instinctive consciousness of similarity."—*F. W. Robertson.* Faces never lie, it is said. Falsehood has not a clear, calm gaze. *The grosser vices leave their mark upon the countenance.* The drunkard, the libertine, the deceiver write the story of their lives upon the *fleshly table* of the

body. The laws of God are written in the nature of things as well as in the Scripture of truth. Mahomet said, "Paradise is under the shadow of swords." All men pay the penalty of their position. A good gained, an ill averted, must reckon with the sweat of the brow or the sweat of the brain. Wise men, who are they but the far-seeing, the foresighted? As those children of Issachar to whom is given *honourable mention*, as being "men that had understanding of the times to know what Israel ought to do" (1 Chron. xii. 32). Nehemiah "saw through" Shemaiah. It needed no miracle to reveal his fraud.

Learn—**I. The supreme importance of truth and uprightness.** The Bible revelation does not make truth, truth; falsehood, falsehood; it only declares what they are. Close your Bible, and still deception will bring disgrace, dishonesty will not be the best policy, judgment will track the wrong-doer. "Be sure your sin will find you out" is written in history and biography.

See—**II. An evidence of the Bible.** The book does not stand alone. The heavens above and the earth beneath, the nature and constitution of man, confirm its truth.

Mark—**III. Confirmation of the doctrine of a judgment to come.** Men are being judged. A book of remembrance each of us is writing. In the failure of falsehood and deception, in the discovery and condemnation of every unrighteous compact, in the fall of dynasties resting upon oppression and bloodshed, in the histories recorded by the daily press, see you not premonition of a day of judgment?

BRIBERY.

vi. 13. *Therefore was he hired, that I should be afraid, and do so, and sin, and that they might have matter for an evil report, that they might reproach me.*

In this paragraph Nehemiah dwells upon the hirelings who were *paid* to do him mischief. The wrong-doer becomes dignified by association with his petty tools, and Tobiah and Sanballat are

exalted into the originals of mischief in contrast with the ready agents who did the mischief for money. *Bribery.*

I. Its existence and varieties. Among heathen states and in the godless

M

associations of the world this guilt is not unnatural, but alas for its commonness in Christian times. From Judas, who took the bribe of thirty pieces of silver, down to the last transaction of the kind yesterday, the world is full of it. 1. *In statecraft.* This golden key finds the wards of more locks than we know of, it buys eloquence in debate, and logic in the newspapers, and valour or cowardice in the field. 2. *In trade.* Talk to any business man about his particular avocations, and get him into the anecdotal strain, and you will find out among what snares an honourable man is compelled to walk day by day. The business man has to battle everywhere with an underground foe. 3. *In morals and religion.* For fear of seeming cynicism let us not pursue this theme. But the purchase system has no respect for sacred things, and the modern temple, like the ancient temple, has its herd of traffickers, which, if driven out with a whip of cords, would leave the Church of God purer and the homes of England safer. In Nehemiah's case the prophets were bought, and the so-called messengers of God were, Balaam-like, guided not by a star from heaven, but by the glitter of golden coins.

II. Its effects. 1. *Personal degradation.* To buy a man in a slave-market is to make him but half a man; but to buy a man's soul in a *conscience-market* is to degrade him from manhood altogether, "for in the image of God made he man." To buy from some poor man his birthright of honour, to take away a man's Christ and leave him thirty

pieces of silver as an equivalent—that is *devil's work in the doer,* and it is *damnation in him in whom the thing is done.* 2. *General disorganization.* The great laws of this world are just, and all departure from them must work downfall. Violation of the laws of health is a wandering towards death. Corruption and jobbing in the state means rottenness and downfall of a nation. Bribery in trade is " a missing of the mark," a sin against the true end of trade, and its revenge is sure. 3. *Hindrance of all good.* The Achan gold-ingot in the tent makes God's army of righteousness weak. "Neither will I be with you any more, except ye destroy the accursed from among you."

III. Its cure. 1. *The first ingredient of the cure is self-denial.* "They all do it" is no matter; *you* had better not. We can only win in this fight by having the courage to lose (1 Sam. xii. 2—5). 2. *The second is resolute unmercifulness to the briber.* For the good of the community and the glory of God let the briber's head be stuck on a pole. 3. *The third is trust in God and faith in right.* God is strong, and if we will honour him he will honour us. He that sitteth in the heavens shall laugh at the petty power of bribery. "Great is truth, and shall prevail," is not a motto to be illuminated on a card, but to be illustrated in a life.

Application. "Seek *first* the kingdom of God and his righteousness." Let that be the guiding law of life and have faith in its success, and it shall succeed.

FIFTY-TWO DAYS' WORK.

vi. 15. So the wall was finished in fifty and two days.

To draw a circumference of fortifications of such dimensions in such short time was no doubt a great engineering feat. The pluck, decision, promptness, and laborious industry and despatch of such a task are very stimulating to read of. *Let us, however, make a parable of the story, and use the text as a motto of a deeper theme.* The circling year furnishes us with fifty-two days of special

work for God. The wall-building of Christian Nehemiahs in the spiritual city of God is mainly done on Sundays, of which the year supplies fifty-two or thereabouts. *Of that fifty-two days and of their work let us speak.* Fifty-two Sundays.

I. How quickly they pass! To a *child* how slow the movement from Sunday to Sunday—what a space in the great time-field! But to a worn, worried, work-wearied *man* a week is but a quick flash of days, " swifter than a weaver's shuttle." Monday with its yawnings and stretchings, Tuesday with its markets, Wednesday with its solid tasks, Thursday with its deeper toil, Friday with its haste " to get it done," Saturday with its summing up and its payments, and then the Sabbath bell and all the associations of the house of God. It is a quick passage from Sunday to Sunday. We soon round a circle of fifty-two. The *first* Sunday of the year, with its cheery, greeting sermon of hope, and then in a little while the *last* Sunday, with its solemn review and reflection. It soon goes, this year of Sundays. 1. *How many circles have you passed?* 2. *How many more do you look for?*

II. What opportunities they furnish! 1. *What opportunities of* REST! The glory of the Sabbath as a rest day, the pillow of the work-wearied world The RIGHTS of MAN in this matter. 2. *What opportunities of spiritual friendship!* The Sabbath a great holiday and reunion of kindred hearts The gathering of the brotherhood of Christians in their souls' home. 3. *What opportunities of Divine instruction!* The lessons rubbed off the slate during the week, or rubbed into indefinite blurs, the new writing of God's word on the tablets of the heart. 4. *What opportunities of moral renewal!* The religious recreative power of Sabbath thoughts and engagements 5. *What opportunities of refreshing* HOPE! God's promises breaking like stars upon the soul escaped from the glare of the world's gas-lamps. God's heaven descending upon the eye of meditation, like the New Jerusalem which John saw End your Sabbath with St. John's vision at the close of Revelation. Fifty-two Sundays! what golden coins from God's mint

III. What results they leave! 1. *In memory* (*a*) Truths taught (*b*) Memories cherished 2 *In life* (*a*) If improved. Growing Christian character —another ring of fortification against the world, the flesh, and the devil. (*b*) If unimproved. A hardening of the moral sense, a deadening of the power of truth, a deepening of the fatal work of worldliness. 3. *For judgment* (*a*) Condemnation, if abused. (*b*) Safety, if used.

Application 1. *Thank God for the day of days.* 2. *Use each day as it comes.* 3. *Determine upon a rounded result for each cycle of fifty-two.*

THE GODWARD SIDE OF THINGS.

vi. 16.　*They perceived that this work was wrought of our God.*

An outer and an inner view. "They all made us afraid, saying, *Their hands shall be weakened from the work, that it be not done*" (ver. 9). The work went on; the wall was finished. "And it came to pass, that when all our enemies heard thereof, and all the heathen that were about us saw these things, they were much cast down in their own eyes for *they perceived that this work was wrought of our God*" (ver. 16). There is an upper and an under side to many things. Work man-ward or work God-ward

I. Work Divinely inspired. "The good hand of God that was upon him," Nehemiah is never tired of recognizing "I heard the voice of the Lord, saying, Whom shall I send, and who will go for us? Then said I, Here am I; send me." —*Isaiah.* "The word of the Lord came unto me, saying, I have ordained thee a prophet unto the nations Then said I, Ah, Lord God! behold, I cannot speak: for I am a child. But the Lord said unto me, Say not, I am a child: for thou shalt go to all that I shall send thee, and whatsoever I command thee thou shalt speak"—*Jeremiah.* "I was no prophet, neither was I a prophet's son; but I was an herdman, and a gatherer of sycamore fruit: and the Lord took me as I followed the flock, and the Lord said unto me, Go, prophesy unto my people Israel"—*Amos.* "I must work the works of him that sent me" "As my Father hath sent me, even so send I you."—*Jesus.* "The Lord spake to Paul in the night by a vision, Be not afraid, but speak, and hold not thy peace."—*Acts of Apostles.* "I was in the Spirit, and heard behind me a great voice, saying, What thou seest, write."—*St. John.* More to the same tune and words in biography of martyr and missionary saint and apostle of modern times. "These great master spirits of the world are not so much distinguished, after all, by the acts they do, as by the sense itself of some mysterious girding of the Almighty upon them, whose behests they are set on to fulfil. And all men may have this; for the humblest and commonest have a place and a work assigned them, in the same manner, and have it for their privilege to be always ennobled in the same lofty consciousness. God is girding every man for a place and a calling" "Every human soul has a complete and perfect plan cherished for it in the heart of God—a Divine biography marked out, which it enters into life to live. This life, rightly unfolded, will be a complete and beautiful whole; an experience led on by God and unfolded by his secret nurture, as the trees and the flowers by the secret nurture of the world; a drama cast in the mould of a perfect art, with no part wanting, a Divine study for the man himself, and for others—a study that shall for ever unfold, in wondrous beauty, the love and faithfulness of God; great in its conception, great in the Divine skill by which it is shaped; above all, great in the momentous and glorious issues it prepares. What a thought is this for every human soul to cherish! What dignity does it add to life! What support does it bring to the trials of life! What instigations does it add to send us onward in everything that constitutes our excellence! We live in the Divine thought. We fill a place in the great everlasting plan of God's intelligence. We never sink below his care, never drop out of his counsel."—*Bushnell.*

II. Workers Divinely helped. "It is not strange that Sanballat saw that the wall-building was wrought of Israel's God. The trouble with God's enemies is not that their knowledge is defective, but that their hearts are alienated. Evidences are multiplying constantly before them, but produce no change in their opposition. Sanballat was vexed because he was thwarted by the Lord God of Israel. Those fifty-two days of wall-building were clearly to his mind a token of Divine assistance; but this knowledge did not stop his opposition." —*Crosby.* Nevertheless the work was hastened; the opposition was resisted; then all was finished. God is at work where he is needed. Our God is a living God. He is a present God. He is a God who inspires men to-day. He is as mindful of us as was Jesus of the hungry, shepherdless crowds of Judæa (Matt. x. 36; xiv. 14—16). God is at work when he is not perceived. The fabric cannot be judged in the loom. Our life is sectional. God sees the end as well as the beginning. There may be periods of life when the thought of God is not forced in upon us. But when life becomes only a consciousness of suffering, what then?

" Be near me when my light is low,
    When the blood creeps, and the nerves prick
  And tingle, and the heart is sick,
    And all the wheels of being slow."

When duty is plain, but the will is wanting, there is stimulus in the remembrance of "God which worketh in you both to will and to do" When the spirit is willing and the flesh is weak, then may we hear the still, small voice of promise: "My strength is made perfect in weakness." And when the tasks of life are completed we shall perceive that "the work was wrought of our God."

ILLUSTRATIVE POEM.

THE BUILDERS.

" ALL are architects of Fate,
    Working in these walls of Time;
  Some with massive deeds and great,
    Some with ornaments of rhyme.

Nothing useless is, or low;
    Each thing in its place is best;
  And what seems but idle show,
    Strengthens and supports the rest.

For the structure that we raise,
   Time is with materials filled ,
Our to-days and yesterdays
   Are the blocks with which we build.

Truly shape and fashion these ,
   Leave no yawning gaps between ,
Think not, because no man sees,
   Such things will remain unseen.

In the elder days of Art,
   Builders wrought with greatest care,
Each minute and unseen part ,
   For the Gods see everywhere.

Let us do our work as well,
   Both the unseen and the seen ;

Make the house, where Gods may dwell,
   Beautiful, entire, and clean.

Else our lives are incomplete,
   Standing in these walls of Time,
Broken stairways, where the feet
   Stumble as they seek to climb

Build to-day, then, strong and sure,
   With a firm and ample base ,
And ascending and secure
   Shall to-morrow find its place.

Thus alone can we attain
   To those turrets, where the eye
Sees the world as one vast plain,
   And one boundless reach of sky."
                         Longfellow.

THE OVERRULING GOD.

vi, 16. *And it came to pass, that when all our enemies heard thereof, and all the heathen that were about us saw these things, they were much cast down in their own eyes : for they perceived that this work was wrought of our God*

If we consult the Jewish history, we soon understand what the work was which is here confessed (though unwillingly, it seems) to have been wrought of God , it was the rebuilding of Jerusalem upon the return of that people to their own land, after a total destruction of the one, and a grievous captivity of the other, by a cruel and unrelenting conqueror. This great and surprising event (a bondage of seventy years having worn out all their hopes, and left them no reasonable prospect of deliverance) must have been brought about in a way very wonderful indeed, and sufficiently astonishing, since, according to the text, whatever favourable circumstances might appear, or second causes be instrumental in it, the hand of God was owned apparently to give effect unto it by enemies, whose malice sought the ruin of their state ; by heathens, whose religion abhorred the object of their worship. What occasioned an acknowledgment so just and so ingenuous, when we consider what was wrought ; so strange and unusual, when we reflect upon the temper and interests of those who, to their shame and disappointment, made it, may be learned, I conceive, from that prevailing instinct in mankind which disposes us to look up for an overruling cause when any extraordinary accidents happen here below. And, indeed, if we do confess any miraculous alterations in the natural, we are obliged to conclude a Divine Power immediately directing the great revolutions of the civil, world.

I God is truly Lord, and his kingdom ruleth over all the earth. Now Christians we know are to suppose this article to be true as having the Word of God himself a voucher for it ; because with them at least no human argument ought to dispute against his authority. The prophecies of the Old Testament prove a Divine prescience, and the promises of the New allow God to be concerned for his Church. It follows then that no contingencies can escape his observation, nor contrivances disappoint his designs. Would we appeal to reason, testimony, or experience, more to satisfy the scruples or to silence the petulancy of other men than to obtain and secure the belief of this point unto ourselves, here also we are safe. 1. *Why so profuse a waste of wisdom and of power in the formation and contrivance of the world, if it might not deserve his future care, who at first condescended to the making of it ?* Or, how indeed could it continue to exist in all that beauty and order which we so much admire had he ever withdrawn his hand, upon whom it always must depend, because it was created by him Hence, if man be the noblest part, he is the peculiar object of the Divine care, nay, he seems to need it most ; and then from the goodness of God we conclude him entitled to the distinguishing protection of it. This cannot be expressed or turned to our use unless all events are under his eye, and all our counsels are submitted to his rule ; considering how little we can foresee of what is to come, able less to provide against it ; how much we are in the dark as to consequences from the management of other men, and at a loss what to promise even from ourselves. This way of reasoning holds stronger yet with regard to public communities than to private persons ; here in this life are they only to be taken notice of, here only, in the visible scenes of human occurrences, can Providence appear concerned for them. And though government be an ordinance and a blessing too from God, yet how often without are fightings and within are fears? And who can prevent or compose these disorders but he alone who restraineth the spirit of princes and stilleth the madness of the people. Then when God giveth quietness who can give trouble? Whether it be done for or against a nation or a man only. 2. *Whatever difficulties the metaphysical considerations of a few, whatever disgrace the superstitious abuses of more, have brought upon it, yet the solemnity of public worship and the sincerity of private prayer, the allowed obligations of an oath, and the unavoidable effects of conscience, declare mankind subscribing to this truth.* In fact, the most desperate and independent tempers, upon some unusual emergencies, have been subdued to a confession of it. To this copious and instructive theme do we owe all those noble sentiments of heathen philosophy which advance human nature above the casualties of fortune, and support the efforts of virtue against the tyranny of fate. From hence did ancient tragedy dress its awful scenes and take its affecting images, to represent a superior dominion over all ; which may mysteriously perplex for a while, yet at last conducts the puzzling incidents to an end, confessing equity and right. What in truth is history but a long detail of God's interfering providence? 3. *We ourselves are living witnesses.* If any of us have ever at a venture drawn our bow, and hit at once surprisingly a mark that others with the most likely skill have often sought to touch in vain, who directed our arrow? If ever the race is not to the swift, nor the battle to the strong, who causes our feet to stumble, and gives success unto the weak? Second causes are the servants of his will, who is truly Lord of what we call nature or mistake for chance.

II. **We may inquire by what characters a work such as the text is speaking of may be perceived to be wrought of our God.** It is not always easy nor even safe boldly to point out what God has done. Yet he does sometimes so *show himself* as that we may perceive his hand. We are often called upon to see the wonderful operations of it. *Where any event comes to pass beyond the reasonable expectations of mankind, or any effect is produced by means altogether unequal to it,* an invisible Mind is plainly concerned in the one, and a supernatural Cause actually gives birth unto the other. *If an event thus strangely brought about eminently consults the honour of God's holy name and the maintenance of true religion and the prosperity of the people,* in these instances God appears. Upon such occasions, doubtless, we may say the arm of the Lord has been revealed, and we have seen the salvation of our God.—*Ross Ley*, 1727.

THE WORLD'S ACKNOWLEDGMENT OF GOD.

vi. 16.   *And it came to pass, that when all our enemies heard, &c.*

The success of Nehemiah *against* such odds proved the success to be Divinely given. They, the enemies, perceived that this work was wrought of God. World's acknowledgment of God.

I. **World's past acknowledgment of God.** 1. *Biblical instances.* The Bible story is the story of God's works and wonders of salvation, and all through that story we see this : — the world struggling like a maniac in paroxysms of wickedness, but now and again bowing down and crying, "It's no use; the Lord he is God, the Lord he is God!" The magicians in Egypt threw down their conjuring tools, and exclaimed of God's miracles by Moses, "This is the finger of God." The heathen peoples of whom we read in the book of Daniel now and then confess the living God, and sob like resisting children whose spirits are broken, "that he is the living God, and steadfast for ever." The sailors in the book of Jonah exemplify the same thing. The people around the cross "smite their breasts" and own, "Truly this was the Son of God." The magistrates and rulers in the book of Acts make tacit or open confessions of the same thing. All through the Bible story we have illustrations of this text. 2. *Later instances.* Early Church history, martyr stories, stories of heathen lands submitting to the gospel, confessions of men who thought themselves infidels, but who were forced like the brute in Balaam's story to speak for God—these furnish exemplifications of this great principle, a rebellious world owning God's presence and power.

II. World's present acknowledgment of God. 1. *Unconscious acknowledgment.* Think of the way Christianity penetrates the life of our modern world; take England for example. Our throne is based on God's word. A representative of the Christian religion gives the Queen her crown. Our legal oath is taken on God's gospel; that little book is "kissed" by the villain in our law courts, and it is supposed that if he ever did speak the truth, he will with that "book" before him. A seventh part of

our time is devoted to education concerning God. Our books, our pictures, our music are full of him. The world gives an unconscious chorus of acknowledgment. 2. *Unwilling acknowledgment.* The testimony of sceptics to the *morals* of Christianity. John Stuart Mill would have the life of Jesus taught in our schools. The "new lights" of our time steal their oil from Hebrew seers and lawgivers and from Christian apostles, and strike their matches on the covers of the Bible, and then run out with their paper lanterns of essays and theories. Oh, the blindness of the fools who are trying to illuminate the world on new systems, and who pretend not to know that the world can see God's word to be the "main pipe" of their illuminations. 3. *Frank acknowledgment.* How many worldlings dare deny God? When Christianity takes them by the button they say, "You are right, and we are wrong, and we shall perhaps come round to you when we have had our fling." "They are cast down in their own eyes, for they perceive that this work is wrought of our God."

III. The world's future acknowledgment. 1. *Willing.* How prophecy lights up the world's future. Men shall confess God. Instance prophecies of this. 2. *Enforced.* The tremendous confession of the last day: "Behold, he cometh in the clouds, and every eye shall see him," &c. What a melancholy thought that men shall fight against God until he has built the wall which fences them out of hope.

Application. 1. *Make acknowledgment of God.* 2. *Now.* "Choose ye this day."

OPPOSITIONS OF INFLUENCE.

vi. 17—19.   *Moreover in those days the nobles of Judah,* &c.

Tobiah, the foe outside Nehemiah's ranks, and "the nobles of Judah" inside, were eminent and influential persons, who were a sore thorn to the good man. He fought against an *influential* opposition, and suggests to us other oppositions of influence.

I. Influence is opposed to God's work. Influence and respectability! A man with a hundred a year may be orthodox in belief, and diligent in Christian work, as in the Sunday-school and in the prayer-meeting, but this man perhaps invents a new kind of blacking, and makes £2000 a year by it, or his aunt dies and leaves him £5000 a year: the man is the *same* man, but his income is changed, and you do not find him in the Sunday-school any more; the night air is dangerous, so he absents himself from the prayer-meeting. Is not this a true story? The man has become an *influential* man Respectability! In one of our law trials a man described another as "respectable" "What do you mean by respectable?" said the judge. "Why," explained the witness, "he kept a gig!" Now it is a fact that such a man's sneer at religion has weight If he had no "gig" I should think him a fool to say what he says; but he *has* a "gig," and his opinion is not to be set aside. I know a man who worked as a schoolmaster for £100 per annum, and he fought Christ's battle then in a ragged school; but he got a berth at £850 per annum as a school inspector, and five months later resigned the ragged school and became "broad" in his views. This is the kind of influence most of us come in contact with, and this is its natural history.

II. **Influence is contemptible in its opposition.** "The kings of the earth set themselves, and the rulers take counsel together, against the Lord, and against his anointed . . . . He that sitteth in the heavens shall LAUGH; *the Lord shall have them in derision.*" 1 *Their power is contemptible.* Crowns, sceptres, swords, cannons, thrones, statutes, put these in one scale, and then put the short, uncertain life of man which a pin-prick can destroy in the other scale. Look through the drapery at the man, and who is he among these everlasting hills of earth, and these rolling histories of the human race, and these solemn eternities of God? What a manikin to play such fantastic tricks before high heaven! Cash-boxes and "gigs" and villas—ah me! as the Chelsea sage would say, what things these are to sway the immortal minds of men! Death breathes on "influence," and then we have a white marble stone with some poetry on it, and that is the last of influence 2 *Their opposition is contemptible.* A Galilean sat down on a green hill-side and talked "golden rules" to a crowd of country-folk, that was how it began. And "Influence" has drawn its sword and bent its bow against Christianity for near 2000 years, and now it gives colour to every lofty thing among the first nations of earth, and millions crowd in fear to own its divinity every Sabbath day, and like a stone down a mountain-side it rolls on its omnipotent course. Do not let us exaggerate "influence."

III. **Influence has to be dealt with.** 1. *Do not let us provoke it* If the lion is asleep and you can pass the den without waking it, let it sleep on. Do not *make* martyrdoms. As a rule, let the martyr's crown come like other honour, *unsought.* But if it come hail it with a doxology. 2. *Do not let us be afraid of it.* (*a*) Its *power is often hollow* The godless judge who tries the prisoner "trembles and says, Go thy way for this time," the King Agrippa of this world says in dainty jest (with a grim reality concealed), "Almost thou persuadest me to be a Christian!" "Influence" sneers at you, and then goes to bed and lies awake all night wondering if you are not right after all. (*b*) *Do not let it sway your convictions.* The bare stern front of God's truth must be more potent with us than any form which presents itself to our eye or our imagination Let no man's life or opinion be a necessary factor with us as we sit solitary, making up the great reckoning of life Do not copy from another's slate You have to do the sum yourself (*c*) *Do not let it damp your hope.* God is strong Truth is mighty. To Jesus Christ "all power is given in heaven and on earth" The crash of fallen "influence" in history is but a feeble prophecy of the downfall of it hereafter. "He *must* reign until he hath put all enemies under his feet."

Application. 1. *Rightly estimate the worth and weight of things temporal.* 2. *Duly ponder the eternal life and power of things Divine.* 3. *Trust simply in God.*

DESERTERS.

vi. 17, 18. Moreover in those days the nobles of Judah sent many letters unto Tobiah, and the letters of Tobiah came unto them. For there were many in Judah sworn unto him, because he was the son in law of Shechaniah the son of Arah; and his son Johanan had taken the daughter of Meshullam the son of Berechiah.

"*Meshullam*" wrought well at the wall-building (iii. 4); but he ensnared himself. "*The nobles*" had not retained a pure faith and an unfaltering patriotism. Under the influence of *personal interests* they forgot the *commonwealth*.

I. **The secret of desertion.** Lot went down to Sodom under the impulse of a worldly choice; and its consequences were that he left part of his family there to encounter the doom-storm, and with the rest brought away the taint of a worldly spirit (Gen. xix.). "Demas hath forsaken me, having loved this present world" (2 Tim. iv. 10). Thus patriarch and apostle bridge the gulf of centuries by a similar experience of the fatal consequences of worldly alliances; Old Testament and New proclaim the need of nonconformity. The nobles were not outwardly at feud with Nehemiah. Their duplicity made them dangerous. Hand and tongue were seemingly engaged in the good cause; heart had long since deserted it. In soul they were men of the world, who had their portion in this life. 1. *In self-cultivation the graver danger is from within.* To repress passion harder than to resist tempter. "The prince of this world cometh and hath nothing in me." Could we say that temptation would be powerless. "Every man is tempted when he is drawn away of his own lust, and enticed." When the tree *is* "desired" it needs hardly a serpent's voice to cause us to "eat of the fruit thereof." 2. *In the prosecution of any good task fear most friends' treachery.* The untiring opposition of foes may be met by sleepless vigilance; the lukewarmness of friends is fatal to progress. We are dependent on co-operation.

II. **Practical unworldliness.** "Be ye not unequally yoked together with unbelievers: for what fellowship hath righteousness with unrighteousness" (2 Cor. vi. 14)? "Have no fellowship with the unfruitful works of darkness" (Ephes. v 11). In some soils the plant of piety cannot thrive. Men pray to be kept from temptation and then boldly enter into it. If in any society I cannot retain my purity, if under any set of circumstances I am unable to maintain my integrity, let me forsake that companionship, avoid that position. Where duty calls follow the sacred voice, and God shall give his angels charge concerning thee. But if pleasure or passion or curiosity bid thee enter, beware. That way ruin lies. Moral deterioration has begun. "Enter not into the path of the wicked, and go not in the way of evil men. Avoid it, pass not by it, turn from it, and pass away" (Prov. iv. 14, 15).

Illustrations:—"What Paul writes concerning false brethren (2 Cor. xi. 26), that has Nehemiah also experienced for his portion. And it is indeed one of the heaviest griefs of the true servants of God, when they must see that those connected with them in religion, yes, indeed, at times their colleagues, who labour with them in the same work, stand in prejudicial intercourse with the enemies of Christ and his Church, and yet wish to be considered as co-members, striving for the honour of God. Those whom God awakens for spiritual building should conduct themselves circumspectly and courageously against the snares of the enemy, and not allow themselves to be frightened off by their slander, but cheerfully proceed. In the end the enemy will be cast down with fear in their consciences, and must acknowledge that the work is of God (Acts v. 39). When we wander in the midst of anxiety God refreshes us, and stretches his hand over the rage of his enemies, and helps us with his right hand (Ps. xcvii. 10)."—*Starke.*

"I care not at all for an open enemy of the Church, such as the Papists, with their power and persecutions; I regard them not, for by them the true Church cannot receive hurt, nor can they hinder God's word, nay, the Church, through their raging and persecution, rather increases. But it is the inward evil of false brethren that will do mischief to the Church. Judas betrayed Christ; the false apostles confused and falsified the gospel. Such are the real fellows through whom the devil rages and spoils the Church."—*Luther*

"What every one is in God's sight, that is he, and no more."—*St. Francis of Assisi.*

"The fervent and diligent man is prepared for all things. It is harder to resist vices and passions than to toil in bodily labours. Be watchful over thyself, stir up thyself, warn thyself, and whatsoever becomes of others, neglect not thyself."—*Thomas à Kempis.*

"Some professors of religion resemble trees, the leaves of which fall off when winter approaches, but appear again when the season becomes more favourable and mild; for in the winter of adversity they conceal their lusts, and restrain their sinful propensities; but when prosperity smiles upon them they break out again, as at the first, and recruit themselves with further supplies of folly and of vanity. This is a genuine evidence of hypocrisy; for nothing is more hateful to a real Christian than such conduct, who in all circumstances, and under very vicissitude, whether public or private, is always the same, and remains unalterably fixed in his God. He preserves an uniform piety both in prosperity and adversity, in poverty and in affluence, steadily cleaving to God, and meeting with resignation every affliction that Providence lays upon him."—*John Arndt.*

THE BAD MAN PRAISED.

vi. 19. *They reported his good deeds before me.*

The nobles of Judah reporting Tobiah's "good deeds" to Nehemiah is a piece of humorous irony often repeated. What heroes this world does select! "Not this man, but Barabbas!" Historians have made rose-coloured villains into heroes. Poets have set to bewitching music names that ought to "blister the tongue." Preachers have written original and beautiful sermons to whitewash poor Cain and Judas and Pilate, and, like the Scotch minister of the story, have looked with almost admiration, at least with sympathy, on the "poor deil." Sometimes this is mawkish perverted sentiment, sometimes cant. The bad man praised.

I. Bad men do get praised 1. *Sometimes this praise is real. (a) No man without some trait of good.* A hand strewed flowers on Nero's grave. The dark rock of guilt may be streaked with a thread of gold or sparkle with some spot of crystal This is the handle for the man's redemption, but not a peg on which to hang draperies to hide real evil. (b) *A bad habit of life may be broken by occasional goodness.* The miser gives money away, the merciless has a tender thought, the bad does a good action contrary to all the common strain of his life. These do not compound for the evil, but are God's calls and strivings asserting and demonstrating themselves. 2. *Sometimes this praise is mistaken. (a) The bad seldom shows a bold front of hardness, but winds a rose garland round his sin and covers* it with hypocritical pretensions. A man can generally give a virtuous explanation of vice, or at least an explanation that leans toward virtue. The "cant" of goodness, of which the world speaks bitterly at times, is nothing compared with the "cant" of badness. (b) *Courteous conciliation of persons often throws dust in the eyes of the world.* A man who bows gracefully to me is in danger of compelling a too favourable interpretation of his deeds to others. Let us not French-polish wickedness. Softened names of things, graceful euphemisms for bad things in place of the "sword-cuts of Saxon speech," have often made blame sound very like praise. 3 *Sometimes this praise is fictitious altogether. (a) In eulogizing a bad man* other men are frequently praising their own likeness. (b) *Eulogy of the evil man* is often a subtle way of reflecting suspicion on moral standards.

II. Bad men are anxious for praise. No bad man wishes to be considered bad. 1. *In this there is a sentence of condemnation.* In hunting for false praise an evil man is but subpœnaing witnesses against his own real inner self. Every sound of undeserved praise is a sentence against the "hidden man of the heart." 2. *In this there is an indirect homage to virtue.* You do not believe evil to be good; you want the evil to be called a good that it is not. To waft the incense of praise to a bad man is to confess there is a noble style of manhood worthy of praise. 3. *In* *this anxiety for praise the bad man is frequently at as much trouble as it would cost him to gain the goodness he seeks credit for.* To *pretend* is nearly as difficult a task as to *be.* If self-defence could kneel down and become prayer, if seeming could break its bonds and strive for reality, the bad man might deserve the character he would like to hold in the estimation of the world.

III. Bad men are not hidden by the praise of the world 1 *Good men detect.* There is a subtle power of penetration in goodness. As the calm eyes of honesty look into the blinking eyes of the liar, the lie stands exposed. And this is a sore trouble to the evil man. He forgets the praise of fifty fools while reflecting on the unspoken censure of one wise man. Cæsar complains in the poem of "that spare Cassius" who "looks quite through the deeds of men." Haman finds that all this honour "availeth him nothing" so long as Mordecai sits with his still dark eye to look into his real soul. 2. *God detects.* 1. *Now.* Amid the music of men's flattery comes the boom of God's censure. In the banqueting chamber the fingers of God write fiery sentences to be read in the pauses of the revel. 2. *Hereafter.* "Every man must give account of himself to God." The ears will soon be stopped to men's praise, the eye will have no power to look on the fawning smile of the flatterer any more; one voice will fill the ear, one sight fix the eye—God—God—God —the "most worthy Judge eternal."

Application. 1. *Do not be discouraged by this misdirected praise.* Live for God's praise. "Be *thy* praise my highest aim, be *thy* smile my chief delight." 2. *Do not be deceived into any lowering of the standard of righteousness.*

ADDENDA TO CHAPTER VI.

Sentences from Old Writers.

I. Opponents (vers. 1—4). "Another let to the good work in hand. That in the fourth chapter was external only; that in the fifth internal only; this here is mixed, that is, partly cast in by the enemies without (those cruel crafties), and partly helped on by the perfidious prophets and ignobles within, conspiring with the enemy against the good of their own country." *The rest of our enemies.* "The Church's enemies are not a few (1 Cor. xvi. 9). She is like unto a silly poor maid, saith Luther, sitting in a wood or wilderness, compassed about with hungry wolves, lions, boars, bears, assaulting her every moment and minute. The ground of all is that old enmity (Gen. iii. 15)." *Sanballat and Geshem sent unto me.* "As if solicitous of my safety, and careful of the common good. Nehemiah well knew that all this pretended courtesy was but dross upon dirt, a fair glove drawn upon a foul hand, a cunning collusion to undo him. He therefore keeps aloof." "Our deceitful hearts do too often draw us away from the prosecution of good purposes, by casting many other odd impertinent matters in our way." "Nehemiah went not, but sent. This was to be wise as a serpent. God calleth us not to a weak simplicity, but alloweth us as much of the serpent as of the dove, and telleth us that a serpent's eye in a dove's head is a singular accomplishment." "Nehemiah was the driver-on of the business. His hands were full of employment. Let the tempter ever find us busy, and he will depart discouraged; as Cupid is said to do from the Muses, whom he could never take idle. An industrious Nehemiah is not at leisure to parley with Sanballat, lest if he let any water go beside the mill he should be a great loser by it. His employment is as a guard or good angel, to keep him both right and safe." *They sent unto me four times.* "As thinking to prevail by their importunity. Sin hath woaded an impudency in some men's faces" "We may style Nehemiah as one doth Athanasius, the bulwark of truth, the Church's champion" "True love teaches us to be angry with none but ourselves. True peace consists not in having much wealth, but in bearing patiently whatever goes against our nature." "If thou canst be silent and suffer, without doubt thou shalt see that the Lord will help thee." "Regard not much who is for thee, or against thee; but mind what thou art about, and take care that God may be with thee in everything thou doest" "It belongs to God to help, and to deliver from all confusion."

II The tongue (vers. 5—9). *It is reported* "And therefore must be true. But who knows not that rumour is a loud liar, and that every public person needeth carry a spare handkerchief to wipe off dirt cast upon him by disaffected persons, that seek to fly-blow their reputation and to deprave their best actions." *Gashmu saith so.* "A worthy wight, a credible witness ! He was known to be one that had taught his tongue the art of lying." "Any author serves Sanballat's turn, who for a need could have sucked such an accusation as this out of his own fingers." "If dirt will stick to a mud wall, yet to marble it will not" "Nehemiah is not over-careful to clear himself This was so transparent a lie that a man might see through it, and was, therefore, best answered with a neglective denial It falls out often that plain dealing puts craft out of countenance." "Faith quelleth and killeth distrustful fear." "These men first mock the Jews, and scornfully despise them for enterprising this building, thinking by this means to discourage poor souls, that they should not go forward in this work; after that they charge them with rebellion. These two be the old practices of Satan in his members to hinder the building of God's house in all ages." "Empty vessels are full of sound, discreet silence, or a wise ordering of speech, is

a token of grace." "Better a mountain fall upon you than the weight of your own tongue." "A pure heart is the tongue's treasury and storehouse." "It is observable, that when the apostle giveth us the anatomy of wickedness in all the members of the body, he stayeth longest on the organs of speech, and goeth over them all : 'Their throat is an open sepulchre ; with their tongues they have used deceit ; the poison of asps is under their lips · whose mouth is full of cursing and bitterness.'" "One reckoneth up twenty-four several sins of the tongue" "Light words weigh heavy in God's balance." "God in nature would show that he hath set bounds to the tongue, he hath hedged it in with a row of teeth Other organs are double ; we have two eyes, two ears, but *one* tongue." "Christianity doth not take away the use of speech, but rule it." "Slanderers are the devil's slaves" "Covetousness sold Christ, and envy delivered him" "Contemplate the life of Jesus, who did not so much as open his mouth against his enemies, nor pour forth any bitter and vehement speeches, but gave blessing and life to those that hated him" "Oftentimes I could wish that I had held my peace when I have spoken" "It is easier not to speak a word at all than not to speak more words than we should"

III False prophets (vers. 10—14). *Shemaiah.* "Fallen, as a star from heaven ! Blazing stars were never but meteors Demas not only forsook Paul, but became a priest in an idol's temple at Thessalonica, if Dorotheus may be believed. A priest Shemaiah was, and would seem to be a prophet, but he proved not right (1 Chron. xxiv. 6). All is not gold that glitters." "Nehemiah went to Shemaiah's house to know what was the matter, supposing him to be a friend, but finding him suborned by the enemy." "Nothing betrays a man sooner than his causeless fear. God helpeth the valiant." *Should such a man as I flee ?* "To the dishonour of God, and the discouraging of the people ? to the scandal of the weak, and the scorn of the wicked ? There is a comeliness, a seemliness, a suitableness appertain;

to every calling and condition of life; and nature hath taught heathens themselves to argue from dignity to duty, and to scorn to do anything unworthy of themselves." " The heavens shall sooner fall than I will forsake the truth," said a martyr. " Life in God's displeasure is worse than death; as death in his true favour is true life." *I perceived that God had not sent him.* " By my spiritual sagacity I smelt him out; as having my inward senses habitually exercised to discern good and evil. What though we have not received the spirit of the world (we cannot cog and comply as they can, yet), we have received a better thing, the Spirit of God, the mind of Christ (1 Cor. ii 12, 16)." *He pronounced this prophecy against me.* " To make my righteous soul sad with his lies, and to bring me to disgrace and danger. Luther was wont to advise preachers to see that these three dogs did not follow them into the pulpit: pride, covetousness, and envy." *Tobiah and Sanballat had hired him* " A minister, as he should have nothing to lose, so he should have as little to get;

he should be above all price or sale." *Therefore was he hired that I should be afraid.* " But they were much mistaken in their aims; this matter was not malleable. Nehemiah was a man of a Caleb-like spirit; he was full of spiritual mettle, for he knew whom he had trusted." " Nehemiah feared nothing but sin, and the fruit thereof, shame and reproach, so great was his spirit, so right set were both his judgment and affections " " We should so carry ourselves that none might speak evil of us without a manifest lie." *The rest of the prophets* " Multitude and antiquity are but ciphers in divinity."

IV Foes foiled (vers 15—19). *So the wall was finished.* " Though with much ado, and maugre the malice of all foreign and intestine enemies. So shall the work of grace in men's hearts; it is perfected there by opposition, and grows gradually, but constantly and infallibly." " God was much seen herein, and the enemies' courage much quailed." " Envy is the devil's disease, and those that are troubled with it can never want woe."

CHAPTER VII.

EXPLANATORY NOTES] " The second section of this book (chaps vii.—xii. 43) furnishes a description of the further efforts of Nehemiah to increase and insure the prosperity of the community in Judah and Jerusalem first, by securing Jerusalem from hostile attacks; then, by seeking to increase the population of the city; and, lastly, by endeavouring to bring the domestic and civil life of the people into conformity with the precepts of the law, and thus to furnish the necessary moral and religious basis for the due development of the covenant people."—*Keil.* It is generally supposed that Nehemiah's return to Persia must be inserted after xii. 43; the remainder of the book narrating his later reforms. Bishop Hervey, however, suggests that the work stopped immediately after the events narrated in vi. 16—19, and that chapter vii. goes on to relate the measures adopted by Nehemiah upon his return with fresh powers. 1—3. *The watching of the city provided for.* I. **Porters . . singers . . . Levites were appointed**] In olden time each had a separate work. *The porters* guarded the gates of the temple They were reckoned by genealogies, and separated into various divisions (see 1 Chron. ix 17—27, xxvi. 1—19). *The singers* had charge of the service of song (1 Chron vi 31), and " their brethren *the Levites* were appointed unto all manner of service of the tabernacle of the house of God " (1 Chron vi 48). " Under the present extraordinary circumstances Nehemiah committed also to these two organized corporations the task of keeping watch over the walls and gates of the city, and placed them under the command of his brother Hanani and of Hananiah, the ruler of the citadel This is expressed by the words (ver. 2), ' I gave Hanani . . . and Hananiah charge over Jerusalem '"—*Keil.* 2 **The ruler of the palace**] The marshal or chamberlain of the vice-regal court which Nehemiah had maintained in Jerusalem —*Jamieson.* 3 **Let not the gates be opened until the sun be hot**] In the East it is customary to open the gates of a city at sunrise, and to bar them at sunset—a rule which is very rarely, and not except to persons of authority, infringed. Nehemiah recommended that the gates of Jerusalem should not be opened until broad day. An earlier opening might expose the city to a sudden surprise. By day the special guard were to watch; by night the inhabitants. **4. The city was large and great, &c.**] Broad on both sides regarded from the centre. After the fashion of Oriental towns, the houses standing apart, with gardens and orchards intervening. **5—69. Genealogy of those who came at the first out of Babylon**] "Nehemiah discovered a register of the first detachment who had come under the care of Zerubbabel. It is transcribed in the following verses, and differs in some few particulars from that given in Ezra ii.; but the discrepancy is sufficiently accounted for from the different circumstances in which the two registers were taken—that of Ezra having been made up at Babylon, while that of Nehemiah was drawn out in Judæa, after the walls of Jerusalem had been rebuilt. The lapse of so many years might well be expected to make a difference appear in the catalogue, through death or other causes, in particular, one person being, according to Jewish custom, called by different names. Thus Hariph (ver. 24) is the same as Jorah (Ezra ii 18), Sia (ver 47) the same as Siaha (Ezra ii. 44), &c. Besides other purposes to which this genealogy of the nobles, rulers, and people was subservient, one leading object contemplated by it was to ascertain with accuracy the parties to whom the duty legally belonged of ministering at the altar, and conducting the various services of the temple; and for guiding to exact information in this important point of inquiry the possession of the old register of Zerubbabel was invaluable."—*Jamieson.* **39—42. The priests**] Only four of the courses returned from the captivity. **43. The Levites**] "Assistants of the priests in Divine worship."—*Keil.* **44 The singers**] Only sons of Asaph returned. **45 The porters**] Door-keepers.— *Keil.* **46—56. The Nethinims**] See on chap. iii. 26. **57—60. Solomon's servants**] "Doubtless those whom Solomon enslaved of the Canaanites (see 1 Kings ix. 20, 21) Their descendants were probably regarded as engrafted into Israel, as were the Gibeonites "—*Crosby.* **70**] "With verse 69 the register ends, and the thread of Nehemiah's history is resumed He was the Tirshatha or governor, and the liberality displayed by him and some of the leading men for the suitable equipment of the ministers of religion forms the subject of the remaining portion of the chapter. Their donations consisted principally in garments. In the East a present of garments, or of any article of use, is conformable to the prevailing sentiments and customs of society." **Drams of gold**] *i. e. darics* A daric was a gold coin of ancient Persia, worth £1 5s. **71. Pound of silver**] i. e. *mina* (sixty shekels, or £9) **73 So** all Israel dwelt in their cities] "The utility of these genealogical registers was thus found in guiding to a knowledge of the cities and localities in each tribe to which every family anciently belonged."—*Jamieson.*

HOMILETICAL CONTENTS OF CHAPTER VII.

FINISHED WORK.

vii. 1—3. *Now it came to pass, when the wall was built, and I had set up the doors, and the porters and the singers and the Levites were appointed, that I gave my brother Hanani, and Hananiah the ruler of the palace, charge over Jerusalem: for he was a faithful man, and feared God above many. And I said unto them, Let not the gates of Jerusalem be opened until the sun be hot; and while they stand by, let them shut the doors, and bar them and appoint watches of the inhabitants of Jerusalem, every one in his watch, and every one to be over against his house.*

THE narrative has traced the progress of the work—its inception, its difficulties, its opponents; now the last stone has been lifted into its place, and Nehemiah looks upon his *finished work*. This is fitting; it is beautiful, but withal uncommon. "God saw everything that he had made, and behold it was very good." And the evening fell upon a *finished world*. "Father, the hour is come. I have glorified thee on the earth: I have finished the work which thou gavest me to do." And when the darkness at the crucifixion rolled away, the sun looked upon a *finished redemption*. Of John the Baptist and Paul the Apostle it is written, they "finished their course," as if there were no incompleteness of character or tasks left undone. Uncommon!

I. **Every man has some work to do.** It is well surely, it is needful certainly, that we be reminded that *business* is a sacred thing, and that *duty* is a bow set in the firmament that is above every one of us. Right and wrong are not theological terms to be accurately defined in Christian pulpits, and spasmodically sought on holy days. The word *work* has all but infinite meanings. It was fitting that the man who perhaps more than any other in our country has taught the sacredness of work should have a medal struck in his honour when he reached the patriarchal age of eighty. That in us which is best and truest says that the man whom we delight to honour is he who can widen our conception of duty, who can cherish in us the faith that this is God's world, not the devil's world, and that life is more important than death. To live in this spirit is no child's play. A merchant who strives to conduct a large business on Christian principles, who endeavours to divest himself of the prejudices of habit and the customs of those around him, will soon discover that the commonplace " honesty is the best policy " is not true in the first and most obvious interpretation which is put upon it. Let any one of us try to take up the petty details of each day's work and ennoble them by the spirit in which they are done, and it shall not be easy. But be it remembered that, after all, the formation of his character is a man's true work. Every work should bear relation to the one indispensable thing, " meetness to be partakers of the inheritance of the saints in light."

II. **Few men leave their tasks complete.** Finished work—that suggests unfinished work. Nehemiah, the rebuilder of Jerusalem, reminds us of David, the projector of Jerusalem. There is much of human feeling in those words of David in which he refers to his *unpermitted purpose.* Shortly before his death—at that period of life when men become prophetic—he assembled the chiefs of the people, and said, " I had in mine heart to build a house of rest for the ark of the covenant of the Lord, and for the footstool of our God, *and had made ready for the building:* but God said unto me, Thou shalt not build a house for my name. Solomon thy son, he shall build my house and my courts " (1 Chron. xxviii.). *Much work is planned but never executed, more is begun which is not completed.* There were brave men before Agamemnon, only no poet arose to sing their deeds. He who, sitting in the hull of some forest tree, first struck out upon the sea was one of the bravest men who ever lived, but his name those who heard it have not transmitted. Yet the art of ship-building had its birth in that man's brain. There is an element of sadness in the fact that David only gathered the materials to build the temple. The idea of that temple floated in his mind, lay concealed there; grew slowly, as all great things grow. Even the pattern was partly conceived. Nothing was wanting but a Divine permission, and that was withheld David was happy in that the work was entrusted to his son Solomon. For that man is honoured who conceives a noble project, and sees his children rise up to carry it out. When in this best and truest sense is fulfilled the old promise that after the fathers shall come up the children, it is well. Such a man may well take a farewell of the world, and say, " Lord, now lettest thou thy servant depart in peace." Perhaps that man is happier who, like Nehemiah, lives to complete his own work. One hardly knows. Of one thing we may be certain—this is the exception, the other is the rule. There are few cemeteries in which you will not find a broken column; broken not by accident, or stress of weather, but by the sculptor's hammer, to indicate that the life of him who sleeps beneath was snapped asunder, his purposes suddenly hindered. As, however, God does not work without a purpose and a plan, there must be, there is, a meaning in this. The world is a huge clock-work. Each man is a part of and necessary to the whole. The individual is insignificant. His work is partial. Division of labour is necessary One man's skill needful to all men's well-being. One country has what another lacks. Life is a series of beginnings. A human life is little more than a beginning. Threescore years and ten are too few in which to accomplish much. " No day without a line " was a motto of Sir Joshua Reynolds. Most men might imitate a famous carver, who when he exhibited his work wrote underneath, " Lysippus has something more to add to this." In the artist's mind the picture is perfect, on his canvas the picture is incomplete. It is only in a relative sense, only with mental reserve and understood apology, that any man can say of himself, " I have finished the work." The story of our *joint work* is pictured in the history of our cathedrals. Norman barons, pious queens, monks of a long-forgotten age, and bishops of to-day have prayed and begged, toiled and given, to make them what they are. This is the conclusion of the whole matter. We work for eternity. We are strangers and sojourners, as all our fathers were.

III. **He that doeth the will of God abideth for ever.** His work may not abide. Nehemiah's did. A builder's work is lasting. All necessary work is not. The eloquence of Chalmers will one day be only a memory ; the bridges of Brunel and Stephenson will tell their tale to many generations. But the influence of Chalmers will abide. Your task may not be permanent ; it has in it some permanent element. What is greater than the work ? The man who does it. An invading army may destroy Nehemiah's wall, but not the memory of Nehemiah's character. The temple of David and Solomon is destroyed, but the Church has preserved their songs and copied their example in building a house for the Lord. They abide for ever. Let us do our work reliant on Him who is the same yesterday, to-day, and for ever.

ILLUSTRATIVE POEM :—

SOMETHING LEFT UNDONE.

" Labour with what zeal we will,
  Something still remains undone,
Something uncompleted still
  Waits the rising of the sun.

By the bedside, on the stair,
  At the threshold, near the gates,
With its menace or its prayer,
  Like a mendicant it waits ;

Waits, and will not go away ;
  Waits, and will not be gainsaid ;
By the cares of yesterday
  Each to-day is heavier made ;

Till at length the burden seems
  Greater than our strength can bear,
Heavy as the weight of dreams,
  Pressing on us everywhere.

And we stand from day to day,
  Like the dwarfs of times gone by,
Who, as Northern legends say,
  On their shoulders held the sky."—*Longfellow.*

THE BEST TESTIMONIAL.

vii. 2. *I gave my brother Hanani, and Hananiah the ruler of the palace, charge over Jerusalem : for he was a faithful man, and feared God above many.*

The *obscure* men and women of the Bible furnish a study as interesting as it is practically inexhaustible. Who was Hanani ? A brother of Nehemiah, who took a journey to Susa to visit his brethren (ch. i. 2). Who was Hananiah ? Ruler of the palace at Jerusalem. No further biographic facts are discoverable. " Apelles approved in Christ" (Rom. xvi. 10). Approved in Christ ; what character lies behind that commendation ! But how little of the private history of Apelles can

investigation furnish   So with Paul's friends in general. *Nehemiah and Hanani.*
Two brothers whose paths diverged. They started in life together : one scaled the
heights until he stood on the steps to the throne ; the other moved in the quiet
vales of lowly life.   Both retained allegiance to the God of their fathers , both
maintained loyalty to conscience ; and each reverenced the other.   A not too
common thing—a brother's testimony to a brother's virtue   For though the
description of a faithful God-fearing man grammatically applies to Hananiah, it is
equally applicable in fact to Hanani   He preferred Jerusalem above his chief joy.
A prophet is often without honour in his own country   " A man's foes shall be
they of his own household."   To be " sympathetic with the loads we see on others,
forgetful of our own," argues no small degree of saintliness.   Nehemiah honoured
himself by honouring Hanani and Hananiah.

I A true man's relation to God.   " Hananiah feared God above many "
Religious reverence, a fear that hath not torment, was the basis of his character.
" The God of my father, the God of Abraham, and *the fear of Isaac* " was Jacob's
description of his God.   Old Testament " fear " melts into New Testament " faith
and love."   Patriarchs and prophets lived under the constraining influence of " the
fear of God ," apostles and martyrs felt the sweet reasonableness of " the love of
Christ "   The phrase is changed, but not the substance.   Life hath its centre not
in self, but in God.   Selfishness is the most ignoble motive of action.   All true
life begins with God.   The cross of our Lord Jesus Christ is the ladder between
the earth on which we stand and the heaven in which God dwells.   Christ came
not to destroy.   He expounded, illumined, fulfilled the descriptions of religious
life he found already.   Do not take old-time reverence out of your holy fear of
God whilst you infuse into it more of the warmth of love and trust   Our God is
more fully revealed to us ; but their God is our God for ever   " Serve the Lord
with fear, and rejoice with trembling," urges the Psalmist ; " Work out your own
salvation with fear and trembling," counsels the Apostle.

II. A true man's relation to his fellows.   " Hananiah, a faithful man."   Firm,
stable, enduring , a trustworthy man   In a judge this is integrity ; in a witness,
truth.   " Fear " and " faithfulness " are inseparable   Our modern equivalents are
profession and practice, creed and conduct   The path reveals the purpose, the life
confirms the lip.   " Faith, if it hath not works, is dead, being alone."   Faulty
conduct does not adorn a faultless creed.   Notable devotion in church must be
supported by noteworthy uprightness in business.   If the temple of our character
rests upon pillars of dishonesty, its rottenness and instability will soon appear.   If
the first table of commandments be written in the chancel, the second table must
be suspended in the counting-house   " Sanctify the Lord God in your hearts."
Only thus can you sanctify him in your lives.   A Christian man ought to be able
to show a bold front to the world   Let him strive ever to keep a conscience void
of offence toward men as well as toward God   If the laws of trade are not com-
patible with the laws of God, so much the worse for the laws of trade.   You may
bend if you will, but alas if you cringe because you must !   You must forgive your
enemies, you must not fear them.   Men of the world seal the lips of (so-called)
Christian men when these show inconsistencies in life.   Would you reprove sin ?
Then your daily life must rebuke it.   Do you desire to maintain the character of a
God-fearing man ?   The penalty you must pay is to deserve the character of a
faithful man.   " He that loveth not his brother whom he hath seen, how can he
love God whom he hath not seen ? "

III. A true man's reward in this world.   " I gave Hananiah charge over
Jerusalem."   Loyalty and royalty are not far apart.   Those who will rule must
learn to obey.   Hananiah had been " faithful over a few things," he was now to
be made " ruler over many things."   No vote of thanks for what he had done
No testimonial raised.   Simply *higher work and more of it.*   Capacity creates
responsibility.   Power demands performance   " To him that hath shall be given."

N

Application. 1. *Graduate in the school of Christ.* There is no limit to your knowledge except your power of acquirement. Do not be content with conventional standards of devotion. Obey conscience, worship duty, fear God *above many.* Thus did Hananiah. 2. *Enter the sacred hierarchy of those who look not every man on his own things, but every man also on the things of others.* Look for virtues in your brethren. Be not like those who, "seeing many things, observe not." Some flowers grow in the shade. Many men like Hanani and Hananiah are hidden until some Nehemiah discovers them. Recognize and reverence goodness wherever you find it. Say not, "Can any good thing come out of Nazareth?" "Are not his mother and his sisters with us?" Thank God for what the man *is,* and aid the purpose of God by placing the man *where he should be.* Thus did Nehemiah.

ILLUSTRATION.

"'*He was a faithful man and feared God above many.*' It is said of Obadiah that he feared the Lord greatly. Every saint fears the Lord, but every saint does not greatly fear him. Oh, there are but few Obadiahs in the world, I mean among the saints on earth. As Paul said of Timothy, 'I have none "like-minded,"' so it may be said of some concerning the fear of the Lord, they have scarce a fellow. Hananiah had got, as to the exercise of and growth in this grace, the start of many of his brethren. He 'feared God above many.' Now, then, seeing this grace admits of degrees, and is in some stronger, and in some weaker, let us be all awakened, as to other graces, so to this grace also: that like as you abound in everything, in faith, in utterance, in knowledge, and in all diligence, and in your love to us, see that ye abound in *this* grace also."—*Bunyan.*

The Spaciousness and Emptiness of the City of God.

vii. 4. *Now the city was large and great: but the people were few therein, and the houses were not builded.*

The spaciousness and emptiness of the city of God! This phrase suggests God's doing and man's misdoing. "With his sword and with his bow" David the warrior-king captured the city; with his wealth he endowed it; to Solomon his son he committed its keeping. Under the hand of Solomon it grew, the great of other nations came to behold its magnificence, silver was as plentiful as stone and cedar trees as numerous as sycamores: it was "the city of the great king." When Nehemiah came it was almost a silent city, as a city of the dead. "The entire number of Jews who returned in Cyrus' day to Jerusalem was small—about 50,000 out of millions. Piety, patriotism, and desire for change were three motives at work in the 50,000. But what a vast mass were unmoved by any of these motives, and were well satisfied with their exile! Some, however, like Daniel, remained from high and holy motives. The Jewish people is a *remnant.*"—*Crosby.*

I. The spaciousness of the city of God. "The Church on earth is called a city. How beautiful the orders, laws, and privileges thereof! God her king dwells in her; angels and ministers are her watchmen and guard; believers are her free CITIZENS, entitled to all the fulness of God; his salvation, providential preservation, and system of sacred government are her *walls* (Isa. lxii. 12). She is called a *great city* because of her extent, and the vast number of her members (Rev. xxi. 10), a *holy city* because of the holiness of her Founder, laws, ordinances, and members, and end of erection (Rev. xi. 2); and the *city of God* because he planned, built, peopled, rules, protects, and dwells in her (Heb. xii. 22)." "Heaven is represented as a *city,* a *city with twelve foundations,* a *holy city.* What glory, order, safety, and happiness are there enjoyed by the multitudes of saints! how perfect and durable their state of felicity! and all of it founded on the purchase of Christ! None but *holy* persons do ever enter it, nor is aught but *holiness* ever practised therein (Heb. xi. 10, 16)."—*Wood. The Church was made for man.* What pages of history have been blurred and blotted in the strife to narrow the entrance, to make the Church for man a Church for men. Not from Rome only, from the east and the west, from the north and the south they have come who would limit the rights of men and monopolize the city of God A city; a kingdom. Whose city? who is the king? "All the ends of the earth," "all nations," "sinners," these are the catchwords of Old and New Testament teaching. The works of men are contracted, the creations of God are broad, limitless. The quiet star-lit sky, how suggestive of boundless space. The all-embracing atmosphere, how emblematic of an all-seeing and all-interested Presence. Everywhere is the only limit that can be assigned to God; to every one the only limit to the offer of his great gifts "According to his glorious riches he shall supply all your need." "He that spared not his own Son, but delivered him up for us all, how shall he not with him also freely give us all things?" *This city is destined to grow* The Church is blessed first inwardly and then outwardly. Religion deepened within her pale, then extension. In the history of the first Church there are the "notes" of the Church's life before the announcement of the Church's increase (Acts ii. 42—47). The Holy Ghost first fell on the assembled disciples, then there were added three thousand souls. The doctrine of justification by faith dawns upon a Luther, and a Reformation follows. The brotherhood of man arrests Wilberforce—"bows the tall soul as by wind"—and the slave-trade is doomed, its extinction is thenceforward only a question of time.

"The golden side of Heaven's great shield is faith,
    The silver reason."

The gospel has an element of Divinity in the comprehensive way in which it claims *all our service* and the *service of all.* None are exempted None are allowed to do partial fealty. "Let the people praise thee, O God; let all the people praise thee."

II The emptiness of the city of God. "Are there few that be saved?" Do you waive that question of curiosity? "Strive to enter in at the strait gate: for many will seek to enter in, and shall not be able." Take heed to thyself "Look to yourselves, that we lose not those things which we have wrought; but that we receive a full reward." Leave the future, busy thyself with the practical, pressing present Now at any rate "few" enough are saved. In any civilized Christian city the population divides into two classes—*the churchgoing and non-churchgoing* If all were disposed to attend Church, they could not *Christian and heathen countries* All are not "soldiers of Christ." What then? Despair? Nay, work, pray, wait. We see not as yet all things put under Christ. But "he must reign." And we understand *a Divine must.*

"Let the echo fly
    The spacious earth around"

The Church has done much; the world needs her to do more. Success has followed missionary effort at home and abroad. A kneeling Church has risen strong in the Lord and in the power of his might to lengthen her cords, strengthen her stakes, and multiply her converts "As Jerusalem, in Nehemiah's time, extended far on both sides, and was scantily populated, so also the city of God in all times has had space for new additions to its population. For, in truth, the rich possessions which God has prepared in his Church for mankind would only then be sufficiently turned to profit when every one called man should enjoy them, and it were itself full and sufficiently built out and all had entered in. For that God, who has made all things for himself, and for that Lord who has redeemed all, the totality alone, from which none is lost, forms a sufficiently great people."— *Schultz* The time is coming when the nations shall stretch out their hands unto God, the kingdoms of the earth sing praises unto the Lord Right shall be predominant when at his name every knee shall bow, and every tongue confess that he is *Lord* The rest is vision. "I beheld, and, lo, a great multitude, which no man could number, of all nations, and kindreds, and people, and tongues, stood before the throne, and before the Lamb, clothed with 'white robes, and palms in their hands." "I heard as it were the voice of a great multitude, and as the voice of many waters, and as the voice of mighty thunderings, saying, Alleluia : for the Lord God omnipotent reigneth."

FAMILY TRADITIONS.

vii. 5. *And my God put into mine heart to gather together the nobles, and the rulers, and the people, that they might be reckoned by genealogy. And I found a register of the genealogy of them which came up at the first.*

When, in Biblical sense, we speak of a family, we may mean a household, a kindred, a division of a tribe, a nation, or the whole family of God in heaven and on earth. "The genealogies occupied an important place in Israel. They contained the certificate of Church-membership for each Israelite. They also contained the claims to official dignity that belonged to priest and Levite. The family-idea thus received a marked emphasis in God's redemptive government—an emphasis which is echoed by Malachi (Mal. iv. 6) and the angel that appeared to Zacharias (Luke i. 17). The appearance of the Nethinim in the genealogies is a forcible illustration of the impartial grace of God. That grace which would bring in all the Gentiles as children was foretokened by the brotherly position of the Nethinim (of Gentile blood) among the people of God—the children of Abraham, Isaac, and Jacob."—*Crosby.* The genealogy was the story of their lives from year to year.

I. **The family-idea.** The corrective of individualism. A natural barrier against selfishness. Father, mother, brother, sister suggest unity in diversity. Differences without disagreement. "There are the two opposite poles of masculine and feminine, which contain within them the entire of our humanity —which together, not separately, make up the whole of man. Then there are the diversities in the degrees and kinds of affection. For when we speak of family affection, we must remember that it is made up of many diversities. There is nothing more different than the love which the sister bears towards the brother, compared with that which the brother bears towards the sister. The affection which a man bears towards his father is quite distinct from that which he feels towards his mother ; it is something quite different towards his sister, totally diverse, again, towards his brother. And then there are diversities of character. First the mature wisdom and stern integrity of the father; then the exuberant tenderness of the mother. And then one is brave and enthusiastic, another thoughtful, and another tender. One is remarkable for being full of rich humour ; another is sad, mournful, even melancholy. Again, besides these, there are diversities of condition in life. First, there is the heir, sustaining the name and honour of the family ; then, perchance, the soldier, in whose career all the anxiety and solicitude of the family is centred ; then the man of business, to whom they look up, trusting his advice, expecting his counsel ; lastly, perhaps, there is the invalid, from the very cradle trembling between life and death, drawing out all the sympathies and anxieties of each member of the family, and so uniting them all more closely from their having one common point of sympathy and solicitude."—*F. W. Robertson.* "Of all the mysteries in the universe, I hardly know of any which is more wonderful than the kind of relationship existing between all of us and our parents. The universal consent of mankind sustains the authority of my conscience, and declares that I—I alone— must be held responsible for whatever evil I commit, and that I am to be praised if I do well. And yet nothing can be plainer than that it is easy or difficult for me to do well, according as my father and my mother, my grand-father and my grandmother, and I know not how far back I may go, were, or were not, temperate, virtuous, upright, good people. As there is this singular and most mysterious relationship be-tween my moral life and the moral life of my parents, there is a relationship equally intimate between my physical and intellectual life and theirs. My voice, the length and shape of my limbs, my height, the colour of my hair, the strength and clearness of my sight, the soundness of my brain, my muscular vigour, whatever constitutes my weak-ness or my power, was largely deter-mined for me by what my parents were."—*R. W. Dale.* The mysteries of life are not so much abroad as at home. The miracle is not in some seldom, far-off event, but in life's daily scenes—noon and night, birth and death, the daily bread, the nightly guardianship. Home, family, a sacred centre, a heaven-made bond.

"Where'er I roam, whatever realms to see,
  My heart, untravelled, fondly turns to thee."

II. Family history. We are heirs of all the yesterdays. An unpayable debt owed to the past. The poets de-scribe virtues more to be valued than "Norman blood." Men prize "Norman blood" notwithstanding. The Jew, "the pilgrim of commerce," turned home-ward with a peculiar ardour of affection. The chosen people. All others Gentiles. Cosmopolitanism a modern idea "My name and the name of my fathers." Jacob "My fathers' God." Moses. "I am not better than my fathers." Elijah. "I am a sojourner as all my fathers were." David. "O thou God of my fathers." Daniel. "I worship the God of my fathers." Paul. The thought which the dying Wesley phrased ran through Hebrew history as a "family tradition"—"*The best of all is, God is with us.*" Their familiar description of God was "the God of Abraham, of Isaac, and of Jacob." The "family tradition" that links us with some event in history is good; the "family tradition" that tells of deeds of heroism and acts of unselfishness is better. Not who we are, but what we are, the pre-eminent consideration.

"My boast is not that I deduce my birth
  From loins enthroned, and rulers of the earth,
  But higher far my proud pretensions rise—
  The son of parents passed into the skies."

The idea of the family is unity; the history of the family suggests continu-ance. "No separation can ever break that fellowship of common love which exists in a home. Its members may be sundered by unknown seas, yet the bands of a common affection and sympathy unite them still. So is the fellowship of the Christian brotherhood unbroken by death. It extends to heaven, and unites it with earth—the whole family in heaven and earth named in Christ."—*E. L. Hull. There is no past.* The ages are inseparably linked together. "One day is with the Lord as a thousand years, and a thousand years as one day." So it shall be with us. Christ hath brought life and immortality to light. We shall stand in the presence of those who were dead, but are alive again and live for evermore. "In my Father's house are many mansions. I go to prepare a place for you. I will come again, and receive you unto myself; that where I am, there ye may be also." The dead will not return to us, but we shall go to them.

THE ENTHUSIASM OF GENEROSITY.

VII. 70—72. *And some of the chief of the fathers gave unto the work. The Tirshatha gave to the treasure a thousand drams of gold, fifty basons, five hundred and thirty priests' garments. And some of the chief of the fathers gave to the treasure of the work twenty thousand drams of gold, and two thousand and two hundred pound of silver. And that which the rest of the people gave was twenty thousand drams of gold, and two thousand pound of silver, and threescore and seven priests' garments.*

This scene reminds us of two similar ones in Hebrew history. Shortly before his death David the king gathered the people together, and by his example and entreaty caused the princes and people to offer willingly (1 Chron. xxix.). Even the abundance of the offerings is less marked than the willing spirit of the offerers. "I know, my God, that thou triest the heart, and hast pleasure in uprightness. As for me, in the uprightness of mine heart I have willingly offered all these things: and now have I seen with joy thy people, which are present here, to offer willingly unto thee. O Lord God of Abraham, Isaac, and of Israel, our fathers, keep this for ever in the imagination of the thoughts of the heart of thy people, and prepare their heart unto thee." Joash gave order to repair the temple with "all the money that cometh into any man's heart to bring into the house of the Lord." "And all the princes and all the people rejoiced, and brought in and cast into the chest, until they had made an end. And they gathered money in abundance" (2 Kings xii.; 2 Chron. xxiv.). The *Jew* and the *Friend* have received honourable mention for their generosity to the poor of their confraternity. The *Jew* has distinguished himself in his devotion to his temple. The pilgrim of commerce has cast some of his commercial gains into the treasury of God

I. Claimants. The cause of God is the cause of humanity. The Church a republican institution. "The rich and poor meet together." "The poor shall never cease out of the land." "The poor ye have always with you." Moses and Jesus, Old Testament and New, recognize what they do not explain— poverty. The Communion Service takes special cognizance of the poor. The offertory sentences cite the golden rule, the laws of analogy, the behests of God It is fitting, it is beautiful that at the feast of love, love should take shape and colour, that a body should be prepared for it. "All ye are brethren." How far-reaching are these simple sayings of Jesus Christ. The cause of God—let not that well-known phrase lose its sharpness by use and familiarity. The cause of God is the cause of righteousness, the cause of the weak and oppressed, the cause of the widow and orphan, the cause of the slave and

aboriginal, the cause of those who in every clime sit in darkness and in the shadow of death.

II. The generous spirit. Motive decides action. "The true measure of sacrifice is not the greatness of the outward act, but the perfectness of the inward motive. We like to do a thing which *seems* to be a great dedication, and which flatters our self-love by its greatness, partly because it is far easier to do a great thing which does not necessitate self-surrender, than a small thing that does. It is the all—*the very heart* of the man—that God asks for; the outward form of the sacrifice is of little worth. It is not the great outward act, but the perfect yielding of the soul, which constitutes the sacrifice which God will not despise."—*E L. Hull.* "The motive and measure." How much shall I give to God? A tithe? "Am I a Jew?" Is the world still in its cradle? Is Christianity a set of rules or a great principle? *How much owest thou unto thy Lord?* "Freely ye have received, freely give." Do not ask, "How little can I give?" Inquire rather how much thou hast received. "In the light of the judgment day" it will be well to be "blameless as the steward of God." When the omniscient Searcher of all hearts pronounces his verdict, blessed will be the man whom he describes as "that faithful and wise steward." Hold your possessions in trust. When need arises and ability be given, cast your uncounted coins into the treasury. "He that hath pity upon the poor lendeth unto the Lord; and look, what he layeth out, it shall be paid him again." "There is that scattereth and yet increaseth; and there is that withholdeth more than is meet, but it tendeth to poverty." "Not getting, but giving, is the way to wealth."

ILLUSTRATIVE POEM :—

"Abou Ben Adhem—may his tribe increase!—
Awoke one night from a deep dream of peace,
And saw amid the moonlight in his room,
Making it rich, and like a lily in bloom,
An Angel writing in a book of gold:
Exceeding peace had made Ben Adhem bold,
And to the vision in the room he said,

'What writest thou?' The vision raised its head,
And with a voice made of all sweet accord,
Replied. 'The names of them that love the
    Lord.'
'And is mine one?' said Abou. 'Nay, not so,'
Replied the Angel. Abou spoke more low,
But cheerily still, and said, 'I pray thee, then,

Write me as one who loves his fellow-men.'
The Angel wrote and vanished. The next night
He came again with a great wakening light,
He showed the names whom love of God had
    blest,
And, lo, Ben Adhem's name led all the rest."
                                    Leigh Hunt.

TOILERS RESTING.

vii. 73. *So the priests, and the Levites, and the porters, and the singers, and some of the people, and the Nethinims, and all Israel, dwelt in their cities, and when the seventh month came, the children of Israel were in their cities.*

Wall built. Reformations about to begin. A breathing-time.

I. Rest after labour. The great human heart of Jesus speaks in Mark vi. 31. "Come ye yourselves apart into a desert place, and rest awhile." More dramatic when we see him weeping tears of friendship by the grave of Lazarus, or tears of regret over the city of Jerusalem. But not more human than this anxiety for his disciples. The people needed teaching and healing, but the disciples needed rest. The circumstances were these. They had been through the cities preaching and healing. Returning to their Lord, "they told him all things, both what they had done, and what they had taught." He orders them to cross the lake and be beyond the tide of human population. After the miracle of feeding he himself "departed into a mountain to pray. And when even was come, he was alone." Putting side by side his precept and example, we have his recorded convictions on the necessity and importance of leisure and loneliness — the needs-be for rest. Body and mind require it. Rest and sleep are Nature's great restorers. Never more than in this day. "One great danger in our time is that every man is so active; every man has so much to think about and to do. Nothing moves slowly. If we had the refashioning of the year, we would make it twenty-four months. If we had the refashioning of the day, we would make it forty-eight hours. If we had our own refashioning, we would kindle in ourselves a fire that would burn forty-eight hours without replenishing. Intensity of life, over-wrought

occupation comes from the very social, political, and commercial conditions in which we live. And, as if this were not enough, we try, by strong stimulus, to wind up the flagging nerve, worn out by too much excitement. We want, in that way, to make twelve hours do the work of twenty-four."—*H. W. Beecher.* One of the penalties we pay for high civilization. The too common history of men in relation to whom work has induced insanity and insanity suicide. Earlier rest would have ministered to many a man's mind in the incipient stages of disease. Moral development retarded by the whirl of business; by the incessant anxiety to make both ends meet. "The cares of this world" and "the deceitfulness of riches" are both harmful. All a Christian's time must not be devoted to others. The sanctuary is necessary. Labour is commendable. But leisure is invaluable. Leisure to remind ourselves that we are immortal, that there is a God for us, leisure for personal examination, contrite confession, private prayer, inward resolve; leisure for physical renewal, mental culture, spiritual advancement. "In these hours of rest and retirement many gentle qualities will spring up which find no place in life; only as flowers and grass find place on a pavement, growing up between the stones. There is many a man whose ordinary life is hard as a stone, and whose taste or culture shows itself only as it steals out through the joints where stone meets stone. It is a piteous thing that men should be so hard; and the habit of being by one's self, the habit of rest and inspection, gives some opportunity for the development of the finer traits of character, which, after all, go far toward making the beauty of holiness in man spring up and bear appropriate fruit."—*H. W. Beecher.*

II Rest before labour. Rest not an end, but a means to an end. The corrective and reward of toil. The true reward of anything consists in having done it more than in its consequences or in men's appreciation of it All who labour may enjoy the earthly paradise of rest. But only when it is the preparation for renewed toil. The life of leisure which some sigh for is not desirable. None more wretched than those who have nothing to do. Work was not imposed as a curse. God put the first man into paradise " to dress it and to keep it." It is expressly noted that "there was not a man to till the ground " Work is as old as the creation. Noble too. God imposed it. The curse consisted in *the toil and its fruitlessness.* "In the sweat of thy face shalt thou eat bread. Thorns also and thistles shall it bring forth to thee." The naturalness of work is seen in the recurrence of day and night. Weary we lie down to rest. Sleep recruits the wasted energies of body; the mind recuperates itself. The morning calls us forth to labour. "Man goeth forth unto his work and to his labour until the evening." All work and no play is a curse indeed. All play and no work is not a blessing. "I must work the works of him that sent me while it is day." So Christ spake. And he gives three reasons for this. It is the accomplishment of his Father's purpose. "He sent me." It is in imitation of his Father. "My Father worketh hitherto, and I work." The opportunity for work will soon be past. "The night cometh, when no man can work."

Speaking of his disciples to the end of time, he said, "As the Father sent me into the world, even so have I sent them into the world." "Labourers together with God " is our appellation. Rest is for a while; work is for life. We find Christ in the city, in the temple, in all the haunts of men. But he soon leaves. His choice seems to be where Nature can speak to him—on the mountain, in the desert, by the sea. He is grander there than when compelled to battle with prejudices. He drank at the pure fount of Nature. So must we. Amongst men we get dwarfed, discontented, disgusted. Meanness, selfishness, the grinding of the weak by the strong, the lip profession belied by the life—all this shakes our faith in goodness. No man can always live in a crowd. We are led by popular opinion, deceived by glitter and show. We shall be superficial in much the same proportion as we neglect solitary converse with ourselves. Too much looking within may be dangerous. That danger is remote. Our danger lies in being strangers to ourselves—looking upward, outward, and onward, but not inward. It is sometimes good for a man to be alone. Some experiences only come to us in solitude. We shall die alone. Friends may smooth our pillow and soothe our pain by their tender ministries of affection; but in the depths of the soul we shall be alone. To every one death is an undiscovered land. Alone in death we must be. And yet not alone. "The Father is with me." Beyond, the labour that does not fatigue, the service that is perfect freedom. "They serve him day and night in his temple." "They rest not day and night, saying, Holy, holy, holy, Lord God Almighty." "They rest from their labours, and their works do follow them."

ADDENDA TO CHAPTER VII.

CITIES.

The classification of the human race into dwellers in towns and nomade wanderers (Gen. iv. 20, 22) seems to be intimated by the etymological sense of the Hebrew words *Ar* or *Ir*, and *Kirjath*, viz., as places of security against an enemy, distinguished from the unwalled village or hamlet, whose resistance is more easily overcome by the marauding tribes of the desert. This distinction is found actually existing in countries, as Persia and Arabia, in which the tent-dwellers are found, like the Rechabites, almost side by side with the dwellers in cities, sometimes even sojourning within them, but not amalgamated with the inhabitants, and in general making the desert their home, and, unlike the Rechabites, robbery their undissembled occupation. The earliest notice in Scripture of city-building is of Enoch by Cain, in the land of his "exile" (Gen. iv. 17). After the confusion of tongues, the descendants of Nimrod founded Babel, Erech, Accad, and Calneh, in the land of Shinar, and Asshur, a branch from the same stock, built Nineveh, Rehoboth-by-the-river, Calah, and Resen, the last being "a great city." A subsequent passage mentions Sidon, Gaza, Sodom, Gomorrah, Admah, Zeboim, and Lasha as cities of the Canaanites, but without implying for them antiquity equal to that of Nineveh and the rest (Gen. x. 10—12, 19; xi. 3, 9; xxxvi. 37). Cities existed in Syria prior to the time of Abraham, who himself came from " Ur," the " city " of the Chaldæans. The earliest description of a city, properly so called, is that of Sodom (Gen. xix 1—22), but it is certain that from very early times cities existed on the sites of Jerusalem, Hebron, and Damascus. The last, said to be the oldest city in the world, must, from its unrivalled situation, have always commanded a congregated population. Hebron is said to have been built seven years before Zoan (Tanis) in Egypt, and is thus the only Syrian town which presents the elements of a date for its foundation. Even before the time of Abraham there were cities in Egypt (Gen. xii. 14, 15; Num. xiii. 22). The Israelites, during their sojourn there, were employed in building or fortifying the "treasure cities" of Pithom and Raamses; but their pastoral habits

make it unlikely that they should build, still less fortify, cities of their own in Goshen. Meanwhile the settled inhabitants of Syria on both sides of the Jordan had grown in power and in number of "fenced cities." In the kingdom of Sihon are many names of cities preserved to the present day; and in the kingdom of Og, in Bashan, were sixty "great cities" with walls and brazen bars, besides unwalled villages; and also twenty-three cities in Gilead, which were occupied and perhaps partly rebuilt or fortified by the tribes on the east of Jordan. On the west of Jordan, whilst thirty-one "royal" cities are enumerated (Josh. xii.) in the district assigned to Judah, one hundred and twenty-five cities with villages are reckoned. But from some of these the possessors were not expelled till a late period, and Jerusalem itself was not captured till the time of David (2 Sam. v. 6—9). From this time the Hebrews became a city-dwelling and agricultural rather than a pastoral people. David enlarged Jerusalem, and Solomon, besides embellishing his capital, also built or rebuilt Tadmor, Palmyra, Gezer, Bethhoron, Hazor, and Megiddo, besides store-cities. Collections of houses in Syria for social habitation may be classed under three heads : (1) cities, (2) towns with citadels or towers for resort and defence, (3) unwalled villages. The cities may be assumed to have been in almost all cases "fenced cities," *i. e.* possessing a wall with towers and gates; and that as a mark of conquest was to break down a portion, at least, of the city wall of the captured place, so the first care of the defenders, as of the Jews after their return from captivity, was to rebuild the fortifications. But around the city, especially in peaceable times, lay undefended suburbs, to which the privileges of the city extended. The city thus became the citadel, while the population overflowed into the suburbs. The absence of walls, as indicating security in peaceable times, combined with populousness, as was the case in the flourishing period of Egypt, is illustrated by the prophet Zechariah (ii. 4). According to Eastern custom, special cities were appointed to furnish special supplies for the service of the state cities of store, for chariots, for horsemen, for building purposes, for provision for the royal table. Special governors for these and their surrounding districts were appointed by David and by Solomon. To this practice our Lord alludes in his parable of the pounds, and it agrees with the theory of Hindoo government, which was to be conducted by lords of single townships, of 10, 100, or 1000 towns. To the Levites cities were assigned, distributed throughout the country, together with a certain amount of suburban ground, and out of these thirteen were specially reserved for the family of Aaron. The internal government of Jewish cities was vested before the captivity in a council of elders with judges, who were required to be priests: Josephus says seven judges with two Levites as officers. Under the kings a president or governor appears to have been appointed, and judges were sent out on circuit, who referred matters of doubt to a council composed of priests, Levites, and elders at Jerusalem. After the captivity Ezra made similar arrangements for the appointment of judges. In the time of Josephus there appear to have been councils in the provincial towns, with presidents in each, under the directions of the great council at Jerusalem. In many Eastern cities much space is occupied by gardens, and thus the size of the city is much increased. The vast extent of Nineveh and Babylon may thus be in part accounted for. In most Oriental cities the streets are extremely narrow. It seems likely that the immense concourse which resorted to Jerusalem at the feasts would induce wider streets than in other cities. Herod built in Antioch a wide street paved with stone, and having covered ways on each side. Agrippa II. paved Jerusalem with white stone. The straight street of Damascus is still clearly defined and recognizable. We cannot determine whether the internal commerce of Jewish cities was carried on as now, by means of bazaars, but we read of the bakers' street (Jer. xxxvii. 21), and Josephus speaks of the wool market, the hardware market, a place of blacksmiths' shops, and the clothes market at Jerusalem. The open spaces near the gates of towns were in ancient times, as they are still, used as places of assembly by the elders, of holding courts by kings and judges, and of general resort by citizens. They were also used as places of public exposure by way of punishment. Prisons were under the kingly government within the royal precinct. Great pains were taken to supply both Jerusalem and other cities with water, both by tanks and cisterns for rain-water, and by reservoirs supplied by aqueducts from distant springs. Such was the fountain of Gihon, the aqueduct of Hezekiah, and of Solomon, of which last water is still conveyed from near Bethlehem to Jerusalem. Josephus also mentions an attempt made by Pilate to bring water to Jerusalem. Burial-places, except in special cases, were outside the city.—*Rev. H. W. Phillott, M.A., in 'Smith's Bible Dictionary.*

GENEALOGIES.

Genealogy, literally the act or art of the γενεαλόγος, i.e. of him who treats of birth and family, and reckons descents and generations. Hence by an easy transition it is often (like ἱστορια) used of the document itself in which such series of generations is set down. In Hebrew the term for a genealogy or pedigree is "the book of the generations;" and because the oldest histories were usually drawn up on a genealogical basis, the expression often extended to the whole history, as is the case with the Gospel of St. Matthew, where "the book of the generation of Jesus Christ" includes the whole history contained in that Gospel. So Gen. ii. 4, "These are the generations of the heavens and of the earth," seems to be the title of the history which follows. Gen. v. 1; vi. 9; x. 1; xi. 10, 27; xxv. 12, 19; xxxvi. 1, 9; xxxvii. 2, are other examples of the same usage, and these passages seem to mark the existence of separate histories from which the book of Genesis was compiled. Nor is this genealogical form of history peculiar to the Hebrews, or the Semitic races. The earliest Greek histories were also genealogies . . . . The frequent use of the patronymic in Greek, the stories of particular races, the lists of priests, and kings, and conquerors at the games preserved at Sparta, Olympia, and elsewhere ; the hereditary monarchies and priesthoods ; the division, as old as Homer, into tribes, fratriæ, and γένη, and the existence of the *tribe*, the *gens*, and the *familia* among the Romans ; the Celtic clans, the Saxon families using a common patronymic, and their royal genealogies running back to the Teutonic gods, these are among the many instances that may be cited to prove the strong family and genealogical instinct of the ancient world. Coming nearer to the Israelites, it will be enough to allude to the hereditary principle and the vast genealogical records of the Egyptians as regards their kings and priests, and to the passion for genealogies among the Arabs, mentioned by Layard and others, in order to show that the attention paid by the Jews to genealogies is in entire accordance with the manners and tendencies of their contemporaries. In their case, however, it was heightened by several peculiar circumstances. The promise of the land of Canaan to the seed of Abraham, Isaac, and Jacob successively, and the separation of the Israelites from the Gentile world ; the expectation of Messiah as to spring from the tribe of Judah ; the exclusively hereditary priesthood of Aaron with its dignity and emoluments ; the long succession of kings in the line of David ; and the whole division and occupation of the land upon genealogical principles by the tribes, families, and houses of fathers, gave a deeper importance to the science of genealogy among the Jews than perhaps any other nation. We have already noted the evidence of the existence of family memoirs even before the Flood, to which we are probably indebted for the genealogies in Gen. iv.

5 ; and Gen. x., xi., &c. indicate the continuance of the same system in the times between the Flood and Abraham. But with Jacob, the founder of the nation, the system of reckoning by genealogies was much further developed. . . According to these genealogical divisions the Israelites pitched their tents and marched, and offered their gifts and offerings, and chose the spies. According to the same they cast the lots by which the troubler of Israel, Achan, was discovered, as later those by which Saul was called to the throne. Above all, according to these divisions the whole land of Canaan was parcelled out amongst them. But now of necessity that took place which always has taken place with respect to such genealogical arrangements, viz., that by marriage, or servitude, or incorporation as friends and allies, persons not strictly belonging by birth to such or such a family or tribe were yet reckoned in the census as belonging to them. The tribe of Levi was probably the only one which had no admixture of foreign blood. In many of the Scripture genealogies, as, *e.g.*, those of Caleb, Joab, Segub, and the sons of Rephaiah, &c., in 1 Chron. iii. 21, it is quite clear that birth was not the ground of their incorporation into their respective tribes. However, birth was, and continued to be throughout their whole national course, the *foundation* of all the Jewish organization, and the reigns of the more active kings and rulers were marked by attention to genealogical operations . . . . . But, however tradition may have preserved for a while true genealogies, or imagination and pride have coined fictitious ones, after the destruction of Jerusalem it may be safely affirmed that the Jewish genealogical system then came to an end. Just notions of the nature of the Jewish genealogical records are of great importance with a view to the right interpretation of Scripture. Let it only be remembered that these records have respect to political and territorial divisions, as much as to strictly genealogical descent, and it will at once be seen how erroneous a conclusion it may be that all who are called " sons " of

such or such a patriarch, or chief father, must necessarily be his very children . . The sequence of generations may represent the succession to such or such an inheritance or headship of tribe or family, rather than the relationship of father and son . . As regards the chronological use of the Scripture genealogies, great caution is necessary in using them as measures of time. What seems necessary to make them trustworthy measures of time is, either that they should have special internal marks of being complete, such as where the mother as well as the father is named, or some historical circumstance defines the several relationships, or that there should be several genealogies, all giving the same number of generations within the same termini. As an indication of the carefulness with which the Jews kept their pedigrees, it is worth while to notice the recurrence of the same name, or modifications of the same name,

such as Tobias, Tobit, Nathan, Mattatha, and even of names of the same signification, in the same family. The Jewish genealogies have two forms, one giving the generations in a descending, the other in an ascending scale. Females are named when there is anything remarkable about them, or when any right or property is transmitted through them. The genealogical lists of names are peculiarly liable to corruptions of the text. The Bible genealogies give an unbroken descent of the house of David from the creation to the time of Christ. The registers at Jerusalem must have supplied the same to the priestly and many other families. They also inform us of the origin of most of the nations of the earth, and carry the genealogy of the Edomitish sovereigns down to about the time of Saul. Viewed as a whole, it is a genealogical collection of surpassing interest and accuracy —*Rev. Lord A. Hervey, in ' Smith's Bible Dictionary.'*

SENTENCES FROM OLD WRITERS.

I. The wall completed (ver. 1). " Nehemiah was not vain-glorious. He was humbly lofty, and loftily humble; humble in heart, and yet high in worth and works." " Those that have a hand in building the spiritual Jerusalem shall be surely crowned and chronicled." " There must be no straining courtesy who shall begin to build, nor must men fear for their forwardness to be styled seraphical and singular." " Not priests and Levites only, but the great men in every country, yea, and the country people too, must work at God's building. Every one must be active in his own sphere; not live to himself, but help to bear the burdens of Church and commonwealth." " All God's work is honourable." " Let us learn at these good men's examples to be bold and constant in well-doing, and not to fear every brag and blast of wind. Let us be as a lusty horse, that goeth through the street, and careth not for the barking of every cur that leapeth forth as though he would bite him; so let us not be afraid of the barking curs, nor look backward, but go

on forth, not changing with every tide; and the mighty Lord will strengthen our weakness with good success to finish his building; for so have all good men done from the beginning."

II. Hanani and Hananiah (ver. 2). " Hanani was a gracious man according to his name, and zealous for his country, which indeed is a man's self." " An honest man of good credit, and more earnest in religion and love to his country than others, because his name is put down in writing, and the others are not." " Hananiah was a man of truth, faithfulness, or firmness; a sure man, and such as one might safely confide in." " He feared God. No wonder, therefore, that he was faithful to men. God's holy fear is the ground of all goodness and fidelity. Hence Jethro, in his well-qualified ruler, places the fear of God in the midst of the other graces, as the heart in the body, for conveying life to all the parts, or as a dram of musk, perfuming the whole box of ointment (Exod. xviii. 21)." " Nothing maketh a man so good a patriot as the true fear of God." " Take away piety, and fidelity is gone." " He cannot be faithful to me (said a king) that is unfaithful to God." " Religion is the foundation of all true fidelity and loyalty to king and country. Hence that close connection, Fear God, honour the king (1 Pet. ii. 17)." " Hananiah feared God above many. This is a singular praise, and by every man to be sought after, to be eminent and exemplary, taller than the rest by the head and shoulders, full of all goodness, filled with all knowledge (Rom. xv. 14), able and active in every good word and work." " That is a low and unworthy strain in some, to labour after no more grace than will keep life and soul together, that is, soul and hell asunder." " God would have his people to be discontentedly contented with the mea-

sures they have received, and to be still adding (2 Pet. i. 5) and advancing (Phil. iii. 14), aspiring to perfection, till they come unto the measure of the stature of the fulness of Christ (Eph. iv. 13)."

III. The city guard (ver. 3). " Set thou watches. He speaketh to the two Hananis, and bids each of them, whose turn it was, see to the well-doing of it. Xenophon saith of Cyrus, that when he gave anything in command he never said, ' Let some one do this,' but, ' Do thou this.' "

IV. An inspired man (ver. 5). " No man ever grew to be greatly good without a Divine instinct." " Every good motion in him, and whatever he thought of that was conducive to the good and welfare of Jerusalem, Nehemiah always ascribed it to God."

CHAPTER VIII.

EXPLANATORY NOTES.] **1. Street]** Rather "square." An open place at the gate of Oriental cities where trials were held and wares set forth for sale.—*Gesenius.* **The water gate]** See addenda to chap. iii. **They spake unto Ezra]** "The assembled people. This reading, then, was desired by the assembly. The motive for this request is to be found in the desire of the congregation to keep the new moon of the seventh month as a feast of thanksgiving for the gracious assistance they had received from the Lord during the building of the wall, and through which it had been speedily and successfully completed, in spite of the attempts of their enemies to obstruct the work. This feeling of thankfulness impelled them to the hearing of the word of God for the purpose of making his law the rule of their life."—*Keil.* **Ezra the scribe]** " In the next verse it is Ezra the priest. This is the first mention of Ezra in the book of Nehemiah. He had come to Jerusalem thirteen years previously. He had forced the Jews to separate from their heathen wives, and had then probably returned to Persia. As we do not meet with his name in Nehemiah till now, it is probable he followed Nehemiah to Judæa to assist him in another movement of reform."—*Crosby.* **2. All that could hear with understanding]** Men, women, and elder children. **The first day of the seventh month]** Distinguished above the other new moon's of the year as the feast of trumpets, and celebrated as a specially sacred festival (Lev. xxiii. 23—25; Num. xxix. 1—6). **3. From the morning]** " From the light till mid-day." About six hours. **4. Pulpit]** A very high platform. **Beside him stood Mattithiah, &c.]** Probably priest. " Perhaps Urijah is the father of the Meremoth of iii. 4, 21; Maaseiah, the father of the Azariah of iii. 23; Pedaiah, the individual named iii. 21, the Azariah to be inserted, according to 1 Esdras, the same named iii. 23; a Meshullam occurs, iii. 4, 6; and a Malchiah, iii. 11, 14, 31 "—*Bertheau.* **6 Ezra blessed the Lord]** Perhaps with a sentence of thanksgiving, as David did (1 Chron. xxix. 10). **7. Also Jeshua, &c. caused the people to understand]** " To instruct by expounding."—*Keil.* **8 So they read, &c.]** *The Rabbis* understand it to be a paraphrase in the Chaldee language for those who were not acquainted with the ancient Hebrew. *Others*, exposition and application. " Perhaps Ezra first read a section of the law, and the Levites then expounded to the people the portion just read; the only point still doubtful being whether the Levites expounded in succession, or whether they all did this at the same time to different groups of people."—*Keil.* **10. Send portions]** See Deut. xvi. 11, 12; Esther ix. 19, 22. **14, 15.]** The law concerning the feast of the tabernacles, of which the essentials are here communicated, is found Lev. xxiii. 39—43. **17. Since the days of**

Jeshua . . . had not the children of Israel done so] The emphasis is on *so* The feast of tabernacles had often been observed, but not in such a way as on this occasion, when the whole community dwelt in booths 18. Also day by day] The law enjoined such a public reading once in seven years at the feast of tabernacles (Deut. xxxi 10, 11).

HOMILETICAL CONTENTS OF CHAPTER VIII.

THE CHURCH'S COMMON SERVICE A PRIMITIVE AND REASONABLE SERVICE.

viii. 4—8. *And Ezra the scribe stood upon a pulpit of wood,* &c.

WE might search long among the different histories of the world before we should find a scene more impressive and affecting than that which is here represented.   A whole people recently re-established by God's mercy in their own country, from which for their sins they had been long banished ; assembled together to hear the solemn reading and exposition of their Divinely-inspired law, now about to be revived amongst them , and bowing down in lowly adoration of the Lord, the great God, from whom they had received it.   So arduous and laborious an enterprise as the resettling of a people in full possession of their own land, and in the complete enjoyment of their several religious, social, and domestic relations, was necessarily a work of time.   Many obstacles were raised to it by the malicious opposition of enemies from without, and many interruptions occurred from a want of spirit and energy within.   The work gradually proceeded.   Under the directions of Zerubbabel, then of Ezra, and lastly Nehemiah, the people had the satisfaction of contributing to the restoration of their dwellings, of their altars, of their temple, and finally of the gates and walls of their city.   But another want remained to be supplied.   The knowledge of their sacred Scriptures had been almost totally lost among the Jews.   Together, therefore, with anxiety and diligence in restoring their material buildings, Ezra, who is recorded to have been " a ready scribe in the law of Moses," combined an equal degree of care and industry in restoring the Holy Scriptures

I. First, then, the reading of the Holy Scriptures thus publicly for the instruction of the people became, from the time of Ezra, a constant practice in the Jewish synagogues   The practice was continued in our Saviour's days, and those of his apostles   " Moses of old time," &c. (Acts xv 21)   And together with the reading of Moses was united that of the prophets (Acts xiii. 15, 27). The *propriety* of this practice might be inferred from our Lord's custom (Luke iv. 16)   The *utility* of the practice may be inferred from the fact, that to this practice has been attributed the preservation of the Jewish people from the idolatrous usages of the neighbouring nations   The practice thus observed in the Jewish Church was continued in the Early Christian   Apparently recognized by St. Paul (1 Thess. v 27 ; Col. iv. 16)   " On the day " (saith Justin Martyr) " which is called Sunday there is an assembly of all those who live either in the cities or in the country, and those things which are written of or by the apostles, and the writings of the prophets, are read as long as time will permit "   Upon this primitive practice is founded that of our apostolical Church.   To the Scriptures of the Old Testament are added those of the New.   The types of the law are accompanied with the antitypes of the gospel.   The promises of the prophets are combined with the historical completion of them recorded by the apostles   Thus by means of the lessons, gospels, and epistles which are read in our churches much benefit accrues to the people. Many persons cannot read the Scriptures themselves. Many who can, will not or do not read them. But no small number of these persons is drawn together to attend the public service of the congregation. And although they may not have the alacrity of the people spoken of here, who " gathered themselves together as one man," and " spake unto Ezra the scribe to bring the book of the law of Moses," yet, when the book of God is brought, they can hardly fail of hearing some portion of its contents, and acquiring some knowledge of the truths which it reveals or records, and the duties which it teaches and inculcates. Not that any man who is able to attain more knowledge of the Scriptures ought to be contented with this. He ought not only to hear, but read, search, search daily— so to study the Holy Scriptures as to know them (John v. 39 ; Acts xvii. 11 ; 2 Tim. iii. 15).

II. **The reading of the law was the express object of the assembly The manner, however, in which this business was undertaken is well worthy o our regard.** " And Ezra opened," &c. (vers. 5, 6). Here is the union which subsists between the reading of the Scriptures to the people and the offering of adoration and thanksgiving to Almighty God. All public service implies this. We assemble and meet together to render thanks to God for the great benefits that we have received at his hands. The union between the devotions of the priest and the congregation. " Amen." Liturgical responses. In those forms of prayer which the Church hath provided we inherit the most valuable examples of Christian piety and devotion, a rich treasury of evangelical doctrine, and perpetual monuments and memorials of practical holiness.

III. **Together with the reading of the law and the accompanying benedictions and adoration, a third service was combined, namely, that of expounding the law to the people.** " So they read," &c. (ver. 8). One cause of difficulty may have been the change of language between the law as originally written by Moses and as now recited by Ezra. A thousand years had elapsed. Religious, political, civil, and domestic revolutions had occurred. From whatever cause, the fact is expressly stated. " The Levites caused the people to understand the law," &c. Practice continued in the service of the synagogue. Sanctioned by the presence and practice of our Lord and his apostles. " When the reader hath done " (continues Justin Martyr), " he that presides in the assembly admonishes and exhorts us to put those good things which we have heard in practice. And afterwards we rise up with one consent, and send up our prayers to God." The sermon—the exposition and application of Scriptural truth.

Application. 1. *Give a reverential attention to the word of God, as read in the public services of the congregation.* Grateful for the mercies of God, and sensible withal of their own manifold infirmities and acts of disobedience, these Jews received the word with lowly expressions of thankfulness, and tokens of humiliation and repentance 2. *With reverential attention to the Holy Scriptures unite a constant and serious participation in the devotions of the Church.* " All the people answered, Amen, and worshipped." If you would derive benefit from God's word, you must derive it through the medium of his grace If you would enjoy his grace, you must solicit it by prayer. 3. *Give attendance to those who are over you in the Lord, and who watch for your souls as they that must give account, that they may do it with joy.* It is no abridgment of your Christian liberty to give heed to those who bear God's commission to instruct you We do not pretend to have dominion over your faith, but we would gladly be helpers of your joy. Let your feet habitually stand within the gates of the temple of God —*Bishop Mant, abridged.*

EFFECT OF EZRA'S PREACHING.

viii. 5, 6. *And Ezra opened the book in the sight of all the people, &c.*

Though in the time of our Lord it was the custom to read the law of God in the synagogues, it does not appear to have been any regular part of the priest's office to preach unto the people. On some occasions we find persons sent through the land of Israel to make known the law; and here we behold Ezra on a pulpit of wood elevated above the people, and surrounded by an immense congregation, who had come together on purpose to hear the word of God expounded to them. Since the introduction of Christianity, the preaching of the gospel to men has been the particular office assigned to men who are set apart for that purpose; and though we must chiefly look to the apostles as our examples, and to the effects of their ministrations as the pattern of what we may expect to see amongst our auditors, yet may we profitably look back to the time of Ezra to learn from him and his ministry.

I. In what manner the word of God should be dispensed. The mode adopted by Ezra, namely, the expounding of Scripture, we conceive to be peculiarly worthy of imitation. It is indeed but little practised at the present day, though at the time of the Reformation it generally obtained; and it has very great advantages above the plan which has superseded it. 1. *It leads the people into a better acquaintance with the Scriptures.* The Scriptures, except as a book for children, are but little read; persons are discouraged from perusing them by an idea that they are unintelligible to common capacities. But a very little explanation would render them, for the most part, easy to be understood by all. And what an advantage would this be! The people studying the word of God at home would be abundantly better qualified to understand it when read in public; and the explanations given to them in public would enable them to study it to better purpose at home; whereas the present plan of

taking only a small passage for a motto, or merely as a groundwork for some general observations, leads to an extreme neglect of the Holy Scriptures, and to a consequent ignorance of them among all classes of the community. 2. *It brings every part of the sacred records into view.* There are some who bring forward the doctrinal part of Scripture exclusively, and leave the practical part entirely out of sight; there are others who insist only on the practical parts, and leave out the doctrinal. There are some also to whom many of the doctrines contained in the sacred volume are perfectly hateful, and who never in all their lives so much as mentioned the doctrines of predestination and election but to explain them away, and to abuse the persons who maintained them. But by expounding whole books of Scripture every doctrine must be noticed in its turn, and the connection between them and our practice must be pointed out. True it is that this mode of preaching would not altogether exclude false doctrine; but it would render the establishment of errors more difficult, because the hearers would be able to judge, in some good measure, how far the true and legitimate sense of Scripture was given, and how far it was perverted. The benefit of this, therefore, cannot be too highly appreciated. 3. *It brings home truth to the conscience with more authority.* The word of man, though true, has little weight in comparison of the word of God; "*that* is quick and powerful, and sharper than a two-edged sword." It is inconceivable what advantage a preacher has when he can say, "Thus saith THE LORD;" then every doctrine demands the obedience of faith, and every precept the obedience of righteousness. When told that the word which is delivered to them will judge them at the last day, the people will not dare to trifle with it, as they will with the declarations of fallible men. Were this matter more attentively considered, we have no doubt but that more frequent appeals would be made to Scripture in our public harangues, and that the obsolete method of expounding Scripture would have at least some measure of that attention which it deserves. But, in considering the word of God as explained to the people of Jerusalem, we are more particularly led to notice—

II. In what manner it should be heard. Truly admirable was the conduct of the people on this occasion. Observe—1. *Their reverential awe.* When Ezra opened the book of God, all the people, in token of their reverence, stood up; and when he blessed God for giving them so rich a treasure, they " all with uplifted hands cried, Amen, Amen ; " yea, they bowed their heads also, "and worshipped the Lord with their faces to the ground." This was a deportment which became sinners in the presence of their God; they did not look to the creature, but to God, whose voice they heard, and whose authority they acknowledged, in every word that was spoken. What a contrast does this form with the manner in which the word of God is heard amongst us ! How rarely do we find persons duly impressed with a sense of their obligation to God for giving them a revelation of his will ! How rarely do men at this day look through the preacher unto God, and hear *God* speaking to them by the voice of his servants ! Even religious people are far from attending the ministration of the word in the spirit and temper that they ought ; curiosity, fondness for novelties, and attachment to some particular preacher too often supply the place of those better feelings by which men ought to be actuated in their attendance on the preached gospel. To "stand in awe of God's word," and " to tremble at it," are far more suitable emotions than those which we usually see around us. The Lord grant that our duty in this respect may be more justly estimated, and more generally performed. 2. *Their devout affections.* " When the people heard the words of the law," they all wept, as feeling that they had sinned greatly against it (ver. 9). And when

they were reminded that, as the design of the present feast was to bring to their view the tender mercies of their God, and to encourage them to expect all manner of blessings at his hands, they ought rather to rejoice (vers. 10, 11), they did rejoice, insomuch that " there was very great gladness " amongst them ; and they rejoiced especially on this account, that " they had understood the words that had been declared unto them" (ver. 12). Now it is in this way that we should hear the word delivered to us. When it shows us our sins, we should weep, as it were, in dust and ashes ; and when it sets forth the exceeding great and precious promises of the gospel, we should rejoice, yea, " rejoice with joy unspeakable." We should have our hearts rightly attuned, so that we should never want a string to vibrate to every touch of God's blessed word. But may it not be said to the generality in the present day, " We have piped unto you, and ye have not danced ; we have mourned unto you, and ye have not lamented " ? Yes ; the gospel has little more power over the affections of men than if it were " a cunningly devised fable." But we entreat you to consider, that if the law when expounded was so powerful, much more should the gospel be, since " it is the power of God unto salvation to every one that believeth." 3. *Their unreserved obedience.* No sooner was it discovered that an ordinance appointed by Moses had been neglected, than they hastened to observe it, according to the strict letter of the law, and actually did observe it with greater fidelity than it had ever been observed even from the days of Joshua to that present hour (vers. 13—18). This showed that the impression made on their affections was deep and spiritual. And it is in this way that we also must improve the ministration of the word. If we attend to the gospel as we ought to do, we shall find out many things which we have neglected, and many that we have done amiss ; yea, many things which are not generally noticed even among the godly will occur to our minds, and show us the defectiveness not of our obedience only, but of the obedience of the best of men. Let us have our minds then open to conviction, and attentive to every commandment of our God   Nor let us be satisfied with paying only customary attention to his revealed will, but let us aspire after higher degrees of purity, and a more perfect conformity to the Divine image   This will serve as the best test of our sincerity, and it will show that neither have you heard in vain nor we dispensed his word in vain.—*Simeon.*

EZRA READING THE LAW.

viii. 9. *And Nehemiah, which is the Tirshatha, and Ezra the priest the scribe, and the Levites that taught the people, said unto all the people, This day is holy unto the Lord your God , mourn not, nor weep. For all the people wept, when they heard the words of the law.*

Ezra and Nehemiah amongst the neglected books of the Bible. Contain no specific prophecies of our Saviour's days nor of the nature of his kingdom. They do not immediately connect themselves with the consideration of our Saviour's ministry, and therefore we are tempted to pass them by. Yet, notwithstanding, they form part of "the whole counsel of God." Their subject-matter   The character of Nehemiah shows how Divine grace, whilst it sustains the lowly, is still the best safeguard to protect those who stand in the high places of the earth. The full and perfect patriotism of Nehemiah's character. Describe the bright contrast which it presents to the base and selfish purposes which are so often sheltered beneath that honourable name.

The people of Jerusalem mourning when they heard the words of the law. The law had not been read to the Jewish people since their return from Babylon. A large stage was erected in the most spacious street of the city, near to the water-gate   Ezra ascended to it with thirteen others of the principal elders Ezra read the law in the Hebrew text, the Levites translated it into Chaldee. This was repeated daily during the entire festival, till they had gone through the whole law.

Observe the impression made upon the people. Their eyes were opened to the clear knowledge of those things which they had before seen only through the partial instruction of teachers in the land of captivity   Their hearts were touched with the consciousness of the great mercies which the Lord their God had wrought for them, and upon the sad return which the history of their own sins and the sins of their fathers presented. They were overwhelmed with sorrow.

The reading of the law revealed the spectacle of Jehovah's creative glory, Jehovah's avenging power, Jehovah's redeeming mercy. Patriarch, prophet, and apostle had been overwhelmed with awe at this spectacle [Story of the past rehearsed again.] Is not *this day* holy unto the Lord our God ? Are *we* not assembled to hear the words of his revealed will? And do not the characters of man's perverseness and rebellion which that revelation depicts stand out in as strong and humiliating contrast with the mercy of God *now*, as they did in the day of Jerusalem's redemption from captivity? Can we listen to the counsels of God's gracious providence unmoved?   Our revelation fuller. Our redemption from a mightier oppressor. We are no longer under the law, but the gospel. Let us take heed, however, to ourselves that in so confessing that truth of Christ which has made us free we mar not the confession by abusing the freedom   We are freed from the law as a covenant ; but we are not freed from the law as a rule. In preaching the law let us not put forth its terrors, in order that men may be affrighted or despair ; but that they may be startled from the slumber of a false security, and fly for refuge unto Christ. "To preach the law alone" (saith Bishop Reynolds) "by itself we confess is to pervert the use of it ; neither have we any power or commission so to do, for we have our power for edification, and not for destruction. It was published as an appendant to the gospel. and so must it be preached ; it was published in the hand of a Mediator, and it must be preached in the hand of a Mediator ; it was published evange-lically, and it must be so preached. We have commission to preach nothing but Christ, and life in him , and therefore we never preach the law but with reverence and manuduction to him." — *Rev. J. S. M. Anderson, M A , abridged.*

The Christian in his Spiritual Joys.

viii. 10 *Then he said unto them, Go your way, eat the fat, and drink the sweet, and send portions unto them for whom nothing is prepared for this day is holy unto our Lord neither be ye sorry ; for the joy of the Lord is your strength.*

A sacred festival "Go your way" They were to return home and refresh themselves He does not forbid the delicacies which they had provided. Eat the fat, and drink the sweet. But all this was to be accompanied with two things. First, *liberality towards the destitute.* "Send portions unto them for whom nothing is prepared." Law of Moses, gospel of Jesus inculcate this Secondly, *with cheerfulness.* "Neither be ye sorry." Joy becomes a feast. And this joy, says Nehemiah, is as important as it is becoming ; for the joy of the Lord is your strength It will strengthen your bodily frame, and, what is more, it will renew the strength of your souls. Let us contemplate the Christian—I. In the Divinity, and, II. In the utility of his joy.

I **The Divinity of it** It is the *joy of the Lord.* So it is called by the Judge of all in his address at the last day. "Well done, good and faithful servant , enter thou into the joy of thy Lord " Now this joy enters the Christian, and as he is so contracted a vessel, he cannot contain much ; but THEN he will enter the joy, and he will find it a boundless ocean. It is the joy of the Lord. 1. His in the *authority* that binds it upon us as a *duty* "Rejoice evermore." "Rejoice in the Lord always." "Rejoice in the Lord, ye righteous." 2. His in the *assurance* which holds it forth as a *privilege.* "The redeemed of the Lord shall return, and come to Zion with songs and everlasting joy " "Blessed are the people that know the joyful sound , in thy name shall they rejoice." 3. His in the *resemblance* it bears to his *own.* Christians are "partakers of the Divine nature." Do we feel the joy of God's salvation? He feels it too ; and this salvation is called "the pleasure of the Lord " 4 His in the *subject.* The material of it. so to speak, is found in him, and in him alone. "Return unto thy rest, O my soul, for the Lord hath dealt bountifully with thee." With him is the fountain of life. We are accepted in the beloved. "I will go in the strength of the Lord God." All his relations are mine. He is my Physician, my Friend, my Shepherd, my Father. All his perfections are mine—his wisdom, his power, his mercy, and his truth. All the dispensations of his providence, all the treasures of his word are mine. All his grace, all his glory is mine 5. His, finally, in the *production* There may be reasons for rejoicing when yet no joy is experienced ; for the mourner may be unable to lay hold of them, and appropriate them to his own use David therefore says, "Thou shalt make them drink of the river of thy pleasures." And he prays, "Rejoice the soul of thy servant " And he acknowledges, "Thou hast put gladness in my heart "

II **The utility of this joy** It is efficacious because Divine. To know the force of an argument, we apply it. To know the power of an implement, we make trial of it. To ascertain the strength of a man. we compare him with others, we task him with some exertion, we judge by the difficulty of the work which he achieves, and especially by the might of opposition which he overcomes Let us examine this joy. Let us bring it to six tests, some of them very severe ones 1. Let us review the Christian in his *profession* of religion. The joy of the Lord is the very strength of this profession. For in proportion as a man possesses it, he feels satisfied with his portion, he glories in his choice, he is ready to avow it. " I am not ashamed, I know whom I have believed." " I will speak of thy testimonies." Let us observe the Christian—2. In his *concern to recommend religion* to others. Godliness must begin at home, but it can never end here. " The joy of the Lord gives us confidence in our addresses. We speak not from conjecture, or opinion, but experience That which we have seen and heard declare we unto you." This also adds conviction and force to our testimony and commendation. Men see what our religion has done for us, and what it can do for them also. Will anything recommend a master more than the cheerfulness of his servants? 3. Let us view the Christian in the *discharge of his duties*. These are numerous, and extensive, and difficult. Fear chills, despondency unnerves, sorrow depresses. But hope is encouragement : joy inspires, excites, elevates. It renders our work our privilege. We not only have life, but have it more abundantly. " I will run in the way of thy commandments when thou shalt have enlarged my heart." 4. Let us view the Christian in his *perils*. Perpetually surrounded with temptations in the world. These flatter him, and would entice him away from God. These he is to resist, steadfast in the faith. How? By constraints? By threatenings? These may indeed induce him actually to refuse the offers and allurements, but not in affection. The joy of the Lord is his strength, and without this a man will only leave the world as Lot's wife left Sodom—she left it, but her heart was still in the place. Prohibition, so far from killing desire, has a tendency to increase it. Having found the pure spring, the Christian no longer kneels to the filthy puddle. Having tasted the grapes of Eshcol, he longs no more for the leeks, and garlic, and onions of Egypt. The palace makes him forget the dung-hill. The only effectual way of separating the heart from the world is to subdue the sense of an inferior good by the enjoyment of a greater. 5 We shall see that the joy of the Lord is his strength if we view the Christian in his *sufferings*. Afflictions try religious principle. 6. This joy of the Lord is the Christian's strength in *death* What but this *can* be his support then? God's comforts delight his soul. What says our subject in a way of practical improvement? 1. Inquire what your joy is 2. See how greatly religion is libelled. 3. What an inducement is here to seek the Lord and his strength, to seek his face evermore. 4. Your religion is to be suspected if you are habitually destitute of joy. 5 Let this joy be a peculiar object of attention to every Christian. Let him never forget that it is his strength 6 Some know the worth of this joy from the want rather than from the experience. Seek, immediately and earnestly, an increase of it.—*Jay, abridged.*

THE JOY OF THE LORD.

viii 10. *The joy of the Lord is your strength.*

A man does not take leave of happiness by knowing Christ. The believer has a sick-bed joy, a death-bed joy—a joy that shall depart with him out of this world, go with him to the judgment, live with him through eternity

I. The nature of the true believer's joy. " The joy of the Lord "—a description 1 *The Lord is its* AUTHOR He creates it and establishes it in the hearts of his people. The joy of true believers is no mere animal sensation. Not " good spirits." Not a natural feel-ing, but a spiritual gift. St. Paul enumerates it among " the fruits of the Spirit," calls it " joy of the Holy Ghost " (1 Thess. i 6) 2 *The Lord is the* SUBJECT *of this joy.* His people not only rejoice by him, but they rejoice in him—they " joy in the God of their salvation. His grace, his gifts, his glories, his perfections constitute the subject-matter of their joy." In his presence is " their fulness of joy " He is the Sun of their souls. And why? What is there belonging to their Lord to give occasion for this joy? (1) The freeness of his great salvation. Here is a daily, hourly song for the believer. (2) The imputation of his justifying righteousness. (3) The Giver of their present privileges, and the Preparer of their future glories.

II. The effects of this joy. "Your strength." 1. Spiritual joy strengthens a man for DUTY. 2. Spiritual joy strengthens a man for SUFFERING.

Application. 1. *To the confident professor.* 2 *To the desponding penitent.* —*Roberts's Village Sermons.*

THE JOY OF THE LORD IS OUR STRENGTH.

viii. 10. *The joy of the Lord is your strength*

The preaching of God's word is a very ancient ordinance. In the context we have a description of the manner in which Nehemiah conducted it. These means of instruction were useful in that day. Nor are they less necessary in every place and age. People need not only reproof for what is wrong, but direction in what is right. The Jews wept bitterly at the hearing of the law; but Nehemiah corrected their sorrow as ill-timed, and exhorted them to rejoice in God, who had done so great things for them.

I. What reason we have to rejoice in the Lord. God is often said to rejoice over his people (Zeph. iii. 17). But the joy here spoken of must be understood rather of that which we feel in the recollection of God's goodness towards us. The Jews at that season had special cause for joy in God. Delivered from Babylon, they had prospered even to a miracle in their endeavours. Their sorrow, however just, was not to exclude this joy. Such reason also have all the Lord's people to rejoice in the Lord. They have experienced a redemption from sorer captivity, and been delivered by more stupendous means. Every day's preservation is, as it were, a miracle. The work of their souls is carried on in spite of enemies; yea, is expedited through the means used to defeat it. Surely, then, they should say, like the Church of old, "The Lord hath done great things for us" (Ps. cxxvi. 3). These mercies are pledges and earnests of yet richer blessings. They may well confide in so good and gracious a God. They have indeed still great cause for sorrow. Yet it is their duty to rejoice always in the Lord. To promote and encourage this we proceed to show—

II. In what respects this joy is our strength. We are as dependent on the frame of our minds as on the state of our bodies. Joy in God produces very important effects. 1. *It disposes for action.* Fear and sorrow depress and overwhelm the soul (Isa. lvii. 16). They enervate and benumb all our faculties. They keep us from attending to any encouraging considerations (Exod. vi. 9). They disable us from extending any relief to others (Job ii. 13). They indispose us for the most necessary duties (Luke xxii. 45). We cannot pray or speak or do anything with pleasure. On the contrary, a joyous frame exhilarates the soul (Prov. xvii. 2). David well knew the effect it would produce (Ps. li. 12, 13). Every one may safely adopt his resolution (Ps. cxix. 32). 2. *It qualifies for suffering.* When the spirit is oppressed the smallest trial is a burthen. In those seasons we are apt to fret and murmur both against God and man. We consider our trials as the effects of Divine wrath. Or, overlooking God, we vent our indignation against the instruments he uses. But when the soul is joyous afflictions appear light (Heb. x. 34; xii. 2). How little did Paul and Silas regard their imprisonment (Acts xvi. 25). How willing was Paul to lay down his very life for Christ (Acts xx. 24). This accords with the experience of every true Christian (Rom. v. 2, 3; 2 Cor. vi. 10).

Application. 1. *Let us not be always brooding over our corruptions.* Seasonable sorrows ought not to be discouraged. But we should never lose sight of all that God has done for us. It is our privilege to walk joyfully before the Lord (Ps. lxxxix. 15, 16; cxxxviii. 5; cxlix. 5). If we abounded more in praise, we should more frequently be crowned with victory (2 Chron. xx. 21, 22). 2. *Let us carefully guard against the incursions of sin.* It is sin that hides the Lord from our eyes (Isa. lix. 2). Joy will not consist with indulged sin (Ps. lxvi. 18). Let us then mortify our earthly members and our besetting sins. Let us be girt with our armour while we work with our hands; nor ever grieve the Spirit, lest we provoke him to depart from us. 3. *Let us be daily going to God through Christ.* If even we rejoice in God at all it must be through the Lord Jesus Christ (Rom. v. 11). It is through Christ alone that our past violations of the law can be forgiven (Col. i. 20) It is through Christ alone that the good work can be perfected in our hearts (Heb. xii. 2). And since all things are through him, and from him, let them be to him also (Rom. xi. 36). —*Rev. Charles Simeon, M A.*

ON RELIGIOUS JOY, AS GIVING STRENGTH AND SUPPORT TO VIRTUE.

viii. 10. *The joy of the Lord is your strength.*

On hearing the words of the book of the law, all the people wept. Nehemiah exhorts them to prepare themselves for serving the God of their fathers with a cheerful mind. These words contain this important truth, that to the nature of true religion there belongs an inward joy which animates, strengthens, and supports virtue.

I. Joy is a word of various signification. By men of the world it is often used to express those flashes of mirth which arise from irregular indulgences of social pleasure. The joy here mentioned signifies a tranquil and placid joy, an inward complacency and satisfaction, accompanying the practice of virtue and the discharge of every part of our duty. A joy of this kind is what we assert to belong to every part of religion; to characterize religion wherever it is genuine, and to be essential to its nature. In order to ascertain this, let us consider—1. *In what manner religion requires that a good man should stand affected towards God.* Rational, enlightened piety presents God not as an awful, unknown Sovereign, but as the Father of the universe, the lover and protector of righteousness, under whose government all the interests of the virtuous are safe. With delight the good man traces the Creator throughout all his works, and beholds them everywhere reflecting some image of his supreme perfection. In the morning dawn, the noontide glory, and the evening shade; in the fields, the mountains, and the flood, where worldly men behold nothing but a dead, uninteresting scene; every object is enlivened and animated to him by the presence of God. Amidst that Divine Presence he dwells with reverence, but without terror. He is under the protection of an invisible guardian. He receives the declarations of his mercy.

Objection. Are there no mortifications and griefs that particularly belong to piety—the tear of repentance, humiliation of confession, and remorse? *Reply.* There may be seasons of grief and dejection, yet this is not inconsistent with the joy of the Lord, being, on the whole, the predominant character of a good man's state; as it is impossible that during this life perpetual brightness can remain in any quarter without some dark cloud. And even the penitential sorrows and relentings of a pious heart are not without their own satisfactions. It is no unusual thing for pleasure to be mixed with painful feelings. And where the mind is properly instructed in religion, it will not long be left in a state of overwhelming dejection, but will return to tranquillity, and repossess again the joy of the Lord. 2. *Consider next the disposition of a good man towards his fellow-creatures.* That mild and benevolent temper to which he is formed by virtue and piety, a temper that is free from envious and malignant passions, is a constant spring of cheerfulness and serenity. 3. *With respect to that part of religion which consists in the government of a man's own mind, of his passions and desires, it may be thought that much joy is not to be expected.* For there religion appears to lay on a severe and restraining hand. Strict temperance and self-denial are often requisite. But in purity, temperance, and self-government there is found a satisfaction. A man is conscious of soundness. There is nothing that makes him ashamed of himself.

II In what respects the joy of the Lord is justly said to be the strength of the righteous 1. *It is the animating principle of virtue, it supports its influence, and assists it in becoming both persevering and progressive.* Few undertakings are lasting or successful which are accompanied with no pleasure. Not until a man feels somewhat within him which attracts him to his duty can he be expected to be constant and zealous in the performance of it. 2. *The joy of the Lord is the strength of the righteous, as it is their great support under the discouragements and trials of life.* A good man's friends may forsake, fortune may fail, his health decay; calumny and reproach may attack his character. Then, when worldly men become peevish, dispirited, and fretful, he can possess himself calm and undisturbed. He has resources within. Much is against us in our endeavours to cultivate this disposition. We must study to correct false ideas, persuade ourselves that there are other things besides riches, honours, and sensual pleasures that are good for man, that there are joys of a spiritual and intellectual nature which directly affect the mind and heart, and which confer a satisfaction both more refined and more lasting than any worldly circumstances can confer. To endeavours of our own for rectifying and improving our taste of pleasure let us join frequent and fervent prayer to God, that he may enlighten and reform our hearts, and by his Spirit communicate that joy to our souls which descends from him, and which he has annexed to every part of religion and virtue as the *strength of the righteous.—Blair, abridged.*

Same Theme.

Joyfulness is the invigorating tonic of the Christian character. The thing that makes you a strong Christian or a weak one is your possession or deprivation of the joy of the Lord. Religion many-sided. Faith, hope, joy. Yet many whose religious principle is strong do not take bright views of Christian service. Some people go to sea because the blood of the sailor is in their veins; they love the sea; almost regret to read in Revelation that in the new heavens and earth of St. John there will be no more sea. Now others go to sea because duty drives them there. If they could go over-land they would; but there is neither bridge nor tunnel, so they must go to sea, and with much fear and sickness they go. It is very like that going to heaven. Some have delight at every step, and that is as it ought to be; some go with the hard constraint of duty upon them, and that is as it should not be. Take, as illustrative of the latter view, two types of religious character that have played an important part in the past of this country—Popery and Puritanism. Roman Catholicism—full of austerities, services mournful; chantings; suffer here or in purgatory, pictures; biographies of the ideal saint; dress of the religious orders, portraits of eminent saints. Whole tone a strange contrast to the "glad tidings of great joy." Puritanism—grand but severe men and women; many fasts, but few festivals. This sentiment of the text about the strengthening power of joy was spoken by one of those grand, all-round honourable men who come as ornaments and saviours of society—Nehemiah. His people had been captive, and were restored, and wept at their restoration, and this was said to cheer them. Bring the thing into our own times. English captive among heathen holding fast to Bible and Christian faith. Patriot rising—a Nehemiah or Garibaldi—to restore. London rebuilt—reading of law. First day of national religious celebration for 150 years. Memories of past bringing tears. But sagacious leader says, "You must above all things keep up your hearts. Weeping will cleanse, but joy is the strengthener." Thankful gladness. Is not our fathers'

God our God? Eat the fat, and send portions to the poor. Weep not, for the joy of the Lord is your strength. They were Jews, and the Jewish religion is a religion of joy. One fast and many feasts. Sabbath joyous. "O be joyful in the Lord." Judaism was, in spite of Sinai, a service of joy. Much more is the gospel joyous. "Glad tidings." "The joy set before him." "We rejoice." "Joy in presence of the angels." Strange, after that, that anybody should have brought gloom into religion. If God did not make his creatures to be happy, why did he make them at all? If God meant us to have no joy on earth, why did he fill earth with beauty and with 'gladness? But he did, for God is love. The joy of the Lord is your strength.

Everybody knows what joy is. Joy means that faculty has seized what it wanted. Now religion aims at perfection; to make most of all life. Hence its attainment is attainment of joy. In this way it takes possession of the body. "Glorify God in your body." Use it for what God has made it. Look at a machine. As those gloriously artistic ribbons come out of the loom you are glorifying, honouring the maker. Sinful gratification is against the laws of the body; for God's laws are written on the body as truly as on the Sinaitic tables of stone. Religious joy is harmony with natural law. Same with active business. Handcraft and head-craft in righteous way. And the righteous way means the right way, and the right way means the true way. There are people who tell you that business on Christian principles means bankruptcy. There are proofs that godliness will actually pay. Golden rule. There is a divinity in business. Paul is as Christian and as holy when he sits at Damascus making tents as when he stands on Mars' Hill and preaches a sermon. To a Christian man all life is holy, all life is joyous. The same is true of intellectual life. Search for truth is pleasant. The tree of knowledge bears good fruits. So with the relative and social aspect. Laughter and jest, wit and humour, are Divine; for Divinity stamped them into us. The laughter of some men is blighting as the laughter of a fiend, and you shrink from it as much; the laughter of another is always against wrong, and on the side of right, and is healing as medicine.

Of course we must wisely distinguish between religion and the joy of religion. Let not a man suppose he is necessarily under the condemnation of God because he lacks brightness and buoyancy. Salvation is one thing, and the joys of salvation are supplementary things:—these we may do without, but that we should not be without. Joy comes out of a steady continuous sense of acceptance with God. But a man may be a true Christian and yet often fail here. For instance, in every-day life a case like this may occur. A man gets for a little while into an unaccountably nervous state. He fears the worst. Friends laugh; doctor examines; the man is assured. Is he really more healthy? No; but still he is stronger. Joy is his strength. A great many Christians act that out in spiritual things. They are safe, if anybody is safe; but oh! for this assurance of safety. If they could believe the word of God joy would come.

Joy then is the proper result of Christian faith. "Believing, we rejoice." Must not forget other side. "Sorrowful, yet always rejoicing." Trivial nature that always wants the countenance wreathed into smiles. Does not deep joy often fly as a resource to tears? Jesus Christ anointed with oil of gladness, and yet acquainted with grief; anointed with oil of gladness, and yet crowned with thorns. So deep and earnest and sympathetic that it must have been thus. Sorrow on surface, and joy in depths. "I have meat to eat that ye know not of." "My joy." "My peace." That joy is our strength.

Then joy is a thing we are exhorted to. Joy is in our power. Not that joy must express itself after one pattern. Two persons watching a spectacle, or listening to music—one jubilant, the other silent. Prospect in nature—one exclamatory, the other still. Both have the deep joy of the scene, each in a form suited to himself. So there are these varying forms of religious experience—silent and speaking, calm and rapturous. Imaged in Revelation—voice of many waters, silence in heaven. Exultation when we say, "Come, let us sing unto the Lord a new song!" "Speechless awe that dares not move." In Book of Genesis it says the vegetables were to increase after their kind, and animals after their kind; and so we must serve God and enjoy his salvation after our kind. The only thing is this, that if we are not enjoying the salvation of Christ we miss the mark more or less. We have not as much as God's love has designed for us. Joy is a controllable thing. We can put ourselves in the shade or in the sunshine. We can be for ever dissecting ourselves, or contemplating Christ. Lack of faith brings joylessness. Not enough confidence in God. A sceptical man cannot be a happy man. Giant Despair's Castle is in the way of scepticism. Sometimes we are afraid to boldly claim all that is ours. "I know whom I have believed." "Now are we the sons of God." Trust Christ, and all is yours. The joy of the Lord is our strength. "A merry heart goes all the day." Band at head of regiment. Do a task you have no joy in, and one that is a delight, and see the difference. Take salvation for granted, and work from it, not for it. And, my brother, yet uncertain as to whether you ought to be a Christian or not, don't be nervous. Christ invites you to joy. A man who has less joy as a saint than as a sinner is a very poor saint, that is all. His ways are ways of pleasantness. The joys of forgiveness are the beginning of heaven. Christian joy is the strength and manliness of all true human character. And when a man enters into the saved state it is as when he enters heaven—he enters into the joy of his Lord.

DAILY BIBLE READING.

viii. 18. *Also day by day, from the first day unto the last day, he read in the book of the law of God.*

Daily reading of the word of God.

I. Why? 1. *Because of its infinite preciousness and value.* "The book of the law of God." Not *a book*, but *the book*. Value it as the gift of a Father's love; as the legacy of the Saviour's grace; as the instrument of the Spirit's power. Dear to all the faithful, because they feel that they hang upon that truth all that is most precious for time and eternity. It comes clothed with the authority of infinite truth, and crowned with the attractions of infinite love. It may be compared to that river that went out of Eden to water the garden, dividing itself into four heads:—"that is it which compasseth the whole land of Havilah, where there is gold;" and it is most significantly added, "and the gold of that land is good." 'Tis a broad land of wealth unknown Study it every day. The Scriptures are styled *oracles*—oracles of God which we may consult for our guidance. Not like the lying oracles of the heathen, which were distinguished for their ambiguity; these are the true sayings of God. It is like the Urim and Thummim, the holy oracle of the Jews, which they were privileged to consult for guidance and direction in all doubtful cases. It is given to be a lamp to our feet. "If any of you lack wisdom, let him ask of God." God gave these oracles to convince of sin, to convert to Christ, to confirm in grace, and to direct and comfort in obedience. The book is called the *Testament*. The Old Testament—a legacy of God to the Jewish Church; the New—a legacy of Christ to the Christian Church. "All the promises are in him yea"—the promises of the Old and the promises of the New. The gospel describes the legacy of blessing Christ has bequeathed to his redeemed people, a legacy for both states of being, and we should study it as an heir to a great estate does title-deeds and documents. If a man does not study it, it is a sign that he does not consider there is any legacy left to him in it. And he who does may be sure to find his name in some codicil or other. "I call that legacy my own." It is called *the book of the law of God.* A man ought to know something of the law of the country in which he lives, and something of the character of the country to which he goes. It is at once the statute book of the King of kings and the great charter of his people's privileges. The law of God's government and the law of God's grace "the law of the spirit of life in Christ Jesus." Study it every day. Revelation, like the sun, must be seen by its own light, and the best of all arguments of its truth are those derived from its own pages. Those parts of the word are most precious which we have made our own by personal examination, inquiry, and experience. It is a law of compensation which obtains in Divine things as well as human, that any species of property obtained by our own effort has a heightened value : an acre of ground cultivated by our own hand, or a plant or flower reared and tended by our own care, exceeds all that we obtain or inherit by the labour or the bounty of others. So one promise examined, prayed over, and applied is more useful than whole books read in a cursory manner. "He that believeth hath the witness in himself." "Now we believe, not because of thy saying !" 2. *Because of its tendency to build up the inner and spiritual life—the life of God in the soul.* Hence compared to manna, to bread, to living water. The life of the natural man is important , of the spiritual man surely not less. "The life I live is by the faith," and the life of faith can only be supported by the word of life. "Man doth not live by bread alone " All life seeks its natural food and aliment. A scientific man reads works of science ; a poet converses in spirit with Chaucer and Milton ; the Christian, the Divine word. "The words that I speak, they are spirit and they are life." There has been a great education of our race going on from the morning of time, by which the souls of men have been trained for eternity, by these Divine words. The humblest Christian, in studying the word, mingles with the greatest minds, with the kingly spirits that have enthroned themselves in the hearts of mighty nations. He makes himself a fellow-student with Moses on the mount ; with Elijah at the cave of Horeb ; with Daniel when he conversed with Gabriel ; with John the Baptist in the wilderness ; with the beloved disciple as he leaned on Jesus' bosom ; nay, with Jesus himself ; and he says, lifting to heaven an unpresumptuous eye, "Truly our fellowship is with the Father, and with his Son Jesus Christ." How can you hope for spirituality without retirement for these purposes ? How can you hope for peace and joy in believing if the closet is deserted and the Bible is unread ? Where is the wonder you complain, "My leanness, my leanness," when you feed only on the husks of worldly opinion and worldly writings, and neglect to sit down at the banquet of truth ? Can you wonder that you are without the comforts of the Spirit when you do not put yourself in communion with the Spirit ? 3. *Because all great revivals of the power of religion have been associated with high reverence for the written word.* It was in the mount that Moses received the tables of stone written by God's own finger. The prophets commenced their addresses by a careful memorial of the time and date of God's manifestation to them : "The word of the Lord came unto me." The finding of the book of the law was the commencement of better times in the later date of the Jewish monarchy. And it was when strengthened by these reports of faith that the ancient worthies wrought righteousness, obtained promises, stopped the mouths of lions, out of weakness were made strong. Our Saxon forefathers valued and prized the word of God King Alfred translated the Psalms for them, and the Venerable Bede the Gospel of John. It was a little leaven, but it served to keep a better faith alive ; a little salt, but it tended to purify the fountains of public opinion. Before Luther the Waldenses held the faith of Christ in the fastnesses of the Alps and in the valleys of Piedmont. Our own countryman Wickliffe gave to the people the whole New Testament in their mother tongue, by which he gave a resting-place to the mind, and widely sowed the seed of the kingdom. So much so that a contemporary says, "You could not meet two people by the way but one of them was a disciple of Wickliffe." This was the crowning work of Luther—the unsealing the fountains of Divine truth to the millions in Germany. In Italy the Reformation dawned in the same manner. If ever the flame of holiness and devotion burn brightly in your bosom, it must be fed by the word. 4. *Because by this word you must be judged.* "God shall judge men by my Gospel." "The words I speak, the same shall judge you at the last day."

II How? Different minds take different courses. Some a chapter of Old Testament in the morning, and New Testament at night; some Psalms; some Gospels, some histories; some epistles. Whate'er is best administered is best. As to states of mind. 1. *With reverence.* "Take off thy shoe!" There should be a pause of solemn seeking and solemn waiting for a spiritual frame. Who feels the sublime dignity of a saying fresh descended from the porch of heaven? Who feels the awful weight of one of the words of the living God? How awe-struck were Isaiah, Jeremiah, Ezekiel, Habakkuk. On the frontispiece of some Bibles is written, "How awful is this place!" "So ought we," as Owen says, "to look upon the word of God with holy awe and reverence for the presence of God in it." 2. *With special affection and prayerfulness.* Go to God by prayer for a key to unlock the mysteries of the word. St. John by weeping got the sealed book open. Daniel by prayer drew an angel down from heaven to give him more light. Bow your knees before you open your Bibles. "Open thou mine eyes, that I may behold wondrous things out of thy law." Honour the prophetical office of Christ. It is the prerogative of the Lion of the tribe of Judah to open the books and unloose the seals. Honour the work of the Holy Spirit. No man can say that Christ is Lord but by the Holy Ghost. 3. *Take time.* Not time? You have time to sin—none to repent? time for the world—none for God? Could God find time to write this book, and will not you to read it? Shall the sick man find no time to read his Physician's prescriptions? the condemned malefactor find no time to read his Judge's pardon? Must Joshua in the midst of war and cares of government find time to meditate on the law; and shall thy shop, or plough, or a few trivial duties discharge you? 4. *Keep the end in view.—Thodey.*

ADDENDA TO CHAPTER VIII.

Festivals.

The religious times ordained in the Law fall under three heads:—(1) Those formally connected with the institution of the Sabbath; (2) The historical or great festivals; (3) The Day of Atonement.

Immediately connected with the institution of the Sabbath are — (a) The weekly Sabbath itself. (b) The seventh new moon, or Feast of Trumpets. (c) The Sabbatical year. (d) The year of Jubilee.

The great feasts (in the Talmud, *pilgrimage feasts*) are — (a) The Passover. (b) The Feast of Pentecost, of weeks, of wheat harvest, or of the First-fruits.

(c) The Feast of Tabernacles, or of ingathering.

On each of these occasions every male Israelite was commanded "to appear before the Lord," that is, to attend in the court of the tabernacle or the temple, and to make his offering with a joyful heart (Deut xxvii. 7; Neh. viii. 9—12). The attendance of women was voluntary, but the zealous often went up to the Passover. Thus Mary attended it (Luke ii 41), and Hannah (1 Sam i. 7; ii. 19). As might be supposed, there was a stricter obligation regarding the Passover than the other feasts, and hence there was an express provision to enable those who, by unavoidable circumstances or legal impurity, had been prevented from attending at the proper time to observe the feast on the same day of the succeeding month (Num. ix 10, 11). On all the days of Holy Convocation there was to be an entire suspension of ordinary labour of all kinds (Exod. xii. 16 ; Levit. xvi. 29 ; xxiii. 21, 24, 25, 35) ; but on the intervening days of the longer festivals work might be carried on. Besides their religious purpose, the great festivals must have had an important bearing on the maintenance of a feeling of national unity. This may be traced in the apprehensions of Jeroboam (1 Kings xii. 26, 27), and in the attempt at reformation by Hezekiah (2 Chron. xxx 1), as well as in the necessity which, in later times, was felt by the Roman government of mustering a considerable military force at Jerusalem during the festivals The frequent recurrence of the sabbatical number in the organization of these festivals is too remarkable to be passed over, and (as Ewald has observed) seems, when viewed in connection with the sabbatical sacred times, to furnish a strong proof that the whole system of the festivals of the Jewish law was the product of one mind Pentecost occurs seven weeks after the Passover ; the Passover and the Feast of Tabernacles last seven days each ; the days of Holy Convocation are seven in the year—two at the Passover, one at Pentecost, one at the Feast of Trumpets, one on the Day of Atonement, and two at the Feast of Tabernacles , the Feast of Tabernacles, as well as the Day of Atonement, falls in the seventh month of the sacred year ; and, lastly, the cycle of annual feasts occupies seven months—from Nisan to Tisri

The agricultural significance of the three great festivals is clearly set forth in the account of the Jewish sacred year contained in Levit xxiii. The prominence which, not only in that chapter, but elsewhere, is given to this significance in the names by which Pentecost and Tabernacles are often called, and also by the offering of "the first-fruits of wheat harvest" at Pentecost (Exod. xxxiv. 22), and of "the first of the first-fruits" at the Passover (Exod xxiii. 19 ; xxxiv. 26), might easily suggest that the origin of the feasts was patriarchal, and that the historical associations with which Moses endowed them were grafted upon their primitive meaning. It is, perhaps, however, a difficulty in the way of this view that we should rather look for the institution of agricultural festivals amongst an agricultural than a pastoral people, such as the Israelites and their ancestors were before the settlement in the land of promise.

The times of the festivals were evidently ordained in wisdom, so as to interfere as little as possible with the industry of the people. The Passover was held just before the work of harvest commenced ; Pentecost at the conclusion of the corn harvest, and before the vintage ; the Feast of Tabernacles after all the fruits of the ground were gathered in. In winter, when travelling was difficult, there were no festivals. After the Captivity the Feast of Purim (Esther ix 20) and that of the Dedication (1 Macc. iv. 56) were instituted. The festivals of wood-carrying, as they were called, are mentioned by Josephus. What appears to have been their origin is found in Neh. x. 34. The term "the Festival of the Basket" is applied by Philo to the offering of the first-fruits described in Deut. xxvi. 1—11.—*Rev. Samuel Clark, M.A., in Smith's 'Bible Dictionary.'*

Sentences from Old Writers.

I. The Reading and Exposition of the Law. *They spake unto Ezra the scribe.* "The people may, if need be, say to Archippus, Look to thy ministry that thou fulfil it. The gifts and abilities of all good ministers are theirs, and they may call for them" (1 Cor. iii. 22). "Ezra knew that the best need hear the law, that they might be kept within the bounds of obedience. Not the unruly colt only, but the horse that is broken, hath a bit and bridle also." "The commandment was a lamp, and the law a light. The Greeks call the law the standing mind of God. And if Demosthenes could say of men's laws, that they were the invention of God; if Xenophon could say of the Persian laws, that they kept the people even from coveting any wickedness; if Cicero durst say of the Roman laws, that they far excelled and exceeded all the learned libraries of the philosophers, both in weight and worth, how much more may all this and more be said of this perfect law of God, the book whereof was here brought forth by Ezra, and read and expounded in the ears of all the people?" *Before the congregation both of men and women.* "Souls have no sexes. In Christ there is no difference." "Little pitchers have ears, and little children will understand much if well principled." "As a scribe Ezra wrote the law; and as a priest he read and expounded it." "Five or six hours they spent in holy duties, whereas the most amongst us think long of an hour; they sit, as it were, in the stocks whiles they are hearing the word read or preached, and come out of the church, when the tedious sermon runneth somewhat beyond the glass, like prisoners out of a gaol." "St Paul laid one text to another, as artificers do the several pieces of their work, that they may perfectly agree the one with the other." "The prophets give us Moses unveiled." "Parallel texts, like glasses, set one against another, do cast a mutual light; like the sun, the Scriptures show other things, and themselves too."

II. Religious Joy. "The joy which has the Lord for its object, and comes from him, is the cause of renewing spiritual strength, so as to run and not be weary, walk and not faint, in the ways of God." "Thou canst not be fully comforted, nor have perfect refreshment, but in God." "It is no hard matter to despise human comfort when we have Divine." *This day is holy unto the Lord your God.* "Your mourning, therefore, now is as much out of season as Samson's wife's weeping was at her wedding." "One being asked whether a good man might not feed upon sweet and delicate meat; eat the fat and drink the sweet, even the choicest wines and chiefest viands? answered, Yes; except God made bees only for fools." "Spiritual joy is such a precious commodity, as that no good can match it, no evil overmatch it." "The peace of a man's conscience will appear in his countenance, as Stephen's did." "To the truly joyous the cross is anointed." *And all the people went their way to eat.* "To do all that they were directed to do. They had been in the furnace of mortification; and now they were willing to be cast into the mould of God's word and to be whatsoever the Lord would have them to be. They were only his clay and wax, a willing people, waiting for his law." *And to make great mirth.* "All kind of honest jollity; for the better exciting their hearts to true thankfulness."

III. Sacred service. *On the second day they were gathered together.* "Divine knowledge is as a great lady, that will not easily be acquainted with us but upon further suit." "Popular men should esteem knowledge as silver, noblemen as gold, princes prize it as pearls" *The priests and Levites.* "These teachers of others took no scorn to learn of Ezra, that perfect scribe." "The greatest part of those things which we know is the least part of the things which we know not." "God will not take up with a careless and slubbered service." "To do nothing for God more than needs must account too little."

CHAPTER IX.

EXPLANATORY NOTES.] "The confession recorded in this chapter uses largely the language of the older Scriptures. For ver. 6 see Ps. lxxxvi 10 , Ex. xx 11, and Deut. x. 14. For ver. 9 see Ex. iii. 7. For ver. 10 see Jer. xxxii. 20. For ver. 11 see Ex. xv. 5, 10. For ver. 12 see Ex. xiii. 21. For ver. 13 see Ex xiii 20 For ver. 15 see Ps cv. 40, 41. For ver. 16 see 2 Kings xvii 14. For ver. 17 see Ps. lxxviii. 11 ; Ex. xxxiv. 6. For ver. 25 see Deut. vi. 10, 11. For ver. 27 see Judges ii. 14, 18. For ver. 29 see Lev. xviii. 5. For ver. 33 see Ps. cvi 6. For ver. 35 and ver. 36 see Deut. xxviii. 47, 48."—*Crosby*. **1. The twenty and fourth day of this month**] Two days after the close of the Feast of Tabernacles. **With fasting and with sackclothes and with earth upon them**] External marks of internal grief. **Sackclothes**] Elsewhere in Eng. version sackcloth for Heb. plural.—*Crosby*. **2. Separated themselves**] Foreigners, "a mixed multitude," had become united with the chosen people by trade and marriage. **3. Stood and confessed and worshipped**] More fully shown in penitential prayer that follows after verse 5. **They read in the book of the law**] Their extraordinary zeal led them to continue this as before. **One fourth part of the day**] For three hours, twelve hours being the acknowledged length of the Jewish day (John xi. 9), so that this solemn diet of worship, which probably commenced at the morning sacrifice, was continued for six hours, i. e till the time of the evening sacrifice.—*Jamieson*. "The general form and phraseology of this prayer place it among the liturgical Psalms of the Old Testament, and show it specially suitable to be used by the whole congregation. **6. All their host**] (Comp. Gen. ii. 1). The host of heaven who worshipped God are the angels (Ps. ciii. 21 ; cxlviii. 2) **7. Abram . . . . Abraham**] (Gen. xvii. 5). **Ur of the Chaldees**] Topography uncertain. Mugheir near the Persian Gulf probable. **8 Canaanites . . . . . Girgashites**] "The Hivites are left out of this enumeration, perhaps to please their descendants, the Nethinim " (see Josh. ix. 7).—*Crosby*. **15. Thou hadst sworn**] Margin—*Lift up thine hand*. Allusion to the ceremony of raising the hand in taking an oath. **17. Appointed a captain**] In Numbers xiv. 4 it is only said that they proposed to appoint, probably they actually carried out their intention, so far as to nominate a leader. **22. Divide them into corners**] "Thou didst divide them (the kingdoms and nations, i. e. the land of these nations) according to sides or boundaries, i. e according to certain definite limits."—*Bertheau*. **The land of Sihon and the land of the king of Heshbon**] Sihon is the king of Heshbon. "Heshbon being the capital city, the passage should run thus :—the land of Sihon, or the land of the king of Heshbon."—*Jamieson*. **29 Withdrew the shoulder**] Like the refractory ox that rebels against the yoke (Zech. vii 11 , Hos iv. 16). **32 Let not all the trouble seem little before thee**] "What seems little is easily disregarded. The sense is, Let our affliction be regarded by thee as great and heavy."—*Keil*. **38. A sure covenant**] Such solemn signing and sealing bespeaks their earnestness. This verse is the first of the tenth chapter in Hebrew.

HOMILETICAL CONTENTS OF CHAPTER IX.

HEBRAIC CONCEPTIONS OF GOD.

THE Bible does not define God. The nearest approach to definitions are in those two remarkable sentences in St. John's Epistle—"God is light , " "God is love." Modern philosophy speaks of God as the Unknowable. One of the oldest books in the world—the Book of Job—teaches that philosophy with a difference. "Canst thou by searching find out God ? canst thou find out the Almighty unto perfection ?" God may be known : cannot be comprehended. The secret of God is as high as heaven, deeper than hell, longer than the earth, broader than the sea St. Paul, the mental philosopher among the twelve apostles, speaks of " that which may be known of God." Bible tells us what God does ; not what God is. Nor does it attempt to prove his existence. "He that cometh to God must believe that he is." Sacred writers assume this. With a " Thus saith the Lord " many of the books open. Every page is instinct with the presence of God. There is no relation to human life in which Eastern poets and prophets did not conceive God. He was in the generation of the righteous; a present help in time of trouble. He was a King to those who believed; a judge of those who rebelled; the helper of those who trusted. They saw God—

I. **In the movements of history.** "Who can utter the mighty acts of the Lord? Our fathers understood not thy wonders in Egypt. He rebuked the Red Sea. He did great things in Egypt, and wondrous works in the land of Ham. Our fathers angered God—not Moses, though him they angered—they angered God at the waters of strife. He gave them into the hand of the heathen, and they that hated them ruled over them. Many times did he deliver them. He made them to be pitied of all those that carried them captive. All nations are before him. Pharaoh's heart he hardens, and Cyrus' sword he employs. He takes hold of the ships of Tarshish. The world's merchandise and hire shall be holiness unto the Lord." These passages are quoted at random. It was hardly necessary to quote at all. The pages of Moses, the songs of David, the prophecies of Isaiah, teem—literally teem—with references to the presence of God in the movements of history. God in history! the seers and songsters of the Scriptures of Truth hardly condescend to say that. God in history? History is God. Men read, "Thou art the Lord the God, who didst choose Abram, and broughtest him forth out of Ur of the Chaldees, and gavest him the name of Abraham; and foundest his heart faithful before thee, and madest a covenant with him to give the land of the Canaanites, the Hittites, the Amorites, and the Perizzites, and the Jebusites, and the Girgashites, to give it, I say, to his seed, and hast performed thy words; for thou art righteous" (ver. 7, 8); and they say, We can see the hand of God in this. Verily there was a God. Then they turn over the pages of English History and read how we emerged out of barbarism; how a fusion of race-stocks has made us what we are—the hardiest, most truth-loving, uprightest nation under the blue sky, and they say, It is history, but they do not say, We see God. Now and then some popular orator turns to the pages of the old Chroniclers and sees how, in the reign of James I., a poor people became enlightened by the word of God, and finding no such phrase in the dictionary as "religious toleration," sped to America; and he adds, I see a Divine hand in this emigration movement. Why not boldly say, "Thou didst divide the sea before them, so that they went through the midst of the sea; and their persecutors thou overthrewest" (ver. 11)? That is the Bible language for the passage of the Red Sea. Surely we, casting our glances towards the West, and noting the magnificent proportions of the American Republic, can see that the language is applicable to the passage of the Atlantic; to the colonization of the New World. Says Bancroft, the American historian, "The pilgrims were Englishmen; exiles for religion; men disciplined by misfortune; cultivated by opportunities of extensive observations; equal in rank as in rights; and bound by no code upon earth but that of religion or the public will." What cast Pharaoh and his hosts into the sea? Nothing—God. Who destroyed the Spanish Armada? Nobody—the storm. Did not, then, the same God direct both storms? What says the prophet, "Seeing many things, but thou observest not." "Seeing ye shall see, and shall not perceive; hearing ye shall hear, and shall not understand," said Jesus the Revealer of truth.

If God had no hand in the Reformation, Martin Luther, the Mansfeld miner's son, the Augustinian monk, the darling of Wittenberg University, was simply an obstinate revolter against authority; whereas he was accustomed to console himself with the thought that the cause was not his, but God's—that God " who stays the waves upon the sea-beach, and stays them with sand." "He that has not God, let him have what else he will, is miserable," was his deliberate opinion. "God will be found there where he has engaged to be," he believed. He loved the second Psalm. The Psalm that tells how God laughs when great men rage he loved with all his heart, "because it strikes and flashes valiantly." The Levites in the olden time sang, "Our fathers were disobedient, therefore thou deliveredst them into the hand of their enemies. Nevertheless, in the time of their trouble, when they cried unto thee thou heardest them from heaven, and according to thy manifold mercies thou gavest them saviours." And shall not we thank God for the "saviours" whom he has raised up to deliver this nation, to burst the shackles of the slave, to flood the dark places of the earth with light? Is it nothing that good Queen Bess and brave, God-fearing Oliver Cromwell once governed these realms? Were not the Puritans ever the friends of popular liberty? Can Scottish Covenanters be forgotten, or the Clapham sect become despised? So long as Nonconformity acts upon its motto, "In things essential, unity; in things doubtful, liberty; in all things charity," it will be the instrument of God for good. When Methodism loses her cunning in spreading Scriptural holiness throughout the land, then—not till then—she will become a by-word and a proverb of reproach among the religious communities of Christendom. On the bead-roll of English worthies men and women in the generations following will look for parson Wycliffe, tinker Bunyan, gentleman Wilberforce, sturdy Howard, and sweet-souled Elizabeth Fry. These were the angels in whose presence the doors flew open, and the iron gate that shut in imprisoned men opened to them of his own accord. Every ray of light that falls upon the darker places of the earth; each blow that is struck for freedom, every the painfulest endeavour of weak men and timid women to teach truth and exhibit the beauty of holiness, is an intimation of a higher presence—a voice from the innermost sanctuary, crying, "Surely the Lord is in this place." In the movements of history the Hebrews saw God; and they heard God. And

II. In the voices of Nature. *The sun* was a globe of light, and more—the visible symbol of the invisible God. The sun brought light and life, and growth and joy, and hope and courage. "The Lord is my light and my salvation; whom should I fear?" "The Lord God is a sun; He will give grace and glory" The sun rode in the heavens like a thing of might; no sign of weariness appeared in him. "Let them that love thee, O Lord, be as the sun when he goeth forth in his might." *The rock* had more than a geological message. It told of strata, growth, history of long-since-buried men; it told too of the strength, patience, endurance of God —"THE ROCK OF AGES." "He is the rock; his way is perfect." "Lead me to the rock that is higher than I." *Clouds* did not merely collect the waters to pour down upon the earth: they were the treasure-houses of God. As the sun shone through them they became luminous as with the shining of the glory of the Lord. They hid the face of the scorching sun from the tired and thirsty traveller. "He spread a cloud for a covering." "His favour is as a cloud of the latter rain." *God was the keeper of the vineyard of the house of Israel.* They saw God—

III. In the lives of men. God writes his will in falling dynasties; in commercial and political changes; in solitary experiences. God speaks to us, works in us, expresses his will through us. Reliant weakness, weariness and worn-outness, trusting in God, have around them an omnipotent arm; they rest on the immoveable rock on which the world reposes. God often means to men terror, fear, law, hatred, hell; too seldom grace, salvation, light, hope, joy, strength, inspiration, courage, help, heaven. "The knowledge of the glory of God is in the face of Jesus Christ." He taught "our Father," and revealed something like "the motherhood of God." A great God we knew before. Tenderness, patience, forbearance, forgivingness, motherliness, he showed us; restated, illustrated what lay in Old Testament less distinctly. Not by his lip only, but in his life. Whom did he seek but the sick and sad? Who sought him but the oppressed and outcast? Whom did he ever send away empty of hope? God is in Nature; God is in history; but the whole of God is in Jesus Christ. Son of man was Son of God.

Application. 1. *My God*—not everybody's God. *God here*—not God everywhere. 2. *When do we think of God?* After wrong-doing? First thing in the morning, last thing at night, there should come to us a word of joy, providence, help—this is what God should be. Let us approach God, who is "a great King," with manly reverence; let us approach God, who is "our Father," with a child's unfaltering trust. "Let us draw near with full assurance," for "our fellowship is with the Father and with his Son Jesus Christ." And as the fellowship grows and deepens there will be revealed to us what is revealable of the infinite secret men call God.

THE STORY OF GOD'S PROVIDENCE RETOLD.

"The invitation to praise God insensibly passes into the action of praising. 'Stand up and bless the Lord your God.' The assembled congregation blessed God. They did so by silently and heartily praying to and praising God with the Levites, who were reciting aloud the confession of sin."—*Keil.* Not as to an unknown God did they cry and make confession. He had been forgotten, but he was still familiar. "Our God," the keynote of Hebrew prayer and psalmody.

I. **A choice and a covenant.** "Thou art Lord alone." "Thou art the God who didst choose Abram." "Thou madest a covenant with him" (ver. 6—8). Around these central themes are grouped illustrations. The independency of God is marked in the making and preserving of all things, in confirmation whereof the host of Heaven worship him. He doeth what he will. When he chose Abram he gave him a new name. "I have called thee by thy name; thou art mine." He who claimed service rendered reward. "Thou foundest his heart faithful before thee, and madest a covenant with him to give the land to his seed." "Abram believed in the Lord; and he counted it to him for righteousness" (Gen. xv. 6). A man of faith will be a faithful man. God's covenants are conditioned. "The meek shall inherit the earth." "With the pure thou wilt show thyself pure; and with the froward thou wilt show thyself froward." "With God word and deed correspond with each other." "Thou hast performed thy words; for thou art righteous."

II. **The word fulfilled.** "Thou sawest the affliction of our fathers in Egypt, and heardest their cry by the Red Sea" (ver. 9—11). The extremes of deliverance. God saw them under the taskmaster's lash; he heard when they fled. The Ever-present *coming down*, the Omniscient *looking*—this is the Biblical anthropomorphism. Admit if you will that this is not God; still it is our necessary conception of him. He is always nigh; but we do not always realize His presence. When I weep assure me that God pities; when I pray tell me that God listens; when I die whisper in my ear that God is nigh. If it be not exact phraseology it is full of comfort, and withal of truth. "He that planted the ear, shall he not hear? He that formed the eye, shall He not see?" Those who are held in the bondage of evil habits, those who are striving to burst the bonds, may take the strength and courage implied in this. The Psalm-book specially exults in the all-seeing eye and ever-listening ear. The romance of reality in the histories of apostles and martyrs, in the stories of saints and sufferers, is derived from the realized nearness of God.

But deliverance is not salvation. The first step of the journey is indispensable, but insufficient. A first implies a second. Possibility is a pledge of performance. Freedom is faculty. The Red Sea opens into the desert, not into the Promised Land.

"Guide me, O Thou great Jehovah,"

is the poetry of the common-place experience of life. "Thou leddest them in the day by a cloudy pillar; and in the night by a pillar of fire, to give them light in the way wherein they should go. Thou camest down also upon Mount Sinai, and spakest with them from heaven, and gavest them laws" (ver. 12—14). Providence without, conscience within. God was in the cloud; duty in the law. "And gavest them bread from heaven, and broughtest forth water out of the rock, and promisedst them that they should go in to possess the land" (ver. 15). A guiding cloud, a directing law, an unfailing supply, an assured promise. "Thou leddest Thy people like a flock."

III. Divine forbearance. "Even the fathers to whom God had shown such favour, repeatedly departed from and rebelled against him; but God of his great mercy did not forsake them, but brought them into possession of the Promised Land" (vers. 16—25). "Words are accumulated to describe the stiffnecked resistance of the people. They hardened their necks; they hardened their hearts. They said one to another, Let us make a captain and return to Egypt. In spite, however, of their stiffneckedness God—a God of pardons—did not forsake them. He did not withdraw his gracious presence, but continued to lead them by the pillar of cloud and fire. The words (ver. 20), 'Thou gavest Thy good Spirit,' &c., refer to the occurrence (Num. xi. 17, 25) where God endowed the seventy elders with the spirit of prophecy for the confirmation of Moses' authority. The definition 'good spirit' recalls Psalm cxliii. 10. The Lord also fulfilled His promise of giving the land of Canaan to the Israelites, notwithstanding their rebelliousness." —*Keil.* They were a community of slaves in process of formation into a nation. God dealt with them as with children. He did not call wrong by any other name, but he compassionated ignorance and pitied weakness. "The mercy of the Lord our God" was celebrated in later times by prophet and priest, seer and scribe. "About the time of forty years suffered he their manners in the wilderness"

IV. Disobedience chastised. "Unto whomsoever much is given, of him shall be much required." In the wilderness they were not without punishments; but there mercy rejoiced against judgment. In the Promised Land, after long experience of the goodness and graciousness of God, their rebellions were less pardonable. So God gave them into the hands of their enemies. Still for his great mercies' sake he did not utterly consume them, nor forsake them (vers. 26—31). They rejected God's law; they slew God's prophets. Yet when they cried he heard; in their distress he sent them saviours. The majesty and mercy of God! "It is a fearful thing to fall into the hands of the living God." "Let me fall into the hand of the Lord, for very great are his mercies; but let me not fall into the hands of man." "The hand of God was very heavy." "The hand of our God is upon all them for good that seek him." "Our God is a consuming fire." "God is love"

V. The past the prophet of the present. "Now, therefore, our God, let not all the trouble seem little before thee" (vers. 32—37). History had repeated itself. The disobedient, God had rejected. Weakened by oppression, they had returned to their own land. In their present distresses they pray to the God of past deliverances—the God who had said of himself that he was unchangeable.

Application. The story of Israel has been always regarded as a parable of life. "The Lord knoweth thy walking through this great wilderness"

ILLUSTRATION.

Egyptian influence on Hebrew character. "Before God gave the Commandments to the Jewish people he wrought a magnificent series of miracles to effect their emancipation from miserable slavery, and to punish their oppressors. He first made them free, and then gave them the law. It might not have been absolutely impossible for the Jews to have kept these commandments even in Egypt, but the difficulties would have been almost invincible. The people were in no condition to receive a Divine revelation. Oppression had broken their spirit, and crushed all the nobler elements of their nature. In the atmosphere which they breathed purity and virtue could hardly live. They had been degraded by the heathenism and by the vices, as well as by the severity of their masters. It was impossible for such a race as the Jews seem to have been at this period of their history to have any vigorous faith in the greatness of the God who had revealed himself to their fathers. The wealth, the greatness, the power of the world belonged to the Egyptians; contempt and wretchedness to the descendants of Abraham and the heirs of the promises. The God of their fathers was either not strong enough to defend them from intolerable evils, or else was indifferent to their distresses. God did not begin by commanding them to acknowledge his greatness and authority, and to show fidelity to himself, and to break at once with the vices to which their external condition almost bound them as with fetters of iron. He began by manifesting his greatness in acts which must have appealed most powerfully to their imagination, and made even their passions— which seem to have been almost the only elements of energy left in them—take the side of faith in himself.—*R. W. Dale, M.A.*

A NATION'S PRAYER.

The three annual feasts instituted by the Mosaic Law were memorials of God's goodness to Israel. His works shall be kept in everlasting remembrance. At the Feast of the Passover the Jews celebrated their deliverance from Egypt; at Pentecost the giving of the Law from Mount Sinai; and at the Feast of Tabernacles the mercies of God during their wilderness journey and the ingathering of the harvest. Never, since the days of Joshua, had the Feast of Tabernacles been celebrated with such solemnity as under the teaching of Ezra and the government of Nehemiah. The services of New Year's Day, or the Feast of Trumpets, had yielded the precious fruits of godly sorrow for sin, and of holy, charitable joy (chap. viii.). One sermon may bring forth great results. The Scripture narrative of the festival closes by informing us "that day by day, from the first day unto the last day, they read in the Book of the Law of God; and they kept the feast seven days, and on the eighth day was a solemn assembly according unto the manner." God's word was the "joy and rejoicing of their hearts;" God's book, the first of books and the best of books. Here we have consolation in sorrow, directions in duty, and armour in the day of battle; a guide-book for every road, and a chart for every sea. In our Lord's time the people pressed upon him to hear the word of God ('Paul's Missionary Journeys' 'Vaudois Christians.' 'Wycliffites.' 'Translation and Diffusion in Modern Times').

The continued and protracted services of the Feast of Tabernacles, the Day of Atonement, and the Feast of Trumpets, produced an extraordinary impression on the public mind. The revival of religion was not merely metropolitan, but national. The deed of Jerusalem was the deed of the whole people; the voice of Jerusalem was the voice of the many thousands of Israel. Immediately upon the close of the services at the Feast of Tabernacles, we read that "the children of Israel were assembled with fasting," &c. (vers. 1—3).

The service of national dedication probably commenced at nine o'clock in the morning with the usual sacrifices. The reading and the exposition for three hours prepared the way for the solemn supplications of the people. These occupied three hours more, and were closed by the offering of the evening sacrifice, and by the public signing of the national covenant. The heads of this form of supplication and dedication were probably drawn up by Nehemiah, who was the first to append his signature. Copies were probably distributed among the Levites, who led the people in prayer. The national dedication opens with solemn worship of God. His great and Infinite Majesty is adored. "Blessed be thy glorious name." Then follows a retrospect of God's mercies to Israel. With this review of mercies was interwoven penitential confession of sin. First they acknowledged the sins of their fathers (verse 16); then they pass on to the transgressions of their fathers under their kings (verse 26). They acknowledged the righteous dealings of God, and their own disobedience to his Word. Thou hast done right, but we have done wickedly ; and they bring before God the one petition in this pathetic appeal : " Now therefore, our God, the great, the mighty, and the terrible God, who keepest covenant and mercy, *let not all the trouble seem little before thee, that hath come upon us,* on our kings, on our princes, and on our priests, and on our prophets, and on our fathers, and on all thy people " They implore mercy, they deprecate judgment, and with one accord resolve to bind themselves unto the service of God, in a perpetual covenant never to be forgotten. This was the conclusion of the whole matter. As the inhabitants of Jerusalem, and men of Judah, they make a solemn promise to God ; and that it might be sure the covenant is written, and as we read in

the thirty-eighth verse, " Our princes, Levites, and priests seal unto it." We are told in the opening of the tenth chapter, that at the top of the eighty-two representative signatures is inscribed NEHEMIAH THE TIRSHATHA, THE SON OF HACHALIAH He had set a noble example to his people, and now, at a time of intense religious feeling, he puts himself in the fore-front to lead them to God. " Happy are the people that are in such a case, yea, blessed are the people who have the Lord for their God."

Have we, as Englishmen, no retrospect to make? Have not we a history to review with thankfulness, and a duty to God and to one another? A nation is made of individuals A national dedication implies personal dedication.—*Rev. J. M. Randall , abridged.*

THE WORLD PRESERVED BY DIVINE PROVIDENCE.

ix. 6. *Thou preservest them all*

The providence of God may be regarded as exercised either in the preservation of the world or in the government of it, to which two main heads all the acts of Divine Providence are reducible.

God's preservation of the world. In that admirable address that is made to God in the name of the Jewish Church, after celebrating him as the great Creator of the universe, are those noble expressions—"Thou, even thou, art Lord alone; thou hast made heaven, the heaven of heavens, with all their host, the earth, and all things that are therein ;" it is added, "and thou preservest them all " The preserving this vast frame of nature, and all things that are therein, is owing to the same omnipotent being that created them. We must not imagine that things, when once put into being, continue to exist independently of him that first created them. It is easily conceivable that the self-existent Jehovah, who existed necessarily from everlasting, must certainly exist to everlasting by the intrinsic excellency of his own most perfect nature. But the case is

otherwise as to contingent beings, who have the source and basis of their existence without them. The works of men's hands may subsist at a distance from the hands which fashioned them , but the creatures can never exist in an absolute separation from God, who is always most intimately and essentially present with his own works. Consider this preservation of all things, which is an eminent act of Divine providence, as extending to the whole inanimate creation, and of all things that have life in their different degrees.

1. *God, by his constant powerful influence, upholdeth the inanimate creation, this huge material system, in all its parts.* As at the first formation of it he put things into a certain order, so it is by his power and wisdom that this order and constitution of things is maintained according to the first establishment. All things in the material world proceed according to a settled rule or method. Sun, moon, and stars; fertile earth, minerals, vegetables As God said at the first creation, " Let the earth bring forth," &c. (Gen. i. 11), so by his pro-

vidential concourse, and according to his appointment, the plants, the herbs, the trees, the flowers in all their tribes, and the various kinds of grain, spring up from their several kinds, and gradually grow up into maturity. The species of them are still continued and kept distinct, and they uniformly preserve their several virtues, their distinct forms and appearances, and bring forth their several productions in the appointed seasons.

2. *God preserveth the beings that have life and sense, with their several capacities and instincts.* "Thou preservest them all" might be rendered, "Thou quickenest them all," or "maintainest them all in life."

God preserveth and upholdeth the inferior brute animals in their several species, which by a wonderful provision are successively propagated according to established laws, and continue to be furnished in all ages with the same organs, powers, and appetites, and the same admirable instincts.

It is God that preserveth the angels in their several degrees. None of them have an independent existence.

In him we exist, or have our being. As he gave us our existence at first, and made us of such a particular order of beings, so by him we are continued in existence, and in that kind of existence which belongeth to us as creatures of such a species. In God we not only exist, or have our being, but in him we live. As it was he that first established the wonderful vital union between soul and body in man, so it is by his care and influence that it subsisteth. To this it is owing that our food nourisheth and strengtheneth us, that the vital functions are carried on, and that we are enabled to exercise our several sensations. "The God of my life." And as it is in God that we exist and live, so it is in or by him that we move. He originally gave us the power of motion, and organs admirably fitted for carrying it on, and it is through him that we are continued in the use and exercise of those organs; so that it may be justly said that we cannot move a foot, or lift up a hand,

without him. And this holdeth equally with regard to the operations of our souls as the motions of our bodies. As he hath endued our souls with the admirable faculties of understanding, with memory, free agency, and hath implanted in us affections of various kinds, so by his providential concourse and support of our faculties we apprehend, judge, reason, remember, and freely determine our own actions. It is he that upholdeth the powers which he gave us, and enableth us to exert those powers. And this he doeth not only when we do good, but when we employ our powers in acting wickedly; and yet this doth not derive the least stain of guilt upon God, or make him the author of our sins. The natural active power and the use of it, which is in itself good, is from God; the abuse of it to sinful purposes is wholly owing to ourselves, and to the corruption of our wills. For if he should withdraw his sustaining influence from men, the moment they attempt to abuse their natural powers, this would be absolutely to hinder them to exercise their liberty, nor could they in that case be accounted free agents at all. As the God of nature he ordinarily upholdeth or sustaineth them in being and in the use of their natural powers, in what manner soever they act; and then afterwards, as the moral governor, he will call them to an account for their actions, and will reward or punish them accordingly.

Practical Reflections. 1. What admiring thoughts should we entertain of God, and what diminishing thoughts of ourselves and all created beings! 2. What a just propriety and dominion God hath on and over us! 3. He is perfectly acquainted with all our thoughts, words, and actions, and all the events which befall us. 4. How strange and inexcusable will our conduct be if we allow ourselves in an habitual neglect and forgetfulnes of the Deity! 5. Since God continually preserveth us he hath an undoubted right to govern us.—*John Leland, D.D.*, 1766, *abridged.*

THE MERCY OF GOD.

ix. 17.   *A God ready to pardon.*

The mercy of God the most delightful subject. It is so in its own nature, and relatively to us who have so great need of it, who have so much depending upon it, who must perish for ever without it. The thought that the greatest Being in the universe is the most compassionate is itself elevating. Mournful that this subject is so little regarded, awakens so little emotion, that all subjects but those immediately relating to duty, affect us. Yet how delightful is it to the Christian when he is brought to apprehend the truth and rest upon it ! That God is ready to pardon, that he waits to be gracious, is a joyful topic to those who know themselves, who have been taught to estimate the value of Divine friendship.

I. A doctrine to be established. There is a strange tendency to doubt it. We speak of news too good to be true ; and under humiliating sense of our own worthlessness are at least ready to make an exception in our own case—"If the Lord would make windows in heaven might this thing be !" The power of unbelief is great, the resistance offered by conscience is great, the prevalence of fear induced by guilt is great. Exodus xxxiv. 6 contains the doctrine and gives mercy pre-eminence. 1. *The direct statements of Scripture.* The object of all revelation is to establish and explain the doctrine of God's mercy. Direct assertions, gracious promises, inspired prophecy. Twenty-nine times in one Psalm "his mercy endureth !"   "Who is a God like unto Thee ?" "The Lord, the Lord God, merciful and gracious" "As the heaven is high above the earth, so great is his mercy toward them that fear him." "Your Father in heaven is merciful." These repetitions show the resistance against it really, the difficulty of believing it, the necessity of being grounded in it. No worship without it, no hope, no love, no joy, no obedience. 2. *The positive facts exhibited in his dispensation.* The gift of his Son.

"Herein is love." "He that spared not his own Son " The gift of his Spirit : Divine revelation, ordinances, heaven at last Discovery of his own character : harmony of attributes, long-suffering to the world in general. Why mitigations of trial ? excitements of hope ?—prodigality of good gifts. This world a great volume of mercy written within and without. 3. *Some striking instances of his readiness to pardon.* Manasseh, Mary Magdalene, thief, prodigal, Paul. "*And such were some of you.*" Every sinner deems himself chief of sinners, and his conversion the greatest miracle, because he knows most of himself

II. A doctrine to be personally applied Not a doctrine for others merely, but for ourselves Go to God for it : " Have mercy upon me." 1. *To produce an immediate appeal to it* We need it deeply. Of no use to know the fact—the business is to build upon it, and say, "I will arise." Approach the mercy-seat by faith in Christ If you doubt it, test it "It is a faithful saying." 2. *To awaken cordial admiration of the method of redemption.* 3. *To check our tendency to distrust and despondency.* Very prevalent in all minds ; specially those newly awakened They do not doubt God's ability, but willingness We have all a great tendency to indulge dishonourable thoughts of God. 4. *To produce affection, contrition, obedience.*

III A doctrine to be carefully guarded from abuse. 1. *The loiterer in religion* To be had at any time, hence delay. 2 *The self-sufficient Pharisee.* Only through the cross. To the truly contrite. 3 *The man who sins that grace may abound.* Always in connection with sanctity. 4. *Those who altogether presume upon it* God is righteous. There is a judgment of God. —*Thodey.*

Illustrations —" It is harder to get sin felt by the creature than the burden when felt removed by the hand of a forgiving God. Never was tender-hearted surgeon more willing to take up the vein, and bind up the wound of his fainting patient when he hath bled enough, than God is by his pardoning mercy to ease the troubled spirit of a mourning penitent."—*Gurnall.*

"God will pardon a repentant sinner more quickly than a mother would snatch her child out of the fire."—*Vianney.*

SAME THEME.

God absolutely incomprehensible : the highest archangel cannot "find him out unto perfection." Yet we are not called to worship an unknown God. All his works praise him, but his word which he hath magnified above all his name peculiarly reveals him. In the sacred volume some clouds and darkness are round about him. Subjects are occasionally intimated which lie beyond the reach of our present faculties, concerning which we may safely follow the advice of the poet : "Wait the great teacher, Death." Scripture renders things plain and obvious in proportion as they are important and necessary. Some truths are written as with a sunbeam—such are those which regard our state as sinners, and are calculated to draw forth our faith and hope in God. For we are saved through faith; we are saved by hope. Man fell by losing his confidence in God; and he is only to be recovered by regaining it. For which purpose we read not only that there is forgiveness with him, but that he is a GOD READY TO PARDON.

I. **What is necessary to render the subject interesting? Three things.** 1. *A conviction of guilt.* "They that are whole need not the physician," &c. "The full soul loathes the honeycomb," &c. In vain we present alms to the affluent, or offer pardon to the innocent. Have you ever lived a day as you ought? Have you not at least been chargeable with sins of omission? The law begins with the object of all adoration, and requires that we serve God alone. Have you never transferred to the creature that supreme regard due to the Creator? If you have daily worshipped the Supreme, has it been in spirit and in truth? never taken his name in vain, "mocked him with a solemn sound upon a thoughtless tongue?" Have you not squandered many precious Sabbath hours? But you are sure you are no murderer! Is there, then, no one dead in whose removal you have

rejoiced? Is there no one alive at whose continuance you have inwardly repined? Have you never been angry with your brother without a cause? You repel with indignation the charge of theft! Is it not pride rather than principle that has sometimes restrained you, or the fear of the consequences rather than a sense of the sin? Are you a stranger to all unjust gain? Always paid fair wages? never robbed the poor? Have you done unto others as you would they should do unto you? 2. *An apprehension of our danger as transgressors.* The present effects of transgression! These only the beginning of sorrow. Can you flee from him who is everywhere; and everywhere the sin-avenging God? There is only one way of deliverance. It is forgiveness. 3. *A discovery of the privileges of a pardoned state.* We talk of happiness. Oh, what a change to be delivered from the wrath to come; to know that God's anger is turned away; that from an enemy he is become a friend—a friend giving us cordial access to all the rights of innocency, and entitling us to a felicity superior to the happiness of Adam in paradise, and even of an angel in glory! "Being justified by faith," &c.

II. **The proofs which establish the truth of the doctrine.** 1. *The provision he has made for the exercise of pardon.* "It became him"—we use his own language—it became him to administer this pardon in a peculiar way. It was necessary that sin should be condemned in the flesh, even while it was forgiven. It was necessary that God's law should not appear so rigid as to require relaxation, or so changeable and weak as to admit of dispensation; but be magnified and made honourable. It was necessary that God's truth should be seen as well as his grace; and his righteousness as well as his mercy. Of his own self-moved compassion he has reconciled us unto himself by Jesus Christ. "He has made him to

be sin for us," &c. "Herein is love," &c.
2. *The promptitude with which he pardons on our return.* "Before they call I will answer, and while they speak I will hear." ('Parable of Prodigal Son.')
3. *His earnestness to excite us to seek after the blessing.* It would be enough to prove that a man was ready to pardon if he yielded immediately upon the offender's submission and application, but God not only waits to be gracious, he comes forward, he beseeches, he urges; yes—by the uneasiness of conscience, by the afflictions of life, by the importunity of friends, by the addresses of ministers—it is as the Apostle says, "As though God did beseech you to be reconciled to God." Seek evidence—4. *In the character of those who have received pardon.* The chief of sinners—Manasseh, the dying thief, the murderers of Christ, the Corinthian converts. Seek evidence—5. *In the number of those who obtain forgiveness.* There are thousands more than we are aware of, even when we send forth Candour to reckon them; and when they shall be all gathered together, out of every kindred, and nation, and tongue, and people, they will be found a multitude which no man can number.

III. The way in which this subject may be abused, and the manner in which it ought to be improved. The subject is abused when it leads us to deny any disposition in God to punish. God is not only to be viewed as a tender father, but a moral governor.

The subject is abused when it encourages us to hope for pardon in ways not warranted by the word of God. For instance—thus, unwarranted is our hope when we expect it *without a reference to the mediation of Christ;* when we expect pardon *without repentance;* when we expect this pardon *by delaying an application for it to the close of life;* when we expect *to find this pardon in another world if we fail to obtain it in this.* But what is the proper improvement we should make of this delightful subject? It should yield encouragement to the broken-hearted, and consolation to those who have believed. It demands not only our admiration and praise, it calls upon us to imitate as well as to admire. Is he a God ready to pardon? "Be ye followers of God, as dear children. Let all bitterness, and wrath, and anger, and clamour, and evil-speaking, be put away from you, with all malice; and be ye kind one to another, tender-hearted, forgiving one another, even as God for Christ's sake hath forgiven you."—*Jay, abridged.*

PROMISES KEPT.

ix. 18—21. *When they had made them a molten calf, and said, This is thy God that brought thee up out of Egypt, and had wrought great provocations; yet thou in thy manifold mercies forsookest them not,* &c.

THE FAITHFUL PROMISER—is not this one of the "surnames" of God?

I. This is the verdict of history. Nehemiah and his Levites knew what they said and whereof they affirmed. Was it not written in the book of Moses (Ex. xiii. 21, 22; Num. xiv. 14), that the pillar of cloud departed not from them by day, neither the pillar of fire by night? Were there not chronicles that told how for their mouth he provided manna, and for their mind instruction (ver. 20)? See Num. xi. 17, 25; Num. xi. 6—9; xx. 2—8. Nothing awanting (ver. 21). God was in Hebrew history: not confined to Hebrew history. England's God. America's God. Men who planted that republic had Bible on their right hand.

II. The statements of Scripture. Psalms in especial addressed to the God of the promises. The psalmists called; he answered. This they make their plea when next they cry—"Doth his promise fail?" "He remembered his holy promise." "Exceeding great and precious promises." "The word of the Lord is tried." Those whom the book canonizes have set to their seal that God is true.

III. The confirmations of experience. "God punishes the persecutors of his people energetically. Our pillar of cloud, which shows us the way to our everlasting fatherland, is the ministry of the Gospel, in which God is truly present and powerful. Although God does not immediately place all the godly in fruitful and pleasant places, nor give them bread from heaven, nor water from the rock; still he gives them, notwithstanding, necessary nourishment and clothing wherewith they should be satisfied."—*Starke.* In despondency trace the footprints of God in the past. "He inclined unto me, and heard my cry." This the strongest confirmation; most unassailable reason.

> What we have felt and seen,
> With confidence we tell;
> And publish to the sons of men
> The signs infallible.

THE HISTORY OF A GENERATION.

ix. 21. *Forty years didst thou sustain them in the wilderness.*

This is the bright side of the story of his people Israel. "The penal portion of the wanderings" (Numbers xiv. 1—39; Hebrews iii.).

I. Every generation inherits the past. "Your children, which in that day" (of rebellion) "had no knowledge between good and evil, they shall go in thither, and unto them will I give it, and they shall possess it" (Deut. i. 39). The fathers sinned; the children suffered. Hereditary diseases. Superstitions, political combinations. "We are the heirs of all the yesterdays."

II. The task of each generation in the present. We receive our fathers' uncompleted tasks. Their plans indicate our power of performance; their aims an index-finger. But new times new methods; a fresh age fresh needs. To-day is not yesterday. Victorian age an advance, calling for all energies "Forward, forward, let us range." Patriarchal times, prophetic period, apostolic age. "Little children; young men; fathers." Parables of growth in Gospels of Jesus. "The righteous shall hold on his way, and he that hath clean hands shall be stronger and stronger." "Grow!" Peter is here not a whit behind his beloved brother Paul.

III. The responsibility of the present generation. We inherit to transmit; we labour to secure blessings for coming generations. The Hebrews of Nehemiah's day found consolation in the memory of God's abounding goodness to their faithless fathers We have inherited freedom; the future will require it at our hands. In this sense is that text applicable—"Hold that fast which thou hast." Pass on the torch of truth to other hands; quench not the Spirit of God. Thy memory will be invaluable; thy work faithfully done a treasure. Let not the chain be snapped—past, present, future. The "continuous purpose" of him who sees the end as well as the beginning! The humblest life is not mean. The tiniest task is not insignificant. The issues of to-day are in the far-off future.

SECULAR PROSPERITY INIMICAL TO SPIRITUAL LIFE.

ix. 25, 26. *They took strong cities, and a fat land, and possessed houses full of all goods, wells digged, vineyards, and oliveyards, and fruit trees in abundance · so they did eat, and were filled, and became fat, and delighted themselves in thy great goodness. Nevertheless they were disobedient, and rebelled against thee, and cast thy law behind their backs, and slew thy prophets which testified against them to turn them to thee, and they wrought great provocations.*

INTRODUCTION.—Let us define our terms. Prosperity—life. Secular— spiritual are here contrasted. Prosperity is outside us. It is the realization of one's hope. The prosperous man has his wishes gratified. "We must distinguish between felicity and prosperity; for prosperity leads often to ambition, and ambition to disappointment."—*Landor.* "A man's *life* consisteth not in the abundance of the things which he possesseth." Secular; spiritual—a distinction and a difference. Often falsely made. All things pertaining to this present world are not secular. "It is not the work that makes the workman holy, but it is the workman's heart that consecrates the toil."—*Cumming.*

I. **The value of prosperity** "They took strong cities," and thus became a strong nation. "Be fruitful and multiply, and replenish the earth, *and subdue it,* and have dominion over every living thing." The earth is the Lord's, but he hath given it to the children of men. "Money answereth all things." Art, science, commerce, civilization, religion, are aided by prosperity. The refinements of life are foes of the lower passions. The devil should not have the best music, nor the best pictures, nor the highest knowledge. Christians! Claim the world for God. It is his; he made it, he upholds it, he sustains it, he redeemed it, he is restoring it. And because it is his it is yours. "Ye shall be my sons and daughters, saith the Lord Almighty." "All things are yours; and ye are Christ's, and Christ is God's."

Illustration.—Riches are the stairs whereby men climb up into the height of dignity, the fortification that defends it, the food it lives upon, the oil that keeps the lamp of honour from going out. Honour is a bare robe if riches do not lace and flourish it, and riches a dull lump till honour give a soul to quicken it.—*Adams.*

II. **The danger of prosperity.** "They became fat, and delighted themselves in thy great goodness. They rebelled against thee." They accepted *God's gifts;* they rejected *God.* "The ground of a certain rich man brought forth plentifully: and he thought within himself, saying, What shall I do, because I have no room where to bestow my fruits? And he said, This will I do: I will pull down my barns, and build greater; and there will I bestow all my fruits and my goods. And

I will say to my soul, Soul, thou hast much goods laid up for many years; take thine ease, eat, drink, and be merry." *My* fruits, *my* barns, *my* goods, *my* soul. Self stood where God should stand. "Am I my brother's keeper?" Are the poor my poor? "Every man for himself." This is the world's policy; the tone, if not the language, of unconsecrated prosperity. Forget God, and you will neglect man.

☞ *Illustrations.*—Prosperity is no friend to a sanctified memory, and therefore we are cautioned, when we are full, lest we forget God. Noah, who had seen the whole world drowned in water, was no sooner safe on shore, and in the enjoyment of plenty, than he forgot God, and drowned himself in wine.—*Gurnall.*

Where one thousand are destroyed by the world's frowns, ten thousand are destroyed by the world's smiles. The world, siren-like, sings us and sinks us, it kisses us and betrays us, like Judas; it kisses us and smites us under the fifth rib, like Joab.—*Brooks.*

It is one of the worst effects of prosperity to make a man a vortex instead of a fountain; so that, instead of throwing out, he learns only to draw in.—*Beecher.*

It is the bright day that brings forth the adder, and that craves wary walking.—*Shakespeare.*

Prosperity most usually makes us proud, insolent, forgetful of God, and of all duties we owe unto him. It chokes and extinguishes, or at least cools and abates, the heat and vigour of all virtue in us. And as the ivy whilst it embraces the oak sucks the sap from the root, and in time makes it rot and perish, so worldly prosperity kills us with kindness, whilst it sucks from us the sap of God's graces, and so makes our spiritual growth and strength to decay and languish. Neither do men ever almost suffer an eclipse of their virtues and good parts, but when they are in the full of worldly prosperity.—*Downame.*

Two things have I required of thee, deny me them not before I die: Remove far from me vanity and lies; give me neither poverty nor riches, feed me with food convenient for me, lest I be full, and deny thee, and say, Who is the Lord? or lest I be poor, and steal, and take the name of my God in vain.—*Agur.*

In all time of our tribulation; *in all time of our wealth,* in the hour of death, and in the day of judgment, Good Lord, deliver us.—*The Litany.*

III. **The safeguard of prosperity.** *Remember thy stewardship.* "What hast thou that thou didst not receive? Now if thou didst receive it, why dost thou glory, as if thou hadst not received it?" "The poor ye have always with you."

"Lay not up for yourselves treasures upon earth," &c. Get to give; gather to scatter. And as the husbandman sows to reap so shalt thou. "The liberal soul shall be made fat." "There is that scattereth and yet increaseth." "Whoso hath this world's good, and seeth his brother have need, and shutteth up his bowels of compassion from him, how dwelleth the love of God in him?" "If a man say, I love God, and hateth his brother, he is a liar for he that loveth not his brother whom he hath seen, how can he love God whom he hath not seen? And this commandment have we from him, That he who loveth God love his brother also."

Illustration — In everything to give and receive is the principle of numerous blessings · in seeds, in scholars, in arts. For if any one desire to keep his art to himself, he subverts both himself and the whole course of things. And the husbandman, if he bury and keep the seeds in his house, will bring about a grievous famine. So also the rich man, if he fails thus in regard of his wealth, will destroy himself before the poor, heaping up the fire of hell more grievous upon his own head. Therefore, as teachers, however many scholars they have, impart some of their love unto each; so let thy possession be—many to whom thou hast done good.—*Chrysostom.*

RESPONSIBILITY OF HONOUR.

ix. 38. *We make a sure covenant, and write it; and our princes, Levites, and priests, seal unto it.*

"Seekest thou great things for thyself? seek them not." These were the words of the Lord by the mouth of Jeremiah to a discouraged man. But because they are the words of a true prophet of God they contain a philosophy. A prophet in occasional Old Testament language is a seer—*one who sees.* Power is good but it exacts penalty.

I. In office and position. "Our princes, Levites, and priests, seal unto it." And the first name was that of NEHEMIAH THE TIRSHATHA. The strongest must carry the burdens; the tallest be exposed to the fire of the enemy. Statesmen, reformers, scientists, preachers, teachers—the best-hated men.

II. In intellectual and moral elevation. The strong must lend an arm to the weak; the wise pour out their treasures to enlighten the ignorant. Those who know the way must guide those who don't. The sun lives for the fields and homes of men. The stars enlighten other worlds. "The Lord *will give* grace and glory; *no good thing will he withhold* from them that walk uprightly." "The Son of man came not to be ministered unto, but *to minister, and to give* his life a ransom for many."

III. In national supremacy. "A strong nation." "A great people." "An increasing territory." "The sun never sets on the Queen's dominions," &c. Every boast implies a duty. "Italian unity;" "German Fatherland;" "American Republic;" "England's sway." Be it ever remembered that with honour comes responsibility; with greatness claims. What then? Biblical fear not! "Thou shalt go to all that I shall send thee. Be not afraid of their faces; for I am with thee." "As I was with Moses, so I will be with thee." "Fear not, thou worm Jacob." Strength without God is weakness; weakness with God is strength. "Where he appoints I go." And thus directed, when I am weak, then am I strong.

ADDENDA TO CHAPTER IX.

SENTENCES FROM OLD WRITERS.

I. From feasting to fasting (ver. 1—3). "There is in this present life an interchange of all things, a succession of feasting and fasting. Of the best whilst here it may be said, unhappy you cannot call him, happy you may not. One compareth him to the Ark, which was ever transportative, till settled in Solomon's Temple; another to quicksilver, which hath in itself a principle of motion, but not of rest." "Deadness of spirit is apt to follow our liveliest joys; but that must be looked to, and security prevented, which is wont to seize upon men after holy duties, like as worms and wasps eat the sweetest fruits." "It was a fast that men appointed, but such a fast as God had chosen. They were restrained from weeping (chap. viii. 9), but now they were directed to weep. The joy of our holy feasts must give way to the sorrow of our solemn fasts when they come. Everything is beautiful in its season." "Confession is the way to the kingdom; walk in it; only it must be joined with confusion of sin, as here. They separated themselves from all strangers, they abandoned their darling sin, they kept themselves from their iniquity." "They that intend by prayers and covenants to join themselves to God must separate themselves from sin and sinners." "Fasting without prayer is a body without a soul." "In the glass of the law we may see our deformities and defilements, and know what to acknowledge and what to amend." "The Word will direct and quicken prayer."

II. A story of Divine guidance (ver. 4—38). *They cried with a loud voice —Unto the Lord their God.* "As being in covenant with them. This shows their faith, as the former their fervency. Faith is the foundation of prayer, and prayer is the fervency of faith." *Then the Levites said, Stand up.* "Gird yourselves and serve the Lord. Be instant, or stand close to the work (2 Tim. iv. 2); set sides and shoulders to it; rouse up yourselves and wrestle with God. In the primitive times the ministers prepared the people to serve God, by saying, Lift up your hearts." *Stand up.* "For though they are before said to stand, yet, through shame and confusion of face, and awe of the Divine Majesty, might be fallen on their faces to the ground." *And bless the Lord your God for ever.* "If we should do nothing else all our days, yea, as long as the days of heaven shall last (said that martyr), but kneel upon our knees and sing over David's psalms to God's praise, yet should we fall short of what we owe to the Lord, who is most worthy to be praised." *And blessed be thy glorious name, which is exalted above all blessing and praise.* "These holy Levites, having called upon the people to bless God, break forth into the performance of this Divine duty themselves. So St. Paul often, exhorting the saints to pray, falls a-praying for them." "When we have done our utmost herein we can never overdo." "As oft as we breathe we are to breathe out the praises of God, and to make our breath like the perfumed smoke of the Tabernacle." *Thou art Lord alone; thou hast made heaven,* &c. "The first article of our Creed is fitly made the first article of our praises." "God's providence extends itself to the highest beings, for they need it; and to the meanest, for they are not slighted by it." "Jehovah is God's incommunicable name; that holy and reverend name of his, which Jews pronounce not, we too oft profane, at least by not considering the import of it, which is enough to answer all our doubts and to fill us with strong consolation, had we but skill to spell all the letters in it" "With great skill and artifice God has made heaven three stories high" (2 Cor. xii. 2; Heb. xi. 10). "Of the heaven of heavens no natural knowledge can be had, nor any help by human arts; for it is neither aspectable nor movable." "God may be read in the great book of nature, which hath three leaves—heaven, earth, and sea." *And foundest his heart faithful.* "He must needs find it so who hath made it so." *And madest a covenant with him.* "Wherever he finds a faithful heart he will be found a faithful God." *And heardest their cry.* "Though mixed with much murmuring So he heard that pitiful poor prayer of David, 'I said in mine haste, I am cut off from thine eyes : nevertheless thou heardest the voice of my supplications, when I cried unto thee.' God heareth the young ravens, though they have but a hoarse and harsh note, making no melody to move pity, and cry but by implication only, and not directly unto him." *And showedst signs and wonders upon Pharaoh.* "That sturdy rebel whom neither ministry, nor misery, nor miracle, nor mercy could possibly mollify." *And gavest them bread from heaven,* &c. "God rained down angels' food, and set the fluid abroach ; and this he did for their hunger, for their thirst, fitting his favours according to their need and request. Besides that, their bread was sacramental, whereof they communicated every day. Their drink also was sacramental, that this ancient Church might give no warrant of a dry communion : for they did all eat of the same spiritual meat, and did all drink the same spiritual drink, the same that we do at the Lord's Supper." *Hearkened not to thy commandments.* ' The word of God they heard, but they did not hearken to God's commandments; and the works of God they saw, but they were not mindful of his wonders." *A God ready to pardon.* " It is our comfort that we have to do with a forgiving, sin-pardoning God, that doth it naturally (Exod xxxiv. 6), plentifully (Isa. lv. 7), constantly (Ps. cxxx. 4). This should be as a perpetual picture in our hearts." *They made them a molten calf, and said, This is thy God.* "These be thy gods (Exod xxxii. 4). It was the serpent's grammar that first taught men to decline God in the plural number : ye shall be as gods" (Gen iii). *They lacked nothing.* " Nor more shall they that seek the Lord lack any good thing. God will not be a wilderness to them, or a land of dark-

ness A sufficiency they shall be sure of, if not a superfluity ; yea, in the midst of straits they shall be in a sufficiency" (1 Tim. vi. 6). *So they possessed the land of Sihon.* " God's favours must not be mentioned in the lump only, and by wholesale ; but particularly enumerated and celebrated." *The land concerning which thou hadst promised to their fathers.* " And they disposed of it by will to their posterity, as if they had been in present possession God's promises are good surehold : the patriarchs would be buried there, though they died in Egypt, and keep possession as they could ; for they knew that all was their own." *So the children went in.* " After that they had been held a long while under the Egyptian servitude. God knows how to command his favours to us; which lightly come by are lightly set by." *And delighted themselves in thy great goodness* "They lived in God's good land, but not by God's good laws." *They wrought great provocations Therefore thou deliveredst them into the hand of their enemies.* " Sin and punishment are tied together with chains of adamant." " They that would not serve God in their own land were made to serve their enemies in a strange land." " It is a pity good land should have bad inhabitants ; but so it was with Sodom." " Fatness and fulness often make men proud and sensual." *After they had rest they did evil again.* " As standing pools breed vermin , as sedentary lives are subject to diseases. If men be not poured out from vessel to vessel, they will soon settle upon their lees. We are commonly best when worst." *And hardened their neck.* " To sinews of iron they added brows of brass " *Thou art a gracious and merciful God* " And this is most seen when misery weighs down, and nothing but mercy turneth the scale." *Behold, we are servants this day.* " A sad change. But see what work sin makes !" *We make a sure covenant,* &c " He that bears an honest mind will not startle at assurances , nor will those that know the deceitfulness of their own hearts think them needless."

CHAPTER X.

EXPLANATORY NOTES.] **Vers** 1—27] "First came the name of the governor, *the Tirshatha,* next *Zidkijah,* perhaps the secretary to the governor Then follow twenty-one names of *priests,* seventeen *Levites,* and forty-four of *the chief of the people.*" **Ver** 28. **The rest of the people**] Represented by the heads of the nations who had sealed the covenant. These sealed, those swore. **All they that had separated themselves**] "The descendants of those Israelites who had been left in the land, and who now joined the new community."—*Keil.* **Ver** 30, 31.] "Besides the general obligation to observe all the commandments, judgments, and statutes of God, two points, then frequently transgressed, are specially mentioned In ver. 30, that we would not give our daughters to the people of the lands, nor take their daughters for our sons In ver. 31, that if the people of the land brought wares or any victuals on the Sabbath day to sell, we would not buy it of them on the Sabbath, or on a holy day, and would let the seventh year lie, and the loan of every hand To the sanctification of the Sabbath pertained the celebration of the Sabbatical year in which the land was to lie untilled and unsown" (Ex. XXIII 10) —*Keil* **Vers** 32—39] Having agreed to keep the law they then resolved to maintain the Temple service **Ver** 32. **The third part of a shekel**] The law required half a shekel, perhaps reduced to one-third in consequence of the people's poverty **Ver** 34 **We cast the lots for the wood offering**] "The carrying of the wood had formerly been the work of the Nethinims. But few of them having returned, the duty was assigned as stated in the text The practice afterwards rose into great importance, and Josephus speaks of the Xylophoria, or certain stated and solemn times, at which the people brought up wood to the Temple."—*Jamieson.* **Ver** 38. **The priest shall be with the Levites when they take tithes**] A prudential arrangement. The presence of a dignified priest would prevent the people deceiving the Levites, or the Levites defrauding the priests.—*Jamieson* **The tithe of the tithes**] The Levites, having received a tenth of all land produce, were required to give a tenth of this to the priests. The Levites were charged with the additional obligation to carry the tithes when received, and deposit them in the Temple stores, for the use of the priests.—*Jamieson.* **Ver. 39 We will not forsake the house**] The people swore to maintain, the priests and Levites to serve, the Temple.

HOMILETICAL CONTENTS OF CHAPTER X.

UNWORLDLINESS.

x. 28—31. *And the rest of the people, the priests, the Levites, the porters, the singers, the Nethinims, and all they that had separated themselves from the people of the lands unto the law of God, their wives, their sons, and their daughters, every one having knowledge, and having understanding; they clave to their brethren, their nobles, and entered into a curse, and into an oath, to walk in God's law, which was given by Moses the servant of God, and to observe and do all the commandments of the Lord our Lord, and his judgments and his statutes; and that we would not give our daughters unto the people of the land, nor take their daughters for our sons and if the people of the land bring ware or any victuals on the sabbath day to sell, that we would not buy it of them on the sabbath, or on the holy day: and that we would leave the seventh year, and the exaction of every debt.*

THEY did not pray to be taken out of the world; they did resolve to keep themselves from its evil Is that biblical unworldliness? St. James says, "The friendship of the world is enmity with God; whosoever therefore will be a friend of the world is the enemy of God." Does the Apostle stand alone in this? Is he carried away by the vehemence of his feelings as public speakers sometimes are? He was pre-eminently a calm man. He weighed his words. The men of his age styled him "the just." He was a man of weight. And the key-note of his epistle is struck in the sermon on the mount Let us listen to the teaching of Jesus, so tranquil in its tone: "No man can serve two masters: for either he will hate the one, and love the other; or else he will hold to the one, and despise the other. Ye cannot serve God and mammon." "Lay not up for yourselves treasures upon earth; but lay up for yourselves treasures in heaven; for where your treasure is, there will your heart be also." "Let your light so shine before men, that they may see your good works." Unfortunately use has dulled the edge of these beautiful words. Could we listen to them as they deserve to be heard they would sound strangely. They distinguish between things that differ—the world and God. They separate the worshippers of the world from the worshippers of God. They tell of a reciprocal influence. If we turn from Christ to Paul the strain is the same. "Be not conformed to this world, that ye may prove what is that good, and acceptable, and perfect will of God." "The time is short: it remaineth, that they that weep be as though they wept not; and they that rejoice, as though they rejoiced not; and they that buy, as though they possessed not; and they that use this world, as not abusing it: for the fashion of this world passeth away." Take one more step—from Paul to John "Love not the world, neither the things that are in the world If any man love the world, the love of the Father is not in him. For all that is in the world is not of the Father, but is of the world."

I. What is the forbidden world? 1. *Not the material world.* "Every creature of God is good" The world is God's · he made it, he gloried in it; he upholds it. It is a mark of God's likeness to enjoy this beautiful world. In the world God is mirrored. When night draws its curtain and hangs up its silvery lamps,

> All things are calm, and fair, and passive. Earth
> Looks as if lulled upon an angel's lap
> Into a breathless dewy sleep so still
> That we can only say of things, they be!

It is said that the first Napoleon was once on the deck of a vessel surveying such a scene when he overheard two of his officers in discussion, and one denying the existence of God. Going towards them he said, "Gentlemen, I heard one of you say there is no God, then pray tell me who made all this?" pointing as he spoke to "the beads of light strung o'er night's dark brow." Think you God has forbidden us to love this beautiful world? Why has he hidden it from us? Why has he made science, art, health, life itself, dependent on the study of it? Is it not that he would have us cultivate its friendship and worm out its secret? and whether we gaze with awe on the worlds upon worlds circling in distant space, or the worlds within worlds in each the minutest creation of God, rise from our daily contemplation, as he rose on the first day of its existence, with the words upon our lips—"It is very good," "He hath done all things well." 2. *Not the men who are in the world.* If the world is dear to God because he made it and sustains it, how much more man, whom he has redeemed with his Son's most precious blood? We have been on the Mount with Christ. Let us revisit it. He shall teach us our relations to the world of men. "Ye are the salt of the earth." "Ye are the light of the world." Did Christ scorn men? He scorned, hated, recoiled from, denounced sin; but the sinner he sought, soothed, taught, won, and rejoiced over. Christ had human affections. Broad enough to embrace a world was the love of Christ, and yet he needed human love. And in selected homes and from selected hearts he got what he wanted God has not outlawed our affections. They will outlast death. Love is of God. Love is eternal. ' If a man say, I love God, and hateth his brother, he is a liar: for he that loveth not his brother whom he hath seen, how can he love God whom he hath not seen? And this commandment have we from him, that he who loveth God love his brother also." 3. *But the spirit of the world.* Our Lord styled it "the evil,"; St. John phrases it, "the lust of the world."

The maxims, the tone, the tendency of a life that shuts out God, ignores death, buries the thought of another life, the godlessness of the world—this is forbidden. The World's Final Court of Appeal is Opinion; the Christian's is God's Word. The one anxiously asks, " What will society say ?" The other fearlessly asks, " What has God said ?" " Will it be discovered ? will shame follow ?" that is one way of meeting a temptation. " Is it right ?" that is the other, the more excellent, way.

II Importance of a correct answer to the question, What is the forbidden world ? A mistake here is fatal. 1. *Some have looked upon this world as accursed.* They have betaken themselves to monasteries and sisterhoods, oblivious of the fact that

> The trivial round, the common task,
> Would furnish all we ought to ask :
> Room to deny ourselves ; a road
> To bring us daily nearer God.

2. *Some have supposed the evil to be in our business.* Here temptation arises ; but the place where the fire breaks out is not the cause of the fire. To be unworldly does not mean to be out of the world. " I pray not that thou shouldest take them out of the world, but that thou shouldest keep them from the evil." St. Paul did not give up tent-making, nor St. Peter relinquish fishing, when they became apostles. They taught their converts to " abide " in their callings. Business is not outside religion ; it must be religiously attended to. The shop should be as sacred as a sanctuary. Work done with right motives and aims is a ceaseless litany. " Whether therefore ye eat, or drink, or whatsoever ye do, do all to the glory of God."

Illustrations :—Let us use worldly things as wise pilgrims do their staves and other necessaries convenient for their journey. So long as they help us forward in our way, let us make use of them, and accordingly esteem them. But if they become troublesome hindrances and cumbersome burdens, let us leave them behind us or cast them away.—*Downame.*

All the water is waste that runs beside the mill , so all thy thoughts and words are waste which are not to the glory of God. A bee will not sit on a flower where no honey can be sucked ; neither should the Christian engage in anything but for his soul's good and God's honour.—*Gurnall.*

Christianity allows us to use the world, provided we do not abuse it. It does not spread before us a delicious banquet, and then come with a " Touch not, taste not, handle not "—*Porteous.*

A Christian is like Jacob's ladder . while his body, that lower part, stands on the ground, the top, his higher and better part, is in heaven. He that hath the living waters of Jesus flowing in his heart, is mad if he stoop to the puddles of vanity, or seek content in the world. Yea, such a one will scarce descend to lawful pleasures, but for God's allowance and nature's necessity ; and then but as the eagle, who lives aloft, and stoops not but for her prey.—*Adams.*

MOSES.

x. 29. *Moses, the servant of God.*

Three periods of forty years :—agreeing with his life in Egypt, Arabia, and the wilderness of the wandering. **I. Birth and education.** Tyranny and cowardice twin-sisters. Pharaoh enslaved the people. Unrighteous power is uncertain power. Pharaoh knew this. Dreading the increasing numbers of the children of Israel, he issued an edict that all the male children should be strangled at birth. Fearing political intrigue, he placed over them Egyptian task-masters. Anxious to crush their spirits, he increased their burdens. *Then* *Moses was born.* Jewish proverb says, " When the tale of bricks is doubled then comes Moses." " Man's extremity is God's opportunity." The story of the child's salvation. His mother his educator. Mother's influence. Augustine and Monica. The mother of the Wesleys. Cowper's poem on seeing his mother's picture. Boyhood of Moses not detailed. Nor childhood of Jesus. Two anecdotes in Stephen's speech. Flight now necessary. **II. Moses kept the flock in the desert near Horeb.** Desert voices—

solitude and thought. Burning bush—
a lesson to the eye; "My people are in
the fire; they shall not be burned."
Voice—a command and a commission.
Reluctance. Moses and Aaron. Our
dependence upon each other. Goes to
Pharaoh

III. His work. Eighty years of preparation. How God can wait! Our
impatience if harvest ripens slowly.
Moses became *deliverer.* Difficulties
from Pharaoh; from people's accustom
edness to bondage. Human sagacity
and Divine help. The order of their
march he indicated, but Hobab a guide.
With the sagacity of a leader Moses
united the courage of a warrior. He
was the *patriarch and judge.* Difficulties he surmounted, and doubts he
resolved. How he bore with them the
history tells. His speech sometimes
song. The *poet* of the nation. Passage
of the Red Sea (Psalm xc.). Farewell
(Deut. xxxii., xxxiii.). The scenes of
this history have passed into proverbs.
Our conceptions of the journey of a
human soul from this land of exile to
its home with God are borrowed from
this narrative. Horeb, Sinai, and Nebo
speak a language understood by thousands. The Red Sea, the city of palm
trees, and the cleft rock have suggested
thoughts of God which have inspired
untold myriads in their pilgrimage.
Such a history can never again be
written. "A man of like passions."
Penalty of passion. He was to see, but

not to enter the land. Forty years he
had toiled to bring them there, and now
he must die outside. How many coveted
objects get just within our reach, and
then are removed as by invisible hands.
A few lines sum up a human life.
"Moses, the servant of the Lord." Few
words, but 120 years in them—the victories and defeats, fears and hopes,
temptations and resistances, dangers and
deliverances of a lifetime. Moses died:
God buried him. The people wept:
Joshua arose. Moses died, but his work
remained—remains. His life is ours to
study. His laws are at the base of
English and American jurisprudence;
and he is with those who have gotten
the victory, who stand on the sea of
glass, having the harps of God, and sing
the song of Moses, the servant of God,
and the song of the Lamb.

Illustrations :—"The life of Moses is probably
the most complete of any man's, either in the
Old Testament or the New—a great, noble,
growing life to the very end, and most clearly
and graphically depicted in the word of God.
But not a single ray of light falls upon his death,
and no man attends his funeral. We only know
that it was well cared for, "the Lord buried
him."—*Ker.*

Moses, pre-eminently one of the greatest men
of all time. Coming from the lowest ranks of
life,—born a slave under the iron tyranny of an
Eastern despot,—he rose to become the emanci-
pator of his people from that bondage, and the
founder of a nation that held the light of heaven
through the darkness of ages; and which, of all
nations, has had the mightiest influence in
advancing the true progress of the world.—
E. L. Hull.

VOLUNTARY TAXATION.

x. 32—39. *We made ordinances for us, to charge ourselves yearly with the
third part of a shekel for the service of the house of our God, &c.*

The old law required the offerings;
but it had been long unread. In the
enthusiasm of the Reformation under
Nehemiah they accepted the neglected
law, and adapted it to their new conditions. Not to enter upon the thorny path
of endowed or voluntary religion, nor to
inquire whether tithes are coeval with
the first man, and binding upon the
present age, let us maintain—

I. That a Church supposes an edifice.

"No particular sort of building, style of
architecture, or ceremony of preparation
is essential. An upper room in Jerusalem,
the abode of the eleven, is the first-
mentioned place of Christian consolation.
The place of pentecostal concourse is
not exactly mentioned, but is called a
house. Afterwards the Christians met
in the temple, probably for public worship; and celebrated the eucharist or
broke the bread in the house. Perhaps

it was in the same place in which the eleven abode that the pentecostal assemblage was held, that the eucharistic bread was broken, that the deacons were installed, and that the apostolic council was held, and which was 'shaken' in answer to prayer."—*Manly.* God may be worshipped in any house. Experience has taught the convenience and value of *a house of God.* The edifice must be built and maintained

II. That a Church requires a minister. "All elders are worthy of honour, the elders that rule well of double honour, the elders that labour in the word and doctrine of special honour The honour consists of either obedience, or maintenance, or of both together. The labourer is worthy of his reward. No man can rightly labour in the word and doctrine without diligent and habitual biblical study; no man can conduct such study without the renunciation of secular pursuits; no man can abandon such pursuits without an adequate and guaranteed salary from the Church in which he teaches and for which he labours; and accordingly it is a wise arrangement, an equitable exchange, a Divine direction, that the bishops or ministers of the churches should be adequately sustained and paid An unpaid ministry must always be an occasional and defective ministry; and a Church that relies on it will droop and decline It is simple justice; and it is God's law that he who is taught in the word should communicate to him that

teacheth in all good things"—*Manly.* The ministry must be sustained.

III. That a Church is a brotherhood. "The rich and poor meet together." "The poor ye have always with you" In a Church sense, "if any provide not for his own house he hath denied the faith" "All ye are brethren."

IV That a Church is a missionary organization It has duties both at home and abroad The word of God must be translated, the masses evangelized, society leavened This is the only "needs-be" for a Church. It gets to give; exists for what it does A praying Church must also be a working Church. A working Church must of necessity be a generous Church. *Jesus stood over against the treasury and saw the rich men casting in their gifts. And he saw also a certain widow casting in the two mites.* "If there be first a willing mind, it is accepted according to that a man hath, and not according to that he hath not." "God loveth the cheerful giver."

Illustration.—Men may say they prefer to give their missionary money nearer home, where they see what becomes of it But remember that it is by setting up standards and beacons, getting hold of a few here and there and Christianizing them, even when results look small, that a great testimony to Christ is finally given. Make the gospel "witness to all nations," before the end comes. The apostles travelled and sailed, casting their bread upon the waters, not too anxious to count up visible results. The great commission was, "Go, preach the gospel to all nations." There is no knowing where the fruit will spring. —*Bishop Huntington*

ZEAL FOR THE SANCTUARY.

x. 39. *We will not forsake the house of our God.*

Israel ordained the guardians of God's spiritual worship, and the repositories of his lively oracles. So long as they kept oracles undefiled and maintained worship undebased God was with them; when they profaned or abandoned the place where his honour dwelt—defiling his worship with superstition and idolatry—he turned to be their adversary He gave up their city to destruction, and their beautiful house, where their fathers had praised him, to utter desolation. They were carried away captive into Babylon. After seventy years of tribulation, God hearkened to their cries. He caused Cyrus to issue a decree of return. Multitudes hastened back. Having rebuilt the temple they kept a solemn festival. They made confessions, and renewed their covenant with God. They bound themselves to restore the tithes and sacrifices which the law ordained Though impoverished and oppressed they undertook to give such things as were needful for the full service of the temple. The whole assembly, in unison with their governor, protested with one mind and one mouth, WE WILL NOT FORSAKE THE HOUSE OF OUR GOD.

Why you should say of " the habitation of God's house," we will not forsake it?

1. *God has clearly ordained public worship.* He made man to be social—social in virtue of his sorrows, his joys, his wants, his affections, his relationships. But if he formed men to be social in things natural, he no less formed them to be social in things spiritual. The isolation of selfishness is of sin; the union of love is of God. But union is cherished by communion, and communion strengthened by united worship. The faithful ought therefore to assemble themselves together in their Master's name. Accordingly, fellowship in worship may be traced from the earliest period. It seems not improbable that, as our great poet has represented, even in paradise the primitive pair had some chosen bower whither they resorted to offer up their stated homage to their Maker. But be that as it may, no sooner do we find men calling upon the Lord after the fall, than we find them calling upon him in fellowship. Where the patriarch pitched his tent, there he built his altar. As soon as ever God had singled out a people for himself, he bade them raise a tabernacle of witness and of worship, giving the minutest instructions for its construction, its furniture, and its ordinances. He added this memorable promise, which remains in all its force, " Wherever I record my name I will come to thee and bless thee." And gloriously did he record his name—first in the tabernacle, and afterwards more gloriously still in the temple. He dwelt between the cherubim, over the mercy-seat, and poured his blessing on all who truly sought him there. Jesus honoured the temple. He loved to resort to his Father's house. He was very jealous of its desecration; the zeal of it ate him up. There he was wont to teach; there he wrought mighty miracles. His disciples met for worship, sometimes in the synagogue, sometimes in the upper chamber, sometimes at the river-side: and no sooner did opportunity serve than they set apart holy places for the ordinances and worship of God. The faithful in every age have desired to dwell in the house of the Lord. If, therefore, any man have the mind of the Spirit; if he love the Saviour and those whom the Saviour loves—he cannot but say of the solemn assembly, " I will not forsake the house of my God."

2. *The special manifestations of the Divine presence, vouchsafed in the congregations of the saints, ought to endear to us such privileged scenes.* Never has the promise failed, " Where two or three are met together in my name, there am I in the midst of them." His chosen have sought and seen his " power and glory in the sanctuary." The history of the Church in all ages is rich in the illustration of this fact. The patriarchal altar was many a time illumined from on high. The cloud of glory often rested on the tabernacle of witness. The mystic splendour which shone between the wings of the cherubim, reflecting a radiance on the mercy-seat —that symbol of the propitiation of Jesus—testified that "God dwelt with man on the earth,"—that " his dwelling-place was in Zion. There, by voices and by visions, by Urim and Thummim," and by secret communications of his grace, he revealed himself to his people. And now—what though the temple with its magnificent ceremonial and impressive ordinances has passed away—what though no visible Shekinah irradiates the simple house of prayer—have we no signs, no tokens left? Have we not the substance instead of the shadow? the spirit in lieu of the letter? If the carnal worshipper sees less—does not the spiritual worshipper see more—abundant glory? " If the ministration of condemnation be glory, much more doth the ministration of righteousness exceed in glory." Are there not still memorials of a present Lord amongst us—memorials sublimely simple, exquisitely expressive?—his blessed gospel—his living sacraments—the preaching of his word? Neither are there lacking demonstrations of his power and love. True it is that they who come not in faith find him not here; but those

who come believingly hear a voice the unbelieving do not hear—feel a presence the unbelieving do not feel—enjoy a blessing the unbelieving cannot receive. If, then, God manifests himself surpassingly in the sanctuary; if he has never failed to bestow his special favour towards the social services of his children, it follows that they who love the Lord and love to meet him cannot but say, " We will not forsake the house of our God."

3 *As the sanctuary has been the place of the Lord's rest, so has it been the scene where he has imparted the richest gifts to his worshippers.* On the day of Pentecost, it was "when they were all with one accord in one place," that "suddenly there came a sound from heaven, as a of rushing mighty wind, and it filled all the house where they were sitting. And there appeared unto them cloven tongues like as of fire, and it sat upon each of them : and they were all filled with the Holy Ghost " Examine the history of the Church ever since, and you will find that of the multitudes of the believing, the largest proportion have been born for eternity in the house of God If not begotten in the sanctuary, the saints have at least been nursed and nourished there. Many a time has the devout worshipper entered the sanctuary in darkness, and left it full of light; entered sorely beset with temptations, returned from it with the snare of the fowler broken ; come perplexed, departed assured ; come burdened, gone back enlarged, come prostrate, gone back exalted, come mourning, returned rejoicing; come cold, gone back enkindled, come secularized, gone back spiritualized; come weary, gone back revived, come earthly-minded, gone back heavenly-minded.

4 *The servant of God will love the courts of the Lord and not forsake them, because in them he tastes most of heaven below.* You cannot form a better conception of heaven than by fixing on the happiest Sabbath, and the happiest hour of worship on the happiest Sabbath, you ever enjoyed in the assembly of the saints Then and there, withdrawn from the world's vanities and disquietudes ; then and there, abstracted from things seen and temporal, and absorbed in things unseen and eternal ; then and there, when all was tranquillity without, and all was calm within ; then and there, faith almost turned into sight and hope into fruition—all earthly distinctions forgotten, the poor and the rich blended in fellowship and love, the whole assembly worshipping in unison, like many instruments all true to one key-note ; then and there, you had a miniature of heaven, you reached the very vestibule of that temple not made with hands, where congregations never break up, and Sabbaths never end He then who loves not such scenes on earth—how could he love the heavenly habitation of holiness ? He who has no taste for the communion and the songs of the saints below, how would he weary of the ceaseless thanksgiving and the eternal communion of the glorified in immortality ! Of all men, the busy, harassed, weary mercantile man—forced to plunge daily into the dust and din of the world's mart—is the very man who most requires the refreshment and savour of the sanctuary. A Sunday passed in worship has an influence on the days of toil. Many are witnesses that, when on the evening of the stated service which forms the half-way well in the week, they have gone up to the house of the Lord, rich has been the return of blessing and comfort. These services interrupt the current of earthly care, and suspend for a little the play of the overwrought machinery of the mind Alas ! with what punctuality do many frequent the counting-house who are seldom seen in the solemn assembly ! What numbers who never think of contenting themselves with a single visit to the warehouse on the Monday, yet content themselves with a solitary attendance at church on the Sunday. What numbers are all alive and alert in the exchange, who are sluggish and uninterested in waiting on God—as though the toys and shadows of time and earth surpassed in magnitude and moment the illimitable realities of immortality.—*Canon Stowell, abridged.*

ZEAL FOR GOD'S HOUSE, EXPRESSED IN A HOLY RESOLUTION NOT TO FORSAKE IT.

x. 39.   *And we will not forsake the house of our God.*

INTRODUCTION. Consider these words as they relate to the Jews at that time. The house of God was once the tabernacle, after that the temple. Tabernacle was forsaken : temple destroyed : worshippers carried away into captivity.

I. A resolution well becoming Christians themselves. "We will not forsake the house of our God." The same zeal and affection which this people expressed to the temple, should be manifested by us to the Church and ordinances of Christ. The material temple was the centre of their unity. Under the gospel there is no such house, unto which all are obliged to repair, and any parts of divine worship are confined. Our house not a material building of wood and stones, of silver and gold, and cedar work ; but a mystical building, a spiritual house, whose maker is the living God, and whose materials are living stones : whose house are we. By this house I mean the Church of God, as it is composed of the faithful in all ages and places of the world ; comprehending his worship and ordinances, with all the concerns of his kingdom, and interests among men. This is that house which we should resolve never to forsake There is doubtless much more intended than is expressed in such forms of speech, and in its full extent this resolution comprehends the three following particulars :—

1. *That we will never cast off the profession of our faith, nor make a defection from the truths and ways of the gospel, for any cause nor upon any account whatsoever.* It's so rare a thing for a nation to change their gods (though really no gods) that the prophet challenges his people to produce a single instance of its being ever done—Hath a nation changed their gods ? But to the everlasting reproach of Israel, they had changed their glory for that which did not profit. They that were the only people under heaven who had no cause to change their God, were of all others the people that had done it. Now it's this defection from the true God and his worship which this people covenanted against.

2. *That we will not neglect the ordinances of Divine worship, nor be wanting in our attendance on them whenever we are called, and have an opportunity of appearing before God in his house.* Thus much is contained in this resolution of these devout and reforming Jews. And the same should be our resolution with respect to the house and worship of God under the gospel ; we certainly are under no less obligations to frequent Christian assemblies and keep up public worship than they were ; we stand in as much need of these helps and advantages as they did. *Jesus Christ, as lord of his own house, has appointed divers ordinances to be observed. There must be an assembly of people meeting together for the public administration of these holy ordinances. There must be some proper and convenient places appointed and agreed upon for such religious assemblies where they can be had.* Some have learned to condemn all assemblies but their own, and every way of worship but what agrees with theirs. I shall leave it to every man's conscience where (according to the best light he can get) he thinks himself obliged ordinarily to worship God. *There are particular times and seasons for the holding these religious assemblies.* Reason tells us, if God is to be worshipped there must be a set time for it. Which day of the week is designed, and ought to be observed, for this stated worship is not agreed among all those that yet are heartily affected to the worship of God itself   Seventh day ? First day ? *There are certain persons, whose work and duty it is to go before others in these holy administrations.* Who they are that have this authority I list not now to contend. Some have

the charity as well as modesty to nullify all administrations besides their own.

3. *That we will promote as far as in us lies the interests of religion, and spread the kingdom of Christ in the world.* It's not the good of this or that particular Church and society only, but the whole interest of Christ as opposed to the devil's kingdom in the world, whose welfare and prosperity we are bound to seek.

II. It is not only lawful, but may be useful and expedient, for Christians in societies to engage themselves to God, and the duties they owe to him and one another. This people agreed together as one man, and bound themselves by a solemn covenant, which was written and subscribed, sealed and sworn to, that they would never forsake the house of the Lord their God. What I would gather from this instance is, that as this people did, Christians may voluntarily agree together, and engage themselves in particular societies to carry on a work for God in such a way as is warranted by his word, and judged by themselves most likely to promote some valuable end. I shall,

III. Offer reasons both for making this resolution and obliging ourselves to make it good. 1. *Because it is God's house.* Everything that is his should be sacred and dear to us. It is his house we are to frequent; they are his ordinances on which we attend. His word is preached and heard. His interest we oblige ourselves to support. They carry his image and superscription; this gives them their worth and value. (1) To forsake God's house would be to forsake our own mercies, and deprive ourselves of the most valuable blessing in the whole world. *In God's house we are sure to meet with the truest pleasure and satisfaction. They that come crowding to God's house, shall be sent away rejoicing to their own, with the greatest benefit and advantage.* Here we may hope to have our doubts resolved, our darkness scattered, and temptations most effectually vanquished. *With that which will prove the firmest and most effectual support to us under all the troubles of life and at the near approach of death.* (2) To leave this house is to forsake the place which God himself hath chosen, and where he delights to dwell. He loveth the gates of Zion. Is it not good for us to be near to God? Has he said, Here will I dwell?—and should not we for that reason say, Here will we dwell? (3) To forsake this house is to forsake God himself. We cannot quit the inheritance of the Lord but in effect we go and serve other gods. To what houses will they resort that have once forsaken God's house? With what company will they associate, and in what assemblies may we expect to find those that have renounced the communion of saints? 2. *Because our particular good is lodged in the public interest.* In seeking we seek ourselves. At the same time that we discharge our duty we consult our interests. No service performed to Christ shall lose its reward. No man shall kindle a fire on God's altar, or shut a door in his house, for nought. It is then likely to go well with our own houses when due care is taken that it may go well with God's house. 3. *This is the noblest way of imitating the great God himself, and conforming to the example of our blessed Saviour.* Thou art good, O Lord, and thou doest good. To be like God is our truest glory, and should be our highest ambition. Herein also we imitate the shining example of Jesus Christ. "The zeal of thine house hath eaten me up." His anger at the profanation of the temple rose up to an holy indignation. 4. *This makes men real blessings to the world.* However they may be esteemed by others, they really are the strength and security of a nation; the stay and support of the public interest: they bear up the pillars of the earth, and keep it from being quite dissolved. For their sakes God sometimes preserves others from those judgments which their crying sins would otherwise pull down upon their guilty heads. Sodom had been preserved for the sake of ten righteous persons, could so many have been found in the place. 5. *This will be our rejoicing and comfort another day. Having* *made this resolution we must oblige our-selves to make it good. Because of the deceitfulness and inconstancy of our hearts. Such engagements will help to fix us more firmly in the interests of religion, and make us more successful in resisting all temptations to apostasy.*

Hereby we are rendered more capable of serving the interests of religion. A force when united becomes the stronger. The joint concurrence of many give a great advantage to a design, and a better prospect of success.—Matthew Clarke 1715 ; abridged.

ADDENDA TO CHAPTER X.

TITHES.

Without inquiring into the reason for which the number ten has been so frequently preferred as a number of selection in the cases of tribute offerings, both sacred and secular, voluntary and compulsory, we may remark that numerous instances of its use are found both in profane and also in Biblical history, prior to, or independently of, the appointment of the Levitical tithes under the law. In Biblical history the two prominent instances are—1. Abram presenting the tenth of all his property, according to the Syrian and Arabic versions of Heb. vii , but as the passages themselves appear to show, of the spoils of his victory, to Melchizedek (Gen. xiv. 20 ; Heb. vii. 2, 6). 2. Jacob, after his vision at Luz, devoting a tenth of all his property to God in case he should return home in safety (Gen. xxviii. 22). These instances bear witness to the antiquity of tithes, in some shape or other, previous to the Mosaic tithe system. But numerous instances are to be found of the practice of heathen nations, Greeks, Romans, Carthaginians, Arabians, of applying tenths derived from property in general, from spoil, from confiscated goods, or from commercial profits, to sacred, and quasi-sacred, and also to fiscal, purposes, viz. as consecrated to a deity, presented as a reward to a successful general, set apart as a tribute to a sovereign, or as a permanent source of revenue. . . . .

The first enactment of the law in respect of tithes is the declaration that the tenth of all produce, as well as of flocks and cattle, belongs to Jehovah, and must be offered to him. 2. That the tithe was to be paid in kind, or, if redeemed, with an addition of one-fifth to its value (Lev. xxvii. 30—33) This tenth is ordered to be assigned to the Levites, as the reward of their service, and it is ordered further, that they are themselves to dedicate to the Lord a tenth of these receipts, which is to be devoted to the maintenance of the high priest (Num. xviii. 21—28).

This legislation is modified or extended in the Book of Deuteronomy, i e. from thirty-eight to forty years later. Commands are given to the people— 1. To bring their tithes, together with their votive and other offerings and first-fruits, to the chosen centre of worship, the metropolis, there to be eaten in festive celebration, in company with their children, their servants, and the Levites (Deut. xii. 5—18). 2. After warnings against idolatrous, or virtually idolatrous, practices, and the definition of clean as distinguished from unclean animals, among which latter class the swine is of obvious importance in reference to the subject of tithes, the legislator proceeds to direct that all the produce of the soil shall be tithed every year (ver. 17 seems to show that corn, wine, and oil, alone are intended), and that these tithes, with the firstlings of the flock and herd, are to be eaten in the metropolis. 3. But in case of distance, permission is given to convert the produce into money, which is to be taken to the appointed place, and there laid out in the purchase of food for a festal celebration, in which the Levite is, by special command, to be included (Deut xiv. 22—27). 4 Then follows the direction, that at the end of three years, *i e* in the course of the third and sixth years of the Sabbatical period, all the tithe of that year is to be gathered and laid up "within the gates," *i.e.* probably in some central place in each district, not at the metropolis; and that a festival is to be held, in which the stranger, the fatherless, and the widow, together with the Levite, are to partake 5. Lastly, it is ordered that after taking the tithe in each third year, "which is the year of tithing," an exculpatory declaration is to be made by every Israelite that he has done his best to fulfil the Divine command (Deut. xxvi 12—14). From all this we gather—1 That one-tenth of the whole produce of the soil was to be assigned for the maintenance of the Levites. 2. That out of this the Levites were to dedicate a tenth to God, for the use of the high priest. 3 That a tithe, in all probability a *second* tithe, was to be applied to festival purposes. 4 That in every third year, either this festival tithe or a *third* tenth was to be eaten in company with the poor and the Levites. . . .

Ewald thinks that under the kings the ecclesiastical tithe system reverted to what he supposes to have been its original free-will character. It is plain that during that period the tithe system partook of the general neglect into which the observance of the law declined, and that Hezekiah, among his other reforms, took effectual means to revive its use (2 Chron. xxxi. 5, 12, 19) Similar measures were taken after the Captivity by Nehemiah (Neh. xii. 44), and in both these cases special officers were appointed to take charge of the stores and store-houses for the purpose The practice of tithing especially for relief of

the poor appears to have subsisted even in Israel, for the prophet Amos speaks of it, though in an ironical tone, as existing in his day (Amos iv. 4) But as any degeneracy in the national faith would be likely to have an effect on the tithe-system, we find complaint of neglect in this respect made by the prophet Malachi (iii 8, 10) Yet, notwithstanding partial evasion or omission, the system itself was continued to a late period in Jewish history, and was even carried to excess by those who, like the Pharisees, affected peculiar exactness in observance of the law (Heb. vii. 5, 8; Matt xxiii. 23; Luke xviii. 12) Among details relating to the tithe payments mentioned by Rabbinical writers may be noticed . (1) That in reference to the permission given in case of distance (Deut. xiv. 24), Jews dwelling in Babylonia, Ammon, Moab, and Egypt, were considered as subject to the law of tithe in kind (2) In tithing sheep the custom was to enclose them in a pen, and as the sheep went out at the opening, every tenth animal was marked with a rod dipped in vermilion. This was "the passing under the rod." The law ordered that no inquiry should be made whether the animal were good or bad, and that if the owner changed it, both the original and the changeling were to be regarded as devoted (Lev. xxvii 32, 33; Jer xxxiii 13). (3) Cattle were tithed in and after August, corn in and after September, fruits of trees in and after January. (4) "Corners" were exempt from tithe. (5) The general rule was, that all edible articles not purchased were titheable, but that products not specified in Deut. xiv. 23 were regarded as doubtful Tithe of them was not forbidden, but was not required.—*Rev. H. W. Phillot, M A., in Smith's 'Bible Dictionary'*

SENTENCES FROM OLD WRITERS.

Now those that sealed were, Nehemiah the Tirshatha —"He is first mentioned, not as a priest, but as a provost, and one that held it an honour to be first in so good a matter. The life of the

prince is the load-star of the people, upon which most men fix their eyes and shape their courses. Great men draw many by their examples, they are as looking-glasses by which others dress themselves. And hence Nehemiah's forwardness here to seal first." "Those that are above others in dignity and power should go before them in the way of God." *The priests*—"They that lead in prayers should lead in every other good work." *The chief of the people.*—"Great men never look so great as when they encourage religion." "They that have interest must use it for God." *All they that had separated themselves.*—"In St Paul's sense 'come out from among them,' from such stand off, stand up from the dead, save yourselves from this untoward generation; shun their sins, lest ye share in their plagues. These holy separates, or proselytes, sealed the covenant, and became free denizens of the commonwealth of Israel." *Entered into a curse.*—"The more to confirm the oath, and to keep their deceitful hearts close to God." "If he that firmly purposeth often faileth, what shall he do that seldom purposeth any thing, or with little resolvedness?" *To walk in God's law.* —"To walk accurately and exactly by line and by rule in all the commandments so far as God should assist them. The bowls of the candlestick have no oil but what droppeth from the olive branches. Condition with the Lord for his strength and grace." *That they would not intermarry.*— "In our covenants with God we should engage particularly against those sins that we have been most frequently overtaken in and damaged by. They that resolve to keep the commandments of God must say to evil doers, Depart." "By the rib, as by a ladder, Satan oft climbs to the heart and corrupts it." "Every man when he marrieth, brings either a good or an evil spirit into his house, and so make it either a heaven or a hell." *If the people of the land bring ware on the Sabbath day,* &c.—"The Sabbath is a market day for our souls." *And the exaction of every debt we would leave.*— "Those are stubborn children indeed that will not mend the fault which they have been particularly corrected for." *Also we made ordinances for us*—"Having covenanted against the sins they had been guilty of, they proceed in obliging themselves to revive and observe the duties they had neglected. We must not only cease to do evil, but learn to do well." *The temple service.*—"Let not any people expect the blessing of God unless they make conscience of observing his ordinances." *The third part of a shekel.*—"Thankfulness is measured, both by God and good men, not by the weight, but by the will, of the retributor. God doth highly accept the small offerings of his weak servants when he seeth them to proceed from great love." *The wood offering*—"They provided the fire and the wood as well as the lambs for a burnt-offering." *The first-fruits.*—"God required to be honoured with the firstlings of all, to show how he sets by our young services." *To bring to the house of our God unto the priests.*—"No man might offer his own sacrifice, though it were never so good, but present it to the priest, who was to offer as well the poor man's lamb as the rich man's ox."

CHAPTER XI.

EXPLANATORY NOTES] "This chapter is intimately connected with chapter vii. 4, showing Nehemiah's plan of increasing the population of the city. The genealogies and then the confession and covenant come in parenthetically—the former as part of the process in the plan, and the latter as chronologically happening while Nehemiah was maturing the plan."—*Crosby*] "The first sentence, ver 1, 'And the rulers of the people dwelt at Jerusalem,' cannot be so closely connected with the next, 'And the rest of the people cast lots,' &c, as to place the rulers in direct contrast to the rest of the people, but must be understood by its retrospect to vii. 4, which gives the following contrast: The rulers of the people dwelt at Jerusalem, but few of the people dwelt there; to this is joined the next sentence· 'And the rest of the people cast lots.' The 'rest of the people' does not mean the assembled people with the exception of the rulers, but the people with the exception of the few who dwelt at Jerusalem. These cast lots to bring one of ten to dwell in Jerusalem."—*Keil.* The holy city] "The predicate, the holy city, occurs here and ver. 18 for the first time Jerusalem is so called, on the ground of the prophecies (Joel iii. 17 and Isa. xlviii. 2), because the sanctuary of God, the temple, was there."—*Keil.* 3 The chief of the province] *i. e.* Judea. "Nehemiah speaks of it as it then was, a small appendix of the present empire"—*Jamieson.* Israel] "This general name, which designated the descendants of Jacob, before the unhappy division of the two kingdoms under Rehoboam, was restored after the captivity, the Israelites being then united with the Jews, and all traces of their former separation being obliterated. Although the majority of the returned exiles belonged to the tribes of Judah and Benjamin, they are here called Israel; because a large number out of all the tribes were now intermingled, and these were principally the occupiers of the rural villages, while none but those of Judah and Benjamin resided in Jerusalem."—*Jamieson.* 11. The ruler of the house of God] "Assistant of the high priest (Num. iii. 32 ; 1 Chron. ix. 11 ; 2 Chron. xix. 11)."—*Jamieson.* 16 The oversight of the outward business of the house of God] Building, furniture, and things necessary for temple worship. 17 The principal to begin the thanksgiving in prayer] The precentor 23 It was the king's commandment] The king is not David, but the Persian king Artaxerxes (Ezra vii 12, *seq.*). 24 Pethahiah . . . was at the king's hand in all matters concerning the people] "This can scarcely be understood of a royal commissioner at Jerusalem, but certainly designates an official transacting the affairs of the Jewish community at the hand of the king, at his court"—*Keil.* 25—36.] "The heads, who with their houses inhabited country districts, are here no longer enumerated, but only the towns, with their adjacent neighbourhoods, which were inhabited by Jews and Benjamites, and even these are but summarily mentioned"—*Keil.* 36 Of the Levites, &c.]—"Rather for the Levites, *i. e.* those who were not resident in Jerusalem were distributed in settlements throughout the provinces of Judah and Benjamin."—*Jamieson.*

HOMILETICAL CONTENTS OF CHAPTER XI.

THE HOLY CITY REPLENISHED.

xi. 1—19. *And the rulers of the people dwelt at Jerusalem: the rest of the people also cast lots, to bring one of ten to dwell in Jerusalem the holy city, &c.*

JERUSALEM is called here the holy city, because there the temple was, and that was the place God had chosen to put his name there Upon this account one would think the holy seed should all have chosen to dwell there. They declined, however. Either—1. *Because a greater strictness of conversation was expected from the inhabitants of Jerusalem than from others, which they were not willing to come up to* Those who care not for being holy themselves are shy of dwelling in a holy city. They would not dwell in the New Jerusalem itself for that reason, but would wish to have a continuing city here on earth. Or—2. *Because Jerusalem, of all places, was most hated by the heathen, their neighbours, and against it their malicious designs were levelled, which made that the post of danger, as the post of honour uses to be, and therefore they were not willing to expose themselves there.* Fear of persecution and reproach, and running themselves into trouble, keeps many out of the holy city, and makes them backward to appear for God and religion; not considering that as Jerusalem is with a special malice threatened and insulted by its enemies, so it is with special care protected by its God, and made a quiet habitation. Or—3. *Because it was more for their worldly advantage to dwell in the country.* Jerusalem was no trading city, and therefore there was no money to be got there by merchandises, as there was in the country by corn and cattle. "All seek their own, not the things that are Jesus Christ's" It is a general and just complaint, that most people prefer their own wealth, credit, pleasure, ease, and safety before the glory of God and the public good. People being thus backward to dwell at Jerusalem now it was poor, we are here told—

I. By what means it was replenished. 1. *The rulers dwelt there.* That was the proper place for them to reside in, because there were set the thrones of judgment, and thither in all difficult matters the people resorted with their last appeals. And if it were an instance of eminent affection to the house of God, zeal for the public good, and of faith, and holy courage, and self-denial, to dwell there at this time, the rulers would be examples of these to their inferiors. Their dwelling there would invite and encourage others to dwell there too. "the mighty are magnetic." When great men would choose the holy city for their habitation, it brings holiness into reputation, and their zeal will provoke very many. 2. *There were some that "willingly offered themselves to dwell at Jerusalem," bravely postponing their own secular interest to the public welfare.* It is upon record, to their honour, that when others were shy of venturing upon difficulty, loss, and danger, they sought the good of Jerusalem, because of the house of the Lord their God : they shall prosper that thus love Zion. It is said the people blessed them. They praised them, they prayed for them, they praised God for them. Many that do not appear forward themselves for the public good will yet give a good word to those that do. God and man will bless those that are public blessings, which should encourage us to be zealous in doing good. 3. *They, finding that yet there was room, concluded, upon a review of their whole body, to bring one in ten to dwell in Jerusalem ; and who they should be was determined by lot, the disposal whereof all knew was of the Lord.* This would prevent strife, and would be a great satisfaction to those on whom the lot fell to dwell at Jerusalem, that they plainly saw God appointing the bounds of their habitations. The proportion they observed of one in ten, as we may suppose it to bring the balance between the city and country to a just and equal poise, so it seems to refer to the ancient rule of giving the tenth to God And what is given to the holy city he reckons given to himself

II. By what persons it was replenished. A general account is here given of the inhabitants of Jerusalem, because the governors of Judah looked upon them as their strength in the Lord of Hosts their God, and valued them accordingly (Zech. xii. 5) 1. *Many of the children of Judah and Benjamin dwelt there.* Originally part of the city lay in the lot of one of those tribes and part in that of the other ; but the greater part was in the lot of Benjamin ; hence more families of that tribe abode in the city. Those of Judah all descended from Perez or Pharez, that son of Judah "of whom as concerning the flesh Christ came." The men of Judah were valiant men, fit for service, and able to defend the city in case of an attack. Judah has not lost its ancient character of a lion's whelp—bold and daring. Of the Benjamites that dwell in Jerusalem we are here told who was overseer and who his second (ver. 9) , for it is as necessary for a people to have good order kept up among themselves as to be fortified against the attacks of their enemies from abroad,—to have good magistrates as to have good soldiers. 2. *The priests and Levites did many of them settle at Jerusalem.* Where else should men that were holy to God dwell but in the holy city? *Most of the priests* we may suppose dwelt there ; for their business lay where the temple was. It is well those labourers were not few (vers. 12—14). It was said of some of them that they were mighty men of valour (ver. 14) ; and so they had need, for the priesthood was not only a work which required might, but a warfare which required valour especially now. Of one of these priests it is said he was "the son of one of the great men," and it was no disparagement to the greatest man they had to have his son in the priesthood ; he might magnify his office, for his office did not in the least diminish him. *Some of the Levites* also came and dwelt at Jerusalem ; yet but few in comparison. Much of their work was to teach the good knowledge of God up and down the country, for which purpose they were to be scattered in Israel. As many as there was occasion for attended at Jerusalem ; the rest were doing good elsewhere.—*Matthew Henry.*

THE HOLY CITY.

xi. 1. *Jerusalem the holy city.*

A sacred temple and a holy city—aids to faith in history of chosen people. Consecrated worshippers befit consecrated place.

I. The sacred city. *Names* —Jerusalem, " the foundation of peace ;" Ariel, " the unconquerable ;" or, as others, " the hearth of God," *i e* the sacred hearth on which the unquenched fire burnt "The Holy City." As here. In later Arabic names. In Matthew's Gospel. *Central position* —" I have set Jerusalem in the midst of the nations and countries round about her " (Ezek. v. 5). In Hereford Cathedral there is a map of the world with Jerusalem as literal centre. " The world is like to an eye ; the white of the eye is the ocean surrounding the world ; the black is the world itself ; the pupil is Jerusalem, and the image in the pupil, the temple." — *Rabbins.* Central to the people of the country. The mother-city. The seat of government. The home of the priests. " Thither the tribes go up." Its " *elevation*," says Dean Stanley, " is remarkable ; occasioned not from its being on the summit of one of the numerous hills of Judea, like most of the towns and villages, but because it is on the edge of one of the highest table lands of the country. To the traveller approaching the city from the east or west it must always have presented the appearance beyond any other capital of the then known world—we may say beyond any important city that has ever existed on the earth—of a mountain city ; breathing, as compared with the sultry plains of Jordan, a mountain air ; enthroned, as compared with Jericho or Damascus, Gaza or Tyre, on a mountain fastness." *An impregnable city.* Ravines and mountains. Natural position accounts for compactness. Hence Scripture references to the Mount of God ; the kings are higher than the kings of the earth ; the mountains are round about Jerusalem ; Zion stands for ever.

Illustrations : " I have set Jerusalem in the midst of the nations and countries that are round about her " " In later times this passage was taken in the literal sense that Palestine, and Jerusalem especially, was actually the centre of the earth ; a belief of which the memorial is yet preserved in the large round stones still kissed devoutly by Greek pilgrims, in their portion of the Church of the Holy Sepulchre. It is one of the many instances in which the innocent fancy of an earlier faith has been set aside by the discoveries of later science In the East probably there are still many points of this kind which have been long surrendered in the more stirring West. But there was a real truth in it at the time that the prophet wrote, which the subsequent course of history makes it now difficult for us to realize. Palestine, though now at the very outskirts of that tide of civilization, which has swept far into the remotest West, was then the vanguard of the Eastern, and therefore, of the civilized world, and, moreover, stood midway between the two great seats of ancient empire, Babylon and Egypt. It was on the high road from one to the other of these mighty powers, the prize for which they contended, the battle-field on which they fought, the lofty bridge over which they ascended and descended respectively into the deep basins of the Nile and Euphrates." —*Stanley*

" Upon the broad and elevated promontory within the fork of the valleys of Jehoshaphat and Hinnom, lies the Holy City. All around are higher hills , on the east, the Mount of Olives , on the south, the Hill of Evil Counsel, so called, rising directly from the vale of Hinnom , on the west, the ground rises gently, to the borders of the Great Wady ; while on the north, a bend of the ridge connected with the Mount of Olives bounds the prospect at the distance of more than a mile. Towards the S.W the view is somewhat more open ; for here lies the plain of Rephaim, commencing just at the southern brink of the valley of Hinnom, and stretching off S.W., where it runs to the western sea. In the N W. too the eye reaches up along the upper part of the valley of Jehoshaphat, and from many points can discern the mosque of *Neby Samuel*, situated on a lofty ridge beyond the great Wady, at the distance of two hours."—*Robinson*.

The Mount of Olives overtops even the highest part of the city by rather more than 100 feet, and the Temple Hill by no less than 300 Its northern and southern outliers—the Viri Galilæi, Scopus, and Mount of Offence — bend round slightly towards the City, and give the effect of standing round about Jerusalem. Especially would this be the case to a worshipper in the temple."—*Grove*.

II. The sacred city a sacred symbol. " The Holy City." " The City of our

God." What is the all-time significance?
A consecrated commonwealth. City and
temple sacred. Festivals and fast-days,
working-days and worshipping-days—all
God's. "Her merchandise shall be holiness to the Lord." "There shall not a
hoof be left behind." On all things
look for the image and superscription of
God. Will the City of Vision descend?
Or shall we ascend to it? The city lieth
four square. Its twelve gates are open
continually. It has no temple. There
is no sacred spot because the city is the
Lord's; and all it contains. Bernard
sings of "Jerusalem the golden."

Illustrations: "Narrow as are its boundaries,
we have all a share in the possession. What
a church is to a city "Palestine is to the world."
—'*Crescent and the Cross.*'

"Not only has the long course of ages invested
the prospects and scenes of the Holy Land with
poetical and moral associations, but these scenes
accommodate themselves to such parabolical
adaptation with singular facility . . . . The
passage of the Red Sea — the murmurings at
the ' waters of strife '—the ' wilderness ' of life
—the 'Rock of Ages,' Mount Sinai and its
terrors—the view from Pisgah—the passage of
the Jordan—the rock of Zion, the fountain of
Siloa, and the shades of Gehenna—the lake of
Genuesareth, with its storms, its waves, and its
fishermen—are well-known instances in which
the local features of the Holy Lands have naturally
become the household imagery of Christendom."
—*Stanley.*

"The Gospel Church is called *Jerusalem* in
her is the peculiar presence of God, in her the
tribes of holy men meet and serve him. O how
beautiful and compact her form !—how firm her
foundation ! — how strongly fortified and protected, by the laws, perfections, and providences
of God !—how rich, wealthy, and free her true
members !—how readily they welcome others to
reside with them ! The heavenly state of glory
is called *Jerusalem*, or the *new Jerusalem*."—
Wood.

The Secular in Sacred Service.

xi. 16. *The outward business of the house of God.*

Outward and inward—a law of life as
of temple service. In the temple of this
world some of us must have the oversight of the outward business of the
house of God. "The priests were chief
managers of the business within the
temple gates, but this Levite was intrusted with the secular concerns of
God's house, that were 'subservient to
its spiritual concerns,' the collecting
of the contributions, the providing of
materials for the temple service, and the
like, which it was necessary to oversee,
else the inward business would have
been starved and stood still. Those
that take care of ' the outward concerns '
of the Church, the serving of its tables,
are as necessary in their place as those
that take care of 'its inward concerns,'
who give themselves to the word and
prayer."—*Matthew Henry.*

I. **It is possible to secularise the
sacred.** When sacred service is entered
upon from secular motives; when it is
performed in a perfunctory manner;
when any object less than God is regarded in its performance, we must
needs pray for the forgiveness of the
iniquity of our holy things. Eli's sons
were in the tabernacle. Priests of all
religions have worshipped at an altar
desecrated by their presence. An unhallowed hand may not bear up an ark.
The grimmest pages of history are associated with holy service marred by
unholy ambitions — by envy, hatred,
malice, and all uncharitableness. A
cowl does not make a monk. High
office cannot elevate a base man.

> " The churl in spirit howe'er he veil
> His want in forms for fashion's sake,
> Will let his coltish nature break
> At seasons through the gilded pale :
> For who can always act? but he,
> To whom a thousand memories call,
> Not being less but more than all
> The gentleness he seemed to be."

"As a man thinketh in his heart, so
is he."

II. **It is necessary to make the
secular sacred.** "He can who thinks
he can." Paul's application of the old
fable in 1 Cor. xii. 14—26, "I had
rather be a doorkeeper," &c. The Christian members of one of our religious
communities annually covenant with
God thus—"Make me what thou wilt,
Lord, and set me where thou wilt; let

me be a vessel of silver or gold, or a vessel of wood or stone, so I be a vessel of honour; of whatsoever form or metal, whether higher or lower, finer or coarser, I am content. If I be not the head, or the eye, or the ear, one of the nobler and more honourable instruments thou wilt employ; let me be the hand or the foot, one of the most laborious, and lowest, and most contemptible, of all the servants of my Lord." Application. 1. *The secret of contentment.* "Self-humiliation is full of truth and reality." The hidden life more secure than the outer life. Circumstances change, character is permanent. Look within. "I know both how to be abased, and I know how to abound," &c. 2. *The law of growth.* Develope thyself. "To be," differs from "to have." Be thy ambition to become pure in thought and feeling, strong in resolve and deed. Serve. Care not how, mind not where. "Inasmuch as ye have done unto one of the least of these, my brethren," &c. And we may add—and inasmuch as ye have rendered *the least service* to the least of these, my brethren, ye have rendered it unto me. But, like the angels, let us serve our brethren "all for love, and nothing for reward."

THE SERVICE OF SONG IN THE HOUSE OF THE LORD.

xi. 22, 23. *Of the sons of Asaph, the singers were over the business of the house of God. For it was the king's commandment concerning them, that a certain portion should be for the singers, due for every day.*

Music is the hand-maid of religion. Were we treating of music in general, and not of it in relation to religious life, we must treat of the science of music as developed in the East and West, as it has been affected in Catholic countries, and influenced by the Reformation. But our text-book is the Bible. The theme is the service of song in the house of the Lord. Music in the sanctuary is the music of the Hebrews, as it has come down to, and been developed in, the Christian Church.

Those who have deeply studied this subject inform us that the science of music amongst the Hebrews is only conjectural. But the practice of music meets us on almost every page of Hebrew history. In Gen. iv. we have an account of the first poet; the first dweller in tents, the first forger of metals, and the first musician—all descendants of Cain. "Jubal was the father of all such as handle the harp and organ"—the harp standing as the representative of all stringed, and the organ of all wind, instruments. Attempts have been made to explain how this discovery of Jubal's was handed down till after the Flood. But, as Mr Aldis Wright, to whose article on music in Smith's 'Bible Dictionary,' I am indebted for these historic facts, says, "Conjectures are worse than an honest confession of ignorance. The Flood did not wash away every musical instrument, and for ever deprive the world of the solace which music gives. The shepherds of the uplands of Syria knew how to chase away care with songs, and thrill the emotions with tabret and harp. 'Wherefore didst thou fly away secretly?' said Laban to Jacob, 'and didst not tell me, that I might have sent thee away with mirth, and with songs, with tabret and harp.' On the banks of the Red Sea, Moses and the children of Israel sang their song of triumphal deliverance, and Miriam led a procession of women chanting in chorus: 'Sing ye to Jehovah, for he hath triumphed gloriously; the horse and his rider hath he thrown into the sea.' The song was accompanied by timbrels and dances; probably Miriam sang the solos, and the women took up the chorus; for it is said, 'Miriam answered them.' "

Music was early employed in the service of idolatry. You will recall the musical instruments when the image of gold was set up in the plains of Dura. An earlier instance is in connection with the golden calf which Aaron made. As Moses and Joshua came down from the mountain on which they had received the two tables of the law, a strange sound saluted their ears. To Joshua it seemed like a war-shout, but Moses said, "It is not the voice of them that shout for the mastery, neither is it the voice of them that cry being overcome, but the noise of them that sing do I hear." Rude and uncultivated must such music have been. Could much variation have been played on those silver trumpets which were used to intimate, the striking of the tents and resuming of the wilderness journeys? Would those rams' horns with which the priests brought down the walls of Jericho, or those trumpets which Gideon's three hundred men blew, have been like the sound of one that had a pleasant voice and could play well on an instrument? The song of Deborah and Barak is metrical, and was probably intended to be sung with musical accompaniment as one of the people's songs, like that with which Jephthah's daughter and her companions met Jephthah on his victorious return. The song with which the women of Israel hailed David after the slaughter of the Philistine was perhaps struck off on the excitement of the moment. "They came out of all cities of Israel, singing and dancing, to meet King Saul with tabrets, with joy, and instruments of music. And the women answered one another as they played, and said, Saul has slain his thousands, and David his ten thousands."

So far there appears, to have been no systematic cultivation of music. When, however, the schools of the prophets were instituted music was taught. Professional musicians were attached to the king's person. David played before Saul. And when David became king he had about him singing men and singing women. Solomon says, "I gat me men singers and women singers." He composed songs. When the ark was brought from the house of Obed-edom there must have been many skilled musicians in the country. With Chenaniah, the master of the song, at their head, David and the Levites brought up the ark with shouting, and with sound of the cornet, and with trumpets, and with cymbals, making a noise with psalteries and harps. Probably the Levites had all along practised music. Living a peaceful life they would be attracted to this peaceful art. It is likely that some SERVICE OF SONG was used in the tabernacle. But be this as it may, David was the patron, and the temple was the school, of music. The three divisions of the tribe of Levi had a representative family in the temple choir. David composed and taught them a chant. For ages it was used as David's, and was sung on three great occasions—before the army of Jehoshaphat, on laying the foundation of the second temple; and by the army of the Maccabees. The chant is Psalm cxxxvi. Women were in the temple choir. We read of Heman's three daughters. Among those who returned from the captivity with Zerubbabel were two hundred singing men and singing women. Amongst the instruments played before the ark were trumpets, which appear to have been reserved for the priests. Being also employed in royal proclamations they set forth by way of symbol, the royalty of Jehovah, and sounded the alarm against his enemies. At the dedication of Solomon's temple one hundred and twenty priests blew the trumpets, while the Levites with their instruments *made one sound to be heard in praising the Lord.* And in the restoration of worship by Hezekiah, when the burnt offering began *the song of Jehovah* began also, with the trumpets, and with the instruments of David, King of Israel. And all the congregation worshipped, and the singers sang, and the trumpeters sounded all until the burnt offering was finished. The altar was, in Scripture phraseology, the table of Jehovah, and the sacrifices were his feasts. And as at kings' tables the musicians play, so at the table of the King of kings was this service rendered. The temple was God's palace, and as the Levite sentries guarded the gates they sang, "Bless ye the Lord, all ye servants of the Lord, which by night stand in the house of the Lord. Lift up your hands in the sanctuary, and bless the Lord." Many of the psalms we know were temple-songs. Of David's influence on Hebrew song let an English poet speak—

> " The harp the monarch-minstrel swept,
> The king of men, the loved of Heaven,
> Which music hallowed while she wept,
> O'er tones her heart of hearts had given,
> Redoubled be her tears, its choids are riven !

> " It softened men of iron mould,
> It gave them virtues not their own ,
> No ear so dull, no soul so cold,
> That felt not, fired not to the tone,
> Till David's lyre grew mightier than his throne !

> " It told the triumphs of our king,
> It wafted glory to our God ;
> It made our gladdened valleys ring,
> The cedars bow, the mountains nod ,
> Its sound aspired to heaven, and there abode !

> " Since then, though heard on earth no more,
> Devotion, and her daughter Love,
> Still bid the bursting spirit soar,
> To sounds that seem as from above,
> In dreams that day's broad light cannot remove."

Solomon provided for the singers with the same munificence with which he adorned the temple.

But although music was consecrated in the temple it was not confined to the temple. Whatever adorns God's service reacts on the homes and haunts of men. Music was enthroned in the temple, but it made its familiar abode in the homes of the Hebrew people. Kings had court musicians. And in the degenerate days of the later monarchs, the prophet tells us of the effeminate gallants of Israel stretched on beds of ivory, covered with perfumes; and as Nero fiddled whilst Rome was in flames, so they amid their nation's wreck chant to the sound of the viol, and invent to themselves instruments of music, like David. But because music may minister to vice that is no reason for deriding it. What may not ? Many a Hebrew home was made joyous after a day of sultry heat, spent among the vines or in the sheep-folds, by family songs. Only when national sin had brought God's curse upon the land could it be said—" All the merry-hearted do sigh. The mirth of tabrets ceaseth, the noise of them that rejoice endeth, the joy of the harp ceaseth. They shall not drink wine with a song." It was when heavy hearts sat by the waters of Babylon that joy-inspiring harps hung on the willows, and cunning hands no longer discoursed sweet music. Their bridal processions were accompanied with music and song. Love had its songs to embody its passion. Sorrow had its funereal chants. The grape-gatherers sang as they gathered in the vintage, and the wine-presses were trodden to the march of music. Women sang as they toiled at the mill. And as long as God smiled approval on the land of the Hebrew people, they were a people of song. Their land was a field which the Lord had blessed.

Music passed into the early Christian Church. Our Lord is found with his disciples singing a hymn. The Man of Sorrows was acquainted with song. " Singing and making melody in your heart to the Lord," is the burden of more than one New Testament passage. Changes it has undergone. By the inroads of barbarians , by the upgrowth of the Reformation ; by modern revolutions ; by persecutions , and by the misguided opposition of conscientious men, the service of song in the house of the Lord has been affected. It has been " chastened, but not killed ; " "cast down, but not destroyed."

Bring song into the sanctuary. The temple choir were Levites. The priests were of the same tribe. Pulpit and choir-gallery both have place. When the preacher fails with the Bible, the choir may succeed with the Hymn Book.

When we pass through the gate into the city we shall sing in. John looked, and lo ! a Lamb stood on the Mount Zion, and with him an hundred and forty and four thousand redeemed from the earth. And he heard a voice as of the voice of many waters, as the voice of a great thunder, and as the voice of harpers, harping with their harps. Let us honour every faculty. Let us cultivate and consecrate our gifts. Let us all use the service of song to praise the Lord, whose mercy— according to David's chant—endureth for ever.

ADDENDA TO CHAPTER XI.

PRIESTS AND THE CONGREGATION.

"It is very worthy of notice that in the numbering of the inhabitants of Jerusalem, not the priests but the tribes of Judah and Benjamin take the lead, and only then follow the priests and Levites ; so much the more worthy of notice, because in the new congregation, following the captivity, according to the entire direction which its development took, and according to everything which was considered as of the greatest moment, the high priests, and the priesthood in general, had a particularly high significance. It is as if the consciousness were indicated, that the priest and Levites, in spite of their distinction, which the Lord hath appointed to them in the affairs of Israel, had been nevertheless nothing at all if they had not had a congregation near and around them, and if they had not succeeded in obtaining satisfactory fruit for their activity, namely, a genuine and true piety, which should substantially prove they were not there in vain. Would also that Christian priests, that is, preachers of the gospel, might preserve a lively consciousness that it is not enough for them to have fellowship with their brethren in office, that they are nothing, and can profit and signify nothing, if not some, if only a small congregation stand by them, in whom the seed which they sow springs up, grows, and bears fruit."

HOLY PEOPLE ON SACRED SOIL.

"When one looks at the space which the Jewish congregation inhabited round Jerusalem, how very small was the territory occupied by the people of God, the only race which possessed a clear knowledge of the only true and holy God ! A few miles, from three to six, north and south, east and west, comprised the entire district. Compared with our countries ; yes, even with our provinces ; this district appears to us almost as a vanishing nothing And nevertheless what powers for the subjugation of entire humanity, for the transformation of all its relations, and for the subduing of all circumstances, has God the Lord been able to put in the people of this oasis, in the, at the same time, insignificant, and in many respects miserable race, which cultivated the ground there, or raised cattle ! If anywhere, surely here arises a testimony for Paul's word, 'God hath chosen the weak things of the world to confound the things which are mighty' (1 Cor. i. 27) A consoling promise also for Christendom in those times, in which it appears as though it were being compressed on all sides, and when it is in truth losing position after position. Let it lose in length and breadth in order afterwards to gain so much the more in height. Even the gates of hell cannot swallow up the Church of the Lord."—*Dr. Schultz, in Lange.*

R

CHAPTER XII.

EXPLANATORY NOTES] "The list of the inhabitants of the province (chap. xi.) is followed by lists of the priests and Levites (xii. 1—26). These different lists are, in fact, all connected with the genealogical register of the whole Israelite population of the province, taken by Nehemiah (vii 5) for the purpose of enlarging the population of Jerusalem . Vers. 1—9 contains a list of the heads of the priests and Levites who returned from Babylon with Zerubbabel and Joshua The high priests during five generations are next mentioned by name (vers. 10, 11). Then follow the names of the heads of the priestly houses, in the days of Joiakim, the high priest; and finally (vers. 22—26), the names of the heads of the Levites at the same period, with titles and subscriptions."—*Keil.* According to *Keil*, "the difference between the names in the two lists of chapters x., xii., is to be explained simply by the fact that the names of those who sealed the covenant (chap. x.) are names neither of orders nor houses, but of heads of houses living in the days of Ezra and Nehemiah Of these names a portion coincides, indeed, with the names of the orders and houses, while the rest are different The sameness of names does not, however, prove that the individuals belonged to the house whose name they bore On the contrary, it appears from xii 13, 16, that of two Meshullams, one was the head of the house of Ezra, the other of the house of Ginnethon " **27. Out of all their places**] The Levites were scattered through the province. **30 Purified themselves . . . people . . . gates . . wall**] This was probably done by the sprinkling of water (Num xix. 18), and the offering of sacrifices (Compare 2 Chron xxix. 21.) "The central point of the solemnity was a procession of two bands of singers upon the wall Nehemiah brought up the princes of Judah upon the wall, and appointed two great companies and two processions These went each upon the wall all in different directions, and stopped opposite each other at the house of God . . . . At the head of one procession went Ezra, the scribe, with one-half of the nobles ; at the head of the second, Nehemiah with the other half "—*Keil.* (See topography of the book of Nehemiah, pages 87—89.) **43 Great sacrifices**] *i. e.* "thank offerings which were eaten by the offerers in a happy feast, after the food of the offering made by fire unto the Lord (Lev iii.)."—*Crosby* With xii. 44, according to *Keil*, Nehemiah's Later Reforms begin, "*at that time* being used in a general sense." *Crosby* differs, referring the phrase to the time of the dedication. *Others* postpone the dedication, making it one of the Later Reforms **44 Portions of the law**] That is, portions prescribed by the law for the priests and Levites (See Num. xviii 20—24; Deut. xviii. 1—8.) **That waited**] Literally, *the ones standing*; that is, standing to minister before the Lord. (Compare Deut x 8.) **45. Kept the ward**] Cared for all that concerned the temple; did their duty faithfully **47 Sanctified unto the Levites**] "To sanctify, said of the bringing of gifts and dues to the ministers of the sanctuary" (comp 1 Chron. xxvi. 27; Lev. xxvii 14) On the matter itself, comp x. 38 *seq*, and Num xviii. 26—29 —*Keil.*

HOMILETICAL CONTENTS OF CHAPTER XII.

THE DEDICATION OF THE WALL.

xii 27—43 *And at the dedication of the wall of Jerusalem they sought the Levites out of all their places, to bring them to Jerusalem, to keep the dedication, &c.*

WE have read of the building of the wall of Jerusalem, with a great deal of fear and trembling; we have here an account of the dedicating of it, with a great deal of joy and triumph. They that sow in tears shall thus reap.

I. We must inquire what was the meaning of this dedication of the wall We will suppose it to include the dedication of the city too—the thing containing for the thing contained; and, therefore, it was not done till the city was pretty well replenished.

1 *It was a solemn thanksgiving to God, for his great mercy to them in the perfecting of this undertaking, which they were the more sensible of, because of the difficulty and opposition they had met with in it.*

2. *They hereby devoted the city in a peculiar manner to God, and to his honour, and took possession of it for him, and in his name.* All our cities, all our houses, must have " Holiness to the Lord " written upon them ; but this city was (so as never any other was) a holy city, the city of the Great King. It had been so ever since God chose it to put his name there, and as such, it being now refitted, it was afresh dedicated to God by the builders and inhabitants, in token of their acknowledgment that they were tenants, and their desire that it might still be his, and that the property of it might never be altered. Whatever is done for their safety, ease, and comfort, must be designed for God's honour and glory.

3. *They hereby put the city and its walls under the Divine protection, owning that, unless the Lord kept the city, the walls were built in vain.* When this city was in possession of the Jebusites, they committed the guardianship of it to their gods, though they were blind and lame ones. With much more reason do the people of God commit it to his keeping who is all-wise and almighty. The superstitious founders of cities had an eye to the lucky position of the heavens, but these pious founders had an eye to God only, to his providence, and not to fortune.

II. **We must observe with what solemnity it was performed, under the direction of Nehemiah.**

1. *The Levites from all parts of the country were summoned to attend.* The city must be dedicated to God ; and therefore his ministers must be employed in the doing of it, and the surrender must pass through their hands. When those solemn feasts were over (chaps. viii. ix.), they had gone home to their respective posts to mind their cares in the country, but now their presence and assistance were again called for.

2. *Pursuant to this summons there was a general rendezvous of all the Levites.* Observe in what method they proceed. (1) They purified themselves. We are concerned to cleanse our hands, and purify our hearts, when any work for God is to pass through them. Themselves they purified, and then the people. They that would be instrumental to sanctify others, must sanctify themselves, and set themselves apart for God with purity of mind and sincerity of intention. Then they purified the gates and the wall. Then may we expect comfort when we are prepared to receive it. " To the pure all things are pure " (Tit. i. 15) ; and to them who are sanctified, houses and tables, and their creature comforts and enjoyments are sanctified (1 Tim. iv. 4, 5). This purification was performed, it is probable, by sprinkling the water of purifying or of separation, as it is called (Num. xix. 9), on themselves and the people, the walls and the gates, a type of the blood of Christ, with which our consciences being purged from dead works, we become fit to serve the living God, and to be his care. (2) The princes, priests, and Levites walked round upon the wall in two companies, to signify the dedication of it all to God, the whole circuit of it. This procession is here largely described ; one end of the ceremony being to affect them with the mercy they were giving thanks for, and to perpetuate the remembrance of it among them.

3. *The people greatly rejoiced.* While the princes, priests, and Levites testified their joy and thankfulness, by great sacrifices, sound of trumpet, musical instruments, and songs of praise, the common people testified theirs by loud shouts, which were heard afar off, farther than the more harmonious sound of their songs and music ; and these shouts coming from a sincere and hearty joy are here taken notice of : for God overlooks not, but graciously accepts, the honest zealous services of mean people, though there be in them little of art, and they are far from being fine. It is observed that the women and children rejoiced ; and their harmonies were not despised but recorded to their praise. All that share in public mercies ought to join in public thanksgivings. The reason given is, that " God had made them rejoice with great joy ; " he had given them both matter for joy and hearts to rejoice ; his providence had made them safe and easy, and then his grace made

them cheerful and thankful. The baffled opposition of their enemies no doubt added to their joy, and mixed triumph with it Great mercies call for the most solemn return of praise, "in the courts of the Lord's house, in the midst of thee, O Jerusalem !"—*Matthew Henry.*

A BOOK.

xii 23 *The chief of the fathers were written in the book of the chronicles.*

THE BOOK OF THE CHRONICLES.

A book is a marvel—why not say a standing miracle?

I A book unites the ages. Brings the past into the present : borrows the future to give the present significance The "sceptred spirits of history " rule us still "The world's grey patriarchs " thought *for us* With books *the poorest enters the highest society · the loneliest need not be solitary.* A good book the truest guide, philosopher, friend.

II. A book reveals life's importance. A book gives permanence to thought, because thoughts sway the world gives permanence to deeds, because if good they encourage, if bad they warn. Life is a writing And with deeper than Pilate's meaning, "What I have written, I have written."

III A book silently anticipates the judgment It is written. A record may be appealed to. Is this thy handwriting? God's "Book of Remembrance."

POSTHUMOUS INFLUENCE.

xii. 24 *The chief of the Levites . . with their brethren over against them, to praise and to give thanks, according to the commandment of David the man of God.*

A man's influence after he is dead. He is still present with his people.

I By his will. "The *commandment* of David." The grip of the dead is on our fields and churches; schools and hospitals.

II. By his writings Immortality of genius. *David's* Psalms. Solomon's proverbs. And outside the circle of sacred history, Shakespeare and Milton, Bunyan, and a thousand others. "Being dead, they yet speak."

III. By his example. "David *the man of God.*" Goodness is greatness. Kind words; good deeds never die. "Let your light shine before men." Intentional influence may fail . unconscious influence cannot For good or evil a man lives. For good or evil his deeds will live after him. "The memory of the just is blessed."

BEGINNING AT THE RIGHT PLACE.

xii. 30 *And the priests and the Levites purified themselves, and purified the people, and the gates, and the wall.*

I A pure Church may make a sound commonwealth. "They purified *themselves.*" Like priest, like people. And as with the people so with the priest. Cleric and laic act and react on each other. Pulpit and pew not two but one All history testifies that an impure priesthood means an impure people "Be ye clean, that bear the vessels of the Lord." Eli's sons. Uzzah may not sustain the ark Jesus swept the temple of the traffickers

II To a pure people all things are pure "They purified the people, and the gates, and the wall " Citizens and city sanctuary and house : God's work and their own

> " All things are sacred
> The eye of God is on them all
> And hallows all "

Jesus revealed God in the minutest. Peter's vision. The present preparatory. "I think our fathers had a better, a grander, a diviner idea even of common life than we have, when they spoke about the trades and professions of men as being their *calling.* We sometimes use the word yet, though it has almost passed out of use. It is a pity, for there is a great thought in it. Why. it makes all the men, streets, shops, and warehouses to me, as I walk along, Divine objects. I feel that I am in a Divine place when I think of the men about me as following their *calling.* I feel that there is a God above men; that there in a God in human society; a God in the shops and counting-houses of London, touching and teaching every human being, and that every man is occupying the place, and putting his hand to the work, to which God has called him. Sometimes you may see a man at a certain calling which is but preparatory. He is meant for something else. Providence opens the way, and he goes up higher and does another thing. God has given us a spiritual vocation—a Divine calling in Jesus Christ, and we are to walk worthy of that vocation, here—doing all worldly things in a spiritual manner, preparatory to a higher calling which shall come one day, when we shall enter upon other forms of duty and service, to which the present inferior forms of duty and service faithfully fulfilled shall gradually prepare and fit us."—*Binney*

A GREAT REJOICING.

xii. 43. *That day they offered great sacrifices, and rejoiced for God had made them rejoice with great joy: the wives also and the children rejoiced · so that the joy of Jerusalem was heard even afar off.*

A great rejoicing as it should be.

I. **Associated with the rites of religion.** "Sacrifices." Holy-day and holiday united. Holy-days joy-bringing times. Holidays not to be dissevered from the sacred nature of those who share them.

II. **The outcome of a great deliverance.** From captivity to freedom : exile to home : heathen surroundings to heaven-chosen city and divinely-built temple. The memory of God's great goodness should awaken joy—a joy that all may share "The wives also and the children rejoiced"

III **The preparation for strong adhesion to the sacred cause.** "The joy of the Lord is your strength." And you must be strong to labour. Sacred festivals not an end but a means to an end. Get to give ; know to communicate; experience to declare, rest to toil; share to serve—this is the will of God concerning us.

TRUE JOY.

xii 43. *That day they offered great sacrifices, and rejoiced.*

I. **Its right** The God who has given us life, wishes also that it shall move joyfully; the God who always anew overwhelms us with favours wishes that they should fulfil their mission; that is, make us happy, in the end holy.

II. **Its occasion.** God's grace, which has strengthened, protected, assured or elevated our lower or higher life. The chief sites in Jerusalem testified to this, and in the Christian Church ; yes, indeed, in our lives, all the heights testify thereof.

III **Its kind** It raises itself to God, is a joy in him, that is, becomes a service to God and our neighbours.—*Dr. Schultz.*

THANKSGIVING AND THANKSLIVING.

xii. 44—47. *And at that time were some appointed over the chambers for the treasures, for the offerings, for the first-fruits, and for the tithes, to gather into them out of the fields of the cities the portions of the law for the priests and Levites : for Judah rejoiced for the priests and for the Levites that waited. And both the singers and the porters kept the ward of their God, &c.*

We have here an account of the remaining good effects of this universal joy that was at the dedication of the wall. When the solemnities of a thanksgiving-day leave such impressions on ministers and people, as that both are more careful and cheerful in doing their duty afterward, then are they indeed acceptable to God, and turn to a good account. So it was here.

I The ministers were more careful than they had been of their work. The respect the people paid them upon this occasion encouraged them to diligence and watchfulness ; "the singers kept the ward of their God," attending in due time to the duty of their office ; the porters too they "kept the ward of the purification," this is, they took care to preserve the purity of the temple, by denying admission to those that were ceremonially unclean. When the joy of the Lord thus engageth us to our duty, and enlargeth us in it, it is then an earnest of that joy which, in concurrence with the perfecting of holiness, will be our everlasting bliss.

II The people were more careful than they had been of the maintenance of their ministers. The people, at the dedication of the wall, among other things which they made matter of their joy, rejoiced "for the priests and the Levites that waited." They had a great deal of comfort in their ministers, and were glad of them ; when they observed how diligently they waited, and what pains they took in their work, they rejoiced in them. The surest way for ministers to recommend themselves to their people, and gain an interest in their affections, is to wait on their ministry, to be humble and industrious, and to mind their business ; when these did so, the people thought nothing too much for them, to encourage them. The law

had provided them their portions ; but what the better were they for that provision, if what the law appointed them either was not duly collected or not justly paid them ?

1. *Care is here taken for the collecting of their dues.* They were modest, and would rather lose their right than call for it themselves ; the people were many of them careless, and would not bring it unless they were called upon ; and therefore "some were appointed" whose office it should be "to gather" in to the treasuries, "out of the fields of the cities, the portions of the law for the priests and Levites," that their portion might not be lost for want of being demanded. This is a piece of good service both to ministers and people, that the one may not come short of their maintenance, nor the other of their duty.

2. *Care is taken that, being gathered in, it might be duly paid out.* They gave the singers and porters their daily portion, over and above what was due to them as Levites ; for we may suppose when David and Solomon appointed them their work, above what was required from them as Levites, they settled a fund for their further encouragement. Let those that labour more abundantly in the word and doctrine be counted worthy of this double honour. As for the other Levites, the tithes, here called the holy things, were duly set apart for them, out of which they paid the priests their tithe according to the law. Both are said to be sanctified. When what is contributed, either voluntarily or by law, for the support of religion, and the maintenance of the ministry, is given with an eye to God and his honour, it is sanctified, and shall be accepted of him accordingly ; and it will cause the blessing to rest on the house, and all that is in it.—*Matthew Henry.*

THE GOOD OLD TIMES.

xii. 46. *The days of old.*

The aged regret, the young despise, these good old times. The old feed on memory, the young on hope. These place the golden age in the future, those in the past.

I. Nothing is necessarily good because it is old. "Hast thou marked the old way which wicked men have trodden?" Habit, education, tradition, prejudice play an important part in history.

II. That which is old is presump-tively valuable. Good lasts. Truth is as old as the hills.

Application. Prove all things. Despise nothing. Gather treasures wherever they can be found. Be not blinded by passion. There is a soul of goodness in things that at first sight seem only evil. The present is a huge borrower from the dead past. Reverence the true word, the saintly deed whenever found. God is all, and in all things bright and good.

CHAPTER XIII.

EXPLANATORY NOTES.] 1. On that day] This is to be understood in the same sense as *at that time*, in chap. xii 44. But no doubt public readings of the law took place frequently during Nehemiah's administration. **Found written**] " The part of the law which forbade mingling with the other nations was specially read on the dedication-day. Deut. xxiii 3 would naturally be read, as also Deut. vii. 1—6. . . . No Moabite or Ammonite family could be admitted to the privileges of Jewry until in the tenth generation after quitting heathenism and formally allying itself with Israel "—*Crosby* **3. They separated from Israel all the mixed multitude**] Non-Israelitish people who followed the Israelites at their departure from Egypt. Here transferred to strangers living among them. **4, 5. Eliashib . . . Tobiah**] Nehemiah left for Persia. Irregularities were permitted. Amongst them this desecration **6 In the two and thirtieth year of Artaxerxes, king of Babylon**] " Probably the 'time set' by Nehemiah and approved by the king (chap. ii. 6), was twelve years. At the expiration of this term he was obliged to leave the superintendence of affairs at Jerusalem and return to the court. Artaxerxes is called 'king of Babylon,' instead of ' king of Persia,' probably because at this time of Nehemiah's return the court was removed to Babylon for some special state reason "—*Crosby.* **After certain days**] No definite interval. Some expositors think a year. No proof. **8 I cast forth all the household stuff of Tobiah**] Nehemiah a man of decision. **10. The Levites and the singers . . were fled**] Their allowance had been withheld. They fled to their own fields for livelihood. **11. Then contended I with the rulers**] They had soon forgotten their vow (chap. x. 39). **I gathered them**] The Levites. **13. I made treasurers**] Managers of the stores. Four faithful men appointed. **14 Wipe not out**] Conceives of his deeds as written in a book. **15. In those days**] When he returned to Jerusalem Sabbath had become desecrated. Work was done and produce brought in **17. The nobles**] Nehemiah reminded them of the unchanged law and the sufferings its visitation had brought upon their fathers (Jer. xvii. 20—27). **20. Lodged without**] The traders forbidden to enter hoped the people would come out to buy **22. Cleanse themselves and keep the gates**] Increasing the sanctity of the Sabbath by making Levites responsible. **23. Jews that had married**] Borderers who by living near the heathen nations had formed alliances. The children's speech was affected. **25**] The action of a governor acting officially. **28. I chased him from me**] Forced him to leave Jerusalem. **30. Thus cleansed I them . . . and appointed the wards of the priests and Levites**] So important did he deem the temple. **31. Remember me**] A repeated supplication. Nehemiah was great and good.

HOMILETICAL CONTENTS OF CHAPTER XIII.

Renewed Purification.

xiii 1—3 *On that day they read in the book of Moses in the audience of the people; and therein was found written, that the Ammonite and the Moabite should not come into the congregation of God for ever, because they met not the children of Israel with bread and with water, but hired Balaam against them, that he should curse them; howbeit our God turned the curse into a blessing. Now it came to pass, when they had heard the law, that they separated from Israel all the mixed multitude.*

The duty of the Church to purify itself constantly anew.

I. In regard to those with whom they assimilate themselves. In the Old Testament, in regard to the Ammonites, &c In the Church, in regard to those who not only go astray, but also who will not allow themselves to be bettered, and who thus exclude themselves.

II. Whereon it grounds itself Not only on the right of self-preservation, but also upon God's word.

III. What it aims at. That the Church set forth more and more what it should be as Christ's spotless bride.— *Dr. Schultz.*

Illustrations The true and grand idea of a Church is a society for the purpose of making men like Christ—earth like heaven—the kingdoms of the world the kingdom of Christ.— *Arnold*

The Irrevocableness of Wrong-doing.

xiii 1, 2. *On that day they read in the book of Moses in the audience of the people, and therein was found written, that the Ammonite and the Moabite should not come into the congregation of God for ever, because they met not the children of Israel with bread and with water, but hired Balaam against them, that he should curse them.*

"The severe exclusion of the Moabite and Ammonite was an enacted token against sin Even these blood relations of Israel were to be kept away as polluted, because they showed no sympathy with Israel, and made a deliberate and vile attempt to plunge Israel into sin. A permanent horror was to be erected between Israel and these monsters of iniquity The key to many of the stern Mosaic statutes is to be found in the necessity of holding up the heinousness of sin, which men are ever ready to make light of "—*Crosby.*

The immortality of evil.

I. It is done—cannot be undone An act has passed into the irreparable past It has become part of the constitution of things Man may forget it, and God forgive it—but it is done. The doer may plead ignorance, prejudice, habit, custom—excuse may busy itself, and regret plead for pity, but the deed is done. Let inexperience remember and

hardness ponder this

II. It has moulded you—you can never again be the same The dyer's hand is subdued to what it works in. A man's trade, profession, or calling is indicated in his features. Habit is a second nature. The beauty of the soul touches the form and face. Vice makes the doer unlovely; stamps its image and superscription upon the otherwise divine form "Be not deceived, God is not mocked," &c

III It has warped others. Their task is rendered more difficult. Their steps will henceforth be more faltering An Ammonite may thwart Israel "Ahab made Israel to sin." That is his title to remembrance—he has an immortality. I am my brother's keeper His path and mine meet I cannot throw off my responsibility. Doing wrong is ruinous Sin is the great foe The wages of sin are duly paid even to the uttermost farthing.

GOOD OUT OF EVIL.

xiii. 2. *Howbeit our God turned the curse into a blessing.*

Nevertheless Balaam's memory is infamous. Evil was intended though God averted it. So in life.

I. Sin. Sin is still sin albeit the sinner is forgiven. God loves not sin. "God hath turned the curse of sin into a blessing. And here it is proper to reflect upon the profound and incomprehensible wisdom of God, who hath made an advantage to us even of our sin and misery. It was truly said by one of the ancients, upon this account, that Job was a happier man upon the dunghill than Adam was in paradise. His holiness indeed was perfect, his happiness was great; but neither of them permanent and indefeasible, as our happiness by the Mediator is. So that in the same sense we may call Adam's fall a happy fall, because ordered and overruled by the wisdom of God to our great advantage. And to this purpose Austin somewhere sweetly speaks. 'O how happily did I fall in Adam, who rose again more happily in Christ!' Thus did the Lord turn a poison into an antidote; thus did that dreadful fall make way for a more blessed and fixed state. Now we are so confirmed and established by Christ in the favour of God, that there can be no more such fatal breaches and dreadful jars betwixt God and his reconciled ones for ever. The bone that's well set is stronger where 'tis knit, than it was before. Blessed be God for Jesus Christ!"—*Flavel.*

II. Sorrow. "God has turned the curse of sorrow into a blessing. Sweet are the uses of adversity! In God's hand indeed they are when he puts his children into the furnace of affliction, it is that he may thoroughly purge away all their dross. A great writer has spoken with great beauty of the resources which God has placed within us for bringing good out of evil, or, at least, for greatly alleviating our trials in the cases of sickness and misfortune. 'The cutting and irritating grain of sand,' he says, 'which by accident or incaution has got within

the shell, incites the living inmate to secrete from its own resources the means of coating the intrusive substance. And is it not, or may it not be, even so with the irregularities and unevenness of health and fortune in our own case?' We too may turn diseases into pearls. But how much more wonderful are the wisdom and mercy of God, in making the spiritual trials and distresses of his people their necessary discipline for their highest good, the means for the greatest perfection and stability of their characters! This is indeed a wonderful transformation. 'God,' says holy Leighton, 'hath many sharp cutting instruments, and rough files for the polishing of his jewels; and those he especially esteems and means to make the most resplendent, he hath oftenest his tools upon'"—*Cheever.*

III. Death. "God hath turned the curse of death into a blessing. It were a waste of words to attempt to prove that death is indeed a curse: it was the woe specially denounced against men as the result of transgression—the ill inflicted on the workers of iniquity. But, through the obedience and death of Christ, the Redeemer, the sting of death has been destroyed, the uncertainty of the future has been dissipated, and, by the destruction of guilt, separation from the world has been revealed, as the beginning of a perfected happiness and an enlarged blessedness to the believer. If it is indeed a blessed thing, for a spirit, weighed down with a sinking mortality, and groaning beneath the load of unnumbered ills, to flee away from its troubles, and soar amid the cloudless light of immortal day, then death has been turned into a blessing, since it merely cuts asunder the chains whereby we are bound to earth, and admits the spirit to a land of peace and joy. If it is indeed a blessed thing for a being long pent up amid the closeness of a dungeon, to exchange its pestilential air for the fragrant breath of paradise, then death has been turned into a blessing, since it serves to dissociate the children of the covenant from the pollution of this world, and advance them to the regions beyond the grave, where the Lamb shall feed them and guide them to fountains of living water, and God shall wipe away all tears from their eyes. I say, if God hath made death the very instrument of exchanging earth for heaven, of

ending the warfare and strife of time, and crowning believers with the unspeakably precious reward, then undoubtedly, while they exultingly proclaim, 'O death, where is thy sting? O grave, where is thy victory?'—they must not cease to remember that death was indeed a crying evil, a bitter curse, but that our God turned the curse into a blessing "—*M'Naughton*.

REFORMATION A SLOW WORK.

xiii. 4—8. *And before this, Eliashib the priest, &c.*

When Nehemiah returned to Persia he left the people penitent and devoted, the temple restored; the priests and Levites at their posts. All were loyal to conscience and God. When Nehemiah came back again to Jerusalem he found Tobiah in the temple, Levites in the fields, tithes in the people's hands, the house of God forsaken, and the Sabbath of God desecrated. And it grieved him sore. He had to build again from the foundations.

I. Reformers are sanguine men. They see the evil, and the needs-be for its removal. Too often they overlook

the herculean task that lies before them.

II. Reformation meets with opposition. The reformers propose to destroy. They confront the selfishness of human nature, and war against the passions of men.

III Reformation must build up after it has destroyed. Building up is slower than pulling down. All reformers have been disappointed. Those whom they have striven to help have been their most determined hinderers. Faith, hope, and courage are indispensable.

PROFANATION OF THE SABBATH.

xiii. 17, 18. *Then I contended with the nobles of Judah, and said unto them, What evil thing is this that ye do, and profane the Sabbath day? Did not your fathers thus, and did not our God bring all this evil upon us, and upon this city? yet ye bring more wrath upon Israel by profaning the Sabbath.*

INTRODUCTION Historical Nehemiah absent, disorder ensued. Among other irregularities profanation of the Sabbath became frequent and flagrant It moved the spirit of Nehemiah not so much that the men of Tyre sold their fish and wares on the Sabbath, which in consideration of their being heathen they might be expected to do, as that they sold them to "the men of Judah," the visible worshippers of God, and "in Jerusalem," the seat of his worship; coming up to the very threshold of his house with their merchandise, as if in contempt of his presence and authority. But we have a more serious concern in this matter than merely to vent our indignation against "the men of Tyre" Our first and main concern is to see that our own garments are clean. Nor is it sufficient that our own habits in respect to our personal observation of the Sabbath are correct. In this respect the nobles of Judah, for aught that appears, were without fault Yet Nehemiah did not hesitate to charge them with the guilt of the profanations which they witnessed "What evil thing is this that *ye do*," said he, "and profane the Sabbath day?" He said this on the assumption that they had the power to prevent the sin, and were answerable for the consequences of their neglect Hence I derive the sentiment that—

MEN OF AUTHORITY AND INFLUENCE INCUR GREAT GUILT, AND BRING WRATH UPON THE COMMUNITY, BY CONNIVING AT PROFANATIONS OF THE SABBATH.

Men of authority and *influence*, because in all countries where the people are the source of power, men in authority can do but little unsupported by men of influence. As men of all classes have their share of influence the responsibility rests in a measure upon all By whatever means the influence of individuals is increased, their responsibility also is enhanced.

1. *Profanation of the Sabbath is a great sin.* The Sabbath is a Divine institution. At the creation, God by His express appointment set it apart from a common to a sacred use This appointment He confirmed and renewed at Mount Sinai. Our Saviour, by the authority vested by him in his apostles, added his sanction to the appointment and made it a law of his kingdom, after the obligation of the Jewish ritual had ceased, with only the circumstantial change of the first instead of the seventh in the series, as the day of rest, in commemoration of his resurrection. Consecrated peculiarly to God's service Wantonly to profane the Sabbath is open contempt of God. This is not a sin of *ignorance*. A few men there may be who seriously disbelieve in the moral obligation of the Sabbath, and others are blinded by custom in regard to the guilt of certain common violations of it, but the great mass know what they do. This sin is an outrage on the rights of men. It opens the door to universal licentiousness, enfeebles the laws of society, tends to destroy our best blessings and blot out our dearest hopes The Sabbath is necessary to the perpetuation of true religion. Some, while they think lightly of religion, profess highly to value free institutions They boast of liberty, and of the sciences, the arts, the enterprise, the universal education of the people, and the general prosperity and happiness which they claim to be its fruits And what is liberty? The unrestricted enjoyment of our rights, so far as this is consistent with the wellbeing of society What liberty then can there be among depraved men, without law to restrain their appetites and passions? or what efficacy can there be in law, without a corresponding moral sentiment in the community to sustain it? or what efficacious moral sentiment without religion? or what religion without the Sabbath? Turn your eyes on those regions of the earth where the Sabbath is unknown, and what do you find the moral, social, and civil condition of men there? See also those portions of the world where the Sabbath is now abandoned, or given up to pastime.

2. *Civil laws to protect the Sabbath from open violation, are just and proper.* In Jewish national code the law of the Sabbath was enforced by civil penalties. On this ground it was that Nehemiah went to the magistrates of Jerusalem and charged them with guilt in forbearing to exercise the authority which God had vested in them to restrain profanations of the day. Equally incumbent is it on every other community, which has authority over its own members, whether it be a family or an empire, to protect the Sabbath from desecration Nor is there anything in this unjust. To enforce a spiritual observation of the Sabbath is not indeed the province of civil authority With duties appropriately religious it has no direct concern. These it must leave to the higher authority of God, and the conscience of every individual. But to protect those who are disposed religiously to observe the Sabbath, in the peaceful enjoyment of the privilege, is no less just and proper, than it is to protect them in the enjoyment of any other right or privilege. They too are the mass of the community Ninety-nine hundred probably would consider a general disregard of the Sabbath destructive to their best interests. Such being the fact, to require that no laws for the protection of the Sabbath be made, or that having been made, they be a dead letter; to require that the mass of our citizens yield to the few, and be governed by their wishes, is

a position which, on any other subject of legislation, would not for a moment be tolerated

3. *For a due execution of these laws, men clothed with the authority and the influence to do this, are answerable to God, and incur great guilt by neglecting it.* They are ministers of God They have taken official oaths. The fact of their being clothed with office, binds them to discharge its duties

APPLICATION. 1 To the friends of Sabbath 2 To fathers and mothers. 3. To the young.—*Noah Porter, D.D , abridged.*

Illustrations —"Each should do what his talent and influence in society enjoin and permit It is the principle upon which I insist If we cannot absolutely shut the gates of our great cities to the entrance of merchandise, we may do something to lessen the evil We may shut the door of our houses—we may prohibit the purchase or reception of articles of consumption by our servants and dependants—we may encourage those upon whom we have any influence, to observe the sacred day Let only the zeal, the courage, the firmness, the disinterestedness of Ezra and Nehemiah be connected with their piety and love to the house of their God, and much would be done."—*Bishop Wilson*

"We find from the beginning of the Christian Church that all days were not alike to Christians, but that one day, the first-day of the week, was singled out and separated from the others as their day of worship The end of the Paschal Lamb was accomplished in the sacrifice of our Lord ; the end of the one Temple has been accomplished , but the end of the Sabbath has not been accomplished, and will not be till toil, and trouble, and sin, and sorrow shall cease Then it will be merged in the eternal Sabbatism which remains for the people of God. But till then the solemn words of our Lord are as a wall of fire around it, to protect its sacredness and integrity ' Verily I say unto you. till heaven and earth pass, one jot or one tittle shall in nowise pass from the law, till all be fulfilled ' "—*John Kennedy, D D*

"The Sabbath is the guardian of every other Divine institution The sin of profaning the Sabbath stamps in the individual, the family, or the nation, which is guilty of it, the character of irreligious, and speedily ripens them for the judgments of God This is the danger of being any way concerned in this iniquity, we are furthering an evil which would ultimately destroy religion itself, and which will assuredly prove as ruinous to the temporal renown, as the spiritual interests, of our country "—*Rev. J A Wylie.*

"It is a most important sentiment, and ought to be kept constantly before the public mind, that religion is the most direct and powerful cause of national comfort, prosperity, and security, and that in its absence all their other causes must be limited and transient in their effects If religion were a mere abstraction of devotion, confined to the closet and the sanctuary, and restricted in its influence to the imagination and the taste, but not having any necessary control over the conscience, the heart, and the life, and not intended to regulate the intercourse of society, if it consisted merely in attendance on the rites and forms of the Church, and began and ended upon the threshold of the house of God, then it would be difficult to point out what a connection such a religion had with the welfare of a country It would, in that case, resemble the ivy, which, though it add a picturesque effect to a venerable fabric, imparts neither stability to its walls, nor convenience to its apartments But if religion be indeed a principle of the heart, an element of the character, the habit of thinking, feeling, and acting aright in all our social relations, the basis of every virtue, and the main prop of every excellence, if it be indeed the fear of the Lord by which men depart from evil; if it be faith working by love; if it be such a belief in the gospel of Christ as leads to a conformity to his example, religion being such as this must secure the welfare of any country. There is not one single influence, whether of law, of science, of art, of learning, tending to the well-being of society, which true religion does not guard and strengthen."—*James*

The Lord's Day.—Stations on the line of your journey are not your journey's end, but each one brings you nearer Such are our Lord's Days A haven is not *home*, but it is a place of quiet and rest, where the rough waves are stayed Such is the "Lord's Day" A garden is a piece of common land, and yet it has ceased to be common land It is an effort to regain Paradise Such is "The Lord's Day" A bud is not a flower, but it is the promise of a flower Such is "The Lord's Day " The world's week tempts you to sell your soul to the flesh and the world "The Lord's Day" calls you to remembrance, and begs you rather to sacrifice earth to heaven and time to eternity, than heaven to earth and eternity to time The six days not only claim you as captives of the earth, but do their best to keep the prison-doors shut that you may forget *the way out* "The Lord's Day" sets before you an open door. Samson has carried the gates away. "The Lord's Day" summons you to the threshold of your house of bondage, to look forth unto immortality, *your immortality* The true Lord's Day is the Eternal life , but a type of it is given to you on earth, that you may be refreshed with the anticipation and foretaste of your rest —*John Pulsford.*

NEHEMIAH.

xii 22 *Remember me, O my God, concerning this also, and spare me according to the greatness of thy mercy*

INTRODUCTION. Historical Every part of Nehemiah's short history shows that the fear and love of God formed the principal motive with Nehemiah. Here is, first—

I An appeal to God's approbation. "Remember me, O my God, concerning this also." Nehemiah often makes appeals of this kind This manner of speaking was an appeal to God—

1 *From man's judgment.* His distinguished abilities had hitherto recommended him to notice in the royal palace, notwithstanding the disgrace of his Jewish faith. But he had now engaged in an undertaking which was likely enough to appear enthusiastic and contemptible in the eyes of his Persian acquaintance. But what then? It was for God's honour, and therefore he despises this shame, casting himself upon the approbation of God This principle it was that influenced Noah, Abraham, Moses, David, Paul It is the principle of faith rendering an unseen God visible. Such men look for a future "recompense of reward," promised by Him who cannot lie. When misunderstood, and undervalued, and misrepresented by the world, they can appeal to God. "Let them curse, but bless thou" Nehemiah makes his appeal to God, secondly—

2. *From man's enmity* While one party satisfied themselves with despising, there was another party in Jerusalem itself, who hated and opposed, his proceedings. These were they who, being Jews, had connected themselves by marriage with heathen families—or the offspring of such marriages. To such persons, the revival of pure Jewish manners was very provoking. Others found that their worldly interests were interfered with by Nehemiah's strict enforcing of the Sabbath It is in reference to their enmity that the appeal in the text is made. Modern enmity. Nehemiah appeals, thirdly—

3. *From man's ingratitude* It was here that this zealous servant of God found his greatest trial He might easily have disregarded man's judgment, or have endured man's enmity. But how painful, when the very persons, whom in God's name he sought to benefit, were cold, reluctant, unfeeling! Nehemiah's was no solitary case.

Is there no danger lest appeals of this kind should lead us to trust in ourselves that we are righteous, and despise others? Not if we make them in the spirit of Nehemiah : for you find in close connection with this appeal—

II A contrite prayer for God's forgiveness "Spare me, according to the greatness of thy mercy." Every real believer, while he habitually labours to have a conscience void of offence, maintains at the same time a deep feeling of humility and of his need of unsparing mercy. Let us endeavour to trace the course of this feeling

1. *After all that he has done for God's service, Nehemiah cannot forget that there is a load of original and actual sin recorded against him, for which no subsequent obedience can make satisfaction* 2. *Nehemiah finds even his religious actions so stained with sin, that though he may appeal from man, he cannot make them a plea of merit before God. 3. He casts himself, with a steadfast faith, on the free grace and covenanted mercies of the Lord.*

APPLICATION. If the despised believer may thus appeal from man to God, what hope can there be for those who compel him so to do?

If the repenting and believing sinner is so graciously spared, how active should he be in serving the Lord, amid a gainsaying and perverse generation!—*Rev. Joseph Jowett, M.A., abridged*

SOLOMON.

xiii. 26. *Did not Solomon king of Israel sin by these things? yet among many nations was there no king like him, who was beloved of his God.*

"It may appear remarkable that one who fell so grievously should contribute at all to the Book of God, nor is there any other instance of the kind; but his sad history adds a peculiar weight of warning to his words; nor are there any books more strongly marked by the finger of God."

"Solomon was chosen of God, and afterwards rejected as Saul had been; he was full of wisdom and understanding, and, what is far more, of holiness and goodness. There is perhaps no one of whom the early promise of good seemed so decisive."

"It has been said, as by St. Augustine, that Solomon was more injured by prosperity than profited by wisdom. Yet we may observe, that his falling away is not in Scripture attributed to his wealth, his power and honour."

"We cannot conclude that Solomon himself did not at last repent; but this has always been considered by the Church as very doubtful, to say the least. All we know is, that Scripture has fully made known to us his falling away from God, but has said nothing of his repentance. The very silence is awful and impressive."

"What more melancholy than the fall of one so great—so wise? What words could have been spoken to him more powerful than his own? What eloquence could describe his fall with more feeling and beauty than his own words? What could more powerfully paint the loveliness of that holiness from which he fell? What the overpowering sweetness of that Divine love which he has consented to give up to feed on ashes? Who can describe the temptations to those very sins by which he was ensnared in a more searching manner than he has done? . . . How must his own sweet and Divine words sound to him like music of Paradise to the lost spirits; yea, as songs of heaven would come back to fallen angels in sad remembrance? . . . . It is very awful to think how God may use men as instruments of good that his Spirit may teach them, and through them teach others, and guide them to the living fountains of waters, yet they themselves at last fail of the prize of their high calling. What a warning for fear."—*From Rev. Isaac Williams' 'Characters of the Old Testament.'*

DIVINE REMEMBRANCE.

xiii. 31. *Remember me, O my God, for good.*

Our Protestant forefathers were fond of the maxim—"They who observe Providences shall never want Providences to observe." The truth of this is eminently seen in the rescue of the Church from the Babylonish Captivity, in the rebuilding of the temple, and in the restoration of the people to the Holy Land. High political considerations rather than religious ones no doubt actuated Cyrus, and Darius, and Artaxerxes, but "the hearts of kings are in the hand of God." So in the Reformation it has been said that God put little thoughts into Henry VIII's mind for great purposes, just as the preservation of the Church in Esther's time was brought about by a single sleepless night of Ahasuerus the king. "This also cometh from the Lord of Hosts, who is wonderful in counsel and excellent in working." The Life and Times of Nehemiah are of much more consequence to the history of the Jewish Church than ordinary readers suppose. Great men are born for great occasions, and eventful times form the training school for public men. Our text is Nehemiah's last recorded prayer, showing us the secret of his strength. It expresses much, but it implies more.

I Nehemiah's delight in the remembrance of God. The remembrance of God the habit of his life. Note the instructive occasions on which the prayer was uttered. Not in the closet for private devotion , not in the family for domestic contemplation ; not in the sanctuary for public worship ; but in the daily walks of life—amidst the toils of his office, amidst the reforms he was carrying on, amidst the hot enmity of the world, amidst the plots that were formed against his life. Again and again he prays, "Remember me, O God." He was in the habit of remembering God, or such a prayer would not have risen spontaneously to his lips.

1. *A test of religious character.* The manner and degree in which devout thoughts mingle with daily thoughts and incorporate themselves with worldly employments the special mark of a child of God Nehemiah specifies this as the distinctive mark of those holy ones who were associated with him—" thy servants, who desire to fear thy name." And Malachi tells us that "a book of remembrance was written for those who feared the Lord, and thought upon his name," and were thus the patterns of distinguished excellence in most degenerate times. Throughout Scripture the remembrance of God is set forth as the active principle of all vice. "The wicked shall be turned into hell, and all the nations that forget God."

2 *A voluntary remembrance* Not enforced The result of a principle. When Solomon says, "Remember thy Creator in the days of thy youth," he appeals to the first and best affections of the human heart, under the impressions of early piety. "In the days of thy youth " some render "in the days of thy choice." Religion is choice. "Choose ye this day whom ye will serve." Not an appeal to fear. God might have compelled our remembrance—by awful judgments ; by outward demonstrations of his power. He asks where he might command , entreats when he might enforce "My son, give me thine heart" So when Jesus says, "Do this in remembrance of me," he appeals to the more generous emotion of inward piety which disposed them to obey at a touch, and yield to the gentler insinuations of Divine grace. Nehemiah's remembrance of God was spontaneous and free . it sprang up on all occasions , like water from a fountain, or music from a bird, or light from the sun It was part of a life—the life of faith and devotion ; a life hid with Christ in God. In your best moments you say, "*The love of Christ constraineth us.*"

3. *A blessed, though difficult, exercise.* It is difficult amidst the active duties of life to keep up a devout remembrance of God , but the blessedness more than compensates its difficulty. It is the advantage of any useful habit that when once formed it becomes easy and spontaneous ; and would require an effort to forego or counteract it "Use is second nature." Same law holds in Christian life. That which we have once determined upon by principle and by choice we continue to do by preference and by affection Well for us when the remembrance of God is the solace and delight of the mind in active and in solitary hours. "Yea, in the way of thy judgments, O Lord, have we waited for thee , the desire of our soul is to thy name, and to the remembrance of thee "

Not an easy attainment. All good men are painfully conscious how great an effort it requires, whilst sedulously engaged with the concerns of time, to give their best hopes and affections to heaven , to carry the spirit of the sanctuary into the cares and vexations of each returning day It is difficult to mind the business of two worlds and to do justice to both to be in the fear of God all the day long.

Difficult : not impossible God enjoins nothing which his strengthening aids will not enable the faithful to achieve "With men this is impossible , but with God all things are possible " The history of the long cloud of witnesses attests the practicability of the religious life amidst all the agitation of this world's cares. Patriarchs, prophets, reformers, and martyrs had as many hindrances in their way to heaven as we have in ours.

II Nehemiah's devout desire for God's remembrance of him. 1. *He set a very high value upon the friendship of God.* Not a matter of indifference to him whether he possessed it or not. It was vital to his enjoyment, vital to his prosperity, vital to his existence. Like a crust to a starving man ; like a plank to the shipwrecked is the love of Christ to a Christian. "Because thy lovingkindness is better than life, therefore my soul seeketh thee." The Psalmist prayed, "Remember me, O Lord, with the favour that thou bearest unto thy people : O visit me with thy salvation." Luther protested that he would not be put off with common things. Much emphasis is in the words, "That I may see the good of thy chosen, and rejoice with thine inheritance"—that I may see it, and partake of it ; have the vision and the fruition of this great goodness.

2. *He had nothing to claim in the way of merit, but everything to hope for in the way of mercy* Not a touch of the Pharisee in Nehemiah. The deepest humiliation characterized his first prayer and his last ; a spirit of self-renunciation and dependence. "I beseech thee, O Lord, the great and terrible God, that keepest covenant and mercy." The only word that seems to look the other way is xiii 14, "Remember me, O my God, for good, and wipe not out the remembrance of my good deeds : " but this was only an earnest appeal to God for his integrity in resisting the tyranny of the nobles of Judah, and maintaining the cause of the poorer among the Levites. As there is a book of remembrance written before God, Nehemiah would not be wiped out of that book He only says, Remember me—not reward it, not record it—yet he was remembered and rewarded too, and his good deeds were recorded as well as remembered. As says Matthew Henry, "Deeds done for the house of God and the offices of it, for the support and encouragement of religion, are good deeds ; there is both righteousness and godliness in them ; and God will certainly remember them, and not wipe them out."

3 *He possessed a happy consciousness of his personal interest in the Divine regards.* Again and again he utters the words, "My God."

4. *He attached much importance to the service of the sanctuary.* He maintained altar and priest.

APPLICATION. How to attain amidst the business of life this pervading principle of spiritual piety. No fixed and invariable rules Every man with the Bible before him must in some respects be a law to himself. Generally—1 Stated seasons of retirement ought to be appointed. 2. Occupy the thoughts in the morning with some leading truth or text of Scripture 3. Form the habit of ejaculatory prayer. 4. Make conscience of your thoughts.—*Thodey*

A LIFE'S WORK REVIEWED.

xiii. 31. *Remember me, O my God, for good.*

I The review is coming. All days point on to the day of judgment

II A review is desirable It *elevates* a man to take a retrospect of his life, judge his motives, broaden his field of vision. To realize the grace of God within him, to mark the purpose of God towards him, and note the work God has given him to do ; all this is well. But here is no elation. Rather is he *humbled.* God is great, and we know him not That he should employ me—such a man may say—is not matter for pride or self-boasting. I am not worthy of the least of all the mercies which he has shown unto his servant And so he *prays* for mercy and grace to be found faithful. Reverence and trust, fear and hope, are in the man who thus pleads with God —*Enlarged from Dr. Schultz.*

THE END

INDEX.

PUNGAY CLAY AND TAYLOR, PRINTERS

Lightning Source UK Ltd.
Milton Keynes UK
UKOW07n0611011217
313643UK00002B/44/P